KENTUCKIANS
IN
ILLINOIS

KENTUCKIANS
IN
ILLINOIS

BY STUART SEELY SPRAGUE

Professor of History·
Morehead State University

GENEALOGICAL PUBLISHING CO., INC.
Baltimore, Maryland 1987

FOREWORD

Kentuckians in Illinois, the third volume in the Kentucky migrants series, is intended to be of use primarily to genealogists seeking ancestors from Illinois of Kentucky descent. However, it will also prove useful to those seeking ancestors of Kentuckians who never left the Commonwealth. The trick is to work through siblings who did.

Kentucky was a classic breeder state, sending her children to newly opened areas where it was believed their prospects would be brighter. So pronounced was this propensity to move on that in the *antebellum* period nearly one-third of all native-born Kentuckians were living out of state. With families being large by modern standards, there could have been few families unaffected by this emigration. Doubtless many of those who moved were of the proverbial rolling-stone variety and put down shallow roots in Ohio, Indiana, Illinois, or Missouri, and finally ended their days farther west.

The information abstracted for this book comes from approximately 140 rare county histories and atlases. The atlases often list patrons by name, birthplace, and year, and give the year they migrated to the county. Thus, post-Civil War migrants as well as early settlers are listed. In county histories the biographical information usually includes the date and county of birth of the biographee. In many cases similar information is provided for the parents.

Arranged in tabular format under county of origin (if the county is unknown, the individual is listed separately), the entries include some or all of the following information: the name of the Kentucky migrant, his/her birthdate, parents' names, dates and places of birth, and date of migration. The division by Kentucky county is useful for several reasons. For the genealogist it provides a small bundle of other surnames, many of which may already be familiar since settlers often migrated in multi-family groups. For local Kentucky libraries and historical societies the information as to sources, visible at a glance, will indicate which county histories might be valuable to them.

Source citations with specific page references are included. Women are listed both by maiden and married name when known. The following symbols are used throughout the work:

( )   maiden name

[ ]   married name

**   born in same county as biographee

/   divides information pertaining to the father from that of the mother

- -   no information

c   circa, as in c1821 (about 1821)

Since the Ohio River was the primary carrier of Kentuckians to the West, and migrants moved frequently and had children even more often, previously published volumes in this series, *Kentuckians in Ohio and Indiana* and *Kentuckians in Missouri*, may also prove helpful. Each additional volume makes the series a more powerful tool. The three volumes published to date abstract information from approximately 400 county histories, atlases, and mug books.

STUART SEELY SPRAGUE
Center for Historical Studies
Clearfield, Kentucky 40313

N.B. Owing to an oversight in the typing of the manuscript, the pages following 95b and 110b are blank.

SOURCES AND ABBREVIATIONS

ACAS   W.R. Brink & Company
Illustrated Atlas Map of Cass County, Illinois.
Carefully Compiled from Examination and Surveys.
Edwardsville: W.R. Brink & Company, 1874.

ACLA   George A. Ogle & Company
Plat Book of Clarke County, Illinois.
Chicago: George A. Ogle & Company, 1892.

ACLY   An Atlas of Clay County, Illinois. From Actual Surveys Under the Direction of B.N. Griffing.
Philadelphia: D.J. Lake & Company, 1881.

AGRU   Warner & Beers Company
Atlas of Grundy County and the State of Illinois.
To Which is Added an Atlas of the United States,
Maps of the Hemisphere &c., &c., &c.
Chicago: Warner & Beers Company, 1875.

AHEN   Atlas of Henry County and the State of Illinois. To
Which is Added an Atlas of the United States,
Maps of the Hemisphere &c., &c., &c.
Chicago: Warner & Beers Company, 1875.

AMCH   Everts, Basken & Stewart
Combination Atlas of McHenry County, Illinois.
Compiled, Drawn, and Published from Personal Exam-
inations and Surveys.
Chicago: Everts, Basken & Stewart, 1872.

AMEN   Illustrated Atlas of Menard County, Illinois. Carefully
Compiled from Personal Examinations and Surveys.
Edwardsville: W.R. Brink & Company, 1874.

AMOU   Atlas of Moultrie County and the State of Illinois.
To Which is Added an Atlas of the United States;
Maps of the Hemispheres, &c., &c., &c.
Chicago: Warner & Beers Company, 1875.

AWOO   Atlas of Woodford County and the State of Illinois.
To Which is Added an Atlas of the United States;
Maps of the Hemispheres, &c., &c., &c.
Chicago: Warner & Beers Company, 1873.

-5-

BCHA   S.J. Clarke Publishing Company
Biographical Record of Champaign County, Illinois. Illustrated.
Chicago: S.J. Clarke Publishing Company, 1900.

BCHI   Wilson & St. Clair Publishers
Biographical Sketches of the Leading Men of Chicago.
Chicago: Wilson & St. Clair Publishers, 1868.

BCHR   Newton Bateman
Historical Encyclopedia of Illinois Edited by Newton Bateman L.L.D., Paul Selby A.M. and History of Christian Co.Edited by Henry L. Fowkes. Illustrated.
Chicago: Munsell Publishing Company, 1918.

BCLA   Newton Bateman
Historical Encyclopedia of Illinois Edited by Newton Bateman L.L.D.,Paul Selby A.M. and History of Clark County Edited by H.C. Bell. Illustrated.
Chicago: Middle West Publishing Company, 1907.

BCSB   Biographical Review of Cass, Schuyler and Brown Counties, Illinois. Containing Sketches of Pioneer and Leading Citizens.
Chicago: Biographical Review Pub. Company, 1892.

BEFF   Newton Bateman
Illinois Historical ... Effingham County, Biographical by Special Authors and Contributors ...
Chicago: Munsell Publishing Company, 1910.

BGLS   Biographical and Genealogical Record of LaSalle County, Illinois. Illustrated.
Chicago: Lewis Publishing Company, 1900.

BHAN   Biographical Review of Hancock County, Illinois. Containing Biographical and Genealogical Sketches of Many of the Prominent Citizens of To-Day and Also the Past.
Chicago: Hobart Publishing Company, 1907.

-6-

BHBU Henry C. Bradsby
  History of Bureau County, Illinois. Illustrated.
  Chicago: World Publishing Company, 1885.

BHDP Rufus Blanchard
  History of DuPage County, Illinois by Rufus
  Blanchard, Illustrated.
  Chicago: O.L. Baskin & Company, 1882.

BHEN S.J. Clarke Publishing Company
  Biographical Record of Henry County, Illinois.
  Illustrated.
  Chicago: The S.J. Clarke Publishing Company, 1901.

BHIQ History of Iroquois County; Together with Historic
  Notes on the North West Geaned from Early Authors,
  Old Maps and Manuscripts, Private and Official Cor-
  respondence, and Other Authentic, Though for the
  Most Part, Out-of-the-Way Sources by H.W. Beckwith.
  Chicago: H.H. Hill & Company, 1880

BKAN S.J. Clarke Publishing Company
  Biographical Record of Kane County, Ill. Illustrated.
  Chicago: The S.J. Clarke Publishing Company, 1898.

BLOG S.J. Clarke Publishing Company
  Biographical Record of Logan County, Ill. Illustrated.
  Chicago: The S.J. Clarke Publishing Company, 1901.

BMCH Biographical Directory of Tax-Payers and Voters of Henry
  County, Containing Also a Map of the County, a Con-
  densed History of the State ... Sketch of the County,
  Its Towns and Villages, an Abstract of ... Laws of
  the State. A Business Directory ....
  Chicago: C. Walker & Company, 1877.

BMCL Newton Bateman
  Encyclopedia of Illinois Edited by Newton Bateman
  L.L.D., Paul Selby A.M.; a History of McLean County
  Edited by Ezra M. Prince and John H. Burnham. Illustrated.
  Chicago: Munsell Publishing Company, 1908.

-7-

BOGL   Newton Bateman
              Historical Encyclopedia of Illinois Edited by Newton
              Bateman L.L.D. and Paul Selby A.M. and History of Ogle
              Co. Edited by Horace G. Kauffman and Rebecca H.Kauffman.
              Chicago: Munsell Publishing Company, 1909.

BRBM   Biographical Record of Bureau, Marshall and Putnam Coun-
              ties, Illinois. Illustrated.
              Chicago: S.J. Clarke Publishing Company, 1896.

BRCM   Biographical and Reminiscent History of Richland, Clay
              and Marion Counties, Illinois. Illustrated.
              Indianapolis: B.F. Bowen, 1909.

BRDK   Biographical Record of DeKalb County, Illinois. Illustrated.
              Chicago: The S.J. Clarke Publishing Company, 1897.

BRJM   Biographical Review of Johnson, Massac, Pope, and Hardin
              Counties, Illinois Containing Historical Sketches
              of Prominent and Representative Citizens ....
              Chicago: Biographical Publishing Company, 1893.

BRKI   Newton Bateman
              Historical Encyclopedia of Illinois Edited by Newton
              Bateman L.L.D. and Paul Selby A.M. and History of Rock
              Island Co. ... by Special Authors ... Illustrated.
              Chicago: Munsell Publishing Company, 1914.

BRMA   Biographical Record of Leading Citizens of Macoupin
              County, Illinois.
              Chicago: Richmond & Arnold Publishers, 1904.

BRML   Biographical Record of McLean County, Illinois. Illustrated.
              Chicago: The S.J. Clarke Publishing Company, 1899.

BROG   Biographical Record of Ogle County, Illinois. Illustrated.
              Chicago: The S.J. Clarke Publishing Company, 1899.

BROC   Biographical Record of Rock Island County, Illinois. Illus.
              Chicago: The S.J. Clarke Publishing Company, 1897.

-8-

BRWS   Biographical Record of Whiteside County, Illinois. Illustrated.
        Chicago: The S.J. Clarke Publishing Company, 1900.

CAOG   Combination Atlas and Map of Ogle County, Illinois.
        Chicago: Evarts, Baskin & Stewart Publishers, 1872.

CASS   Newton Bateman
        Historical Encyclopedia of Illinois Edited by Newton
        Bateman L.L.D. and Paul Selby A.M. and History of
        Cass County Edited by Charles A.E. Martin.
        Chicago: Munsell Publishing Company, 1915.

CBKA   Commemorative Biographical and Historical Record of Kane Coun-
        ty, Illinois, Containing Full Page Portraits and Biogra-
        phical Sketches of Prominent and Representative Citizens
        of the County Together with Portraits and Biographies
        of the Governors of Illinois and of the Presidents of
        the United States. Also a History of the County, From
        Its Earliest Settlement to the Present Time.
        Chicago: Beers, Leggett & Company, 1888.

CELW   Combined History of Edwards, Lawrence and Wabash Counties, Illi-
        nois. With Illustrations Sescriptive of the Scenery and Bio-
        graphical Sketches of Some of their Prominent Men & Pioneers.
        Philadelphia: McDonough & Company, 1883.

CHAM   Newton Bateman
        Historical Encyclopedia of Illinois Edited by Newton Bate-
        man L.L.D. and Paul Selby A.M. and History of Champaign
        County, Edited by Joseph O. Cunningham.
        Chicago: Munsell Publishing Company, 1905.

CHDI   J.S. Lothrop
        Champaign County Directory 1870-1871, With History of the
        Same, and of Each Township Therein.
        Chicago: n.p., 1871.

CMCD   S.J. Clarke
        History of McDonough County, Illinois, Its Cities, Towns
        and Villages with Early Reminiscences, Personal Incidents
        and Anecdotes and a Complete Business Directory of the Co.
        Springfield: D.W. Lusk, 1878.

COLE   History of Coles County, Illinois; Containing a History of
the County, Its Cities, Towns, &c.; a Directory of Its
Tax-Payers; Portraits of Early Settlers and Prominent
Men; General and Local Statistics; Map of Coles County;
History of Illinois Illustrated; History of the Northwest
Illustrated; Constitution of the United States; Miscella-
neous Matters, &c., &c. Illustrated.
Chicago: William LeBaron Jr. & Company, 1879.

CSBR   Combined History of Schuyler and Brown Counties, Illinois,
with Illustrations Descriptive of their Scenery, and Biographical Sketches of Some ... Prominent Men and Pioneers.
Philadelphia: W.R. Brink & Company, 1882.

DUPA   History of Du Page County, Illinois. Compiled Under the Direction and Supervision of the Board of Supervisors 1876.
Aurora: Knickerbocker & Hodder, 1877.

ECHA   Melton W. Mathews and Lewis A. McLean
Early History and Pioneers of Champaign County, Illustrated
by 115 Superb Engravings by Melville Containing Biographical
Sketches of the Early Settlers, the Early History of the
County Obtained from the Most Reliable Sources, and Many
Graphic Scenes ... from the Bright and Shady Sides of...Life.
Urbana: Champaign County Herald, 1886.

EFAY   Newton Bateman
Historical Encyclopedia of Illinois Edited by Newton
Bateman L.L.D. and Paul Selby A.M. and the History
of Fayette County, Illinois, Edited by Robert W. Ross
and John J. Bullington.
Chicago: Munsell Publishing Company, 1910.

FSTE   Pioneer Publishing Company
In the Footsteps of the Pioneers of Stephenson County,
Illinois; A Genealogical Record.
Freeport: The Pioneer Publishing Company, 1900.

FUST   Addison L. Fulwider
History of Stephenson County, Illinois; a Record of
Its Settlement, Organization and Three Quarters of a
Century of Progress.
Chicago: The S.J. Clarke Publishing Company, 1910

GHHA Thomas Gregg
    History of Hancock County, Illinois; Together with
    an Outline History of the State and a Digest of
    State Laws Iluustrated.
    Chicago: C.C. Chapman, 1880.

GPPD Lewis B. Gross
    Past and Present of DeKalb County, Illinois. By Pro-
    fessor Lewis M. Gross, Assisted by an Advisory Board
    Consisting of H.W. Fay, G.E. Congdon, F.W. Lowman and
    Judge C.A. Bishop Illustrated with Historic Views.
    Chicago: The Pioneer Publishing Company, 1907.

GRUND History of Grundy County, Illinois. Containing a History
    from the Earliest Settlement to the Present Time, Em-
    bracing Its Topographic, Geological, Its Physical and
    Climactic Features; Its Agricultural, Railroad Inter-
    ests &c., Giving an Account of the Country, Its Aborigi-
    nal Inhabitants, Early Settlement by Whites, Pioneer In-
    cidents, Its Growth, Its Improvements, Organization of
    the County, the Judicial History, the Business and Indus-
    tries, Churches, Schools &c. Biographical Sketches, Por-
    traits of Some of the Early Settlers, Prominent Men, &c.
    Chicago: O.L. Baskin & Company, 1882.

HADM History of Adams County, Illinois, Containing a History of
    the County, Its Cities, Towns, Etc. A Biographical
    Directory of Its Citizens, War Records of Its Volun-
    teers in the Late Rebellion; General and Local Statis-
    tics, Portraits of Early Settlers and Prominent Men,
    History of the Northwest, History of Illinois, Map of
    Adams County, Constitution of the United States, Miscel-
    laneous Matters &c., &c. Illustrated.
    Chicago: Murray, Williamson & Phelps, 1879.

HCAR History of Carroll County, Illinois Containing a History of Its
    Citizens, War Record of Its Volunteers in the Late Rebellion,
    General and Local Statistics, Portraits of Early Settlers
    and Prominent Men, History of the Northwest, History of
    Illinois, Map of Carroll County, Constitution of the United
    States, Miscellaneous Matters, &c., &c. Illustrated.
    Chicago: H.F. Kett & Company, 1878.

HCAS William Henry Perrin
    History of Cass County, Illinois. Illlustrated.
    Chicago: O.L. Baskin & Company, 1882.

HCHA   History of Champaign County, Illinois. With Illustrations
       Descriptive of Its Scenery, and Biographical Sketches
       of Some of Its Prominent Men and Pioneers.
       Philadelphia: Brink, McDonough, 1878.

HCHR   History of Christian County, Illinois with Illustrations
       Decriptive of Its Scenery, and Biographical Sketches
       of Some of Its Prominent Men and Pioneers.
       Philadelphia: Brink, McDonough & Company, 1880.

HDEW   History of De Witt County, Illinois. With Illustrations De-
       scriptive of Its Scenery and Biographical Sketches of
       Some of Its Prominent Men and Pioneers.
       Philadelphia: W.R. Brink and Company, 1882.

HEDG   History of Edgar County, Illinois, Containing a History
       of the County--Its Cities, Towns, &c.; Directory of
       Its Tax-Payers; War Record of Its Volunteers in the
       Late Rebellion; Portraits of Early Settlers and Promi-
       nent Men; General and Local Ststistics; Map of Edgar
       County; History of Illinois. Illustrated; History of
       the Northwest Illustrated.
       Chicago: William LeBaron, Jr. & Company, 1879.

HENR   Henry L. Kiner
       History of Henry County, Illinois. Also Biographical
       Sketches of Many Represntative Citizens of the County
       Illustrated.
       Chicago: Pioneer Press, 1910.

HFAY   History of Fayette County, Illinois. With Illustrations
       Descriptive of Its Scenery, and Biographical Sketches
       of Some of Its Prominent Men and Pioneers.
       Philadelphia: Brink, McDonough & Company, 1878.

HFUL   History of Fulton County, Illinois; Together with Sketches
       of Its Cities, Villages and Townships, Educational,
       Religious, Civil, Military, and Political History;
       Portraits of Prominent Persons and Biographies of
       Representative Citizens; History of Illinois Embracing
       Accounts of the Pre-Historic Races, Aboriginies, French,
       English, and American Conquests and A General Review of
       Its Civil, Political, and Military History, Digest of
       State Laws, Illustrated.
       Peoria: Charles C. Chapman & Company, 1879.

HGJR History of Greene abd Jersey Counties Illinois; Together with Sketches of Towns, Villages and Townships, Educational, Civil, Military and Political History; Portraits of Prominent Individuals, and Biographies of Representative Men; History of Illinois, Containing Accounts of the Pre-Historic, and Historic Races, and a Brief Review of Its Civil and Military History. Illustrated.
Springfield: Continental Historical Company, 1885.

HGRU Newton Bateman
Historical Encyclopedia of Illinois Edited by Newton Bateman L.L.D., Paul Selby A.M. and History of Grundy County (Historical and Biographical) of Special Authors and Contributors.
Chicago: Munsell Publishing Company, 1914.

HGSH History of Gallatin, Saline, Hamilton, Franklin and Williamson Counties Illinois. From the Earliest Times to the Present; Together with Sundry and Interesting Biographical Sketches, Notes, Reminiscences, Etc., Etc. Illustrated.
Chicago: Goodspeed Publishers, 1887.

HHEN The History of Henry County, Illinois; Its Taxpayers and Voters; Containing Also a Biographical Directory; A Condensed History of the State; Maps of the County; A Business Directory; An Abstract of Every-Day Laws; War Record of Henry County; Officers of Societies, Lodges, Etc., Etc.
Chicago: H.F. Kett & Co., 1877.

HJAC History of Jackson County, Illinois, With Illustrations Descriptive of Its Scenery and Biographical Sketches of Some of Its Prominent Men and Pioneers.
Philadelphia: Brint, McDonough & Company, 1878.

HJOD The History of Jo Daviess County, Illinois, Containing a History of the County, Cities, Towns, etc. A Biographical Directory of Its Citizens; War Record of Its Volunteers in the Late Rebellion, General and Local Statistics; Portraits of Early Settlers and Prominent Men; History of the Northwest; History of Illinois; Maps of Jo Daviess County; Constitution of the United States; Miscellaneous Matters. Illustrated.
Chicago: H.F. Kett & Company, 1878.

-13-

HLAS   History of LaSalle County, Illinois; Together with Sketches of Its Cities, Villages and Towns, Prominent Persons, and Biographies of Representative Citizens, and a Condensed History of Illinois Embodying Winnebago and Black Hawk Wars, and a Brief Review of Its Civil and Political History. Illustrated. Chicago: Inter-State Publishing Company, 1886.

HLOG   History of Logan County Illinois: Its Past and Present; Containing A History of the County; Its Cities, Towns, Etc. A Biographical Directory of Its Citizens; War Record of Its Volunteers in the Late Rebellion; Portraits of Its Early Settlers and Prominent Men; General and Local Statistics; History of the North West; History of Illinois; Constitution of the United States; Map of Logan County; Miscellaneous Maters, Etc., Etc. Chicago: Donnolley, Loyd & County, 1878.

HMAC   History of Macoupin County, Illinois; With Illustrations Descriptive of Its Scenery and Biographical Sketches of Some of Its Prominent Men and Pioneers. Philadelphia: Brink, McDonough & Company, 1879.

HMAD   History of Madison County, Illinois. Illustrated with Biographical Sketches of Many Prominent Men and Pioneers. Evansville: W.R. Brink & Company, 1882.

HMCD   History of McDonough County, Illinois; Together with Sketches of Towns, Villages and Townships, Educational, Civil, Military, and Political History; Portraits of Prominent Individuals, and Biographies of Representative Citizens. History of Illinois Embracing Accounts of the Pre-Historic and Historic Races, and a Brief Review of Its Civil and Military History. Springfield: Continental Historical Company, 1885.

HMCH   Portrait and Biographical Record of Hancock, McDonough and Henderson Counties, Illinois. Containing Biographical Sketches of Prominent and Representative Citizens of the County Together with Biographies and Portraits of All the Presidents. Chicago: Lake City Publishing Company, 1894.

HMCL   The History of McLean County, Illinois, Containing a History of the County--Its Citizens, Towns, &c.; Portraits of

of Early Settlers and Prominent Men; General Sta-
tistics; Map of McLean County; History of Illinois,
Illustrated; History of the North West, Illustrated;
Constitution of the United States; Miscellaneous
Matters, &c., &c. Illustrated.
Chicago: William LeBaron, Jr. & Company, 1879.

HMEM   The History of Menard and Mason Counties, Illinois.
Containing a History of the Counties, Their Cities,
Towns, &c.; Portraits of Early Settlers and Prominent Men, General Statistics, Map of Menard and Mason Counties, History of Illinois, Illustrated; History of the North West, Illustrated; Constitution of
the United States; Miscellaneous Matters, &c., &c.,
Illustrated.
Chicago: O.L. Baskin & Company, 1879.

HMER   History of Mercer County, Together with Biographical Matter, Statistics, Etc., Gathered from Matter Furnished
by the Mercer County Historical Society, Interviews
with Old Settlers, County, Township and Other Records,
and Extracts from Files of Papers, Pamphlets, and Such
Other Sources as Have Been Available. Containing Also
a Short History of Henderson County.
Chicaho: H.H. Hill, 1882.

HMOR   History of Morgan County, Illinois; Its Past and Present,
Containing a History of the County, Its Cities, Towns,
Etc.; a Biographical Directory of Its Citizens; War
Record of Its Volunteers in the Late Rebellion; Por-
traits of Early Settlers anf Prominent Men; General and
Local Statistics; History of the North West; History of
Illinois; Constitution ofthe United States; Map of Mor-
gan County; Miscellaneous Matters, &c., &c. Illustrated.
Chicago: Donnelley, Loyd & Company, 1878.

HPEO   The History of Peoria County, Illinois, Illinois. Contain-
ing a History of the Northwest--History of Illinois--
History of the County, Its Early Settlement, Growth,
Development, Resources, Etc., Etc. A Sketch of Its
Cities and Towns, Their Improvements, Industries, Manu-
factories, Churches, Schools, etc., etc.--A War Record
of Its Volunteers in the Late Rebellion--General and
Local Statistics--Biographical Sketches--Portraits of
Early Settlers and Prominent Men--Map of Peoria County--
Constitution of the United States--Miscellaneous Matters--
Tables, Etc., Etc.
Chicago: Johnson & Company, 1880.

-15-

HPIK   History of Pike County, Illinois; Together with Sketches
                of Its Cities, Villages and Townships, Educational,
                Religious, Civil, Military and Political History;
                Portraits of Prominent Persons and Biographies of
                Representative Citizens. History of Illinois, Em-
                bracing Accounts of the Pre-Historic Races, Abor-
                igenes, French, English and American Conquests, and
                a General Review of Its Civil, Political and Milit-
                ary History. Digest of State Laws, Illustrated.
                Chicago: C. Chapman & Company, 1880.

HPPB   George B. Harrington
                Past and Present of Bureau County, Illinois, by
                George B. Harrington, Together with Biographical
                Sketches of Many of Its Prominent and Leading Citi-
                zens and Illustrious Dead.
                Chicago: Pioneer Publishing Company, 1906.

HSAN   History of Sangamon County, Illinois; Together with
                Sketches of Its Cities, Villages and Townships, Edu-
                cational, Religious, Civil, Military and Political
                History; Portraits of Prominent Persons and Biogra-
                phies of Representative Citizens. History of Illi-
                nois, Embracing Accounts of the Pre-Historic Races,
                Aborigenes; Winnebago and Black Hawk Wars and a
                Brief Review of Its Civil, Political and Military
                History. Illustrated.
                Chicago: Inter-State Publishing Company, 1881.

HSTC   History of St. Clair County, Illinois, with Illustrations
                Descriptive of Its Scenery, and Biographical Sketches
                of Some of Its Prominent Men and Pioneers.
                Philadelphia: Brink, McDonough & Company, 1881.

HSTE   The History of Stephenson County, Illinois, Containing a
                History of the County, Its Cities, Towns, &c., Bio-
                graphical Sketches of Its Citizens, War Records of
                Its Volunteers in the Late Rebellion, General and
                Local Statistics, Portraits of Early Settlers and
                Prominent Men, History of the North West, History
                of Illinois, Map of Stephenson County, Constitution
                of the United States, Miscellaneous Matters, &c.,
                &c., Illustrated.
                Chicago: Western Historical Company, 1880.

HWAS   History of Washington County, Illinois, Descriptive of
                Its Scenery and Biographical Sketches of Some of Its

Prominent Men and Pioneers.
Philadelphia: Brink, McDonough & Company, 1879.

HWCL   History of Wayne and Clay Counties, Illinois. Illus-
       trated.
       Chicago: Globe Publishing Company, 1884.

KANE   Newton Bateman
       Historical Encyclopedia of Illinois Edited by
       Newton Bateman L.L.D. and Paul Selby A.M. and
       History of Kane County Edited by General John S.
       Wilcox.
       Chicago: Munsell Publishing Company, 1904.

KNOX   History of Knox County, Illinois; Together with Sketches
       of the Cities, Villages and Townships; Record of
       Its Volunteers in the Late War; Educational, Reli-
       gious, Civil and Political History; Portraits of
       Prominent Persons and Biographical Sketches of the
       Subscribers; History of Illinois, Abstract of the
       State Laws, &c., &c., &c. Illustrated.
       Chicago: Blakely, Brown & Marsh, Printers, 1878.

LOGA   History of Logan County, Illinois; Together with Sketches
       of Its Cities, Villages and Towns, Educational, Re-
       ligious, Civil, Military and Political History.
       Portraits of Prominent Persons and Biographies of
       Representative Citizens. Also a Condensed History
       of Illinois, Embodying Accounts of Prehistoric Races,
       Indian Wars and a Brief Review of Its Civil and Po-
       litical History. Illustrated.
       Chicago: Inter-State Publishing Company, 1886.

MACL   History of Marion and Clinton Counties, Illinois, With Il-
       lustrations Descriptive of the Scenery and Biographi-
       cal Sketches of Some of the Prominent Men and Pioneers.
       Philadelphia: Brink, McDonough & Company, 1881.

OCHA   George A. Ogle & Company
       Plat Book of Champaign County, Illinois.
       Chicago: George A. Ogle & Company, 1893.

OPLO   George A. Ogle & Company
       Plat Book of Logan County, Illinois.
       Chicago: George A. Ogle & Company, 1893.

PAUP   William Henry Perrin
                        History of Alexander, Union, and Pulaski Counties,
                        Illinois. Illustrated.
                        Chicago: O.L. Baskin & Company, 1883.

PBAD   Portrait and Biographical Record of Adams County, Illi-
                        nois, Containing Biographical Sketches of Prominent
                        and Representative Citizens, Together with Biogra-
                        phies and Portraits of All the Presidents of the
                        United States.
                        Chicago: Chapman Brothers, 1892.

PBCO   Portrait and Biographical Album of Coles County, Illi-
                        nois, Containing Full Page Portraits and Biographi-
                        cal Sketches of Prominent and Representative Citi-
                        zens of the County ...
                        Chicago: Chapman Brothers, 1887.

PBCW   Portrait and Biographical Record of Clinton, Washington,
                        Marion and Jefferson Counties, Illinois; Containing
                        Biographical Sketches of Prominent and Representa-
                        tive Citizens of the Counties, Together with Biog-
                        raphies and Portraits of All the Governors of the
                        State and the Presidents of the United States.
                        Chicago: Chapman Publishing Company, 1894.

PBDK   Portrait and Biographical Album of DeKalb County, Illin-
                        ois, Containing Full-Page Portraits and Biographical
                        Sketches of Prominent and Representative Citizens of
                        the County Together with Portraits of All of the Gov-
                        ernors of the State and Presidents of the United
                        States; Also Containing a History of the County,
                        From Its Earlies Settlement to the Present Time.
                        Chicago: Chapman Brothers, 1886.

PBDP   Portrait and Biographical Album of Dewitt and Piatt Coun-
                        ties, Illinois, Containing Full Page Portraits and
                        Biographical Sketches of Prominent and Representative
                        Citizens of the County, Together with Portraits and
                        Biographies of All the Presidents of the United States
                        and Governors of the Stste.
                        Chicago: Chapman Brothers, 1891.

PFAY   Plat Book of Fayette County, Illinois.
                        Chicago: Alden, Ogle & Company, 1891.

-18-

PBHE Portrait and Biographical Album of Henry County, Illinois, Containing Full-Page Portraits and Biographical Sketches of Prominent and Representative Citizens of the County. Together with Portraits and Biographies of All the Governors of Illinois, and of the Presidents of the United States. Also Containing a History of the County from Its Earliest Settlement to the Present Time.
Chicago: Biographical Publishing Company, 1885.

PBJD Portrait and Biographical Album of Jo Daviess and Carroll Counties, Illinois, Containing Full-Page Portraits and Biographical Sketches of Prominent and Representative Citizens of the County, Together with Portraits and Biographies of All of the Governors of the State and Presidents of the United States.
Chicago: Chapman Brothers, 1889.

PBKN Albert J. Perry
History of Knox County, Illinois: Its Cities, Towns and People; by Albert J. Perry. Illustrated.
Chicago: The S.J. Clarke Publishing Company, 1912.

PBMA Portrait and Biographical Record of Macoupin County, Illinois. Containing Biographical Sketches of Prominent and Representative Citizens of the County. Together with Portraits and Biographies of All of the Governors of Illinois, and of the Presidents of the United States. Also Containing a History of the County from Its Earliest Settlement to the Present Time.
Chicago: Biographical Publishing Company, 1891.

PBMB Portrait and Biographical Record of Montgomery and Bond Counties, Illinois. Biographical Sketches of Prominent and Representative Citizens, Together with Biographies and Portraits of All the Presidents of the United States.
Chicago: Chapman Brothers, 1892.

PBMC Portrait and Biographical Record of Macon County, Illinois, Containing Biographical Sketches of Prominent and Representative Citizens, Governors of the State of Illinois and Presidents of the United States.
Chicago: Lake Publishing Company, 1893.

-19-

PBML   Portrait and Biographical Album of McLean County, Illinois,
Containing Full-Page Portraits and Biographical
Sketches of Prominent and Representative Citizens of
the County, Together with Portraits and Biographies of
All the Governors of Illinois, and of the Presidents
of the United States.
Chicago: Chapman Brothers, 1887.

PBMO   William Henry Perrin
History of Bond and Montgomery Counties, Illinois.
Chicago: O.L. Baskins, 1882.

PBPE   Portrait and Biographical Album of Peoria County, Illinois.
Containing Full Page Portraits and Biographical Sketches
of Prominent and Representative Citizens of the County,
Together with Portraits and Biographies of All the Presi-
dents of the United States and Governors of the State.
Chicago: Biographical Publishing Company, 1890.

PBRI   Portrait and Biographical Album of Rock Island County, Illi-
nois, Containing Full-Page Portraits and Biographical
Sketches of Prominent and Representative Citizens of
the County, Together with Portraits and Biographies of
All the Governors of Illinois and of the Presidents of
the United States. Also Containing a History of the
County from Its Earliest Beginnings to the Present Time.
Chicago: Biographical Publishing Company, 1885.

PBRJ   Portrait and Biographical Record of Randolph, Jackson, Perry,
and Monroe Counties, Illinois, Containing Biographical
Sketches of Prominent and Representative Cities of the
County Together with Biographies and Portraits of All
the Presidents of the United States and Governors of
Illinois.
Chicago: Biographical Publishing Company, 1894.

PBSM   Portrait and Biographical Record of Shelby and Moultrie Counties, Illinois, Containing Biographical Sketches of Prominent and Representative Citizens of the Counties, Together with Portraits and Biographies of All the Governors of the State and Presidents of the United States.
Chicago: Biographical Publishing Company, 1891.

PBWA   Portrait and Biographical Album of Warren County, Illinois,
Containing Full Page Portraits and Biographical Sketches

of Prominent and Representative Citizens of the County, Together with Portraits and Biographies of the Governors of Illinois and Presidents of the United States. Also Containing a History of the County from the Earliest Settlements up to the Present Time. Chicago: Chapman Brothers, 1886.

PBWH Portrait and Biographical Album of Whiteside County, Illinois, Containing Full Page Portraits and Biographical Sketches of Prominent and Representative Citizens of the County Together with Portraits and Biographies of All the Governors of Illinois and Presidents of the United States. Also Containing a History of the County from the Earliest Settlements to the Present Time. Chicago: Chapman Brothers, 1885.

PBWO Portrait and Biographical Record of Winnebago and Boone Counties, Illinois, Containing Biographical Sketches of Prominent and Representative Citizens, Together with Biographies of All the Governors of the State and of the Presidents of the United States. Chicago: Biographical Publishing Company, 1892.

PCHR Portrait and Biographical Record of Christian County, Illinois, Containing Biographical Sketches of Prominent and Representative Citizens Together with Biographies of All the Governors of the State of Illinois and Presidents of the United States. Chicago: Lake Publishing Company, 1893.

PFAY Alden, Ogle & Company
Plat Book of Fayette County, Illinois.
Chicago: Alden, Ogle & Company, 1891.

PHCC William Henry Perrin
History of Crawford and Clark Counties, Illinois.
Chicago: O.L. Baskin, 1883.

PHEF History of Effington County, Illinois, Illustrated.
Chicago: O.L. Baskin & Company, 1883.

PHKX Albert J. Perry
History of Knox County, Illinois: Its Cities, Towns, and People by Albert J. Perry. Illustrated.
Chicago: S.J. Clarke Publishing Company, 1912.

PHPI   Emma C. Piatt
                History of Piatt County, Together with a Brief His-
                tory of Illinois from the Discovery of the Upper
                Mississippi to the Present Time with Map and Illus-
                trations.
                Chicago: Shepard & Johnston Printers, 1883.

PJEF   William Henry Perrin
                History of Jefferson County, Illinois, Illustrated.
                Chicago: Globe Publishing Company, 1883.

PLAS   The Past and Present of LaSalle County, Illinois, Con-
                taining a History of the County--Its Cities, Towns,
                &c., a Biographical Directory of Its Citizens, War
                Record of Its Volunteers in the Late Rebellion,
                Portraits of Early Settlers and Prominent Men, Gen-
                eral and Local Statistics, Map of La Salle County,
                History of Illinois, etc., etc.
                Chicago: H.F. Kett, 1877.

PPDM   Past and Present of the City of Decatur and Macon Coun-
                ty, Illinois, Illustrated.
                Chicago: S.J. Clarke & Company, 1903.

PPME   Robert Don Leavy Miller
                Past and Present of Menard County, Illinois, Ill-
                ustrated.
                Chicago: S.J. Clarke Publishing Company, 1905.

PPLA   The Past and Present of Lake County, Illinois, Contain-
                ing a History of the County, Its Cities, Towns, &c.
                A Biographical Directory of Its Citizens, War Rec-
                ord of Its Volunteers in the Late Rebellion, Por-
                traits of Early Settlers and Prominent Men, General
                and Local Statistics, Map of Lake County, History
                of Illinois, Illustrated, History of the North
                West, Illustrated, Constitution of the United States,
                Miscellaneous Matters, &c., &c.
                Chicago: William Le Baron & Company, 1877.

PPPI   Charles McIntosh
                Past and Present of Piatt County, Illinois; Together
                with Sketches of Many Prominent and Influential Ci-
                tizens, Illustrated.
                Chicago: S.J. Clarke Publishing Company, 1903.

PPRI   The Past and Present of Rock Island County, Illinois,
           Containing a History of the County--Its Cities,
           Towns, etc., a Biographical Directory of Its Ci-
           tizens, War Record of Its Volunteers in the Late
           Rebellion, Portraits of Early Settlers and Prom-
           inent Men, General and Local Statistics, Map of
           Rock Island County, History of Illinois, Consti-
           tution of the United States, Miscellaneous Mat-
           ters, &c., &c.
           Chicago: H.F. Kett & Company, 1877.

PPVE   The Past and Present of Vermilion County, Illinois,
           Illustrated.
           Chicago: S.J. Clarke & Company, 1903.

PPWA   The Past and Present of Warren County, Illinois, Con-
           taining a History of the County--Its Cities,
           Towns, etc., a Biographical Directory of Its Ci-
           tizens, War Record of Its Volunteers in the Late
           Rebellion, Portraits of Early Settlers and Promi-
           nent Men, General and Local Statistics, Map of
           Warren County, History of Illinois, Constitution
           of the United States, Miscellaneous Matters, &c.,
           &c.
           Chicago: H.F. Kett & Company, 1877.

PPWO   The Past and Present of Woodford County, Illinois, Con-
           taining a History of the County--Its Cities, Towns,
           etc.; a Directory of Its Taxpayers; War Record of
           Its Volunteers in the Late Rebellion; Portraits
           of Early Settlers and Prominent Men; General and
           Local Statistics; Map of Woodford County, History
           of Illinois, Illustrated; History of the North
           West, Illustrated; Constitution of the United
           States; Miscellaneous Matters, &c., &c.
           Chicago: W. Le Baron, jr., 1878.

PSTC   Portrait and Biographical Record of St. Clair County,
           Illinois, Containing Biographical Sketches of Prom-
           inent and Representative Citizens, Together with
           Biographies and Portraits of All the Presidents of
           the United States.
           Chicago: Chapman Brothers, 1892.

PSTE   Portrait and Biographical Album of Stephenson County,
           Illinois, Containing Full Page Portraits and Bio-
           graphical Sketches of Prominent and Representative

Citizens of the County, Together with Portraits
and Biographies of All the Governors of Illinois
and of the Presidents of the United States.
Chicago: Chapman Brothers, 1888.

PVED   Portrait and Biographical Album of Vermilion and Edgar Counties, Illinois, Containing Full Page
Portraits and Biographical Sketches of Prominent
and Representative Cities of the Counties, Together with Portraits and Biographies of All the
Governors of the State and of the Presidents of
the United States.
Chicago: Chapman Brothers, 1889.

TAZE   History of Tazewell County, Illinois; Together with
Sketches of Its Cities, Villages and Townships,
Educational, Religious, Civil, Military, and
Political History, Portraits of Prominent Per-
sons and Biographies of Representative Citizens.
History of Illinois Embracing Accounts of the
Pre-Historic Races, Aborigenes, French, English,
and American Conquests, and a General Review of
Its Civil, Political and Military History. Di-
gest of State Laws. Illustrated.

VTBU   The Voters and Taxpayers of Bureau County, Illinois,
Containing Also, a Biographical Directory; a
History of the County and State, a Business Di-
rectory.
Chicago: Henry F. Kett & Company, 1877.

WHWI   George H. Woodruff
History of Will County, Illinois, A History of
the County--Its Cities, Towns, &c.; a Directory
of Its Real Estate Owners, Portraits of Early
Settlers and Prominent Men; General and Local
Statistics; Map of Will County; History of Il-
linois, Illustrated; History of the North West,
Illustrated; Constitution of the United States,
Miscellaneous Matters, &c., &c. Illustrated.
Chicago: William Le Baron, jr. & Company, 1878.

WINN   The History of Winnebago County, Illinois: Its Past
and Present Containing a History of the County.
Its Cities, Towns, etc., A Biographical Direct-

ory of Its Citizens, War Record of Its Volunteers
in the Late Rebellion, Portraits of Early Settlers
and Prominent Men, General and Local Statistics,
History of the North West, History of Illinois,
Constitution of the United States, Map of Winnebago County, Miscellaneous Matters, etc., etc.
Chicago: Henry F. Kett & Company, 1877.

BIRTHDATE	NAME OF BIOGRAPHEE	PARENTS/BIRTHPLACE/BIRTHDATE	SOURCE/PAGE	DATE
00 000 0000	J.H. Abell		HCHR 260	----
12 Feb 1801	James H. Abell		PBWO B311	----
12 Sep 1805	John R. Abell		BCHR 830	----
28 Mar 1815	John L. Anderson		CMCD 595	----
00 000 1833	John J. Banks		HADW 856	1839
15 Jan 1806	Lorina A[Banks]		CMCD 595	1835
16 Apr 1804	Vandever Banks	Vandever & Elizabeth(Walford)Md/Va	HMCD 626	----
14 Dec 1801	Richard Batterson	Amor & Frances	AMEN 39	1818
22 Nov 1827	Martha Baxter[Fletcher]		HSAN 764	----
15 Dec 1832	William Bowyer		HNOR 632	1833
00 000 0000	Mary Burton[Brockman]		CSBR 260	----
15 Dec 1797	William Butler		HSAN 520	1828
23 Jul 1817	William A. Butler	Nathan M. & Mary(Hardin) Va/Ky	HSAN 855	1824
22 Feb 1836	L.C. Cheek[Whitaker]		HMEM 851	----
14 Jan 1808	Levi Conover	Levi	CASS 869	----
17 Aug 1807	Charles Creel		CMCD 596	1836
00 000 1818	Silas Creel		CMCD 596	1833
00 Apr 1829	William H. Dawson		CMCD 596	1832
00 000 0000	William H. Dawson		HMCD 1052	1832
29 Jan 1814	Elisha Fargusson	Stephen & Nancy	HMCD 1033	1833
00 000 0000	Malinda Fletcher[Tongate]		HNAC 275	----
12 Mar 1824	Loven Garrett	Robert & Catherine(Yates) Va/Va	HMCD 1139	1834
02 Sep 1808	George G. Gun		CMCD 597	1836
00 000 1828	S. Hamilton		CMCD 597	1831
05 Aug 1826	Harrison Hamilton	Levi & Malinda(Creel)	HMCD 1020	c1835
00 000 1820	Green Harding	Abel & Julia(Bettisworth) Ky98/Va91	GHHA 554	1831
29 Jul 1799	Eli Hartley		AMEN 46	----
00 000 0000	Nathan Hartley	Eli 1799/x	PPME ---	----
00 000 0000	Nathan Hartley		AMEN 22	1852
07 Aug 1817	John Hills		HMCD 650	1829
00 000 0000	Colonel H. Lester		CSBR 392	1829

Date	Name	Parents / Notes	Origin	Code	No.	Year
09 Feb 1820	Dolly A. Lightfoot[Lanterman]			BLOG	580	----
19 Apr 1817	Gordon Lightfoot	Henry F. & Mary L(Jones)	Ky/Ky	HSAN	1025	1833
00 000 0000	Rebecca J. Logan[Jenning]	John		CSBR	385	1835
00 000 1802	John Lyon	John		HMCH	557	1835
00 000 1807	John McClain			HPIK	553	----
00 000 0000	Thomas McClure	John	Va/x	HMCH	236	----
00 000 0000	Susan McCrosky[Walker]			CSBR	378	1834
14 Feb 1842	James McDowell	John & Lucinda(Rippetoe) **09/**11		PEMO	B286	1860
01 Dec 1822	William A. McElvair	Samuel & Penelope(Abell)	Va/Va	HSAN	763	1828
00 00c 1796	Solomon Miller			HSAN	1011	----
14 Jun 1822	B.F. Montgomery	Samuel & Mary(Bailey)		HMEM	700	1829
30 Jun 1820	---- Montgomery	Samuel & Mary(Bailey)		HMEM	699	1829
08 Dec 1850	Robert O. Morris			HPIK	463	1874
04 Oct 1831	William H. Mourning	Lewis & Ann(Jones)		HMCD	591	----
15 Mar 1801	Benjamin F. Naylor			QMCD	599	1833
00 Mar 1801	Benjamin T. Naylor			HMCD	668	----
21 Apr 1834	L. Naylor	Benjamin		HMEM	794	1835
00 000 0000	Resin Naylor			HMCD	308	----
00 000 0000	Ruth Parr[Way]			HCAS	301	----
06 Dec 1828	C.C. Patterson	J.W. & Jane(Ramsey)		HMEM	735	----
00 000 0000	Harriet J. Patterson[Leach]			CSBR	377	----
11 Dec 1811	William B. Pile			QMCD	599	1833
31 Dec 1799	Andrew Pinkerton	James & Mary(Foster)	Ire/Va	HGJR	1006	----
01 Oct 1814	Isaiah Rucker	Carter & Nancy		BOGL	1007	1833
10 Sep 1827	J.J. Sheppard	Thornton & Ellinor		HMOR	672	----
00 000 0000	J.C. Smith			HMAC	272	1840
27 Dec 1823	James B. Smithers			CMCD	600	1833
27 Jan 1823	Thomas T. Smithers			CMCD	600	1833
00 000 0000	E.C. Steith			AMEN	36	1839
16 Oct 1829	Stephen Stone	John & Lucy(Preston)	Ky/Ky	HMEM	742	1830
13 Oct 1858	Dr. Charles E. Taylor	Dr.J.G. & Sallie(Elliott) **/**		BLOG	550	1872
26 Mar 1814	Hon. James C. Taylor	Dr. James G.& Sallie(Elliott)**/**		BLOG	558	1872
01 Sep 1814	Harriet Tinsley[Vincent]			HMCD	1006	----
00 000 0000	Mary H. Trabue[Lester]			CSBR	392	1829
00 000 0000	Allen H. Walker			HMCD	713	----

A D A I R   C O U N T Y   (C O N T.)

BIRTHDATE	NAME OF BIOGRAPHEE	PARENTS/BIRTHPLACE/BIRTHDATE	SOURCE/PAGE	DATE
29 Jun 1824	Andrew H. Walker	Cyrus	CMCD	601	1833
25 Sep 1832	Cyrus Walker	Cyrus	HMCD	724	----
00 000 0000	Elizabeth Walker[Bailey]	James	HMCD	271	1833
29 Apr 1819	John M. Walker		CMCD	600	1833
00 000 0000	Joseph M. Walker		AMEN	19	1830
18 Jun 1815	Pinkney H. Walker	--- & Martha(Scott)	HMCD	383	1834
00 000 0000	Judge P.H. Walker		CSBR	378	1834
20 May 1814	Quintus Walker	Alexander & Mary M(Hammond) Va/NC	HMCD	1016	----
00 000 0000	Quintus Walker		CMCD	601	1830
30 Jan 1830	Samuel T. Walker		HMEM	851	1853
26 Feb 1819	Rev.Thos. M. Walker	Alexander & Margaret(Frost) Va/x	GHHA	838	----
00 000 0000	Fannie R. Wheat[Borden]		CJRI	250	----
23 Dec 1813	William Whitlock	William & Rosanna(Shelton)	HGJR	975	----
04 Aug 1825	William B. Worth	John D & Elizabeth(Hopkins) Va/Va	HSAN	1039	----

A L L E N   C O U N T Y

BIRTHDATE	BAME OF BIOGRAPHEE	PARENTS/BIRTHPLACE/BIRTHDATE	SOURCE/PAGE	DATE
00 000 0000	Elizabeth Brewster[Cook]		MACL	295	1827
00 000 0000	Rebecca Byars[Stonecipher]		MACL	295	1827
00 000 1809	Leander J. Clark	Va/x	BRJM	399	----
17 Feb 1842	James P. Frost	William B & Sarah(Holloway) Ky/x	CELW	275	1860
00 000 0000	James P. Frost		CELW	347	1860
00 000 0000	Sarah F. Garrison[Smith]		HMAC	275	----
13 Nov 1812	Zachariah W. Gatton Thomas	Md1774/x	CASS	887	----
14 Jun 1820	Charles L. Holliday		HMOR	718	1828
00 000 0000	Emma J. Howser[McCollom]		HMAC	275	----

BIRTHDATE	NAME OF BIOGRAPHEE	PARENTS/BIRTHPLACE/BIRTHDATE	SOURCE/PAGE		DATE
25 Dec 1822	Elijah Jennings	Joseph & Elizabeth(Shadowens) NC/TN	BRJM	172	----
22 Oct 1847	Rebecca Jones[Morrison]	Ambrose & Mary	BRMA	171	1851
00 000 0000	Eleanor Jordan[Keen]		CELW	356	1803
10 Jul 1861	Dr.Albert R. Lyles	Moses M & Sarah J(Walker) **/**	CASS	920	1844
00 000 0000	Catherine[Maxwell]		HWAS	85	----
18 Nov 1824	James M. Manlon	Abel & Rebecca NC1794/Ga1800	HFAY	76	----
22 Apr 1820	James C. Overbee	James & Lucretia(Wade)	HWCL	B27	----
04 Nov 1813	William T. Rigg	Richard & Elizabeth(George) Va1813/Ky	CSBR	277	----
00 000 0000	William T. Rigg		CSBR	391	1831
00 000 0000	Jasper Server		HFAY	96	1831
00 000 0000	Mary Server		HFAY	96	1831
00 000 0000	Mary F Spilman[Goss]		HGRU	818	----
28 Nov 1823	James H. Thaxton	Thomas & Hannah(Williamson) SC/SC	HSAN	911	----
00 000 0000	Thomas Thaxton		HWAS	85	1839
22 Nov 1802	Judge William Thomas		HMOR	318	----
22 Nov 1802	William Thomas		EFAY	522	----
00 000 1833	William C. Travelstead	Frederick & Mary(Burton) NC/SC	HGSH	662	----
02 May 1832	William G. Warden		PEMO	B184	----
30 Nov 1823	Mathinsey O. Witherspoon	Hardy & Nancy(Motley) NC/NC	HWCL	B209	----
12 Dec 1830	Rev.William J. Young	James D. & Eleanor(Harrison)Va1809/Ky	PEMB	434	1849

ANDERSON COUNTY

BIRTHDATE	NAME OF BIOGRAPHEE	PARENTS/BIRTHPLACE/BIRTHDATE	SOURCE/PAGE		DATE
00 000 1832	Edwin R. Alexander		BCLA	670	1834
23 Nov 1825	Darius R. Elliott	John & Melville(Berry) Va/Ky	PESM	488	----
29 Jul 1823	Levi E. Hancock		PBDP	695	----
00 000 0000	Martha A[Joiner]		HMAC	274	1842
07 Mar 1821	Thomas Joiner	George & Polly(Pullem) Va/Va	HMAC	139	----
00 000 0000	Thomas Joiner		HMAC	274	1842
00 000 0000	Robert McAllister		HMOR	667	1840
10 May 1853	Thomas M. Morgan	--- & Martha E(Watson) Ky/Ky	PVED	750	----

A N D E R S O N   C O U N T Y   (C O N T.)

BIRTHDATE	NAME OF BIOGRAPHEE	PARENTS/BIRTHPLACE/BIRTHDATE	SOURCE/PAGE	DATE
28 Aug 1841	W.D. Mountjoy	George & Frances M(Stout) Ky/Ky	PBOO 382	----
27 Mar 1823	William R. Parker		COLE 573	1828
18 Jan 1826	James N. Rigg	Richard & Margaret(Utterback) Va/Va	BCSB 287	1831
11 Mar 1830	Peter Rigg	Richard W & Elizabeth(George)Va1789/Va	BCSB 309	1831
25 Feb 1838	Henry W. Sharp	Francis & Amanda(Residen) **/Va	BCHR 980	----
10 Mar 1807	William Tinsley		COLE 580	1831
25 Mar 1868	Dr. George A. Wash	Allen & Susan(Alstoot) Ky1813/1834	BRMA 364	----
11 Jun 1841	Dudley J. Watson	Dudley G & Jane(Robison) **1812/x	HCHR 188	----
00 000 0000	Salena M. Yates[Holden]		HCHR 267	----

B A L L A R D   C O U N T Y

BIRTHDATE	NAME OF BIOGRAPHEE	PARENTS/BIRTHPLACE/BIRTHDATE	SOURCE/PAGE	DATE
29 Sep 1860	George P. Bird	John H & Virginia J(Ward)	PAUP B319	----
00 000 0000	Sarah [Sams]		HJAC 74	1811
00 000 0000	Thomas M. Sams		HJAC 78	1811

B A R R E N   C O U N T Y

BIRTHDATE	NAME OF BIOGRAPHEE	PARENTS/BIRTHPLACE/BIRTHDATE	SOURCE/PAGE	DATE
00 000 0000	E. Davidson Abereen[Eter]		HMAC 275	1844
00 000 1822	J.H. Atkinson		CMCD 595	1834
00 000 1806	William S. Barry	John & Elizabeth(Robinson)	PBMO B291	c1834
00 000 0000	Judge Downing Baugh		PJEF B3	----
16 Dec 1828	William A. Berryman		HMOR 567	----

-30-

Date	Name	Parents / Spouse	Origin	Code	No.	Year
08 Jun 1806	Willis H. Black		Ky/x	PBWB	316	----
05 May 1821	Alexander Black	Andrew R & Sarah B.	Ky/Va	PPWO	595	1831
09 Feb 1829	Lydia Blunt[Samuell]	Thomas F.		HMEM	818	----
06 Jul 1814	Daniel Burner			PBKN	521	----
00 000 0000	Rachel[Campbell]			HADM	806	1826
00 Dec 1805	Henry Clark			HMEM	693	----
03 Mar 1831	Robert Council	Hardy & Jane		HMEM	719	----
08 Nov 1824	Alexander Crews	Matthew & Nancy(Blair)	Va1794/x	HWCL	B96	----
00 000 1796	Caleb Davidson			PPWO	538	1831
00 000 0000	C.C. Davidson			AWOO	5	----
00 000 0000	Hezekiah Davidson			HCHR	265	----
16 Sep 1813	Col.James W. Davidson	Hezekiah & Eleanor(Wilson)	NC/Ky	PBWA	664	----
24 May 1823	M.E. Davidson	Caleb & Martha		PPWO	537	----
01 Mar 1822	Adam Eaton			PVED	667	----
09 Aug 1847	Charles T. Farrell			PLAS	622	----
12 Jan 1840	J.W. Farrell			PLAS	397	1856
00 000 0000	Edward Flatt			HGJR	828	----
26 Apr 1801	Catherine Gardner			PPWA	301	1848
29 Sep 1810	Dr. B. Greenwood	John & Triphena(Garretson)	Va/Va	PCHR	365	----
00 000 0000	A.S. Greer			HCHR	265	----
05 Nov 1824	Fletcher Haines	Christopher & Myra(Galewood)	Va/x	HCHR	228	----
30 Apr 1837	Michael W. Hall	Robert S & Julia(Harber)	**/x	PBWA	557	----
14 May 1819	Andrew Harding	Martin & Isabella(Beard)	Va1792/Tnl794	BCSM	548	----
00 000 0000	Paschal Harding			ACAS	40	----
17 Dec 1817	Peyton Harding	Martin & Isabella(Beard)	Va1792/Tnl794	BCSB	548	----
00 000 0000	Sarah Harding	Martin & Isabella(Beard)	Va1792/Tnl794	BCSB	548	----
00 000 0000	William Harding	Martin & Isabella(Beard)	Va1792/Tnl794	BCSB	548	----
00 000 0000	I.E. Hardy			HMAD	558	----
08 Mar 1825	J.E. Hardy	Isham & Martha(Edwards)	Va/Ky	HMAD	404	1837
03 Feb 1805	Wesley Harlen	Jacob & Sarah(Combs)	Va/Va	CMCD	371	1825
11 Mar 1812	Henry Harmon			CJRI	803	1836
20 Dec 1827	Dr.Baxter Haynes	Rev.William & Anne(Hensley)	NC/SC	PBWB	286	----
00 000 0000	Martha Hicks[Johnson]			HADM	793	----
00 000 1774	William Higgins			HSAN	898	1817
15 Nov 1813	Daniel Holstlaw	Richard & Mary(Smith)	Va/x	BRCM	184	1830
00 000 1813	Daniel J. Holstlaw			BRCM	160	----

BIRTHDATE	NAME OF BIOGRAPHEE	PARENTS/BIRTHPLACE/BIRTHDATE	SOURCE/PAGE		DATE
24 Oct 1819	Alexander Johnson		HMOR	757	----
04 Jul 1852	Louis A. Jones		HSAN	742	----
04 Feb 1816	William H. Jones	John & Mary(Young) Va/Ky	BLOG	227	----
16 Jan 1803	William McHenry	Daniel & Elizabeth(Jones) Ky/Ky	PBHE	436	1812
00 000 0000	Albert Mansfield		HMAC	275	1856
00 000 1827	J.B. Mansfield		HMOR	644	1830
01 Jan 1856	Dr. J.A. Martin	F.M. & Mary J(Newberry) Ky1831/Ky1834	PHCC	312	----
00 000 0000	Candis Miller[Hall]	John & Permilla(Tapscott) **/**	PBWA	558	----
00 000 0000	Rachael Mills[Harris]		HMAD	565	1830
00 000 0000	Ellen Monroe[Dunbar]		COLE	518	----
24 Sep 1811	Hon. John Monroe		COLE	527	----
00 000 0000	Rachel[Mullican]		HADM	806	----
14 Dec 1818	Vickrey National	Isaac NC/Va	KNOX	697	1835
00 000 0000	William Nevil		HMEM	806	----
00 000 0000	T. Newell[Fletcher]		HCHR	265	----
19 May 1818	Harvey O'Neal	Bennet & Sallie(Emery) Va/Va	HMEM	809	----
22 Nov 1827	Rev.William M.Owen	James & Susannah(Monroe) Va/SC	HWCL	B100	----
11 Sep 1825	Thomas P. Parrott	Josiah & Nancy G(Bransford) Md00/Va07	BCSB	227	1831
11 Feb 1839	James T. Poynter	--- & Elizabeth(Davis)	PHEF	B135	----
05 Nov 1824	Fletcher Raines	Christopher & Myra(Gatewood)Va1795/Ga	BCHR	893	----
14 Jul 1817	John Rhea		HSAN	969	----
28 Feb 1818	John G. Rogers	James & Rachel(Jolleff)	EFAY	456	----
00 000 0000	Ezekiel Rush		HFAY	96	1830
00 000 0000	Leonard Rush		HFAY	96	1830
22 Dec 1825	Jonathan R. Shelton		PPWA	346	1837
06 Sep 1821	Samuel T. Shelton	David & Patsey Ky1792/Va1795	PBWA	555	----
00 00c 1808	Nancy Sherley[Hall]		HGSH	702	----
25 Aug 1811	Jemima Simms[Timberlake]		HHEN	346	----
26 Jan 1832	John W. Staples	William & Elizabeth(Thacker)	HEDG	705	----
00 000 1834	S.F. Sutton	James & Elizabeth A Ky/Vt	HPIK	735	----
20 Aug 1819	Joseph Taylor		HMEM	797	1836
00 000 0000	Dr. E.P. Toney		MACL	300	1861
29 Nov 1814	Iverson I. Twyman		CMCD	600	1836

B A T H   C O U N T Y

BIRTHDATE	NAME OF BIOGRAPHEE	PARENTS/BIRTHPLACE/BIRTHDATE		SOURCE/PAGE		DATE
00 000 0000	Eliza J. Alkire			AMEN	19	1827
02 Apr 1805	Cleanthes Arnett	John & Rebecca(Whitecraft)	Va/Tn	HFUL	827	----
27 Mar 1832	J.H. Arnett	Cleanthes & Margaret(Dean)	Ky/x	HFUL	783	----
00 000 0000	Rachel Arnick[Whitecraft]			PCHR	226	1835
01 Jan 1826	A.M. Barnes			HLOG	471	----
13 Jan 1825	George W. Becker	A.L & Elizabeth(Kinkaid) Fleming/Ky06		PBWA	309	----
18 Jan 1825	George W. Becker			PPWA	266	1852
10 Mar 1849	Henry C. Beckrer			PPWA	266	1852
20 Aug 1846	John L. Bliss	Charles A & Mary A(Badger)	Ky/Ky	HSAN	1062	----
04 Jun 1812	Thomas H. Boyd	Drury B & Elizabeth(Hurd)		PBWA	260	----
00 000 0000	Abigail Bracken[Hornback]	Robert & Elizabeth(Mappen)		PPME	453	1825
00 000 0000	George W. Bracken			AMEN	22	1828
04 Mar 1822	James H. Bracken	Theophilus	Va1???/x	PBDP	774	----
00 000 0000	N.W. Bracken			AMEN	22	1828
28 Feb 1831	O.P. Bradley	Elijah & Martha(Hornback)	Ky/Ky	HMEM	729	1853
00 000 0000	Nancy [Brown]			HGHA	183	1868
28 Feb 1818	Thomas B. Burbridge	Robert	Ky/x	HPIK	590	----
00 000 1787	Ann P Caldwell[Kincaid]			AMEN	35	1834
05 Dec 1814	Carlisle H. Canterbury			PPME	343	1826
00 000 0000	Ann Dean[Parr]			PBWA	235	----
20 Nov 1815	Michael Dean			PPWA	267	1840
16 Jul 1824	Walker R. Donaldson			PPME	213	----
16 Jul 1824	W. Richardson Donaldson	Alexander & Sarah(Power)	Ky/Ky	PPME	203	1850
16 Jul 1824	W.R. Donaldsor	Alexander & Sarah(Power)	Ky/Ky	HMEM	729	1850
00 000 0000	William Donaldson			AMEN	19	1849
00 000 0000	William R. Donaldson			AMEN	19	1849

BIRTHDATE	NAME OF BIOGRAPHEE	PARENTS/BIRTHPLACE/BIRTHDATE	SOURCE/PAGE	DATE
01 Feb 1826	Hon. John R. Eden	John P & Catherine(Carr) Md1796/Ky00PBSM	PBSM 191	1831
10 Sep 1820	Joseph E. Eden	John P & Catherine(Cann) Md/**	PBSM 249	1831
01 Oct 1822	Dr. William L.England Jesse & Hannah(Mershon) Va/NJ		HSAN 905	----
28 Jan 1820	Elizabeth Estill[Cantrall] William & Mary(Williams)		HMEM 719	----
00 Dec 1804	Ann Foster[Iles]		HSAN 1062	----
18 Oct 1837	Thomas J. George	Henry & Ann(Sharp) Va/Ky	PPVE 1116	c1850
02 May 1835	William O. Ginter		PHEF B158	1855
01 Aug 1845	William R. Grimsley Nimrod G & Frances(Moreland)Va1813/Ky		PPME 442	----
00 000 0000	Elmore Grinssley		AMEN 19	1865
00 000 0000	N. Grinssley		AMEN 19	1865
00 000 1833	Elizabeth Groves[Thompson] John R & Louisa		HSAN 962	----
00 000 0000	Albert Hagaman		HMAC 274	1863
00 000 0000	Charlotte H[Hagaman]		HMAC 274	1868
27 Nov 1821	Louisa Hale[Kincaid]		PPME 314	----
17 Jun 1842	George W. Hardin	William Ky/x	HGHR 171	1860
28 Nov 1809	John Hendrix	Jacob & Catherine(Thompson)	PBCO 394	----
22 Apr 1822	Sarah E. Hornback[Killion] John & Abigail(Bracken) Ky/Ky		HMEM 744	----
00 000 1807	Fielding House	William & Ann(Whitecraft) Md/x	PBMC 663	----
26 May 1807	Fielding House	William	PBMC 303	1835
01 Jun 1829	Margaret House[Kincaid]		PBMC 664	----
00 000 0000	Elizabeth Iles[McDannold] Thomas Pa/x		CSER 373	----
00 000 0000	Washington Iles		HSAN 1062	----
00 000 0000	Cynthia [Johnson]		AMEN 22	1823
08 Jan 1801	William Johnson		PPME 193	1823
00 000 0000	William Johnson		PPME 461	1823
00 000 0000	William Johnson		PBDP 774	----
15 Nov 1822	David G. Jones	Andrew & Eleanor(Goodan) Va1785/Pa83	HSAN 879	----
00 Aug 1805	Jacob Keithley		HMCD 627	----
00 000 1810	Andrew Kincaid		HMCL 928	1836
00 000 0000	J.K. Kincaid		AMEN 22	1832
00 000 0000	Mrs. J.K. Kincaid		AMEN 22	1823

Date	Name	Parents / Notes	Code	No.	Year
30 Jun 1808	John K. Kincaid	Andrew & Ann P(Caldwell) Pa1791/**87	AMEN	35	---
30 Jun 1808	John K. Kincaid	Andrew & anna P(Caldwell) Va/x	PPME	204	---
30 Jun 1808	J. Kennedy Kircaid	Andrew & Ann P(Caldwell)	HMEM	737	1832
00 000 0000	John T. Kincaid		AMEN	26	1843
15 Oct 1822	Thomas Kincaid	Andrew & Ann P(Caldwell)	HMEM	723	1834
00 000 0000	Thomas Kincaid	Andrew & Ann P(Caldwell) Pa1791/**87	PPME	226	1834
03 Nov 1815	W.C. Kincaid		AMEN	22	1834
00 000 0000	William C. Kincaid	Andrew & Ann P(Caldwell) Pa/**	PPME	314	1834
00 000 0000	William C. Kincaid		AMEN	19	1834
00 000 0000	Ann Lukins [Kincaid] Jesse		AMEN	22	1834
03 Nov 1838	Elizabeth McCausland[Craft]		HMCL	928	1836
05 Jul 1826	Thomas A. McDannold	John & Elizabeth(Iles) Kyc1800/**	HJOD	805	1845
05 Jul 1826	Thomas L. McDannold	John Montgomery1797/x	GSBR	373	---
00 000 0000	Thomas L. McDannold		BGSB	246	---
00 000 0000	W.P. McDonald		GSBR	392	1845
25 Nov 1852	Vermilion J. Meredith	Thomas E & Elizabeth(Anderson) Oh/In	AMEN	19	1848
00 000 0000	Mary J Meteer[Morse]		CHAM	993	1867
26 Jun 1811	Andrew K. Mitchell		BGHR	949	---
00 Oct 1800	John B. Moffett		HGJR	897	---
00 000 1800	John R. Moffett		PBWC	506	---
00 000 0000	Thomas Moffett		PBWC	367	1818
31 Oct 1820	E.H. Morton		HSAN	78	---
00 000 0000	Jane Perkins[Lenton]	Edmond & Elizabeth(VanLandingham)**/Ky	HEDG	587	---
09 Dec 1819	Charles B. Pettgh	Samuel & Elizabeth Va/c1795	BHAN	66	---
00 000 1821	Uriah Prather	Jonathan & Sarah(Ritter) Va/Pa	PBWH	584	---
00 000 0000	Jonathan H. Pugh		PPVE	504	---
00 000 0000	E.C. Reed		HSAN	77	1823
00 000 0000	Nannie Ryan[Crowning] Moses & Dulcina		AMEN	19	1833
00 000 0000	Nettie Shumake[Trimble]		HLOG	347	---
03 Oct 1834	James M. Simpson	Thomas & Caroline(Badger) Va/Ky	HSAN	895	---
01 Feb 1828	Catherine Stephens[Stuart]		PCHR	353	1835
07 Feb 1823	Chambers M. Stuart		HMCL	839	---
00 000 0000	E.L. Swiney		HMCL	839	1862
28 Jul 1823	E.L. Seiney		AMEN	22	1828
			HMEM	741	1835

BIRTHDATE	NAME OF BIOGRAPHEE	PARENTS/BIRTHPLACE/BIRTHDATE		SOURCE/PAGE	DATE
00 000 0000	William C. Swiney	Edward & Elizabeth A(Caldwell)		PEDP	333	----
02 Sep 1840	Walker B. Tackett	William & Isabella	Ky/Ky	BCHA	74	----
17 Oct 1816	A.A. Taylor	Charles	Pa/x	HCHR	168	----
00 000 0000	Benjamin Thompson			HFAY	96	----
00 000 1808	Martha S. Thompson[Power]			HMEM	744	1829
00 000 0000	Rachel A.N.[Vieten]			HCHR	265	----
00 000 0000	Catherine Whaley[George]			HCHR	172	----
00 Aug 1830	George W. Whitecraft	John & Rachel(Arnett)	**/**	HSAN	726	1835
11 Jan 1819	John A. Whitecraft	John & Rachel(Arnett)	Tn/Clark	HCHR	163	----
11 Jan 1819	J.A. Whitecraft	John		PCHR	225	----
10 Mar 1824	John C. Whitecraft	John & Rachel	Tn/Ky	HCHR	167	----
06 Mar 1828	Silas M. Whitecraft	John & Rachel(Arnet)		HSAN	726	1835
04 Jan 1823	Andrew Wiggenton			HLOG	526	1828
13 Jan 1804	Nancy Wilcockson[Power]			HSAN	910	1821
00 000 0000	Cynthia Williams[Johnson]			PEDP	774	----
00 000 0000	Cynthia Williams[Johnson]			PPME	193	1823
00 000 0000	Cynthia Williams[Johnson]			PPME	461	1823
11 Sep 1808	Col. John Williams	James & Hannah(Mappin)	Va/Pa1776	HSAN	728	1823
11 Sep 1808	Col. John Williams	James & Hannah(Mappin)		HMEM	727	1823
11 Sep 1808	John Williams			EFAY	591	----
23 Nov 1829	Robert A. Young	William P & Margaret(Young)	Ky/Va	PPME	432	1836

B E L L   C O U N T Y   (N O N E)

B O O N E   C O U N T Y

BIRTHDATE	NAME OF BIOGRAPHEE	PARENTS/BIRTHPLACE/BIRTHDATE	SOURCE/PAGE	DATE

Date	Name	Parents	Origin	Ref	No.	Year
00 000 0000	Arminta Adams[Dawson]			HWCL	851	---
00 000 0000	Arramintia Adams[Dawson] Mathew			PBWL	933	---
00 Jul 1832	Zebulon Allphin	Reuben	Ky/1801	BCSB	143	---
15 Jul 1827	Eliza Anderson	Thomas & Sarah(Myers)		HWCL	B225	---
27 Aug 1814	Daniel Baldwin	Daniel & Mary A(Peak)	Va/NJ	LOGA	454	---
15 May 1839	Francis H. Bates	Horace & Mary(Carpenter)		HADM	754	1847
07 Jun 1828	Joseph W. Botts	Absalom		BHAN	569	---
29 Jan 1852	William L. Brumback	Peter W & Ann E(Estes)	Va1801/1809	BCSB	504	1864
18 Sep 1826	Elizabeth Burt[Quisenberry]			TAZE	491	---
00 000 1810	James E. Campbell			HPEO	812	---
12 Dec 1812	John Campbell	Alexander & --- (Dooley)		CHAM	891	---
18 Dec 1812	John W. Campbell	Gilbert & Mary		HPEO	804	---
28 Jan 1868	Milly J. Clarkson[Williams]			HADM	907	---
27 Aug 1829	Marcellus M. Cleek	Benjamin & Martha(Harris)	Ky1800/x	BCSB	403	1834
02 Nov 1832	Benjamin F. Clore	Abram		PBRJ	363	1836
22 Nov 1830	Harrison Clore	Abraham & Sarah(Cornelius)	Va/Ky	PBRJ	456	1867
00 000 0000	Adam Crisler			HJAC	129	1867
00 000 0000	Alm Crisler			HJAC	129	---
00 000 0000	Silas Crisler			PBRJ	375	---
15 Mar 1807	Nicholas Darnall			HMCL	936	1829
17 Dec 1828	Joseph N. Datin	Noel & Nancy(McDonald)		GHHA	962	1829
00 000 1794	James R. Dawson			PBWL	937	---
19 Jul 1831	Joseph Donaldson	Andrew	Va/x	PHEF	B156	---
00 000 0000	Joel G. Garnett	William		HMCH	380	1834
00 000 0000	Elizabeth Gibson[McGinnis]			HSAN	931	1826
00 000 0000	Ann E. Graves[Garnett]	Reuben	Va/x	HMCH	380	---
15 May 1834	Thomas J. Grimsley	John B. & Julia A(Johnson)	Va1800/**	PBWL	1021	1824
31 Jul 1821	William B. Hawkins			COLE	635	1837
00 000 0000	A.M. Henderson			ACLY	50	---
16 Mar 1822	David Henline	John & Mary(Darnell)	1787/1791	PBWL	875	---
00 000 0000	James J. Henline			PBWL	894	---
20 Dec 1823	William B. Herline	John & Mary(Darnell)	1781/1791	BMCL	1091	1828
20 Dec 1823	William B. Herline	John & Mary	1787/1791	PBWL	928	---
00 000 1835	W.H. Higgins	William & Nancy	Ky/Ky	GJRI	515	---
19 Oct 1832	William Huey	John & Matilda(Rice)	Ky/Ky	HMCH	318	1834

B O O N E   C O U N T Y   (C O N T.)

BIRTHDATE	NAME OF BIOGRAPHEE	PARENTS/BIRTHPLACE/BIRTHDATE	SOURCE/PAGE	DATE
23 Jul 1817	E.W.S. Hume		HEDG 663	----
00 Nov 1808	J.J. Johnson		HSAN 1025	----
27 Apr 1825	Mary W. Johnson[Carter]	David & Sybella(Allen) Ky/Ky	HSAN 1025	----
00 000 0000	Catharine Livingston[Allin]		PBML 399	----
07 Jul 1823	William McGinnis	David & Eliza(Gibson) Mercer1798/**	HSAN 845	1827
15 Aug 1821	Noble C. Newport	Joseph & Maria(Scholes) Pa/Eng	HLAS B163	1836
00 000 0000	Sarah A. O'Kerson[Peters]		HDEW 344	1848
00 000 0000	William M. Peck		HCHR 263	1866
00 000 0000	William Pierson		HJAC 130	----
00 000 1827	William A. Powell	Hezekiah & Lucy(Ealer)	CJRI 547	----
17 Sep 1847	Dr. D.D. Roberts		HEDG 709	----
15 Apr 1847	Dr. M.L. Saunders		HGAR 424	----
02 Feb 1816	Moses Scott	William & Mary(Kyle)	HMCH 346	1850
00 000 0000	Mary Shafer[Crisler]		PBRJ 375	----
00 000 0000	Hilan Soverns		HMAD 562	1863
24 Oct 1842	James T. Stansifer	Henry & Lucy(Richardson)	PBWB 140	----
00 000 0000	Elizabeth Stevens[Peck]		BCHR 263	1848
16 Jun 1826	Joseph W. Stevens	Samuel & Elizabeth(Powell) Va/Va	BCHR 993	----
13 Sep 1822	James F. Thompson		HMCL 917	1829
02 Nov 1805	Martha Thorp[Bondurant]		PBDP 980	----
30 Sep 1831	Wesley Walton	Frederick M & Emily(Rice) Va/x	HMCH 320	----
30 Sep 1831	Wesley Walton	Frederick M & Emily(Rice) Ky/Ky	GHHA 591	1835

B O U R B O N   C O U N T Y

BIRTHDATE	NAME OF BIOGRAPHEE	PARENTS/BIRTHPLACE/BIRTHDATE	SOURCE/PAGE	DATE
00 000 1804	Harmonas Alkire	Adam & Margaret(Hornbeck)	HSAN 901	----
00 000 0000	Ira Allen[Taylor]		PPVE 116	----
00 000 1806	Iva Allen[Taylor]		PPVE 654	----

00 000 0000	Gilmore Anderson		HMAD 464	1816
04 Mar 1808	Martha R. Archer[Brown]		COLE 594	----
29 Jun 1828	W.T. Baker	James **/x	HCHR 238	----
00 000 0000	Abraham Banta	Henry **/x	PVED 939	----
00 000 0000	J. Henry Banta	Abraham **/x	PVED 509	----
15 Oct 1810	Alexander L. Barnett	John & Sallie(Kenney) Va1781/x	HDEW 177	1845
00 000 0000	James Barnett		HDEW 345	----
08 Nov 1820	James Barnett	John	PBDP 673	----
09 Nov 1820	James Barnett	John	PBDP 958	----
21 Jan 1818	T.J. Barrett		HMCL 870	1832
00 0c 1800	Michael Barr		PVED 943	1812
00 000 0000	Jane Beckett[Brown]		BCSB 280	----
00 0c 1813	William Blakemey		PVED 495	----
00 000 0000	Barbara Flankenbaker[Bayne] Nicholas		HMCH 331	----
00 000 0000	Elizabeth Booth[Colvin]		HADM 801	----
03 Jan 1828	Mary Booth[Durman]		HADM 803	----
00 000 1794	John Boulden	Thomas	BRJM 498	----
28 May 1823	B.F. Bowen		HEDG 562	----
25 Aug 1834	N.A. Bowen		HEDG 562	----
13 Mar 1825	David Bowles	Hughes & Elizabeth(Payne) Va/Va	BLOG 264	----
25 Oct 1812	Mourning Bowles[Nichols]		HADM 806	----
00 Nov 1807	Nancy Bowles[Roberts]		COLE 630	----
27 Sep 1829	William Fowles		HADM 908	1830
05 Oct 1829	William T. Bowles	Hughes Va1786/x	LOGA 533	----
23 Jun 1823	Nancy J. Bradley[Booth] Hiram & Mary(Markwell) **/Fleming		PBAD 169	1844
07 Jul 1834	James E. Breckenridge Oliver H.P. & Nancy(Ellis)		PBHE 626	----
05 Aug 1807	Preston Breckinridge		HSAN 877	----
28 Dec 1826	Elizabeth A.Bridges[Stewart] John & Eliza(Ellis)		CHAM 1033	----
25 Jul 1828	J.C. Bryan	James & Margaret(Burris)	PHCC 10	1830
00 000 0000	Mary J. Buchanan[Metcalf]		HMAC 276	1833
11 Apr 1829	James L. Campbell Lewis & Elizabeth(Wallace) **90/**99		PBKN 237	----
00 000 0000	James O. Campbell John & Jane(Wallace) Va/Va		PBDP 937	----
01 Aug 1813	Rev. Johr G. Campbell James & Nancy A V&/Va		PBML 1128	----
00 000 0000	Rev. Johr G. Campbell		PBML 293	----
00 000 0000	Sallie A. Campbel[Campbell]		PBML 293	----
24 Aug 1805	Zebulon Cantrall		LOGA 568	----

BIRTHDATE	NAME OF BIOGRAPHEE	PARENTS/BIRTHPLACE/BIRTHDATE	SOURCE/PAGE	DATE
00 000 0000	Artemisia Carl[Mills]		HDEW 341	1860
21 Mar 1808	Kitty Carter[Nichols]		HADM 926	----
30 Sep 1809	David W. Clark	John & Nancy A(Isgrig) NJ1779/Md83	BLOG 590	----
12 Oct 1812	H.P. Clendenen	George W & Mary	HGJR 850	----
01 Mar 1847	Dr. J.A. Clutter		CJRI 795	1830
11 Apr 1829	Amos Conaway		PHEF B153	1830
00 000 0000	Amos Conaway		PHPI 504	1829
01 Feb 1830	Stephen F. Corrington Rev. Elijah & Ailsie(Gray)		HGJR 714	----
13 Dec 1819	E.R. Couchman	Benjamin & Millicent(Riggs)	HMEM 708	1825
24 Dec 1819	E.R. Couchman	B.F.	PPME 427	1825
00 000 0000	E.R. Couchman		AMEN 23	1852
00 000 0000	M. Couchman		GHHA 598	----
00 000 0000	John Coughlan		PHCC 13	----
02 Sep 1812	Thomas Crawford		BHAN 401	----
10 Feb 1855	W. Keen Crockett	William & Eliza(Ware) Ky/Ky	PBRI 557	----
03 Jun 1813	Montgomery Crumbaugh Solomon		PBML 1064	1841
08 Jun 1791	John Darnelle		HSAN 827	----
23 Apr 1829	Screpta Daugherty[Crawford]		BHAN 401	----
00 000 1794	James R. Dawson		PBML 933	----
25 Dec 1868	Lillie David[Coyle]		BWGL 986	----
02 Oct 1820	Mitchell Dazey		HADM 849	1820
25 Feb 1833	Martha A. Dickey[Wallace] T. Lyle **/x		PLAS 383	1839
00 000 0000	T. Lyle Dickey		PLAS 362	1834
23 Feb 1794	Joseph Duncan		PBMA 131	----
05 May 1831	Samuel S. Elder	Samuel & Phebe(Clinkinbeard)	HSAN 660	1834
22 Feb 1808	James Faris		COLE 586	----
00 Jan 1831	John M. Forden	John & Evaline(Snyder)	HSAN 665	1831
02 Nov 1800	Isaac Forman	Joseph & Mary(Landers) 1775/1782	HSTC 291	----
27 Sep 1810	William B. Forman		HWAS 50	----
00 000 0000	William B. Forman		HWAS 569	----
16 Oct 1806	Joseph Fry		HMGH 193	1865

Date	Name	Parents	Origin	Code	No.	Year
00 000 0000	Dr. W.M. Garrard			CELW	350	1856
00 000 1808	George R. Givens			CSBR	266	1831
09 Aug 1815	David C. Gooden			HCHR	173	---
25 Feb 1817	Levi H. Graves	James & Margaret(Blackburn)		PVED	556	1828
00 000 0000	Dr. William G. Gray			CSBR	385	1850
00 000 0000	Sarah Griffith[Thomas]			HPIK	736	---
00 000 0000	Sarah F. Hardesty[Ballard]			HMCL	990	---
17 Mar 1811	Isaac Harness	Jacob & Christina(Smith)	Va/x	PBML	1103	1832
17 Mar 1811	Isaac Harness	Jacob & Christina(Smith)	Va/x	BRML	189	---
00 000 0000	Mary N. Headleston			HSAN	672	---
05 Nov 1827	Catherine T. Hedges[Moreland] Peter & Susan(Miller)		**/**	PVED	673	---
00 000 0000	Dorcas Hedges[Banta] James		Eng/x	PVED	940	---
00 000 0000	Mary E. Hedges[Colvin]			HADM	802	---
28 Feb 1824	Andrew G. Henry	John & Betsey		PBMO	B16	1827
28 Feb 1824	Judge A.G. Herry	John & Betsey(Mills)	SC/Ky	PBMB	255	1827
25 Jul 1808	Greenup Henry	--- & Elizabeth(Alexander)		HMOR	573	---
00 000 0000	Jacob Hersman			CSBR	386	1834
11 Aug 1811	Jacob Hersman	Henry & Elizabeth(Fry)	Va/Ky	HEDG	263	1834
22 Mar 1833	Junius B. Hildreth	A.K.	Fleming02/x	HEDG	662	1834
20 Oct 1829	William H. Hildreth	A.K.		PVED	662	1832
00 000 0000	William H. Hildreth	Alvin K & Sally(Ritter)	Ky/Ky	HLAS	793	---
13 Jun 1810	Col.Daniel F. Hitt	Rev. Martin & Margaret(Smith)	Va63/x	OGLE	A532	---
22 Jan 1799	Samuel M. Hitt			PBWA	687	---
07 Dec 1816	Msrtha Holloway[Rankin] George			PBWA	216	---
26 Sep 1829	Hon.Robert Holloway George		Va/x	PBWA	623	---
03 Feb 1798	Garrett V. Hopkins Lemuel		Pa/x	HFUL	440	---
14 May 1809	Dr. Samuel A. Hopkins Samuel & Nancy(Harney)		Mdl774/De	HPEO	661	---
03 Feb 1798	John Hornback			PPME	453	1825
25 Jul 1800	David Housh			KNOX	682	1803
00 000 0000	Drusilla Hudson[East] William			HDEW	347	1843
15 Sep 1821	W.W. Hughes William			BHAN	370	---
00 000 0000	Mary E. Ingles[Pritchett] William			PBMC	374	---
01 Jan 1837	Nathan H. Ingles William & Parmelia(Jacoby)		Ky/Ky	HSAN	797	1855
05 Aug 1827	Elizabeth J. Irvin[Barnett] John & Sarah(Wilson)		**/**	PBDP	673	---
00 000 0000	Elizabeth J. Irwin			HDEW	345	1846
30 Dec 1822	Dr. Henry D. Jenkins			COLE	647	1855
00 000 0000	Mary Jones[Gooding]			PSTC	365	---

BOURBON COUNTY (CONT.)

BIRTHDATE	NAME OF BIOGRAPHEE	PARENTS/BIRTHPLACE/BIRTHDATE	SOURCE/PAGE	DATE
18 Aug 1812	Henry S. Kemp		HADM 723	1831
00 000 1812	Henry S. Kemp	Charles Pa/x	PBAD 529	---
06 Feb 1814	William C. Kennett	Dixon H & Fanny(Wilson) Md1782/Pendletn	HGJR 1058	---
13 Jun 1831	Malinda J. Kenney[Bowles]		HLOG 443	---
10 Sep 1826	John King		PBWO B225	1854
00 000 1805	Thomas Kirkpatrick		PBWL 506	---
25 Jul 1818	Elizabeth B. Laughlin[Yeargin]		HADM 907	---
00 000 0000	Philip Linn		HMEM 808	1865
00 000 1815	Joseph Liter		HMOR 736	1839
12 Feb 1822	Rev. John W. Lock	Rev. George	PJEF B24	---
00 000 1842	Martha E. McConnell[Henry]		HMOR 664	---
16 Nov 1814	James McCrory	James & Sarah(Vance) Ire/Va	PBCQ 333	---
00 000 0000	Mahala McDavid[Linn]		HMEM 808	1865
00 000 0000	Jane McDowell[Sandusky]		PVED 747	---
25 Dec 1791	Samuel McIntosh	John & Sarah(Bennett) Scotland/NJ1753	CELW 296	---
00 000 0000	John McKinney		PHPI 488	---
00 000 0000	John A. Magner	William & ---(Hopkins) In/In	HGRU 856	---
00 000 0000	James Mahan		PBWA 393	---
00 000 0000	James Mahan		HMAC 261	c1834
16 Dec 1793	Valentine R. Mallory		HSAN 852	---
01 Apr 1820	David Martin	James & Catherine(Layton) Va/De	PBWC 326	---
25 Oct 1804	Preston Martin	William & Amie(Hopper) W/**	HMCH 530	1836
00 000 0000	Sarah D. Maxwell[Reading]		PCHR 433	---
00 000 0000	Jacob H. Miller	John A & Jane(Levesque) Ky/x	PBWC 213	---
09 Sep 1831	John R. Miller	John & Jane(Levesque) Ky/Ky	PPDM 718	---
09 Sep 1831	John R. Miller	John & Jane(Levesque} Ky/x	PBWC 213	---
16 Dec 1825	Uriah K. Miller		HADM 806	---
10 Dec 1827	John H. Mills	Nathan & Catherine(Jamison) Va/Va	PBDP 722	---
00 000 0000	Hannah V. Mock[Stump]	Charles & Sarah S.	PBAD 180	---
05 Apr 1835	John Mock	Abraham & Cynthia(Wilson) Ky/Ky	HMCH 339	---
00 000 0000	Margaret Moreland[Sandusky]	Thomas & Catherine T(Hedges)Ky/	PPVE 259	---
00 000 0000	Susan Moreland[Sandusky]	Thomas & Catherine(Hedges) Ky/Ky	PVED 504	---

Date	Name	Parents/Spouse	Origin	Code	No.	Year
00 000 0000	Sarah M. Morrow			HDEW	345	1850
11 Feb 1822	Abijah D. Nea_			PBCO	270	----
28 Jan 1812	George W. Nea_	Tavener	Va/x	PBDP	344	----
05 Sep 1795	John T. Neal	Jacob & Ann(Yeamin)		PBCO	270	----
01 Nov 1817	William Neal	James M & Matilda	Ky/Ky	CJRI	359	1827
00 000 1816	William Neal			COLE	258	----
00 000 1841	H. Clay Nicholas			HADM	670	1852
11 Sep 1799	James Nichols			HADM	806	----
20 Apr 1829	John P. Nichols	James & Margaret(Wallace)	**1799/x	PBAD	332	----
20 Apr 1829	John P. Nichols			HADM	806	1833
29 Jan 1826	L.W. Nichols	James & Margaret(Wallace)		PBAD	509	----
29 Jan 1826	Lewis W. Nichols			HADM	807	1833
25 Oct 1793	Margaret Norton[Darnelle]			HSAN	827	----
00 000 0000	Lewis L. O'Neal			HMAC	271	1837
16 Feb 1810	Grayson Orr			HADM	852	----
14 Aug 1819	Milly Orr[Selby]			HADM	853	----
00 000 0000	Josella Parker[Talbott]			PVED	463	----
00 000 0000	Martha Payne[Riley]		Ky/x	CHAM	1012	----
23 May 1830	Thomas A. Pritchett	William & Lydia(Wilson)	Ky/Ky	PBWC	374	----
00 000 0000	Nancy Rain[Neal]			PBDP	344	----
00 000 1807	Hon. James H. Ralston			HADM	679	c1828
25 Jan 1801	Joseph N. Ralston			HADM	680	1832
00 000 1810	James W. Reno			BRMA	328	1843
25 Feb 1807	Isaac Roberts	Azariah	Ky/x	COLE	629	----
00 000 0000	Robert Robertson			BGLS	28	----
22 Oct 1830	Z. Robertson		c1775/x	COLE	554	----
00 000 0000	William O. Rogers			HDEW	345	1856
00 000 0000	J.A. Rogers			HSTC	375	----
00 000 0000	Jane Rogers[Deventer]			BCSB	285	----
09 Sep 1836	W.O. Rogers	John & Elender(Hildreth)	Ky1800/x	HDEW	318	----
28 Sep 1814	Catherine Ruddell[Hendry]			HADM	806	----
28 Sep 1814	Catherine Ruddell[Nichols]			HADM	806	----
26 Dec 1821	George H. Ruddell	William & Armen(Phelan)		HMOD	584	1829
11 Mar 1849	J.D. Ruddell	George & Martha(Neal)	Ky/Ky	PHCC	253	1853
28 Sep 1812	Hon. John M. Ruddell	Rev.Stephen & Susan(David)	Va68/Va80	PBAD	461	----
09 Feb 1847	Zalmon Ruddell	George & Martha(Neal)	Ky/Ky	PHCC	253	----
00 000 0000	Jacob Ruggles	Thomas & Rachel(Freeland)	NC/Md	BHAN	426	----

BIRTHDATE	NAME OF BIOGRAPHEE	PARENTS	BIRTHPLACE	BIRTHDATE	SOURCE/PAGE	DATE
24 Mar 1833	Abraham Sandusky	Abraham & Jane(McDowell)		**1793/**1792	PVED 473	----
00 000 0000	Abraham Sandusky				PVED 747	----
17 Jul 1817	James Sandusky	Isaac & Euphemma(McDowell)	Ky/Ky		PVED 495	----
19 Nov 1826	William Sandusky				PVED 500	----
11 Mar 1829	William T. Sandusky	William & Julia(Earp)	Ky/Va		PVED 378	1829
01 Mar 1829	William T. Sandusky	William & Julia(Earp)	Ky/Va		PPVE 352	1828
00 000 1802	Samuel Sconce				PVED 191	1829
00 000 1802	Samuel Sconce				PPVE 181	----
01 May 1823	William H. Sconce				PVED 698	----
00 000 0000	F.L. Scott				HCHA 179	1830
27 Jan 1807	Fielding L. Scott	Patrick & Ann(Campbell)	Pa/Ire		HCHA 128	----
27 Jan 1807	Fielding L. Scott	Patrick & Anna(Campbell)	Pa/Ire		ECHA 48	----
00 000 0000	Jane Scott[House]	Arthur	1777/x		PBWC 303	----
30 Mar 1823	Levin P. Scrogin	John & Patsey(Mills)	Md/Va		PBWL 1006	1828
00 000 1801	Drusilla Sebby[Compton]	Jeremiah & Nancy			CELW 298	----
00 000 0000	S.H. Segester				ACLY 50	1853
01 Aug 1820	Lewis V. Selby				HADM 853	----
02 Oct 1803	William M. Shawhan	John & Margaret(McCune)			ECHA 80	----
21 Oct 1821	Hannah Shrout[Honn]				HEDG 618	----
10 Dec 1833	George P. Sidener	George P.			HSAN 1009	1852
21 Oct 1861	Harlan W. Six	Presley & Mary E(Palmer)	Ky/Pa		CHAM 1027	1870
08 Dec 1839	Benjamin F. Snowden	William & Mary(Pigg)	Clark/Clark		PVED 309	----
00 000 0000	Rawser Spicer		Va/x		PBAD 281	1831
00 000 0000	James P. Stockton				HJAC 129	1875
08 Dec 1822	M.E. Stribling[Lurton]	Rev.W.D. & Mahala			HMOR 699	----
11 Jun 1826	William J. Tackett	John & Enfield(Mason)			PBSM 453	1829
00 000 0000	Augustine Talbott				PVED 463	----
04 Aug 1834	Joseph D. Taylor	John H & Eliza(Liter)		**1809/**	BCHA 467	1861
00 000 0000	Nancy P. Taylor[Seekman]				CSBR 390	1844
10 Dec 1832	Reuben Terry	Reuben & Elizabeth(Dazey)			PBSM 656	1833
00 000 0000	Isaac Thomas	James & Abigail(Langsford)	Ky/Ky		BHAN 383	----
30 Jan 1827	Andrew T. Thompson	John & Elizabeth(Furguson)			HSAN 962	1836

Date	Name	Parents / Notes	Origin	Code	No.	Year
09 Nov 1814	Judge Anthony Thornton Anthony & Mary(Towles)		Va/Va	PBSM	240	----
09 Nov 1814	Anthony Thornton			EFAY	522	----
00 000 1825	Franklin Todd John P & Mary		Vt/Pa	HPIK	416	1832
00 000 1819	Robert Todd John & Mary		Md/SC	HPIK	416	1832
00 Oct 1810	Hon. Arthur H. Trimble			HADM	798	1830
00 000 0000	Catherine Troxell_Swearingen]			HDEW	345	1826
13 Jun 1809	George Trotter James & Elizabeth(Keeney)		Va1770/x	PSTE	340	----
12 Feb 1826	Pence B. Truitt[Stone] Littleton		Md/x	PBSM	574	----
09 Oct 1816	Harness Trumbc Adam & Mildred(Foster)		**/**	HSAN	1066	1828
06 Sep 1814	Eliza Trunmel[Egbert]			PPWO	497	----
05 Dec 1840	Dillard B. Tucker Osborn & Cynthia(Bathershell)Oh/Ky			PVED	1033	----
00 000 0000	Edward W. Turrer			HGAS	221	----
00 Apr 1805	Robinson Turpin			HSAN	929	----
00 000 0000	Caleb Underhill			HCHA	184	1872
00 000 0000	E.B[Underhill]			HCHA	184	1872
06 May 1815	Cyrus W. Vanderen Bernard & Eliza(McKee)			HSAN	848	1834
00 000 0000	Mary Wagoner[Wortman]			HGAS	274	----
00 Aug 1806	Margaret Wallace[Nichols]			HADM	806	----
05 Mar 1814	Armistead Ward John & Nancy(Billington) SC/Oh1796			CJRI	549	----
00 000 0000	Louis Ward			BCHR	888	----
17 Jun 1826	Charlton D. Weters Silas & Shannah(Conway)			BRML	411	----
00 000 1808	Nancy Waters[Sconce]			PVED	191	1828
00 000 1808	Nancy Waters[Sconce]			PPVE	181	1829
00 000 0000	C.W. Wayne			HMAC	277	1844
03 Feb 1816	Churchill W. Wayne Benjamin F & Nancy(Tankesly) Va/Ire			HMAC	187	----
28 Jan 1829	Elizabeth A. Weathersford[Cawby] Henry & Mary(Lighter)			HMAC	275	1857
29 Dec 1809	Richard O. Wells			COLE	619	----
28 Jan 1829	Catherine E. West[Hendrick] Henry & Mary(Lightner)			HMCL	921	----
01 Jul 1834	Martha West[Hendrick] Henry			BMCL	1086	----
30 Jan 1827	Hon. Simeon H. West Henry & Mary(Liter) Mason/**			BMCL	766	----
30 Jan 1827	Simeon H. West H. & Mary(Liter)			BMCL	1340	----
00 000 0000	Simeon H. West			HMCL	933	1851
23 Aug 1827	John Wiggintor			HLOG	400	----
23 Aug 1827	John Wiggintor Peter & Margaret		Va/Va	LOGA	907	1827
00 000 0000	Drucilla Williams[Adams]			HDEW	341	1830
00 000 0000	Wesley Williams			BHAN	669	----

BIRTHDATE	NAME OF BIOGRAPHEE	PARENTS/BIRTHPLACE/BIRTHDATE		SOURCE/PAGE	DATE
00 000 0000	William Wright	Hugh	Va/x	PVED 291	1828
25 Oct 1829	James A. Yingling	Joseph	Pa1792/x	HADM 913	1831
17 Dec 1787	Jacob Yocum			HSAN 1045	----

B O Y D   C O U N T Y

BIRTHDATE	NAME OF BIOGRAPHEE	PARENTS/BIRTHPLACE/BIRTHDATE		SOURCE/PAGE	DATE
21 Jan 1841	Landrum Burchett	William & Emily	Ky/Ky	LOGA 872	----

B O Y L E   C O U N T Y

BIRTHDATE	NAME OF BIOGRAPHEE	PARENTS/BIRTHPLACE/BIRTHDATE		SOURCE/PAGE	DATE
12 Feb 1865	James Anderson			HMOR 762	----
00 000 1811	Nathan Beadles	Rice & Sarah(Adams)	Va/Va	HFUF 785	----
02 Jun 1825	Mary J Briscoe[Meade]	George H & Eliza K(Ewing)		BCSB 201	----
02 Nov 1842	Mary E. Bruce[Bright]	Henry & Mary E(Pope)		PBML 234	----
02 Nov 1842	Mary E. Bruce[Bright]	Henry & Mary E(Pope)		BRML 521	----
12 Dec 1864	John H. Bright	William M & Mary E(Bruce)Lincoln35/**42		BRML 521	----
00 000 0000	John Crow			HGJR 729	----
07 Oct 1828	Dr. James M. Davis	Dr.Cyrus A & Anna R(Montague)		HGJR 725	----
14 Feb 1806	Samuel F. Dodds	Samuel		PSTE 740	----
09 Apr 1841	Robert Drury	John J.	Nelson/x	PBMA 854	----
10 Jun 1837	H.R. Fields			BHIQ B205	----
00 000 0000	Dr.Willis D.Green	Dr. Duff & Lucy		PBCW 241	----
00 000 0000	Susan Jones[Lucas]			PVED 504	----
00 000 1853	John T. Lillard			HMCL 801	----

BIRTHDATE	NAME OF BIOGRAPHEE	PARENTS/BIRTHPLACE/BIRTHDATE		SOURCE/PAGE	DATE
01 Apr 1852	John T. Lillard	Thomas M & Mary(Bright)		BMCL	1162	----
00 000 0000	Mary Little[Crow]			HGJR	729	----
29 Dec 1805	Walter Nichols		RI/x	HMCL	994	----
23 Dec 1792	David Shelton			PBWA	555	----
01 Feb 1834	Dr. Joshua N. Speed	William & Elizabeth(Nicholas)Casey/RI		CSBR	240	1854
00 000 0000	Mary Speed[Warren]			CSBR	378	1855
00 000 0000	John Taylor			HSAN	787	----
27 May 1841	William A. Webb	William R & Jane(Moore)	Va/Ky	PBSM	716	----

B R A C K E N   C O U N T Y

BIRTHDATE	NAME OF BIOGRAPHEE	PARENTS/BIRTHPLACE/BIRTHDATE		SOURCE/PAGE	DATE
18 Jun 1800	Dr. Thomas Bottle	John & Ann(Thome)	Pa/Scotland	GHHA	771	----
30 Apr 1813	Cynthia Craig[Megeath]			PHCC	282	----
00 000 1816	E.T. Currens			COLE	542	----
23 Oct 1847	Andrew M. Darrough			BHIQ	B194	1851
10 Apr 1827	Bertrand Dawson	John & Cory(Jones)	Va1791/Nicholas01	HSAN	958	----
05 May 1827	Dr. J.W. Dora			COLE	544	----
30 Mar 1813	Andrew Dunn			BEFF	747	1853
00 000 1845	Dr. Thomas J. Dunn Andrew		**1813/**1812	PHEF	B126	----
04 Aug 1812	Sarah A. Elliott[Dunn]			BEFF	747	1853
20 Sep 1827	Andrew Feagan	Richeson & Martha(Dunn)	Va/Pa	PBCO	219	----
04 Dec 1823	Margaret Field[Gillespie]			PHEF	B219	----
00 000 1805	Hiram D. Gregg			PBCO	470	----
00 000 0000	Nancy Harmon[Ellis]	Samuel & Elizabeth	Ky/Ky	BCSB	304	----
00 000 0000	Levi Houston	Joseph & Delilah(Weldon)	Md/Md	PVED	930	----
30 Apr 1820	Benjamin Howard	Joseph	Ky/x	PBDB	266	----
00 000 0000	Rachel Howard[Buckner]			HDEW	340	1836
00 000 1807	Elizabeth Humlong[Gregg]			PBCO	470	----
29 Mar 1823	Stephen King	William B & Anna R(Geening)	Va/Va	HSAN	1054	1830
17 Sep 1810	Uriah Mann	Peter & Elizabeth(Gaterel)	Va/Va	HSAN	859	1831
17 Sep 1810	Uriah Mann			HSAN	853	1831

BRACKEN COUNTY (CONT.)

BIRTHDATE	NAME OF BIOGRAPHEE	PARENTS/BIRTHPLACE/BIRTHDATE	SOURCE/PAGE	DATE
04 Jun 1841	A.M. Peddicord	Nelson & Rebecca	BRCM 176	c1855
10 Oct 1833	J.W. Philp	Thomas & Elizabeth(Baltzell) Eng/Oh	PJEF B148	----
09 Jan 1846	Euphrasia Reynolds[Kirk]	Witt & Lucretia	PBML 1122	----
00 000 0000	John T. Walton		HMGL 830	----
20 Jul 1803	N.E. Walton		VTBU 376	1812
28 Sep 1813	Harrison Washburn		HADW 810	----
00 000 1799	John A. Wells	Eli & Elizabeth(Coles)	PBCO 415	----
24 Jul 1825	James Wiley	John A & Ruth(Wells) **1799/Ky	PBCO 415	----
02 Feb 1798	Robert Wright		PBCO 337	----

BREATHITT COUNTY (NONE)

BRECKINRIDGE COUNTY

BIRTHDATE	NAME OF BIOGRAPHEE	PARENTS/BIRTHPLACE/BIRTHDATE	SOURCE/PAGE	DATE
04 Sep 1826	Samuel Adkison	Jeremiah & Nellie(Johnson) Va/x	PHCC 77	----
10 Oct 1830	William Adkison		PPWA 263	1836
21 Oct 1838	Sarah A Anderson[Miller]		HADW 806	----
02 Feb 1814	J.B. Barger	Jacob & Elizabeth(Seaton) Pa1784/Ky1787	HGSH 525	----
25 Feb 1844	George W. Barr	Elias & Sallie A(Beauchamp)**07/Hardin	BHAN 21	----
00 000 1851	Dr. John A. Barr	Charles & Sarah(Beauchamp) Ky/Ky	GHHA 845	1859
17 Feb 1849	Dr. John A. Barr	Elias & Sallie(Beauchamp)	HMCH 404	1869
00 000 0000	Dr. D.H. Baysinger		HJAC 128	1869
00 000 1833	R. Baysinger		HSTE 721	1846
28 Nov 1825	Harmon Brown	Albert G & Mary(Murdoch) Ky/Ky	PBKN 854	1830

Date	Name	Parents	Birthplaces	Code	No.	Year
13 May 1823	Samuel Brown	Alfred & Mary(Mordock)	Ky/Ky	HMER	622	c1830
21 Nov 1827	T.M. Brown			PPWA	288	1832
00 000 0000	Thomas Bruington			PBWA	648	---
13 May 1807	Thomas Bruington	James & Jane(McGlothin)		PBWA	464	---
13 May 1807	Thomas Bruington			PPWA	288	1840
09 May 1830	A.J. Bruner	Abraham & Nancy(Penick)	Ky/Va	PBCO	514	---
28 Dec 1833	Francis M. Bruner	Henry & Matilda(Claycomb)		KNOX	658	1834
14 Oct 1844	George F. Bruner	John & Susan(France) **1804/Va		PBWA	528	---
12 Dec 1812	Henry Bruner	Henry & Eves(Frymire)	Ky/Ky	KNOX	658	---
10 May 1814	Peter Bruner			PPWA	230	1836
00 000 0000	Polly Bruner[Frymire]			PPWA	231	---
14 Feb 1805	Otho Carr			PPWA	317	---
00 000 1812	A. Claycomb	Coonrad & Nancy(All)	Ky/Ky	GHHA	899	---
04 Feb 1828	George W. Claycomb	Frederick & Mary Ann(Claycomb)		PBWA	548	---
14 Jan 1805	Nancy Claycomb[Carr]			PBWA	317	---
00 000 1820	John M.J. Cox	Benjamin & Elizabeth Pa1774/Va		GHHA	826	---
05 Apr 1824	John M.J. Cox	Benjamin & Elizabeth(Midcap) Pa1775/x		HMCH	372	1833
04 Oct 1828	Jane Crawford[Horney]			CSBR	380	1837
15 Nov 1806	John H. Frymire			PPWA	231	1837
22 Jul 1842	William Frymire			PPWA	231	---
15 Oct 1837	Elizabeth A. Crant[White]			FAUP	B117	---
00 000 0000	John R. Gregory	William & Sarah(Pierce)	Va/NC	HSAN	967	1848
29 Mar 1849	William Hall	Sylvester & Mary(Hall)	Va/Va	PBCO	549	---
00 000 0000	Elizabeth Huckelby[Walker]			CSBR	381	1836
00 000 0000	Lucy E. Johnson[Campbell]			COLE	561	---
30 Apr 1828	Major Samuel Johnson	William & Mildred(Idson)	Ky/Va	MACL	271	---
00 000 0000	Samuel Johnson			MACL	299	1844
27 Aug 1855	Dr. William T. Lampton	Henry T & Mary C(Browne)	Ky/Ky	CJRI	758	---
17 Aug 1844	Richard Lewis	Thomas & Sarah(Nattingly)	W/Ky	BRCM	178	1846
30 May 1812	John A. McClernand	Dr. John & Fatima		HSAN	121	---
00 000 1812	Maj.Gen. John McClernand	John & Fatima		HSAN	318	---
08 Sep 1810	Elizabeth[McGlothin]			PPWA	291	1847
24 Jun 1839	Thomas H. Manren	Sidney S & Eliza A(Walton)	Ky/Ky	PJEF	B98	---
08 Dec 1818	Mary Meadows[Kilgore]			PVED	969	1831
20 Dec 1826	Dr. N.P. Merritt	Dr.John W & Lucretia(Pyle)	Va/Md	HWCL	B111	---
24 Dec 1812	Jane Moredock[Pruitt]			PPWA	292	---

BIRTHDATE	NAME OF BIOGRAPHEE	PARENTS/BIRTHPLACE/BIRTHDATE	SOURCE/PAGE	DATE
22 Mar 1814	William G. Nevitt	William & Mary(Edlin)	PBWH	659	1819
22 Nov 1849	Dr. T.V. Noakes		HADM	872	1875
29 Aug 1843	O.P. Norris	Joseph & Rebecca R.W.(Morris) Ky/Pa	PJEF	B99	----
00 000 1845	E.W. Parks	Seth & Mary(McCoy) NY/Va	CJRI	519	----
01 Jul 1837	William C. Parks	Seth & Mary(McCoy) NY/Va	CJRI	519	----
00 000 1838	M.H. Perrin	William & Sally D(Hardin) Va/Ky	CJRI	520	1864
17 Feb 1819	W.H.K. Pile		COLE	553	1855
00 000 1859	Daniel T. Ray	Thomas L & Mary(Barr) **1827/**1838	BHAN	27	----
02 Jan 1833	Bainbridge H. Roberts	James E & Sarah M(Cox) Tn/Pa	HMCD	640	----
16 Aug 1822	Elizabeth Shrewsbury[Harris]	Samuel & Polly(Kurrens)Va/NC	HWCL	B109	----
13 Nov 1822	Fendol P. Snider	Henry P & Verlinda(Dowell) Va/Va	CJRI	560	----
00 000 0000	John Waltrip		PBCO	577	----
29 Jan 1824	Francis Wheatley	Thomas & Susan(Mattingly) **c81/**87	HMCH	408	----
21 May 1853	Dr. W.G. White	Dr. Jacob S. Oh1824/x	PAUP	B117	----
00 000 0000	Susan Williams[Waltrip]		PBCO	577	----
21 Feb 1815	William Williams	Norris & Elizabeth(Miller) Pa/Pa	PBCO	510	1836
07 Apr 1839	Jesse M. Wright	David & Elizabeth(Jacob)	PBRJ	394	----

B U L L I T T   C O U N T Y

BIRTHDATE	NAME OF BIOGRAPHEE	PARENTS/BIRTHPLACE/BIRTHDATE	SOURCE/PAGE	DATE
00 00c 1830	L.L. Alexander		HWCL	171	----
09 Jul 1804	Col.John Cofer	Thomas & Sarah Va/Md	COLE	640	----
09 Jul 1804	Col. John Cofer	Thomas & Sarah(Winn) Va1781/Md	PBCO	305	----
00 000 0000	Mary A. Crow[Kermicle]		CJRI	829	1882
00 000 0000	John H. Felker		CELW	357	1844
00 000 0000	Harrison Grant	Noah	BHAN	363	----
01 Sep 1822	Samuel A. Ricketts	Jonathan & Nancy(Stevenson)	HMGH	438	----
03 Sep 1809	Cephas Simmons	Richard & Sophia	HPIK	564	1827
18 Mar 1813	John E. Stallings	William & Nancy Ky/Va	CJRI	360	1815

24 Dec 1818   Vincent Stewart   Reuben & Della(Owen)   HEDG 603 ----
03 Nov 1806   John Stringer   HPEO 782 ----
02 May 1835   James Watson   James & Rachel(Young)   Pa/Pa   PVED 894 ----

B U T L E R   C O U N T Y

BIRTHDATE	NAME OF BIOGRAPHEE	PARENTS/BIRTHPLACE/BIRTHDATE	SOURCE/PAGE		DATE
12 Oct 1812	Delpha Anderson[Moore]	George & Jennie(Worrell)	PBCW	324	----
11 Nov 1803	Moses K. Anderson		HSAN	815	----
29 Jan 1822	S.H. Ashmore		COLE	559	1826
06 Sep 1816	N.N. Borah	Pa/x	HWCL	B117	1818
00 May 1807	J.C. Caldwell	George	HMOR	540	1827
01 Aug 1833	Mary A. Davis[White]	George & Rhoda(Bishop)	PBJD	270	----
00 000 0000	William Embrey		HMAD	583	1845
04 Dec 1849	B.N. Ewing	Ky/Ky	TAZE	516	----
00 000 1845	Samuel Y. Ewing		EWCL	1022	----
25 Aug 1845	Samuel Y. Ewing	Nathaniel & Nancy(Young) **/Logan	PEWL	745	----
06 May 1853	William W. Ewing		HMCL	936	1853
00 000 1798	George B. Hargrave		HGSH	544	----
00 000 0000	Martha Hartis[Briggs]		HLOG	451	----
04 Sep 1857	D.H. Holman	Joseph & Rebecca(Given) Tn/x	HWCL	B98	----
00 000 1824	William H. Keown		HMAD	574	----
24 Oct 1826	Thomas N. Laurance	Henry C. 1807**/x	BRJM	341	----
00 000 0000	William McDade		HPIK	720	----
15 May 1807	George C. McMackin	John	HWCL	B24	1822
28 Apr 1827	Thomas G. May	Stephen U & Elizabeth J(Allen) x/Ky	HCHR	127	----
24 May 1838	Dr. E.G. Neel	Wade & Lucy(Wand) **1805/Warren1815	HGSH	732	----
11 Dec 1841	Jane E. Porter[Crain]	Benjamin & Nancy(Hutchinson)	PEWL	274	----
13 May 1846	James H. Reed	John & Susan **/**	HMOR	578	----
00 000 1853	George W. Stone	Silas H. NC/x	BRJM	318	----

BIRTHDATE	NAME OF BIOGRAPHEE	PARENTS/BIRTHPLACE/BIRTHDATE	SOURCE/PAGE	DATE
00 000 0000	James Baker		HGSH 591	----
29 Aug 1810	Eliza A. Campbell[Davis] David	SC/x	PBWC 473	----
30 Aug 1822	Benjamin C. Carter		PPWA 266	----
00 000 0000	D.T. Clark		CELW 353	1854
00 000 1832	F.E. Clinton	John & Sarah(Shelby) SC1791/Livingston	HGSH 771	----
30 Jan 1819	Nancy J. Dodds[Drennan]		HSAN 981	----
00 000 0000	Frank P. Drennan		HCHR 260	1856
15 Mar 1853	Franklin P. Drennan	John L & Henrietta(Wimburley) Ky/Ky	PCHR 321	----
00 000 0000	John G. Drennan		HCHR 260	1856
24 Dec 1854	John G. Drennan	John L & Henrietta(Wimburley)	HCHR 139	----
14 Nov 1836	Hon. John L. Drennan	Eli & Margaret(McDowell) SC1800/x	PCHR 330	1856
14 Nov 1826	John L. Drennan	Eli & Margaret(McDowell) SC/**	HCHR 256	----
00 000 0000	John L. Drennan		HCHR 265	1856
18 Feb 1808	John L. Drennan		HSAN 981	----
03 Dec 1854	Jonathan G. Drennan	John L & Henrietta(Wimburley)	PCHR 314	1856
00 000 0000	F.W. Duckwell		HCHR 265	----
20 Jun 1828	James Durning	John & Jane(Maxwell) Pa1802/**1805	PBWC 562	----
00 000 0000	Lucy Hunter[Self]		CELW 345	----
28 Dec 1824	Oliver V. Jones	Fountain W & Mary A(Vanlandigham)Tn/Ky	HSTC 344	1830
00 000 0000	Edden Lewis		HSAN 984	----
00 000 0000	Jiney G. Lyon[Hoxsey]		HWAD 565	1843
00 000 0000	Cinderella McCaslin[Gwyn]		PBWB 339	----
00 000 0000	Gray McCaslin	James	Ire/x	PBWO B65	----
00 000 0000	Hugh McCaslin	James	Ire/x	PBWO B65	----
00 000 0000	James McCaslin	James	Ire/x	PBWO B65	----
00 000 0000	Jane McCaslin	James	Ire/x	PBWO B65	----
00 00c 1807	John O. McCaslin		Ire/x	PBWO B65	----
00 000 0000	Martha McCaslin	James	Ire/x	PBWO B65	----
00 000 0000	Mary McCaslin	James	Ire/x	PBWO B65	----
00 000 0000	Rachel McCaslin	James	Ire/x	PBWO B65	----
06 Jan 1825	William R. McCaslin	Thomas & Sallie(Robinson) Tn/Tn1794	PBWO B75	----

BIRTHDATE	NAME OF BIOGRAPHEE	PARENTS/BIRTHPLACE/BIRTHDATE		SOURCE/PAGE		DATE
00 000 1811	William M. Orr	Hewey	Ire/x	BRJM	537	----
23 Jun 1827	Robert Rankin	Elias & Elizabeth		HADm	911	1852
00 000 1827	Robert Rankin	Elias & Elizabeth(Herron) Scotland/NC		PBAD	389	----
00 000 0000	Pressley Robinson			HMAC	276	1835
00 000 1841	J.D. Sanders			HMAC	276	----
00 000 0000	May F. Sanders[Duckwell]			HCHR	265	1851
03 Mar 1825	Lucy Scoot[O'Neal]			HSAN	800	----
00 000 1823	Francis M. Scoot	James & Mary	Va/Ky	HMOR	650	1830
10 Feb 1828	Dr. Elijah S. Shirley	Samuel & Phoebe(Cook)	Va/NC	HWCL	B167	----
00 00c 1826	S.P. Shirley			HWCL	B167	----
00 Feb 1824	Samuel K. Smith	William & Rebecca(Maxwell)	Ky/Ky	PPDM	472	----
00 000 0000	John Tartt			HMAD	557	1836
00 000 1824	Dr. Josiah Whitney	John	Yn/x	BRJM	393	----

C A L L O W A Y   C O U N T Y

BIRTHDATE	NAME OF BIOGRAPHEE	PARENTS/BIRTHPLACE/BIRTHDATE		SOURCE/PAGE		DATE
04 Feb 1844	Nathan L. Chester	John & Elizabeth(Frizell)	Christian16/x	BRJM	608	----
11 Nov 1846	Thomas B. Humphrey	Alfred	NC/x	BRJM	405	----
11 Apr 1838	Louis N. Marby	Alfred & Martha(Freeman)	Va/Va	PHCC	244	----
19 Dec 1833	James A. Metcalf	Thomas F & Jane(Graham)	Ky/Ky	PAUP	B307	----
23 Oct 1839	Robert E. Metcalf	Thomas F & Jane A(Graham)	Ky/Ky	PAUP	B307	----
00 000 0000	Reuben P. Starkes	Josiah		BRJM	456	----
20 Jan 1830	John F. Thomas	Henry	Tn/x	HWCL	121	----
06 Jul 1821	Joseph P. Woodside	William & Mary(Rowlet)	1775/x	BRJM	268	----
00 000 1841	Miles J. Yandell	Philander & Frances(Rushing)	NC1813/Tn	BRJM	378	----

C A M P B E L L   C O U N T Y

BIRTHDATE	NAME OF BIOGRAPHEE	PARENTS/BIRTHPLACE/BIRTHDATE		SOURCE/PAGE		DATE
00 000 1813	Squire Baker	Nicholas & Susanah(Carroll)	Pa/Va	TAZE	678	1837
00 000 1815	Elizabeth Clark[Baker]			TAZE	678	1837

BIRTHDATE	NAME OF BIOGRAPHEE	PARENTS/BIRTHPLACE/BIRTHDATE	SOURCE/PAGE		DATE
11 Dec 1817	John R. Craig	James & Mary(Barrickman) Pa/x	PBSM	455	c1818
00 000 0000	Charles Ducker		ACLY	49	1877
22 Apr 1832	Eli D. Gilliham	Robert & Elizabeth(Walker) Ky/Ky	BHAN	673	----
17 Jun 1823	John Gillham	Robert & Elizabeth(Walker) SC/Md	GHHA	645	1835
00 000 0000	Susan E[Harrold]		HDEW	341	1839
11 Apr 1827	James T. Johnson	George & Nancy(Botta) Va/Va	GHHA	647	----
05 Nov 1797	John Johnson	William & Eunice	HPEO	774	----
20 Sep 1862	John M. Kiser	Wilson & Mary(Johnson) **/**	BHAN	312	----
00 000 0000	Catherine Light[Rardin]		PECO	530	----
00 000 0000	Julia V. Martin[Hull]		MACL	296	1853
03 Jul 1337	Mortimer M. Miller	Frederick A & Sarah A. Pa/Bourbon	PBPE	946	1857
10 Feb 1842	Gustine Parker	William & Rebecca J.	GHHA	650	----
22 Apr 1824	Nancy Rardin[Gollady]	Samuel & Catherine	COLE	625	1842
22 Apr 1824	Nancy Rardin[Johnson]	Samuel & Catherine	COLE	625	1842
00 000 0000	Samuel Rardin		PBCO	530	1842
00 000 0000	D.F. Robbins		HDEW	341	1835
00 000 0000	John Searl	James & Anna(Mayall) NY/x	HFUL	928	1834
00 000 0000	Jennie Slack[McQuinn]		MACL	293	1866
00 000 0000	Dr. James E. Smith		CELW	356	1875
11 Dec 1838	Dr. James E. Smith		CELW	297	----
24 Jul 1828	William Stephens	James & Margaret(Peck) Ky1801/1808	HMCD	964	----
04 Aug 1859	Frank J. Stillwell	John W & Sarah(Templeton) **/x	PBSM	621	----
00 000 0000	Mary Ann Stillwell[Parker]		BRDK	375	----
23 Nov 1830	Nancy Stilwell[Graham]	Joseph & Martha(Barrackman) Ky/Ky	PBDK	353	----
20 Mar 1845	Dr. Noble Vance	Arthur & Lavinia(Noble)	PBDP	743	----
21 Mar 1827	Henry M. Walker	George & Rachel(Clark) Md/Pa	GHHA	780	1833
15 Feb 1822	Presley Williams	Presley & Rebecca(Buchanan) x/Va	PBDP	309	----

C A R L I S L E   C O U N T Y   (N O N E)

C A R R O L L   C O U N T Y

BIRTHDATE	NAME OF BIOGRAPHEE	PARENTS/BIRTHPLACE/BIRTHDATE	SOURCE/PAGE	DATE
30 Jan 1843	Turner J. Bowling	George W. **1804/x	PHEF B150	1863
00 000 1835	Barbara Campbell[Johnson]	William & Ellen(Pegs)	CJRI 499	----
17 Aug 1822	John Dunn		CJRI 255	----
01 Aug 1836	George V. Elliston	Benjamin S & Susan	PHEF B251	1842
28 Aug 1853	John A. Gladson	Richard & Sarah(Scruggs) Val832/Jeffer	BEFF 764	----
13 Oct 1834	Dr. Sidney W. Scanland	Thomas B & Agnes W(Searcy) Ky/Ky	BCSB 261	1840
00 000 0000	R.C. Seanland		HPIK 699	----
05 Sep 1834	B.R. Spencer	David & Rachel(Long)	CJRI 336	----
06 Feb 1815	W.M. Tandy		HADM 809	----
03 May 1812	Agnes Searcy[Seanland]		BCSB 262	----
30 Sep 1834	Joseph Wallace	James & Mary	HSAN 533	----
00 000 1823	W.F. Wayland		CMCD 601	1832
00 000 0000	Delia White[Coachmar]		GHHA 598	----
19 Mar 1826	John M. Wilcox	Benjamin & Flora(McCormick)Shelby/Fayett	HMCD 964	----
19 Mar 1826	John M. Wilcox	Benjamin & Flora(McCormick) Shelby96/x	HMCH 261	----
19 Mar 1826	John M. Wilcox		CMCD 601	1836

C A R T E R   C O U N T Y

BIRTHDATE	NAME OF BIOGRAPHEE	PARENTS/BIRTHPLACE/BIRTHDATE	SOURCE/PAGE	DATE
06 Oct 1848	Rev. David Coale	Henry J & Eleanor(Rowe) Val818/x	PVED 731	1863
06 Oct 1848	Rev. David Coale	Henry J. 1818/x	PVED 1054	----
00 000 0000	Elexor Rowe	Edward & Elenor(Littleton)	PVED 1054	----
00 000 0000	Ann Willim[Coale]	Edward & Clara C(Duncan)	PVED 732	----

C A S E Y   C O U N T Y

BIRTHDATE	NAME OF BIOGRAPHEE	PARENTS/BIRTHPLACE/BIRTHDATE	SOURCE/PAGE	DATE
00 Mar 1818	Dr. Meredith C Archer		HMCD 408	----

BIRTHDATE	NAME OF BIOGRAPHEE	PARENTS/BIRTHPLACE/BIRTHDATE		SOURCE/PAGE		DATE
00 000 0000	Elizabeth Canady[Waters]			HMAC	274	1847
09 Jan 1806	Elizabeth Canady[Waters]			PBMA	892	----
13 Sep 1819	William Clifton	Nehemiah & Margaret		PBMC	659	----
20 Apr 1812	George W. Davenport	William	Ky/x	PBDP	805	----
01 Nov 1842	Madison Davenport	William & Rebecca	Ky/De	HMOR	542	1863
25 Aug 1825	William C. Drake	Hiram		PBMA	292	----
14 Sep 1809	Sarah Hickman[Lawhorn]			FUST	B507	1832
00 000 0000	A.D. Holliday			HMAC	271	1849
02 Aug 1804	William Lawhorn			FUST	B507	1832
06 Dec 1815	John Mason			PVED	817	----
06 Dec 1815	John Mason	William & Mary(Spoonamore)		HEDG	702	1838
01 Feb 1812	James Mullican			HADM	806	1836
00 000 1848	Elizabeth Pledger			HDEW	346	----
29 Apr 1831	Benjamin Scott	Welcome & Elizabeth(Allen)	Ky/Ky	HGJR	883	----
00 000 0000	Elizabeth J Sweeney[Gobble]			HMAC	275	1855
16 Sep 1819	Robert D. Warriner			HPIK	867	----
06 Mar 1825	William C. Waters	Zachariah & Elizabeth(Canaday)		HMOR	563	1825
07 Jan 1805	Rev. Z. Waters			PBMA	892	----
00 000 0000	Rev. Zachariah Waters			HMAC	274	1847
08 Feb 1844	Emanuel Webb	Henry & Louisa(Spiecer)	Eng/Eng	PSTC	468	----
00 000 0000	Dr. R.F. Williams	Samuel & Letta(Mason)	1798/1800	PHCC	105	----
11 Jun 1832	C. Wilson			CMCD	601	1834

C H R I S T I A N   C O U N T Y

BIRTHDATE	NAME OF BIOGRAPHEE	PARENTS/BIRTHPLACE/BIRTHDATE		SOURCE/PAGE		DATE
00 000 0000	C.H.C. Anderson			HMAC	267	1834
29 Jan 1819	Crittenden H.C. Anderson	Col.James C & Ann R.		PBMA	215	----
00 000 0000	Erasmus S. Anderson	Col. James C.	Va/x	PBMA	279	----
00 000 0000	Erasmus S. Anderson			HMAC	121	1834

Date	Name	Parents	Origin	Code	No.	Year
00 000 0000	M.M. Anderson			HMAC	267	1834
24 Dec 1830	Malcolm M. Anderson Col. James		Va/x	PBMA	261	----
11 Jan 1817	John Bain John & Martha(Brooks)		NC/x	BRJM	174	1821
00 000 0000	Mahala Barnes[Padfield]			HSTC	351	----
00 000 0000	George W. Barrett William		Ky/x	BRMA	89	1835
00 000 0000	Margaret Bond[Ricks]			PCHR	354	----
00 000 0000	Lucy W. Boddie[Anderson]			BRMA	43	----
00 000 0000	Elizabeth Boyd[Fruit]			PBDP	252	----
03 Dec 1816	George Boyd Hardy & Mary(Torian)			PPWO	536	----
00 000 0000	G. Boyd			AWOO	5	1850
14 Jun 1849	Lucy A. Boyd[Major] George & Elizabeth(Pierce)		Ky/Ky	PBWO	276	----
00 000 0000	Susan Boyd[Gresham]			PPWO	600	1850
25 Feb 1837	Alfred B. Bozarth			PBML	486	----
15 Jan 1832	Milton Bozarth John & Cynthia(Taylor)			PBML	849	1839
15 Jan 1832	Milton Bozarth John & Cynthia(Taylor) Ky1799/Ky1807			HMCL	1008	1839
14 Mar 1817	Martha A. Bright[Caldwell]			HMEW	709	----
00 000 0000	Cater Bunch			PAUP	B243	----
00 000 0000	Esther M. Campbell[Ulm]			CELW	358	1817
16 Oct 1812	Nathaniel Carr			HADM	908	----
00 000 0000	A.L. Clark			HCHR	260	----
22 May 1827	A.I. Clark			HCHR	139	1843
00 000 0000	J.H. Clark			HCHR	260	1844
06 Apr 1819	Dr. Joseph H. Clark James C & Hannah(Henderson)		Va/SC	HCHR	138	----
00 000 0000	Mary M. Clark[Valentine] James C & Hannah			BCHR	1002	----
02 Sep 1842	Louis H. Coleman H.H & Barbra A.		Ky/Ky	HSAM	661	----
00 000 0000	R.R. Cooper			HMAC	175	1853
22 Jan 1828	Robert R. Cooper Edward L & Mary(Perry)		Va/Va	HMAC	161	----
22 Jan 1818	Robert R. Cooper Edmund L & Mary M(Perry)			PBMA	662	----
30 Oct 1821	William P. Courtney John T & Melinda(Harrison) Va/Woodford			PAUP	B303	----
00 000 0000	George Coventry			HMAD	445	1863
31 Aug 1816	Judge J.M. Davidge Rezin		Md/x	PAUP	B314	----
18 Jul 1835	Prof. E.W. Dickinson Elijah & Mary Ann Va1795/Va1800			PPWO	598	1835
03 Nov 1842	Lana Donagan[Outland]			HLOG	369	----
00 000 0000	Catherine Ewing[Worrell] Nathaniel & Sophia(Wallace) NC/NC			PBML	1143	----
00 000 0000	William Farmer			HFAY	97	1829
03 Mar 1808	William Farmer Absalom & Ailey(Heyatt)		NC/NC	HFAY	89	----

BIRTHDATE	NAME OF BIOGRAPHEE	PARENTS/BIRTHPLACE/BIRTHDATE		SOURCE/PAGE		DATE
21 Sep 1823	Edmund F. Fruit	Thomas & Elizabeth(Thompson)	NC1784/x	HDEW	251	----
21 Sep 1823	Edmund W. Fruit	Thomas & Elizabeth(Thompson)	NC1784/NC	PBDP	251	----
00 000 0000	John Fruit			HMAD	584	1817
00 000 0000	Matilda T. Fruit[Cooper]			HDEW	344	1834
00 000 0000	Martha[Geest]			HMAD	582	1861
00 000 1821	Anna Gibson[Hewitt]			PCHR	253	----
16 Sep 1827	William B. Goode	William H & Jinsa(Walker)	Va/Tn	HGJR	947	----
12 Oct 1817	Jerome R. Gorin	John D & Mattie(Thomas)	Va/x	PBMC	585	----
12 Oct 1817	Jerome R. Gorin	John D & Mattie(Thomas)	Va/x	PPDM	173	----
00 000 0000	R.H. Graham			AWOO	3	1850
00 000 1828	Elizabeth Gresham[Venable]			HPIK	736	----
23 Jun 1815	Isaac Guliher	George & Sarah(Gibson)		KNOX	678	----
09 May 1830	J.T. Gunnell			HMGL	1038	1834
16 Feb 1832	James L. Gunnell		Va/NC	TAZE	517	----
16 Nov 1819	D.D. Haggard	Dawson & Charity(Baldwin)	Va/Va	HMGL	730	----
00 000 0000	Dovey E. Hannah[Grey]			MACL	295	1840
00 000 0000	Jane Hannah[Grey]			MACL	295	1840
07 Apr 1826	Columbus Harlan	James & Catherine	Ky/x	HMAC	164	----
22 Dec 1810	E. Harlan	John & Frances(Ranch)	Va/Md	HMAC	164	----
00 000 0000	Elijah Harlan			HMAC	268	1834
00 000 0000	J.N. Harlan			AWOO	5	1833
22 Mar 1821	Mildred Harvey	Joel & Frances(Harvey)	Al/Ga	PBWL	859	----
12 Jan 1825	Peter G. Hay	John & Celia	Va/Ky	TAZE	549	1835
05 Oct 1823	James W. Herndon	Benjamin & Nancy	Va/Va	TAZE	549	1835
00 000 0000	Mary M. Hester[Shearer]	John & Elizabeth(Matthews)	Va/Ky	BRJM	321	1852
19 Feb 1849	Aurelius M. Hewitt	William T & Andronica(Gibson)	Va/x	PCHR	289	----
00 000 0000	Matilda Hinch[Harrington]			HMAD	576	1817
00 000 0000	Lucinda A[Houck]			HMAC	270	----
00 000 0000	Phebe E Huey[Jones]			MACL	299	1828
00 000 0000	Elijah Hunsaker			CSBR	392	1867
00 000 0000	Elizabeth J. Husband[Yowell]			HMAC	277	1841
00 000 0000	James Huston			HMAD	527	1819
09 Apr 1845	E.T. Hutchinson			HMGL	789	----

Date	Name	Parents / Notes	Code	No.	Year
00 000 1788	John Johnson		MACL	211	----
00 000 0000	Martha Jones[Huey]		MACL	299	1828
00 000 0000	William Jones		HGJR	949	----
00 000 0000	W.S. Jones		MACL	299	1834
00 000 0000	A.G. Kinkead		HMAC	275	1851
13 Nov 1818	Preston B. Knight		LOGA	490	1819
04 Apr 1828	Charles W. Lander	Samuel & Sally(Haggard) Clark98/Clark05	BMCL	1147	----
21 Oct 1834	Grace F. Lander[Muelheim]	Henry & Elizabeth(Purcell)Ky/**	PSTC	249	----
23 Feb 1857	Roy S. Lander	William D & Ann W(Rogers) Ky/Ky	PBCW	550	----
17 Jan 1824	John D. Landers		HMCL	954	1835
00 000 0000	Elizabeth Lewis[Johnson]		HGSH	711	1793
04 Sep 1803	Elizabeth Lindley[Harbour] Simon		HSAN	191	1807
05 Dec 1813	Elizabeth L. Lindsey[Neville] James		BMCL	1218	1834
15 Jun 1821	Elder John Lindsey	James A & Jean(Scott)	TAZE	556	1836
00 000 0000	Rev. John Lindsey		AWOO	3	1849
00 000 0000	Laura Long[Gilberson]		HMAC	277	1869
15 Jan 1851	Winston L. Long	John C & Rebecca S(McCormick)Muhl/NC12	PCHR	251	----
00 000 0000	Rev.Charles A. McCord		PBWO	B24	----
26 Jul 1817	Judge Hugh McGee	Benjamin & Nancy(Armstrong) Tn1794/1800	PAUP	B306	----
00 000 0000	Dr. John M. Major		HMCL	804	1835
23 May 1827	William Major	Ben & Lucy(Davenport) Ky1796/Ky02	PPWO	604	1834
00 000 0000	James H. Means		HWAS	84	1847
00 000 0000	Joseph W. Messick	Abraham	PBWA	307	----
17 Aug 1831	William T.M. Miller	James & Isabella(Moore) Va/Va	PBML	337	1835
00 000 0000	James Minnis		BCHR	947	1828
00 000 0000	James Minnis		HCHR	136	1828
00 000 0000	Andrew J. Moore		BRJM	242	----
00 000 0000	Mrs. G.L. Muelheins		HWAS	84	1853
26 Apr 1826	Jacob W. Myers		BRML	621	----
00 000 1831	Constant H. Oglesby	Walker & Sarah(Durham) Va/x	LOGA	801	c1840
28 Dec 1812	James K. Orendorff	William & Sarah	PBWL	227	----
00 000 0000	Hester A. Outhouse[Minnis]		HCHR	136	----
00 000 0000	Langley Pernecy[DeCamp]		HCHR	263	1828
20 Sep 1809	John Pugh	Thomas & Beulah(Hall)	PBSM	630	1820
25 Jan 1809	Abner Pyle	Abner & Sarah(Hall)	HMAD	470	1820
00 000 0000	Abner Pyle		HMAD	562	1847

BIRTHDATE	NAME OF BIOGRAPHEE	PARENTS/BIRTHPLACE/BIRTHDATE	SOURCE/PAGE		DATE
02 Jun 1828	Albert Quisenberry	Edward S & Nancy(Thoroughkill) Va/Va	BLOG	528	1835
19 Oct 1823	Allen Quisenberry	Edward S & Nancy	LOGA	710	----
29 Aug 1835	Arthur Quisenberry	Edward S & Lucy(Cator) Va/Va	LOGA	508	1835
29 Aug 1835	Arthur Quisenberry	Edward S & Lucy(Catour)	BLOG	642	----
30 Sep 1833	R.N. Radford	Benjamin J & Frances T(Lawrence)Va/Va04PPWO	BLOG	606	----
00 000 0000	R.N. Radford		AWOO	5	1834
17 Apr 1814	R.R. Rees	Hampton & Catherine	HJAC	109	----
00 000 0000	Amos Richardson		BCHR	969	1829
00 000 0000	Louisa[Richardson]		HCHR	264	1841
00 000 0000	William S. Ricks		PCHR	354	----
26 Oct 1805	Judge Urbane E. Robinson	James & Sarah Va/x	HJAC	75	1809
15 Dec 1827	Henry L. Samuell	Andrew & Sarah(Braddus) Va/Va	HMEM	818	1834
20 Aug 1818	John Small	John & Mary(Mason) Va/Va	TAZE	430	----
00 000 0000	William R. Smith		BCHR	989	----
23 Oct 1835	Adlai E. Stevenson		EFAY	507	1852
23 Oct 1835	Adlai E. Stevenson		HMCL	821	1852
00 000 0000	James B. Stevenson		HMCL	821	1853
15 Aug 1840	W.W. Stevenson		HMCL	821	1851
02 Apr 1817	John Summers	Henry & Mary(Fleming) Va1772/x	PPWO	607	1836
22 Oct 1785	Edmond Taylor		HSAN	913	----
00 000 0000	Elizabeth Taylor[McClure]		HMCD	816	----
00 000 0000	Mary A. Thompson[Haines]	William	PBRJ	611	----
00 000 0000	George Tindall	Thomas & Martha(Wall)	HMAD	539	----
00 000 0000	Lewis Tindall	Thomas & Martha(Wall)	HMAD	539	----
00 000 0000	Richard Tindall	Thomas & Martha(Wall)	HMAD	539	----
03 Apr 1838	Lloyd A. Underwood	John & Lucy(McAtee) Ky/x	FSTE	204	----
20 Apr 1816	Peter H. Vance	James & Jane B(Hay) Ky/Ky	PPBO	614	----
07 Apr 1826	Columbus Wheeler	James & Catherine(Harlan)	PBWA	415	----
00 000 0000	Ann E. Wilson[Blackford]		CELW	358	1844
00 000 0000	Sarah[Wood]		HMAD	562	1819
00 000 1822	John H. Wristen	Thomas & Hannah(Boggess) Ky/Va	GHHA	546	1851

BIRTHDATE	NAME OF BIOGRAPHEE	PARENTS/BIRTHPLACE/BIRTHDATE		SOURCE/PAGE		DATE
12 Sep 1840	John M. Artis	Robert & Fannie(McDonald)	De/Ky	PBML	1036	1859
12 Jul 1841	Nannie Artist-Bohrer]			HMCL	831	----
00 Jan 1819	Linville Ballard	John & Nancy(Bybee)		HFUL	479	----
02 Feb 1833	James Battershell	William & Elizabeth(Wills)	Ky/Ky	BCHA	233	1839
13 Mar 1811	John Battershell	John & Abigail(Rector)	Md/Ky	HPIK	451	1829
01 Jul 1827	Samuel Brandenburg	David		PBDP	445	----
00 000 1818	Alexander H. Brooking			CMCD	595	1833
23 Jan 1833	William F. Brookshier	Martin & Amanda(Cummings)	Ky/x	PBMC	323	----
23 Dec 1833	William F. Brookshier	Martin & Amanda(Cummings)	Ky/x	PPDM	655	----
13 Apr 1821	Dr. Addison M. Browning			HSAN	941	----
00 000 1817	David Bybee	Thomas & Rachel(Hogans)		HFUL	730	----
00 000 0000	Elizabeth M. Bybee[Emerson]		Ky/Ky	PBML	729	1830
00 Sep 1798	Thomas T. Bybee			HFUL	481	----
15 Jun 1832	John A. Campbell	Benjamin F & Dolly(Bateman)	Va/x	PBML	909	----
00 000 0000	Sarah Campbell[Magner]	Robert & May(Key)	Scotland/Md	HGRU	856	----
23 Feb 1840	Caleb Capps	John & Sallie T(Gilmer)	Va/Ky	PBMA	857	1826
11 Feb 1811	Ambrose B. Cass	Robert & Mary(Boggs)		HSAN	809	1850
08 Dec 1822	John S. Clinkenbeard	John	**/x	HSAN	923	1830
23 Oct 1818	George W. Constant	Isaac & Amy(Dean)	Ky/Va	HSAN	1051	----
03 Apr 1789	Isaac Constant			HSAN	1046	1826
13 Sep 1781	John Constant	Isaac		HSAN	803	1827
00 000 1826	Dr. John Constant			BKAN	269	----
24 Jul 1848	T.J. Daniel	Willis & Sarah G(Jackson)	Ky/Ky	PSTC	415	1851
29 Oct 1833	John T. Didlake			HMCL	991	----
00 000 0000	James M. Dooley			BRML	824	----
11 Nov 1830	J.M. Dooley	William	**/x	HMCL	1001	1852
11 Nov 1830	J.M. Dooley	William & Minerva(Morris)	Ky/Ky	PBML	1101	1851
20 Sep 1837	O.G. Dooley	William	**/x	HMCL	1001	1852
00 Sep 1837	Obadiah G. Dooley	William		BMCL	1008	1852
15 Aug 1834	William H. Dooley	William		HMCL	880	1851
15 Aug 1834	William H. Dooley	William & Minerva(Morris)		BMCL	1009	1851
15 Aug 1834	William H. Dooley	William & Minerva(Morris)	**1804/**10	PBML	266	----

BIRTHDATE	NAME OF BIOGRAPHEE	PARENTS/BIRTHPLACE/BIRTHDATE	SOURCE/PAGE	DATE
29 Dec 1830	Elizabeth Dunniway	David & Anna	HPIK 434	1836
13 Apr 1792	William F. Elkin		HSAN 510	1841
00 000 1792	William F. Elkin		PBMC 315	----
22 Nov 1802	Uriah Elledge	Boone	HPIK 536	1823
30 Sep 1819	F.M. Emerson	William & Polly(Tuggle) Va1787/Va90	PBML 729	----
00 000 0000	Polly Emerson[Knight]		PBML 257	----
00 000 1825	James C. Evans	Ky/Ky	PPPI 206	----
23 Jul 1822	R.M. Ewing	William & Sarah(Coombs)	HDEW 239	----
24 Jun 1834	Cassius C. Epperson	Green & Thirza(Woods) Madison/Madison	COLE 596	1807
08 Jun 1821	Jacob Fesler		HPIK 762	----
17 Nov 1797	Hon. Isaac Funk	Adam & Sarah(Moore)	PBML 1148	1807
27 Dec 1824	James H. Garner		HPIK 762	1840
15 Oct 1816	Jacob Goldman		HPIK 540	1829
00 000 1822	Henry H. Groom	William & Nancy(Haney) Va/Pa	GHHA 613	----
00 000 0000	Abraham Gudgel		CELW 352	1859
29 Oct 1839	Dr. J.R. Haggard	David J & Sarah A(Edmonson) Ky/Ky	BHDP B98	1840
00 000 1805	Sallie Haggard[Lander]	David Va1763/x	BMCL 1147	----
12 Nov 1819	Dr. Lucien W. Hammer		PHEF B221	1828
12 Nov 1819	Dr. Lucien W. Hammer		BEFF 667	1826
02 Nov 1817	William L. Hammer	Frederick & Elizabeth(Webb) Ky/Ky	PBMC 211	----
02 Nov 1817	Judge William L. Hammer	Frederick & Elizabeth(Webb)	PPDM 871	----
00 000 0000	Angeline B. Hay[Hull]		MACL 296	1867
00 000 0000	Mary J. Hooton	Nicholas	PBML 348	----
08 May 1822	James W. Judy		HMEM 715	----
00 000 1809	Paris Judy	Wineforth Germany/x	PBAD 336	----
04 Dec 1811	Paris T. Judy		HADM 903	----
28 Mar 1852	Thomas F. Kennedy	George F & Nancy E(Railsback) Ky/Ky	BMCL 1129	----
23 Mar 1852	Thomas F. Kennedy	George & Nancy E(Railsback) **/**	PBML 580	----
22 Apr 1809	Thomas A. King	William B & Annie R(Greening) Va/Va	HSAN 856	----
03 Jan 1824	Thomas Lackey	John Ky/x	PHCC 309	----
21 Jan 1798	Samuel Lander		BMCL 1147	----

BIRTHDATE	NAME OF BIOGRAPHEE	PARENTS/BIRTHPLACE/BIRTHDATE	SOURCE/PAGE	DATE
00 000 0000	Carolyn Laugh_in[Kemp]		HADM	723	---
15 Jul 1800	Jesse Lott		HMCL	971	---
00 000 0000	Sarah G. Mart_n[Taylor]	George T & Mary E(Mott)	BMCL	1320	---
00 000 0000	Robert H. Max_ield		HMAC	276	1831
00 000 0000	Susan J. Nels_n		BRML	824	---
24 Jan 1820	W.B. Owen	Francis	WHWI	850	---
00 Sep 1812	Nelson Raker	Daniel M & Susan E(Chaney) NC/NC	HFUL	837	---
28 Feb 1801	James D. Rawl_ns		HJOD	713	---
00 000 0000	Sarah M. Ride_s[Cver]		CELW	349	1841
21 Feb 1809	James M. Slus_		HEDG	644	---
00 000 0000	Lucy E. Smith_on[Hclloway]		HMAC	275	1863
12 Nov 1825	Nathan Tucker		HEDG	715	1829
22 Jan 1818	Osburn Tucker		HEDG	715	---
23 Oct 1810	Dr. John B. V_vion	Harvey & Mildred(Ryon) Va/Va	KNOX	712	---
23 Oct 1810	Dr. John B. V_vion	Henry & Mildred(Ryan) Va/Va	PHKX	B454	---
00 000 1796	Eliza Young[M=Carn]	James Va/x	PBDP	230	---
22 Oct 1829	John L. Young		HMCL	1008	1852

C L A Y   C O U N T Y

BIRTHDATE	NAME OF BIOGRAPHEE	PARENTS/BIRTHPLACE/BIRTHDATE	SOURCE/PAGE	DATE
00 000 0000	George L. Pige		HCHA	180	---
00 000 0000	William Walte_s		OGRU	12	1843

C L I N T O N   C O U N T Y

BIRTHDATE	NAME OF BIOGRAPHEE	PARENTS/BIRTHPLACE/BIRTHDATE	SOURCE/PAGE	DATE
00 000 0000	J.W. Coventry		HMAD	555	1813
22 Nov 1832	John M. Jones	Wilson L.	HWCL	B186	---
00 000 1796	Urias Martin		PAUP	B77	---

C L I N T O N   C O U N T Y   (C O N T.)

BIRTHDATE	NAME OF BIOGRAPHEE	PARENTS/BIRTHPLACE/BIRTHDATE	SOURCE/PAGE	DATE
00 000 0000	John Ragland		HSTC 373	----
00 Jun 1847	John Vigels		HMOR 653	----
00 000 1800	Keziah Williams[Martin]	Rev. Hardin	PAUP B77	----
11 May 1814	David B. Wood	James SC/x	BRMA 50	1832
00 000 0000	J. Wood		HCHR 265	----
25 Oct 1845	J. Willis Wood	John & Sarah(Crouch) Tn1791/Tn	HCHR 259	----
00 000 0000	Mahala Wright[Johnston]		HMAC 267	1863

C R I T T E N D E N   C O U N T Y

BIRTHDATE	NAME OF BIOGRAPHEE	PARENTS/BIRTHPLACE/BIRTHDATE	SOURCE/PAGE	DATE
22 Jul 1823	William Baird	Simon SC/x	PBMA 634	----
00 000 0000	William Baird		HMAC 270	1845
29 Nov 1844	Joseph M. Butler	Amsted & Margaret(Green) Va1815/x	HGSH 602	----
03 Sep 1851	J.J. Butler		HGSH 603	1862
18 Dec 1848	Andrew J. Crisp	John & Leah(Brantley) Ky/Ky	HGSH 774	----
01 Jun 1851	Joseph E. Hickman	William B & Eliza A(Witherspoon)	PBMO B148	1851
00 000 1838	Walker P. Hickman	William & Elizabeth(Witherspoon)	PBMO B196	----
09 Mar 1836	W.A. Hughey	John R. Va/x	PJEF B52	----
00 000 0000	Dr. J.S. Lewis	George L & Amy E(Weldon) Il1829/Ky30	HGSH 632	----
27 Apr 1853	Dr.William J.J.Paris	Dr. J.L & Nancy S(Smart) Tn/NC	BRJM 617	----
30 May 1822	Francis M. Winders		BRJM 369	----

C U M B E R L A N D   C O U N T Y

BIRTHDATE	NAME OF BIOGRAPHEE	PARENTS/BIRTHPLACE/BIRTHDATE	SOURCE/PAGE	DATE

Birth Date	Name	Parents	Origin	Code	No.	Death
31 May 1803	Robert Allen			HPIK	523	----
15 Apr 1789	Rev. John Antle			HSAN	1012	----
15 Jan 1829	Jacob Austin			HFAY	74	----
25 Jul 1816	William J. Bennett	Richard & Mary(Odell)	Va/NC	PBDP	292	1868
00 000 0000	Emeline Brents[Ray]	Gabriel E & Polly(Summers)	Va/Ky	HJAC	128	1827
21 Aug 1824	H.G. Bristow			GHHA	656	1834
00 000 1812	James Cheatham	Elijah & Susanna	Ky/x	HPIK	452	1825
09 Jan 1813	John Cole	Richardson		VTBU	248	----
09 Jan 1812	Rev. John Cole	Samuel & Mary(Brown)	1778/1779	BHBU	486	----
09 Jan 1830	Frank H. Colenan	James M & Mary(Cliff)	Va1782/Md1790	PBMC	318	1830
16 Oct 1835	Edward G. Creal	Elijah & Temperence S(Wilburn)		HGSH	869	1830
09 Nov 1810	Nancy Davidson[McCollom]			BHAN	465	----
07 May 1802	Benjamin Ferguson			HMOR	680	----
00 000 0000	Elizabeth J[Foster]			HMAC	272	1830
01 May 1793	Sarah Foster[Scott]			HSAN	813	1830
08 Aug 1830	Capt.John P. Higgins	Durrett & Mary(Graves)		PPWA	557	----
23 May 1816	Nancy Higgins[Yates]			HSAN	937	----
24 Jan 1836	George W. Hutchins	William & Jane(Pace)		HMCD	966	1853
00 000 0000	James Jenkins			HJAC	128	1818
00 000 0000	James Johnston			HMAC	267	1863
00 000 0000	Mary Jones[Rice]			HMAC	271	1831
00 000 1808	Eliza D. McClure[Kinkade]			HMCD	729	----
23 Jun 1811	Samuel L. McClure			HMCD	816	1835
10 Feb 1813	Henry B. McCollom			BHAN	465	----
00 000 0000	Elizabeth Morrison[Pointer]			HMCD	1004	----
00 000 0000	James A. Obanion			HJAC	128	1868
00 May 1809	William I. Pace			HMCD	715	----
30 Nov 1810	William Pointer	Cornelius & Rebecca(Snow)	Pulaski/Md	HMCD	750	1829
00 000 0000	G.W. Ray			HJAC	128	1868
00 000 1828	John Rowland	Wade & Winfred	Va/Va	HFUL	766	----
06 Apr 1791	Dallas Scott			HSAN	813	----
00 Oct 1817	Adaline M. Semple_Bradford]	John	NC/x	HSAN	645	----
01 Nov 1806	James Smith			HWAS	60	----
00 000 0000	L.B. Smith			HMAC	275	1850
03 Sep 1835	Prof.Adoniram J. Thomson	Herbert C & Louise W(Hail)	Va/Ky	KNOX	710	1838

BIRTHDATE	NAME OF BIOGRAPHEE	PARENTS/BIRTHPLACE/BIRTHDATE	SOURCE/PAGE		DATE
00 000 1834	David L. Thurman	James & Polly(Robinson) Ky/SC	HPIK	467	1837
14 Dec 1830	Allen T. Vawter	Beverly & Elizabeth(Hutchins)Va1782/NC	BHEN	306	1833
07 Jan 1812	Capt.John H.Welch	Richard & Jane(Jones) Va/NC	HFAY	73	----
00 000 0000	John H. Welch	Va/x	HFAY	96	1829
00 000 0000	Martin Welsh	Richard W.	EFAY	824	----
00 000 0000	Martin Welsh		HFAY	97	1829
25 Aug 1805	J.S. Wilburn		HMEM	799	1820
00 000 0000	James E. Wood		HMAC	270	1832
25 Dec 1804	Samuel Wood	James	PBMA	747	----

DAVIESS COUNTY

BIRTHDATE	NAME OF BIOGRAPHEE	PARENTS/BIRTHPLACE/BIRTHDATE	SOURCE/PAGE		DATE
08 Nov 1852	Dr. N.B. Allen	N.B. **/x	CJRI	800	----
25 Dec 1798	Anna Brown[Hedges]		HSAN	930	----
00 000 1845	Louis A. Burk	Edward A & Nancy(King) Ky/Ky	PBML	1085	1848
00 000 0000	Eliza J. Crawford[Vandever]		CELW	348	1858
00 000 0000	Priscila Crawford		CELW	348	1855
00 000 0000	Remea Davis		HDEW	344	1836
00 000 0000	Elizabeth F. Dawson[Bond]		CELW	345	1858
00 000 1830	William A. Durk		HLOG	519	----
22 Nov 1836	John W. Eddy	James & Burilla	LOGA	700	1856
19 Feb 1840	Ezekiel Field	John & Nancy(Allen) Ky/Ky	PAUP	B304	----
00 000 0000	Nancy J. Frazer[Ritter]		MACL	301	1872
00 000 0000	Mary Galloway[Guyot]		CELW	348	1855
00 000 0000	Silas Hart		COLE	653	----
16 Mar 1821	Elizabeth A[Lowry]		HCAR	485	1839
02 Jun 1812	Hiram McNamer		HCAR	486	1835
00 000 1802	Jacob Myers	Abraham Ger/x	PBMC	637	----
00 000 0000	Elizabeth[Nave]		HFAY	98	1837
00 000 0000	Mary A[Reincke]		HMAC	274	1833

00 000 0000	James R. Roby			CELW	348	1854
01 Jan 1858	I.N. Taylor	Thomas & Maria(Norris)	Oh/Oh	PAUP	B296	----
09 Jan 1838	A.L. Wall	A.S & Elizabeth(Allen)		HWCL	B70	----
00 000 0000	C.M. Wall			ACLY	50	1864

E D M O N S O N   C O U N T Y

BIRTHDATE	NAME OF BIOGRAPHEE	PARENTS/BIRTHPLACE/BIRTHDATE		SOURCE/PAGE		DATE
00 000 1835	I.M. Capps	John & Miriam(Cole)		PBWA	441	1864
22 Sep 1830	Andrew J. Catton	Abel & Lively(Harrington)	Tn/Ky1808	PBWA	494	----
13 Sep 1829	James Gardner	Thomas & Catherine(Lair)	W/Barren	PBWA	628	----
12 Nov 1819	Jackson Houchin			HMEM	838	----
02 Oct 1821	Lucinda Houchin[Taylor]			HMEM	797	----
00 000 0000	Lev M. Lee			PHPI	302	----
00 000 1817	William D. Leeper	Arthur A.	Ky/x	BCSB	330	1829
00 000 1826	Elza Majors	Thomas & Polly	Va/Ky	HFUL	764	1854
29 Feb 1832	Andrew J. Nash	Lewis C & Millie(Oller)Pulaski107/Ill4		PBMO	B248	----
06 Feb 1828	M.B. Ray	Garland & Sarah(Lee)	Ky/Ky	PBWA	370	----

E L L I O T T   C O U N T Y   (N O N E)

E S T I L L   C O U N T Y

BIRTHDATE	NAME OF BIOGRAPHEE	PARENTS/BIRTHPLACE/BIRTHDATE		SOURCE/PAGE		DATE
03 Jul 1851	James W. Adams	Berryman & Cynthia A(Moppin)	Va/Va	BRML	551	1869
00 000 0000	Lucinda Carver[Wilcoxen]			HFUL	503	----
00 000 0000	Amanda F. Crabb[Snowden]	Whitney & Maria(Bellis)	x/**	PVED	310	----
13 Sep 1812	William D. Darnall			HEDG	570	1822
00 000 0000	Bettie A. Dozier[Horgham]	Ephraim & Huldah(Benton)	Ky/Ky	BWCL	1103	----

BIRTHDATE	NAME OF BIOGRAPHEE	PARENTS/BIRTHPLACE/BIRTHDATE	SOURCE/PAGE		DATE
00 000 0000	Brutus C. Epperson	Green & Thirza(Woods) Madison/Mad1800	COLE	596	----
27 Nov 1817	Elijah Jennings	NC/NC	HFUL	831	----
22 Jan 1858	John W. Webb	Daniel & Debbie(Willcoxen)	BCSB	487	----
10 Dec 1825	Anna A. Willcoxen[Ray]	Elijah & Salle A(Brinagar) Ky1827/Ky41	HFUL	838	----
10 Dec 1825	Anna A. Willcoxen[Vail]		HFUL	838	----
12 Mar 1817	Maj. E. Calloway Willcoxen	Capt.Elijah & Charlotte(Calloway)	HFUL	840	----
00 000 1829	J.C. Willcoxen	Elijah & Charlotte(Calloway) NC/NC	HFUL	817	1830
05 Nov 1827	Marshall Ney Willcoxen	Elijah & Charlotte(Calloway)NC89/NC	HFUL	841	----
31 Dec 1819	Mary Willcoxon[Cope]	Elijah & Charlotte(Calawan) NC/NC	PBKN	285	1830
00 000 0000	J.C. Wilson		EMCL	1295	----

F A Y E T T E   C O U N T Y

BIRTHDATE	NAME OF BIOGRAPHEE	PARENTS/BIRTHPLACE/BIRTHDATE	SOURCE/PAGE		DATE
00 Feb 1810	Elizabeth Armstrong[Bennett]	Thomas	PHCC	261	----
00 000 0000	John Baker		HSTC	95	1829
13 Nov 1840	Robert S. Bishop	E. & Laura	HEDG	557	----
13 Aug 1867	William H. Bowles	Lemuel & Sarah(Bosworth) Ct/x	BRKI	1037	----
02 Apr 1865	William M. Bridgett	Thomas & Mary(Shaffer) Pa/In	PPVE	132	----
00 000 0000	William Bristow		PAUP	B302	----
01 Mar 1810	James Brown		EFAY	722	1819
00 000 0000	John Brown		BCSB	280	c1831
18 Aug 1798	Joseph Brown		HPIK	843	----
00 000 1817	Edwin F. Bull		PHCC	229	----
17 Sep 1798	Nancy C, Bullen[Brown]		HPIK	843	----
30 Nov 1832	Dr.Thomas R. Burris Hiram H.	Ky/x	BRJM	265	1850
00 000 0000	Asa Butler		PVED	226	1834
18 Oct 1787	James Butler		PBCO	402	----

Birth Date	Name	Parents	Origin	Code	No.	Death
07 Mar 1844	A.R. Candy	John & Celeste F(Robert)	Eng/x	PBCO	317	----
00 000 0000	John Garr			HGJR	682	----
00 000 0000	R.T. Cassell			AWOO	3	1839
00 000 0000	James W. Cheaney			PPME	523	----
24 Jun 1827	Samuel Chowning			COLE	585	1831
05 Feb 1847	Benjamin Chrisman	Jefferson & Jennette	**/Jessamine	HMCL	841	----
00 000 0000	Mary E. Chrisnand[Guess]			CELW	353	1870
00 000 0000	Benjamin A. Clark	James	Ire/x	PBWA	256	----
20 Apr 1806	John Clark	William		HGJR	856	1815
22 May 1820	R.B. Clark	Samuel B.		HMAC	257	c1830
18 Jun 1834	H.L. Clay			HMOR	479	----
03 Sep 1816	George M. Coons			HCAS	327	1825
29 Jul 1809	Mary A. Coons[Phelps]	John & Polly(Crosswhite)		COLE	602	1830
13 Mar 1811	Isaac Cope			PBKN	285	----
14 Jul 1818	Col. William D. Crockett			PPRI	399	1868
00 000 0000	Nathaniel Cutright			HPEO	638	----
00 000 0000	Sarah E. Duncan[Barnett]			HDEW	340	1838
00 000 0000	C.M. Dunlap			CSBR	385	1838
00 000 0000	Charles M. Dunlap	Rev.Latin W & Rebecca M(Bell)	NJ/**	BCSB	491	1837
02 Jul 1821	George N. Dunlap	William & Onie(Green)	Va/x	BRML	548	----
24 Jun 1829	J.H. Devore			HMOR	482	1831
11 Apr 1805	U.J. Devore	John & Margaret(Devore)	Pa/Va	HCAS	661	1830
01 Jul 1827	William S. Douglass			PBKN	305	----
00 Oct 1809	John Eads		Md/x	CASS	744	----
06 Jul 1798	Dr. Andrew Elder	1749/1757		HSAN	762	----
17 Nov 1786	Henry Ellis	John & Sarah(Parrish)		HCHR	930	----
00 000 0000	Ann E[Emerson]			HCHR	263	1854
00 000 0000	Richard N. Emerson			PCHR	263	1854
17 Feb 1825	Richard N. Emerson	Perry & Catherine(Aldridge)	x/Ky	PCHR	305	----
00 000 0000	Elizabeth Ann Endicott[Mahan]			PBWA	393	----
00 000 1823	Amanda Ervin[Allen]	Elias & Martha(Eaton)	Md/Ky	PBCO	194	----
08 Oct 1811	Frances M. Estes[Pinnell]			HEDG	622	----
03 Mar 1827	C.P. Ford	Thomas & Malinda(Hackett)		HDEW	209	1829
03 Jul 1824	William R. Ford	Daniel & Mary(Randolph)	NJ/Ky	HSAN	796	1838
25 Nov 1799	Thomas Foutch	John & Nancy(Wherritt)	Va1776/Md1778	HSAN	934	----

BIRTHDATE	NAME OF BIOGRAPHEE	PARENTS/BIRTHPLACE/BIRTHDATE		SOURCE/PAGE	DATE
07 May 1829	John H. Francis	Littleburg & Polly(Hubbard)	Ky/Ky	PBPE 196	----
00 000 0000	Elizabeth Fry[Harris]			HMAC 271	1850
20 Sep 1799	Gen. Jacob Fry	Bernhardt		HGJR 702	----
17 Feb 1826	Mary E. Galloway[Miller]			PBMC 214	----
17 Apr 1803	Flora Gates			CMCD 597	1835
00 000 0000	Edwin George			BCHR 888	----
00 000 0000	Rebecca Gillespie[Gould]			CBLW 351	1819
00 000 0000	James Glenn			HHEN 258	1835
00 000 0000	James Glenn			AHEN 14	1835
24 Jul 1847	John W. Goss	Charles & Margaret		PBHE 229	----
00 000 0000	Mary Gordly[Lee]			HMEW 807	----
00 000 1837	Elisha J. Graham			PHKX B431	----
00 000 0000	Edward Grimes			HMAC 272	1852
00 000 0000	John Grimes			HMAC 272	1852
10 Sep 1821	Merrill F. Hackett			COLE 568	1829
19 Dec 1858	Dr. Alonzo Hall	James H & Sallie A(Pritchett)	Ky/Ky	PBMC 379	----
00 000 0000	Mary E. Halsted[Case]			MACL 298	1830
08 Jul 1806	John R. Haney	William & Margaret	Md/Md	HMOR 663	1819
00 000 0000	Maria Hanning[Levitt]	Daniel	Va/x	HWCL B231	----
00 000 0000	Catherine Hanson[Craig]			PBCO 493	1828
27 Oct 1832	John S. Harper	Cyrus A & Harriet(Sterling)	Ky/Va	PBML 622	----
07 Feb 1801	Dr. Charles Hay	John	1779/x	BHAN 11	----
00 000 1801	Dr. Charles Hay	John & Jemima(Coulter)	Va/Pa	GHHA 661	----
03 Jul 1817	Milton Hay			HSAN 123	1832
00 000 0000	Simon Hedden			BCHR 900	----
00 000 0000	Agnes[Helms]			HCHA 178	1854
00 000 1827	E.R. Henry			HMOR 564	1835
09 Jun 1809	John T. Henry			HMOR 664	1830
31 Oct 1797	Richard Henry			HMOR 664	1830
00 000 0000	Sarah E. Hersman[Baxter]			GSBR 386	1854
19 Jun 1809	Rodney Hickman	Lewis	1776/x	HDEW 257	----

Date	Name	Parents/Spouse	Birthplace	Code	No.	Year
20 Mar 1828	Thomas G. Hickman	Col. Thomas B.		EFAY	759	----
11 Dec 1817	John L. Higgins	John		PPPI	115	----
24 Mar 1809	Jesse Hill	James & Mary C(Cope)	Pa/Md	PBWL	265	----
00 000 0000	Mary A. Hill			BCHR	928	1837
00 000 0000	Phebe L. Hill[Beatty]			HDEW	340	----
00 000 0000	Mary J. Hoffman[Juett]	Michael & Syba		BCSB	535	1851
06 Jan 1831	Rev. B.D. Howk			CSBR	384	----
00 000 0000	Dr. Thomas B. Hunt	Silas W & Elizabeth C(Wilson) **/**		HMCH	143	----
30 Aug 1827	Bartlett H. Ingels			CSBR	383	1830
04 Jan 1817	Dr. Charles N. Irwin	John M.C & Martha(Nourse) **/Mercer	NC/Ky	BCSB	441	----
00 000 0000	George W. Jeffers	Robert & Nancy(Tapp)	Va/x	CJRI	556	----
00 000 0000	J.M. Jenkins	Elijah		PBCO	362	----
00 000 0000	Ann Johnson[Dyer]			BWCL	1014	----
29 Aug 1835	Peter Keenan	Patrick	Ire/x	PBML	395	----
27 Nov 1855	Ann E. Keiser[Emerson]	James L & Abigail(Stipp)		PCHR	306	----
10 Jan 1833	Thomas Keiser	James I & Emily G(Stipp) **/**		BCHR	916	----
00 000 1801	Sarah E. Kenpe[White]			COLE	591	----
00 000 0000	Henry Kent	Henry & Mary		HPIK	594	1836
00 000 0000	John Lee			HMEM	807	----
00 000 0000	Michael Levitt			HWCL	B231	----
00 000 0000	Catherine Lite-			HMOR	736	----
00 000 1788	Neal McCann	Plaza	Ky/x	PBDP	230	----
17 Aug 1813	Perry McConathy			PBWB	276	----
00 000 1825	Joseph M. McKenzie	John & Sarah(Milligan)		GHHA	559	1838
23 Jan 1848	Mary McPheeters[Sruman]	Major Addison		PBSM	658	----
17 Nov 1830	Hon. John A. Mallcry	Ambrose	Va/x	HMEM	771	1835
00 000 0000	Nancy Martin[Jenkins]			PBCO	362	----
24 Jun 1832	Dr. Joseph Marshall	Robert & Elizabeth(Evans) **00/**1804		HMCL	974	----
30 Aug 1840	Tabitha Mason[Shoemaker]			COLE	638	----
07 Jun 1797	Joseph Meek	Bazel & Ellen(Roberts)		PPWO	541	----
00 000 1822	William Miller	James & Sarah(O'Hara)	Ky/Ky	PBCO	568	----
29 Mar 1808	Charles Miner	Rufus & Betsey(White)	Ct/Va	HCHA	120	----
23 Mar 1835	George W. Morgan	James & Belinda(Raney)	Ky/Ky	PCHR	307	1837

BIRTHDATE	NAME OF BIOGRAPHEE	PARENTS/BIRTHPLACE/BIRTHDATE	SOURCE/PAGE	DATE
31 May 1814	Susan P. Morton[Ferguson] Charles S.		COLE 520	1829
00 000 1833	George A. Mure		HPIK 556	----
15 Mar 1836	W.J. Neely	Robert F & Mary(McCoart) Scotland/Ire	HIAS A547	----
08 Nov 1797	John P. Nichols	Thomas & Elizabeth(Perkins) Va/Md	HADM 926	----
06 Dec 1842	W.J. Parrott	Ky1812/x	HMOR 730	1835
01 Jan 1810	John Patrick	R.D & Sarah(Bonham)	CMCD 599	1835
01 Jan 1810	John Patrick		HMCD 700	1835
00 000 0000	Margaret Patterson[Jennings]		GSBR 385	----
00 000 0000	J.C. Payne		HMAC 270	----
02 Feb 1831	John C. Payne	Sanford K & Frances(Cragg) **/Woodford	HMAC 155	----
07 Sep 1814	Lucy A. Payton[Springer]		COLE 645	1835
00 000 1826	Dr. J.G. Phillips	Joseph M & Nancy(Miller) Pa/Ky	HPIK 502	----
16 Mar 1824	Rev.Lewis A. Pilcher J. & Nancy	Va1783/Va87	HJOD 764	1836
00 000 0000	William Porter	William Md/x	PVED 434	----
00 000 1818	Catherine Poston[James]		PBDP 795	----
00 000 0000	Margaret Powell[Darnell]		BRML 671	----
08 Sep 1804	E.D. Power	William & Elizabeth(Stogedill) Md/Md	HMEM 744	----
18 Feb 1798	George Power	James & Eleanor(Dedman)	HSAN 910	1821
00 000 0000	Mary Power[Darnell]		BRML 671	----
29 Jul 1788	Robert Price		PVED 317	----
00 000 0000	Abraham Prickett		HMAD 334	1808
30 Apr 1815	Dr.Caleb W. Reid	Benjamin & Mary(Prall) Md/NJ	HWCL B82	----
00 000 1800	Joseph L. Reynolds		HGSH 651	1817
31 Mar 1836	Justin W. Richardson Henry & Lucy(Fisher) Ma/Ma	BGSL 719	----
00 000 1811	Hon. William A. Richardson		HADM 414	----
00 000 0000	William A. Richardson		GSBR 149	----
00 000 0000	James Ritchey		GSBR 387	1834
28 Nov 1834	William T. Ritter	James & Rebecca(Woodgate) Jessamine/**	BLOG 400	1864
00 000 0000	Eleanor D. Robards[Myers]		HSAN 698	----
14 Jan 1843	L.W. Roberts	Rev. Richard B.	BHIQ B116	----

Birth Date	Name	Parents / Spouse	Origin	Ref	No.	Yr
00 000 0000	Sarah H. Robinson[Parks]	James & Phoebe(Coulter)	NY/NJ	GSBR	390	1835
00 000 1809	Samuel Rose			GHHA	619	1830
03 Jun 1844	James W. Ross	Samuel B & Betsy(Baskin)	Ire/Ire	BRKI	1388	----
15 Feb 1798	Susan Sandusky[Ferguson]			HMOR	681	----
20 Jan 1840	Matthew T. Scott	Isaac W.		PPPI	101	----
24 Feb 1828	Matthew T. Scott			EFAY	472	1874
00 000 0000	Isaac W. Scott			PHPI	393	1831
16 Apr 1814	James H. Self			HMOR	671	----
31 Dec 1822	John G. ShanElin	John & Jenett(Green)	Va/Lincoln	PPDM	786	1843
00 000 0000	Mrs. Samuel[Shirley]			HFAY	95	----
17 May 1812	Milton Shryock	Christian & Rebecca(Graham)		HFUL	500	1805
00 000 0000	John Simpson	Maj. William		BRJM	489	----
16 Mar 1796	John Sinnet			HCHR	31	----
10 Mar 1796	John S. Sinnet			EFAY	481	----
00 000 1817	Henry Smith	Nicholas & Anna	Eng/Va	KNOX	706	1817
04 Apr 1814	John Blair Smith			EFAY	524	1833
00 000 0000	Thomas C. Smith			MACL	296	----
13 Feb 1808	J. Springer			COLE	645	----
22 Apr 1831	Samuel A. Stcops	John & Rosanna(Kephart)	Pa/Md	PBWL	922	----
22 Apr 1831	Samuel P. Stcops	--- & Rosanna(Kephart)	Pa1787/Md1802	HMCL	1026	----
00 000 0000	Purnel Stout			PBWC	199	----
10 Nov 1807	John T. Stuart	Robert & Hannah(Todd)	Va/x	HSAN	110	----
16 Nov 1807	John T. Stuart	Robert		EFAY	511	----
12 May 1818	Richard Summers		De/x	PBAD	186	----
07 Nov 1803	Hiram Tatman			HMCD	1142	----
00 000 0000	Berryman Taylor			HMAC	277	1855
00 000 0000	Jane E[Taylor]			HMAC	277	1855
27 Apr 1787	Dr. John Todd			HSAN	522	----
27 Apr 1787	Dr. John Todd			EFAY	524	----
10 Apr 1807	Dr. Joshua O. Tomlinson	Ambrosio & Mary(Dykes)		HPEO	734	1824
24 Jun 1820	James R. True			WINN	616	----
00 000 0000	Nancy Truax[Cosalt]		1747/x	PPVE	775	----
20 Oct 1782	Benjamin Tyler	William & Letty(George)		PBMC	528	----
00 000 0000	Rev. John W. Tyler	Benjamin & Susamah(Shores)	**1782/x	PPDM	316	----
27 Sep 1808	John W. Tyler			PBMC	528	----

FAYETTE COUNTY (CONT.)

BIRTHDATE	NAME OF BIOGRAPHEE	PARENTS/BIRTHPLACE/BIRTHDATE		SOURCE/PAGE	DATE
24 Jul 1780	William Tyler	William & Letty(George)	1747/x	PBWC 528	----
05 Nov 1815	William A. Whitesides	Charles & Elizabeth(Graves)	Va85/**88	HSAN 1010	1854
05 May 1837	William P. Whiting	William & Margaret(Robison)		HWCL B59	----
07 Jul 1833	Thomas R. Wilcox		Va/Ky	CWCD 601	1835
00 000 0000	William Wyatt			HCAS 354	----
22 Feb 1828	William M. Wyatt	James & Sarah(Stevenson)	Ky/Ky	BCSB 408	1830

FLEMING COUNTY

BIRTHDATE	NAME OF BIOGRAPHEE	PARENTS/BIRTHPLACE/BIRTHDATE		SOURCE/PAGE	DATE
00 000 0000	J.M. Allen			AWOO 3	----
00 000 0000	Louisa Ashley[Stokes]			HCHR 264	1854
00 000 0000	Evan Baird			HSTC 377	----
18 Dec 1804	Evan Baird			HSTC 260	----
23 Mar 1817	Matilda F. Belt[Dunlap]	Fielding & Margaret	Va1782/Pa91	PBKN 323	----
17 Nov 1847	James M. Biddle	Stephen & Elizabeth(Shockey)	Ky/Ky	PBWC 545	1863
26 Mar 1806	Robert M. Bonham			CWCD 595	1839
00 000 0000	Ethel E. Bowlings[Armstrong]			HCHR 265	1869
00 000 0000	Elizabeth Bruce[Morgan]	William		HCHA 133	----
25 Aug 1830	Stephen B. Burris	Hiram D.	**/x	BRJM 225	----
27 Aug 1819	Capt. John T. Canterbury	Asa & Margaret(Hornback)		HSAN 902	1826
21 Jul 1824	Oliver P. Canterbury			HSAN 903	1855
04 Feb 1830	James W. Cheaney	Edward & Sarah(Neal)		PPME 543	----
28 Mar 1848	Dr. Cassidy Chenoweth	Dr.W.J.		PBWC 202	----
06 Sep 1788	William Cline			HMCD 991	----
00 000 1815	Ross Cochran[Summerville]	James	Va/x	PVED 1075	----
16 Nov 1816	Jacob R. Cooper			PBWO B102	----
22 Aug 1817	W.G. Culbertson			HEDG 677	----
22 Aug 1817	William G. Culbertson	James & Sarah(Weaver)	Mason/x	PVED 812	----
00 000 0000	Elizabeth Deering[Maddux]	William & Anna(Rogers)	Va/Va	BRML 255	----

Date	Name	Parents/Spouse	Code	No.	Year
00 000 0000	Dr. G.W. Cornwall		PHEF	B153	----
00 000 0000	Dr. G.W. Cornwall		BEFF	664	----
00 000 0000	J.W. Davis		HMAD	581	1862
00 000 0000	Harriet Debell Means]		GSBR	261	1858
00 000 0000	Elizabeth Deering[Maddux]	William & Anna(Rogers) Va/Va	BRML	255	1841
00 000 0000	I.T. Dillon		MACL	295	1825
25 Sep 1808	James Dinsmore		HPIK	591	----
22 May 1837	W.W. Duley	Rev.Hiram & Sophia(Northcott)x/c1810	PPVE	1016	----
24 Mar 1811	Edmund P. Dunlap		PBKR	323	----
10 Feb 1811	Stephen Dunlap		HMOR	696	1840
04 Jul 1810	Col.A.P. Dunbar	A.	COLE	518	1828
12 May 1846	Alexander W. Dunn		HLOG	499	----
12 Oct 1821	A.A. Dunseth		COLE	564	----
09 May 1820	Joseph S. Eakins		PBDP	642	----
30 Aug 1794	William Estell		HMEM	743	1824
06 Mar 1823	J.W. Estill	William & Mary(Williams) Barren94/**	HMEM	720	----
17 Oct 1817	T.W. Evans	Robert & Rhoda(Wilson)	HMCL	833	----
26 Nov 1829	William Evans	Jesse & Hannah(Pitts) Val795/Ky1800	PBWL	458	----
16 Jan 1800	Isaac Fulton		AMEN	46	----
00 000 1804	James Fulton		CMCD	597	1830
00 000 1804	James Fulton		HMCD	985	1830
07 Nov 1796	Martha Fulton[Clire]		HMCD	991	----
19 Nov 1826	William W. Fuqua		HEDG	699	----
01 Oct 1806	B.N. Galliher		HADM	868	----
00 000 0000	Harrison Glass		MACL	302	1840
22 Apr 1825	John P. Glasscock	Asa & Mary(Penquite) Va/Pa	PBSM	208	----
00 000 0000	Robert Gooding	Cornelius	PSTC	365	----
06 Jan 1820	Joshua Graham	Nathaniel & Sarah(Harbor) Pa/Ky	HSAN	1002	1826
00 000 0000	V.H. Harrison		AMEN	19	1863
28 Feb 1822	O.D. Hawkins	Gregory R & Elizabeth(Ballard) Md/Ky	COLE	600	1830
28 Feb 1822	Oliver D. Hawkins	Gregory & Elizabeth(Ballar) Md89/Ky93	PBCO	262	1864
24 Dec 1843	Joan Hayden[Kiss-ck]		VTBU	318	1824
19 Oct 1801	Elijah Hendrick		HMCL	927	1824
00 000 1801	Elijah Hendrick		BMCL	1086	1824
00 000 1868	J.W. Hilligoss		PHPI	608	----
01 Oct 1841	J.W. Hilligoss	Thomas Ky1818/x	PBDP	281	----

BIRTHDATE	NAME OF BIOGRAPHEE	PARENTS/BIRTHPLACE/BIRTHDATE	SOURCE/PAGE	DATE
01 Oct 1841	John W. Hilligoss	Thomas & Mary(Darnall) Ky/Ky	PPPI 85	----
00 000 0000	J.S. Howe		CJRI 813	----
03 Jan 1829	Elder Daniel T. Hughes James		HMEM 731	1830
14 Jul 1844	Elizabeth[Ingle]		HMCL 1017	1851
23 Oct 1860	Kirby S. Johnson	John S & Luellen(Bradley) Ky1817/Ky18	PPME 190	----
10 Aug 1822	Abbie Jones[Pittman]		HADM 677	1847
01 Nov 1816	Lewis E. Kelly	Francis Vt/x	HFUL 660	----
16 Jun 1818	W.G. Kelly		HFUL 660	----
24 Jul 1838	W.L. Kenner	L.W & Mary H(Bell) Ky/Ky	HMCD 1060	1864
30 Aug 1837	Francis M. Kissick		VTBU 318	1864
00 Jan 1833	Jesse LaForgee	Ayers & Dorinda(Cassity) Ky/Ky	PPDM 838	----
00 000 0000	D.D. Lanterman		CELW 351	1818
04 Sep 1817	Peter Lanterman		BLOG 580	----
00 000 0000	William A. Lanterman	Daniel A & Sarah(Luman) Pa/Va	HMAD 577	1819
26 Nov 1815	William A. Lanterman	--- & ---(O'Connell)Holland/NY	HMAD 487	----
24 Mar 1832	Hannah C. Lewellin[Petrie]		HMEM 734	----
05 Nov 1823	John D. Lewis	Peter B & Catherine B(Ringo) Va89/1798	PBWL 560	----
27 Dec 1827	Minerva W. Lewis[Riggs] William D & Nancy		HMCL 904	----
00 000 0000	J.W. Lightfood		AGLY 50	1880
00 Mar 1811	Samuel M. Little	Samuel & Mary(Newcomb)	HSAN 1063	----
00 Feb 1811	Samuel N. Little		HSAN 690	1818
18 Oct 1793	Robert E. Lockhart		PBWH 653	----
00 000 0000	G. Lukins		AMEN 19	1830
11 May 1811	Gregory Lukins	Peter & Ann(Rector)	AMEN 39	----
14 Feb 1836	John T. Luckins	Jesse	HMCL 928	1837
10 Jan 1825	Polly M. McCullough[Perry] Peter		HMCL 1012	1826
04 Feb 1808	Thomas L. McKinnie	Lewis & Nancy(Saunders)	HSAN 1026	1826
20 May 1810	William P. McKinnie	Lewis & Nancy(Saunders)	HSAN 1026	1826
24 May 1832	Dr. C.A. McLean	James & Charlotte M.A(Argo)	PBWC 677	----
24 May 1832	Dr. Chambers A. McLean James & Charlotte M.A(Argo) **/**		PPDM 360	----
17 Mar 1859	James O. McKee	Hiram & Sarah(Ledford)	PPME 366	----

Date	Name	Parents/Notes	Origin	Code	No.	Year
23 Jul 1832	William Maddux	Edward D & Elizabeth(Deering) Ky/**		BRML	255	----
00 000 0000	Lorana B. Marks[Ycurgman]			CRJI	583	----
00 000 1823	Eliza Markwell[Skirvin]			HADM	906	----
30 Jul 1817	Nancy Markwell[Judy]			HADM	903	----
18 Oct 1833	Sarah A. Markwell[Walls]			HRDG	691	1867
00 000 0000	Arthur Marriott			CELW	347	1879
00 000 0000	M.J[Martinie]			HGHA	181	----
21 Jul 1830	Andrew W. Mers	Samuel & Tenna(Plank) **1797/x		BGLS	611	----
00 000 1818	T.O. Mershon			HQAR	457	----
00 000 1815	David K. Moore	Jacob & Rebecca(Paddicks) Ky/Ky		TAZE	646	1857
24 Aug 1824	Eliza M. Morga[Little]	Daniel & Mary(Woods)		HSAN	1063	1828
20 May 1808	Jacob Morgan	Charles		HSAN	960	1826
29 Dec 1853	William B. Morgan			HMEM	770	c1861
07 Sep 1840	John Moss	William H.H & Mary(Chrisman) **/**		PVED	979	----
25 Jul 1837	John A. Moss			COLE	653	----
04 Apr 1827	Elizabeth[Nuckles]			PVED	1050	1831
18 Apr 1805	William Orange			HMCL	916	----
28 Oct 1838	Lewis Page	Allen & Clarinda(Lawrence) Ky/Ky		HMEM	734	1858
08 Feb 1856	John A. Petrie	David A & Hannah C(Lewellen)NY29/**32		PPME	546	----
00 000 0000	Martha J. Pierce[McGary]			PPME	366	----
15 Jul 1831	Samuel Plummer			PBKN	316	----
00 000 0000	William Pointer			HMCD	1004	----
19 Sep 1819	John C. Power	John Val787/x		HSAN	531	----
25 Dec 1827	LaFayette Proctor	William & Sarah(McKee) Pa/**		PBML	841	----
00 000 0000	William Raney			PVED	581	----
31 May 1836	Austin Rawlings	John E & Polly(Scott)		PBML	1169	1837
18 Oct 1810	John E. Rawlings	Thomas & Mary(Triby) Va/Va		PBML	707	----
18 Oct 1810	John E. Rawlings			HMCL	1019	1837
00 000 0000	A.J. Reed			AMEN	19	1833
00 000 0000	Darius B. Reid	James C & Susan(Lee) Md/x		PVED	634	----
11 Dec 1827	George W. Riggs	William M & Nancy(Pitts) Md1803/Ky06		PBML	716	1830
11 Dec 1827	G.W. Riggs	William M.		HMCL	904	----
15 Mar 1845	James Routt	Byram & Eleanor C(Riggs) Ky/Ky		HMEM	810	----
24 Jun 1838	John Routt	Byram Ky/Ky		HMEM	809	----
00 000 0000	Jonathan R. Saunders	Gunnell & Mary(Mauzy) Val783/Val784		HSAN	713	----
00 000 0000	Samuel Scott			PVED	913	----

BIRTHDATE	NAME OF BIOGRAPHEE	PARENTS/BIRTHPLACE/BIRTHDATE	SOURCE/PAGE	DATE
30 Jan 1813	Arthur C. Shriver		COLE 533	----
06 Feb 1816	William H. Smith		HPEO 794	1835
00 000 0000	W.C. Smoot		AMEN 22	1831
13 Feb 1830	W.S. Smoot	Colman & Rebecca(Wright) 1791/1795	HMEM 746	----
00 000 0000	Harrison Sousley		PVED 979	----
27 Aug 1829	Mary A. Sousley[Rardin]		COLE 629	----
00 00c 1798	George W. Strode		PAUP 845	----
00 000 0000	Peter J. Sutton		HDEW 344	1855
00 Apr 1812	John Swain		HSAN 929	----
23 Nov 1819	Nathan Swain	Nathan & Nancy(Nolan) Md/Md	PBRI 526	----
20 Jan 1853	John W. Terhune	James & Ann E(Harrison) Ky/Ky	PPME 300	1853
20 Oct 1812	William S. Tout		HADM 899	1824
15 Jan 1815	Serena Truitt[McKinley]		PPWA 269	----
11 Aug 1826	Deborah Van Kirk[Beckner]		PPWA 266	----
14 Dec 1817	George W. Van Sandt		PPMO B255	----
25 Oct 1820	James R. Wallingford	James & Sarah(Reed) Va/Pa	HMCD 936	----
00 000 1865	Jane Washburn[Starkey]		HDEW 346	----
00 000 0000	John Wheeler		HMAC 274	1834
00 000 0000	Frances Williams[Osborn]		PVED 887	----
15 Dec 1826	John S. Williamson	Abraham & Keziah(Smith) NJ/Ky	HMEM 811	1844
00 000 0000	William N. Wilson	John & Margaret(Newcomb) **/**	PVED 1000	----

F L O Y D   C O U N T Y

BIRTHDATE	NAME OF BIOGRAPHEE	PARENTS/BIRTHPLACE/BIRTHDATE	SOURCE/PAGE	DATE
26 Jan 1834	William F. Auxier		HMEM 843	----
08 Apr 1839	Mial M. Crum		HHDG 693	1852
08 Oct 1825	Hiram Frasier	Weeks & Anna(Sammons)	PVED 772	----
25 Jun 1817	George W. Haws		HHDG 716	1820

08 Feb 1823	T.J. Martin		CJRI 501	---
11 Jul 1813	Judith Mayo[Driskell]		HEDG 570	---
00 000 0000	Margaret Priest[S-zemore]		HEDG 674	---
00 000 1835	Francis M. Hall	George & Rachel(Hay) Ky/Ky	EMCL 1068	---

F R A N K L I N   C O U N T Y

BIRTHDATE	NAME OF BIOGRAPHEE	PARENTS/BIRTHPLACE/BIRTHDATE	SOURCE/PAGE	DATE
20 May 1852	Mary Ahern[Harris]		HSAN 767	---
00 000 0000	Ann E. Brown[Mahan]		HMCL 857	---
10 Feb 1830	George P. Brown	Robert & Permelia(White) Ky/Ky	PBML 766	---
11 Dec 1823	George S. Brown	Bedford & Caroline(Springer)	PBWA 665	---
02 Oct 1815	Lucy W. Buck[Harris]		OGLE 820	---
22 Aug 1803	James M. Camptell	John R & Margaret F(Self) Va/Va	GNCD 327	---
22 Aug 1803	James M. Camptell	John R & Margaret F(Self)	HMCD 277	1809
18 Jul 1789	Thomas Carlin		PBWA 135	---
00 000 0000	Margaret Clark[Ross] John		BGLS 156	---
00 000 0000	Adelia M. Damer[Swiney]		HDEW 346	1877
00 000 0000	Moses Deere		HCHA 180	1830
15 Apr 1809	Ninian W. Edwards	Ninian	HSAN 93	---
00 000 0000	George Edgar		BCSB 137	---
09 Dec 1835	Temp Elliott	John & Jane E(Taylor) Va/Ky95	HSAN 659	1834
00 000 0000	William T. Elliott		PEMO B140	---
00 000 1799	Letitia Ewing[Spears] Baker		PPME 346	---
07 Nov 1831	Sanford Faught		BHAN 107	---
00 000 1801	W.W. Graham		HEDG 630	---
29 Jan 1837	William Grimes	Thomas W & ---(Wheeler)	PJEF B50	---
00 000 0000	George M. Hart		PHKX B499	1843
15 Sep 1831	Capt.James S. Jackson	William & Sarah(Mayhall) **/x	MACL 265	1851
22 Oct 1830	James S. Jackson	William & Sarah(Mayhall) Ky1798/Ky	PBCW 395	---
04 Nov 1817	John U. Lyons		PBML 456	1839
00 000 0000	Col.Thomas A.Marshall	William & Catherine(Eddings) Va/x	COLE 526	---
25 Dec 1812	Samuel W. Mayhall		BRBM 473	---
	Hiram B. Menough		BGLS 679	---

F R A N K L I N   C O U N T Y   (C O N T.)

BIRTHDATE	NAME OF BIOGRAPHEE	PARENTS/BIRTHPLACE/BIRTHDATE	SOURCE/PAGE	DATE
00 000 0000	Ellen I. Miles[Marshall]	Dr. James I.	COLE	526	1839
01 May 1825	Traleton C. Miles	Dr. James I.	COLE	527	1845
00 000 0000	J.L. Myers		AWOO	3	1835
00 000 0000	Mrs. M.R. Myers		AWOO	3	1835
21 Mat 1842	Thomas M. Page	Thomas S & Jane B(Julian) NY1800/x	BGLS	427	----
22 Feb 1814	William B. Potts	Richard F.	PEMO	B230	----
27 Jun 1825	James D. Reed		PBKN	470	----
00 000 1800	Sallie Scofield[Vaughan]		PHCC	129	----
28 Feb 1835	Manlieus T. Shepherd	William & Eveline H(Bell) Val794/x	PBSM	663	1859
00 000 0000	Peter Silver		PPVE	232	----
21 Jul 1827	Joseph S. Smith	Joseph Val794/x	HSAN	970	----
00 000 1825	J. Taylor Smith	Joseph & Sally(Taylor) Va/x	HSAN	716	1834
19 Feb 1808	Milton Smith	William & Obedience(Brown) Pa/x	PBWL	968	----
19 Feb 1808	Milton Smith	William & Obedience(Brown) Pa/x	PBWL	984	----
23 May 1827	William M. Smith		EFAY	489	----
00 000 0000	John J. Stephens		HJAC	77	----
00 000 0000	Charity Watson[Ravenscraft]		CSHR	388	1848
00 000 0000	James H. Whitehurst		HCHA	181	1852
25 Dec 1804	Elizabeth Williams[Powell]		PBAD	377	----

F U L T O N   C O U N T Y

BIRTHDATE	NAME OF BIOGRAPHEE	PARENTS/BIRTHPLACE/BIRTHDATE	SOURCE/PAGE	DATE
12 Jan 1850	William T. Morley	Nathaniel & Amanda(Burgess) Va/Tn	HGSH	565	----

G A L L A T I N   C O U N T Y

BIRTHDATE	NAME OF BIOGRAPHEE	PARENTS/BIRTHPLACE/BIRTHDATE	SOURCE/PAGE	DATE

BIRTHDATE	NAME OF BIOGRAPHEE	PARENTS/BIRTHPLACE/BIRTHDATE	SOURCE/PAGE	DATE
00 000 0000	Laura Brumfield[Applegate]		CELW 353	1867
00 000 0000	Louisa Brumfield[Applegate]		CELW 353	1867
00 000 0000	John H. Clements		HCHA 181	1860
00 000 0000	Daniel Dillman		ACLY 49	1851
01 May 1840	Martin L. Dorman	Peter & Lucy(Kemper) Va/Owen	BCHR 877	----
17 Jan 1834	John W. Dunniway	David & Annie(Crow)	HPIK 432	1836
00 000 0000	Lucille Gex[Pullen]		MACL 301	1857
09 Sep 1809	Dr.James H. Gibson	David & Mary(Marrow)	HSAN 935	----
00 000 0000	Rosanna Hampton[Mack]		HPEO 662	----
25 Jan 1811	John S. Holiday		CMCD 597	1832
00 000 0000	Samuel Jack		HPEO 662	----
00 000 0000	Edward Kern		PBSM 646	----
22 Mar 1849	D.I. Lillard		HEDG 583	----
31 Aug 1843	Dr.V.T.Lindsay	Michael & Martha A. Ky/Ky	HSAN 690	----
03 Apr 1836	W.J. Peak		COLE 572	----
00 Apr 1836	Dr. Willis J. Peak	Grigg & Susan(Crow) Va/Pa1802	PBCO 412	----
30 May 1854	Dr. B.I. Poland	Isaac & Martha(Duncan) Tn/**	PPVE 137	1861
00 000 0000	Polly A. Rice[Kern]		PBSM 646	----
30 Oct 1847	Catherine W. Richey[Rodgers]		COLE 590	----
04 Jun 1825	H.C. Skirvin		HADM 898	----
00 000 0000	Lucy D. Taylor		MACL 302	1834
14 Jan 1815	John M. Wilson	James & Bridget(Custer) Pa1772/Va1775	MACL 738	----
00 000 0000	Minnie L. Winn[Bookhardt]	Henry & Mary(Flack) Ky/Ky	BEFF 728	----
18 Jan 1818	Gov. Richard Yates	Henry Va1786/x	EFAY 603	----
18 Jan 1818	Richard Yates		HSAN 507	1831
18 Jan 1818	Richard Yates		HMOR 382	1831
14 Mar 1811	Thomas Yates		HSAN 937	1836

GARRARD COUNTY

BIRTHDATE	NAME OF BIOGRAPHEE	PARENTS/BIRTHPLACE/BIRTHDATE	SOURCE/PAGE	DATE
00 000 1840	R.D. Anderson		HADM 914	1860
14 Jan 1812	Capt. Joseph F. Ballinger		PBWA 351	----
21 Mar 1849	Huston J. Barton	Oliver T & Susannah W(Walker) Ky/Ky	PPDM 806	----

BIRTHDATE	NAME OF BIOGRAPHEE	PARENTS/BIRTHPLACE/BIRTHDATE		SOURCE/PAGE		DATE
09 Sep 1822	Samuel L. Boyd	Andrew	Pa/x	PBWA	385	----
00 000 0000	Bentley Brown			HGHA	183	1868
00 000 0000	John F. Callison	Absalom & Anna(Flack)	WV/x	PBDP	276	----
00 000 0000	Nancy J. Casey[Stipe]			HGHR	264	----
30 Sep 1842	George M. Clinton			HEDG	678	----
00 000 0000	Elizabeth Ray[Fitzgerrell]			PJEF	B139	----
05 Jun 1831	Elizabeth Fletcher[Kearby]	Thomas & Mary(Lear) **1792/Va99		HMCL	1010	----
00 000 1831	Elizabeth Fletcher[Kearby]	John	Ky/x	BWCL	1127	----
00 000 0000	Nancy[Hall]			HMAC	272	1855
00 000 0000	Sidney Hall			HMAC	272	1855
24 Sep 1799	Samuel Harbour			HSAN	828	1817
21 Nov 1797	Levi Harbur			HSAN	828	1818
15 Jan 1833	John P. Henderson	James Harvey	Va/x	PBWA	557	----
16 Nov 1793	Col. William H. Henderson			HPPB	956	----
16 Nov 1793	William H. Henderson			BRBM	10	----
00 000 0000	S.A. Kennedy			ACLY	50	1865
09 Apr 1822	Henry C. Layton	William & Mary A(Yator) SG1783/Ky1787		PBCO	277	----
29 Sep 1827	Martha J. Logan[Layton]	Hugh & Elizabeth(Layer)	NC/Va	PBCO	278	----
00 000 1801	John McCoy	Daniel & Agnes	Va/Va	PBAD	504	----
00 000 0000	Catherine McDonald[Bramwell]			PBML	366	1811
00 000 0000	Jacob H. Merriman			CELW	349	1876
00 000 1822	William E. Moberly	John & Mahala	Md/x	PAUP	B136	----
00 000 0000	J.C. Myers			HDEW	340	1875
08 Aug 1858	Dr. Joseph C. Myers	Jordan & N. Amelia(Banton)	Ky/Ky	PBDP	478	----
10 Mar 1840	Jeremiah P. Nicholson	John & Elizabeth(Henry)		PBWC	489	----
00 000 0000	Elizabeth Onstadt[Callison]			PBDP	276	----
18 Jun 1816	Benjamin W. Patton	John & Margaret(Wiley)	NC/x	PBML	913	----
01 Feb 1826	Frederick Payne	Robert & Sarah(Stipe)	Ky/Ky	PCHR	316	----
08 May 1831	Elizabeth Roerty[Peugh]			HHEN	411	----
00 000 1842	William B. Rose	George W & Eliza(Champ)	Ky/x	HMCH	439	----
05 Oct 1843	John M. Rothwell	Thomas & Matilda	Va/Ky	BLOG	263	1865
00 Mar 1836	James B. Sneed	John H & Elizabeth	Va/In	HMCL	912	----
28 Jul 1819	Sarah Sublet[Shields]			PBCO	469	----

BIRTHDATE	NAME	PARENTS/BIRTHPLACE		SOURCE	PAGE	DATE
24 Nov 1814	James Wallace	Allen		PBAD	401	----
28 Mar 1821	James A. Wallace			HADM	770	1835
31 Dec 1817	Origen Wallace	Allen & Ann		HADM	751	----
07 Nov 1815	Lytle R. Wiley		Va/Ky	HMCL	1046	1818
24 Aug 1813	William Wiley	John & Hannah(Sampson)	Md/x	PBML	804	----
30 Nov 1834	Dr. N.M. Williams	Andrew & Levina(Wood)	Va/SC	HWCL	B138	----
22 Jan 1839	Dr. Eberle Wilson			HGJR	737	----
00 000 1844	Stephen S. Wilson	James F & Elizabeth(Stewart)	WV/WV	GHHA	767	1849
16 Nov 1822	D.J. Wylie	John & Mary(Thompson)	Ky/Ky	GHHA	769	----

G R A N T   C O U N T Y

BIRTHDATE	NAME OF BIOGRAPHEE	PARENTS/BIRTHPLACE/BIRTHDATE		SOURCE/PAGE		DATE
00 000 0000	Zebulon Allphin	Reuben & S.Brumback	Ky/Va	CSBR	384	----
00 000 0000	Joseph Anderson			AGLY	50	1847
01 Sep 1819	Joseph Anderson	Joseph & Patsie D(Henderson)		HWCL	B224	----
14 Feb 1852	Dr. John R. Barnert	Thomas A & Amarias(Vance)		BLOG	244	1856
14 Feb 1852	Dr. John R. Barnert	Thomas A & Amarias(Vance)	Ky/Ky	LOGA	324	1867
16 Sep 1868	Dr. Charles F.Burkhardt	William & Nancy E(Arnold)	Pa/**	BFF	728	----
08 Aug 1814	Elizabeth Buskirk[Haselwood]	Thomas		PBAD	225	1836
00 000 1835	Dr.James W.Carlton	George W & Maranda(Tull)	Ky/Ky	GHHA	698	1842
00 000 1854	Joseph P. Carter	Landon S & Sally	**/**	PPPI	298	----
05 Jul 1821	Dr. Childers			HADM	932	1831
08 Jul 1820	Washington Corbin	James & Jane(Briggs)	Va/x	PBAD	165	----
13 Jan 1822	J. Daniel Curry	Nicholas & Elizabeth(Robinson)	Ire/Ky	BLOG	440	1829
13 Jan 1841	John W. Fugate			HSAN	934	----
00 000 0000	James Haselwood			PBAD	225	1836
00 Feb 1840	William K. Haselwood	Thomas A & Frances A(Dance)		PBAD	511	1857
00 000 0000	G.A. McMillen			HMAD	556	1876
22 Dec 1830	Dr. Samuel Mileham	Ebenezer & Ann(Dougherty)	NC/Ky	PBAD	462	----
00 000 0000	James Mills			HDEW	341	1860
00 000 0000	John H. Mills			HDEW	341	1860
00 000 0000	W.A.A. Mills			HDEW	341	1860
20 Jul 1844	Enoch K. Nelson	William K & Mary(Edmonson)		CJRI	546	1855

BIRTHDATE	NAME OF BIOGRAPHEE	PARENTS/BIRTHPLACE/BIRTHDATE	SOURCE/PAGE	DATE
00 000 0000	John A. Points		CSBR 382	1834
00 000 1827	Ezekiel Rucker	Morning & Julia(Reese) Va/Va	BHAN 50	----
31 Dec 1822	Hamilton Skirvin		HADM 906	1833
29 Nov 1829	Jamison Wilson	John R & Rachel(Junip)	BCSB 133	1836

G R A V E S   C O U N T Y

BIRTHDATE	NAME OF BIOGRAPHEE	PARENTS/BIRTHPLACE/BIRTHDATE	SOURCE/PAGE	DATE
21 Sep 1831	Samuel Briley	John & Lavina(Anderson) Ms/x	PAUP B218	----
00 000 0000	James W. Heaton	James W & Lorinda J(Lindsay)Henry/Henry	BRJM 408	----
00 000 0000	L.S. Lamb		MACL 302	1857
12 Aug 1838	Lemuel L. Laurence	Henry G Va1807/x	BRJM 464	----
06 Aug 1833	Hon.Francis M. McGee	Benjamin F.	BRJM 495	1835
17 Dec 1839	Archibald T. Mozley	John N & Agnes(Golloway) Tn/NC	BRJM 173	----

G R A Y S O N   C O U N T Y

BIRTHDATE	NAME OF BIOGRAPHEE	PARENTS/BIRTHPLACE/BIRTHDATE	SOURCE/PAGE	DATE
27 May 1810	Charles T. Askins	Philemon & Philenor(Stayton) Va/Md	HSTC 257	----
00 000 0000	Charles T. Askins		HSTC 377	----
26 Feb 1827	Abram D. Attebury		PBWO B124	1850
00 000 0000	F.M. Atteberry	Stout & Annie L(Crask) SC/Ky	HWCL B140	----
20 Jan 1847	William A. Beatty	Joseph & Sarah(Akres) **1823/Ky c26	PBWO B235	----
01 Mar 1829	Mitchell T. Bruster	Thomas & Martha(Jeffers) Va/Va	CURI 529	----
09 Aug 1822	William Burtle	William & Sarah(Ogden) Md1780/Md1786	HSAN 788	1826
09 Aug 1822	William Burtle	William & Sarah(Ogden)	HSAN 761	1826
03 May 1846	John T. Cain	Abraham P.	PBWA 201	----
24 Jun 1831	Robert Chism		PBWO B124	----

Date	Name	Parents / Spouse	Origin	Code	No.	Year
00 000 0000	Stephen Coonroe			HCHR	179	---
11 Jul 1802	James T. Cunningham			COLE	543	1830
19 Sep 1831	Judge J.R. Cunningham	John & Elizabeth(Yates)	Va/Md	PBCO	492	---
06 Jan 1828	John Cunningham	James T & Elizabeth C(Yocum)**/**		HMCD	911	---
00 000 1801	Sarah Day[Johnston]			PBHE	578	---
29 Dec 1835	David T. Dickey	Samuel & Elizabeth(Cooper)	Pa1804/Oh	COLE	634	1860
12 Dec 1827	S.C. Doran	Thomas & Nancy(Cleaver)	Nelson/Washing	PBMB	255	---
20 May 1856	S. Lee Elliott	George & Lucina(Kessinger) **/**		PBMB	464	---
20 May 1856	S. Lee Elliott	George & Lucina(Kessinger) **/**		PBCO	331	---
20 Jul 1826	John J. Gannaway	John & Elizabeth(Williams)	Va1789/x	COLE	588	---
02 Mar 1841	Ann M. Hackley[Jeffris]		Ky/Ky	PBCO	341	---
02 Mar 1841	Ann M. Hackley[Jeffris]	John & Susan(Thomas)		PBCO	398	---
25 Apr 1849	Elizabeth Hackley	John R & Susanna		COLE	587	1855
25 Nov 1842	James L. Hackley		Ky/Va	COLE	585	---
02 Jun 1847	Kittie B. Hackley[Diehl]		Ky/Ky	COLE	652	---
18 Jun 1846	James L. Hart	Oliver & Zoranda	**1825/Hardin1823	HLAS	B451	---
01 Jul 1818	Oliverhill Havenhill	George		COLE	585	---
23 Feb 1824	Mary E. Jeffris[Diehl]			COLE	588	1831
17 Mar 1821	James Jeffris			HDEW	344	1858
00 000 0000	Mary J. Johnson[Winslow]	John & Zillah(Van Metre)	Md87/Ky92	HGJR	886	---
17 Jan 1817	Etersa Keller[Corrington]	William L.	Hart/x	PBMB	256	---
00 000 0000	Lucina Kessinger[Elliott]			COLE	585	---
02 Aug 1816	Sally Matthews[Diehl]			PJEF	B137	1817
00 000 0000	John Milner			HWCL	B127	1817
25 Sep 1812	Nathan A. Morris	Isaac & Mary		PBMB	276	1819
07 Jan 1819	Matilda J. Olverson[McConathy]			HMAC	271	1846
00 000 0000	Maria[Rafferty]			HGJR	463	---
00 000 0000	Elizabeth Redcash[Elliott]	Beal & Mary		HWCL	B127	---
10 Mar 1816	Sarah A. Reid[Morris]			HMAC	272	1834
00 000 0000	Charles Rhoade			HMAC	252	---
12 Aug 1819	Charles Rhoade	Samuel V & Jane(Pennybaker)	Hardin191/x	PBWA	729	---
11 Aug 1824	Charles C. Rhoads	Henry & Mary(Cleaver)	**/Meade	HMAC	235	---
11 Aug 1824	Charles C. Rhoads	Henry & Mary		HMAC	271	1855
00 000 0000	Edmund[Rhoads]			HMAC	271	1855
00 000 0000	Frances[Rhoads]			ACLY	49	1851
00 000 0000	Dreaury Rose			BRCM	345	1856
00 000 0000	Drury Rose		Ky/x	ACLY	49	1850
00 000 0000	G. Smith			ACLY	49	1851
00 000 0000	S.L. Smith					

BIRTHDATE	NAME OF BIOGRAPHEE	PARENTS/BIRTHPLACE/BIRTHDATE		SOURCE/PAGE		DATE
28 Mar 1812	Richard Stoddert			COLE	532	1838
28 Feb 1815	Thomas Stoddert	Benjamin & Mary		COLE	533	1836
00 000 0000	B.C.W. Utterback	Thomas	Ky/x	ERCM	23	1836
08 Nov 1824	Dr. Samuel Van Meter	John & Catherine(keller)		COLE	535	----
05 Oct 1831	John H. Walker	Felix & Rachel(Watts) Breckin1804/1804		BCSM	538	1837
00 000 0000	Samuel Walker			AMEN	26	1827
01 Mar 1815	Robert E.Y. Williams	William L & Mary(Gannaway)	Va/Va	PBCO	361	----
03 Nov 1821	Silas Wilson	Samuel	Va/x	HWCL	B59	----
18 Nov 1830	Eliza A. Wortham[Doran]			COLE	634	1860

BIRTHDATE	NAME OF BIOGRAPHEE	PARENTS/BIRTHPLACE/BIRTHDATE		SOURCE/PAGE		DATE
30 May 1809	Jane L. Anderson[Eccles]	Pouncey & Nancy(Lynch)	Va/Va	PEWO	B103	----
29 Nov 1832	Abigail Bale[Hawks]	Solomon		HMEM	856	----
26 Dec 1828	Rev. John R. Barbee	John & Mary(Ray)		PEWO	B259	1864
00 000 0000	L.B. Bays	John W.		HFUL	785	----
00 000 0000	Mary Black[Davis]			PBCW	475	----
02 Jul 1821	S.G. Cartright			ACLY	49	1861
13 Jan 1817	George Brent			HSAN	737	----
00 Feb 1846	Samuel W. Caldwell	John & Elizabeth(Conover)		HMEM	708	----
00 000 0000	Abraham Calhoun		Ky/Ky	HMOR	569	1851
00 000 0000	S.G. Cartright			ACLY	49	1861
01 Dec 1823	Dr. William J. Chenoweth	John S & Elizabeth(Ross)	Shelby/x	PBMC	483	----
01 Dec 1823	Dr. William J. Chenoweth	John S & Elizabeth(Ross)		PPDM	735	----
27 Dec 1826	H.C. Clark	Howard & Eliza J(Wilson)		HMAC	170	----
00 000 0000	William B. Cloe			AMEN	26	1829
03 Apr 1840	George Cole	William & Mary(Bolin)	Ky/Ky	HGJR	797	1845
00 000 1798	Ellen Colelasure[Hardin]			HWCL	B218	----
00 000 0000	Frances Crow[Armitage]			BCHR	837	----

18 Sep 1824	Rev. H.P. Curry	George & Mary(Wilcox)		HMEM	692	1827
CC 000 0000	William Davis			PBCW	475	---
13 Sep 1842	Jesse H. DeSpain	Sedas & Abigail(Edwards)	Ky/x	PERJ	482	---
CC 000 0000	W.C. Dickey			AHEM	15	1855
CC 000 1805	Joseph Dobson			HFUL	947	---
18 Jun 1820	S.S. Douglas	Charles & Polly(Smith)	Va/Va	PBHE	244	---
00 000 0000	I.H. Ellis			ACLY	50	1849
19 Jan 1838	David Ellmore			HMEM	789	1858
19 Dec 1828	J.V. Ellmore			HMEM	788	1855
00 000 1797	William Faulkner			PBCW	239	---
00 000 0000	Z.J. Gibson			HMAC	268	1853
11 Jun 1839	Zachariah J. Gibson	John & Elizabeth		BRMA	253	c1848
09 Sep 1818	E.M. Goff	William & Amy(Trent)	Ky/Ky	HMEM	738	1825
29 Aug 1832	William Goff	William & Amy(Trent)	Ky/Ky	HMEM	739	1825
29 Aug 1832	William Goff	William & Amy(Trent)	Ky/Ky	PPME	198	1825
00 000 0000	J.B. Goldsby			AMEN	22	1830
26 Oct 1818	William M. Golcsby	James & Elizabeth(Hingley)		HMEM	695	---
00 Apr 1823	Bedford Graham	Hampton & Maria	Va/NC	HMCD	638	---
00 000 0000	Mary Greene[Watkins]			PPME	403	---
00 000 0000	Sarah Graham[Lewis]			BCSB	223	---
00 000 0000	Emeline C. Griffen[Alexander]			HSTC	378	---
27 Apr 1813	Benjamin D. Grasty	Benjamin & Nancy(Dunn)	Md1781/Pa1782	CSBR	372	1830
00 000 0000	J.B. Gum			AMEN	23	1822
07 May 1807	William P. Harris			HMQR	547	1829
25 Nov 1823	James L. Hawks	Charles & Sarah		HMEM	856	1849
29 Sep 1815	Martha Haycraft[Renc]			BRMA	328	---
00 000 0000	Elias Hohimer			AMEN	26	1824
07 Aug 1818	John M. Holmes			CMCD	598	1835
00 000 0000	A. Hunley			ACLY	49	1868
00 000 0000	T.S. Hutchason			HDEW	340	1856
27 Jun 1826	Lucy A Hutchason[wilson]			COLE	537	1857
00 Sep 1834	Lewis Jones	Judge George	Va/x	PPVE	1065	---
13 Aug 1824	William B. Larie		France/x	HMER	824	1832
17 Feb 1817	William D. Leeper	Robert A & Frances(Summers)	Ky/Ky	HCAS	291	1829
13 Nov 1847	Richard W. Lobb	Chapman & Ann(Horton)	Va/c1818	BRMA	369	---

BIRTHDATE	NAME OF BIOGRAPHEE	PARENTS/BIRTHPLACE/BIRTHDATE	SOURCE/PAGE	DATE
28 Nov 1820	William G. McCubbin	Joseph & Eleanor	GHHA	872	1834
13 Jan 1802	Nancy[Logan]		CMCD	598	1828
04 Jun 1820	Benjamin P. Miller		HCAR	393	---
25 Mar 1819	Edmund P. Miller	Maj. William & Martha(Winlock)Va90/Va88	HCAS	252	---
04 Jan 1832	Col. James Monroe	Dr. Byrd & Margaret(Linder) Ky/Ky	PBCO	442	1834
05 Jan 1848	James B. Montague	George W & Margaret S(Moore)	LOGA	501	---
01 Feb 1821	James S. Moore	John N & Phebe(Scott)	HMEM	723	1822
19 Jan 1847	Dr. W.A. Mudd	Henry L & Arabella S(Cass) 09/Clark16	PPME	336	---
20 Sep 1813	John B. Murray	William Md/x	HMCD	632	1834
09 Dec 1842	Milom A. Murray	William NC/x	HMCD	610	1849
26 May 1811	Moreau J. Phillips		HSAN	700	1829
00 000 1797	Polly Price[Martin]		BCHR	933	---
07 Sep 1812	James Purkipile		PPME	381	---
20 Sep 1819	D.K. Raffety	James & Elizabeth(Kean)	HEDG	654	---
16 Dec 1817	John Raffety	James & Elizabeth(Kean) NC/x	HEDG	654	---
00 000 0000	Jasper Rice		HMAC	271	1832
00 000 0000	Sarah P. Rice[Kyle]	Benjamin	HMCD	409	---
07 Feb 1837	William B. Roberts	William C & Mary(Gilmore) Pa/x	HMAC	253	1831
14 Oct 1816	Hiram Russell		CMCD	600	1832
08 Dec 1808	John L. Russell		CMCD	599	---
31 Oct 1819	Margaret Russell[Phelps]		CMCD	600	---
09 Mar 1815	Merritt A. Russell		HSAN	974	---
16 Jan 1804	Elisha Sanders		EFAY	474	1818
05 Jan 1798	James Semple		HMAD	401	1818
05 Jan 1798	Gen. James Semple	John W & Lucy(Robertson) Va/Va	HASN	691	1822
03 Jan 1810	Ann Short[McCormick]	James & Lucretia SC/SC	HMAC	275	1860
00 000 0000	Joseph A. Smith		AMEN	22	1824
00 000 0000	George Spears	1764/1762	PPME	266	1824
09 Mar 1805	George Spears	George & Mary(Neely)	HMEM	717	---
18 Apr 1822	George C. Spears	Jacob & Letitia S(Ewing)	HMEM	717	---

BIRTHDATE	NAME OF BIOGRAPHEE	PARENTS/BIRTHPLACE/BIRTHDATE		SOURCE/PAGE		DATE
00 000 0000	George C. Spears			AMEN	23	1849
18 Apr 1822	George C. Spears	Jacob & Letitia(Ewing)Linc85/Franklin99		PPME	346	----
00 000 0000	John H. Spears			AMEN	22	1827
12 Jun 1818	Zarel C. Spears	John & Rebecca(Conover)		PPME	470	c1828
21 Jun 1827	James F. Speer	James & Elizabeth(Grant)	Ky/Ky	PPME	482	----
00 000 0000	S.F. Stanley			ACLY	50	1848
17 Dec 1807	R.D. Timberlake	James & Anne(Douglas)	Va/Va	PPME	214	1833
00 000 0000	C.P. Tongate			HMAC	275	1837
00 000 0000	R.D. Tongate			HMAC	275	1837
00 000 0000	Thomas Watkins			PPME	403	----
23 Aug 1827	Thomas Watkins	Elijah & Lydia(Montgomery)		CASS	978	1829
00 000 0000	James W. Watt	James		HMAD	440	1817
01 May 1849	Charles E. Wilson			COLE	537	----

GREENUP COUNTY

BIRTHDATE	NAME OF BIOGRAPHEE	PARENTS/BIRTHPLACE/BIRTHDATE		SOURCE/PAGE		DATE
04 Mar 1818	John R. Chapman	John & Mary		OGLE	784	----
00 000 0000	I.M. Deputy[Benton]			CSBR	378	1834
00 000 0000	A.G. Dupuy			CSBR	378	1834
00 000 1824	Margaret Edwards[Todd]			HPIK	416	----
00 000 0000	Eugene Hockady			HCHA	182	1870
21 Aug 1873	Dr. Charles P. Hoffman	John E & Carrie(Eberwein)	1844/x	BCHA	629	----
00 000 0000	L.A. Miller			CELW	355	1854
04 Dec 1836	Robert P. Miller	Erastus	Ky/x	HMAC	229	----
14 Oct 1810	Thomas H. Rice	James & Ann(Hopkins)	Va/**	PBWA	387	----
00 000 0000	Robert J. Rigg			CELW	358	1837
00 000 0000	Thomas J. Rigg			CELW	354	1836
07 Jun 1821	Russell Riggs	Samuel & Nancy	Md/SC	HMCD	700	1828
22 Dec 1819	Thomas D. Tennery	Thomas & Jane(Wilson)	Tn/Tn	PHEF	B206	1820
16 Aug 1844	William A. Tower	William & Frances(Barker)	Va/x	HMCH	186	1855
00 000 0000	J. Traylor			CELW	350	1855

BIRTHDATE	NAME OF BIOGRAPHEE	PARENTS/BIRTHPLACE/BIRTHDATE	SOURCE/PAGE	DATE
05 Feb 1837	B.I. Ulen	Samuel & Margaret(Thompson)Va98/Mason10	PAUP B280	----
19 Jun 1831	Frederick G. Ulen	Samuel & Mary A(Thompson) WV98/Md	PAUP B324	----
16 Sep 1830	John Virgin	John	HMOR 726	----
16 Sep 1830	John Virgin	John H & Margaret(Hughes) 1796/x	HMOR 731	----

H A N C O C K   C O U N T Y

BIRTHDATE	NAME OF BIOGRAPHEE	PARENTS/BIRTHPLACE/BIRTHDATE	SOURCE/PAGE	DATE
07 Oct 1823	Joseph L. Allison	William L & Elizabeth B(Lewis)Ky94/**95	PHCC 3	1825
00 000 0000	Aurelia F. Blain[Fletcher]		GJRI 744	----
24 Jan 1846	John N. Carman		HMEM 754	c1856
24 Aug 1823	Isaac Hale		HMOR 756	1845
00 000 0000	Virginia A. Lyons[Barnett]		PPWO 548	----

H A R D I N   C O U N T Y

BIRTHDATE	NAME OF BIOGRAPHEE	PARENTS/BIRTHPLACE/BIRTHDATE	SOURCE/PAGE	DATE
00 000 0000	Noah Adams		HJAC 130	1863
14 Feb 1803	U.R. Allen	Elijah & Elizabeth(Scott)	HCHR 170	----
18 Jun 1831	James T. Amis	William & Fannie(Davis)	PVED 407	1852
00 000 0000	James Anderson		HMAC 271	1852
00 000 0000	Phebe Armour[Peat]		BCHR 959	----
00 000 0000	John Baird		CELW 357	1816
19 Oct 1838	V.A. Baker	William & Caroline(Utterback)	HCHR 220	1843
00 000 0000	Martha Barron[Powell]		GSER 381	1838
04 Dec 1808	Sallie A. Beauchamp[Barr] Jerry B.		BHAN 21	----

Date	Name	Parents	Loc.	Code	No.	Yr.
00 000 1819	W.B. Bolding	William & Elizabeth(Alphin)	Va/SC	CJRI	794	1832
20 Apr 1820	James Brandenburg			COLE	609	1823
23 Sep 1823	Thomas Bradley	William & Elizabeth(Crowder)	Va/NC	PCHR	259	1832
22 Jul 1832	Daniel Brown			COLE	693	1854
12 Mar 1843	Joseph N. Carter			HADM	609	----
12 Mar 1843	Hon.Joseph N. Carter	William P & Martha(Mays)		PBAD	233	1873
00 000 1839	James P. Clancey			HJAC	130	----
20 Jul 1839	Thomas N. Cofer	Col. John & Eleanor(Magill)		PBCO	285	----
00 000 0000	Thomas N. Cofer			COLE	641	1834
00 000 1797	Lydia Coffman[Clark]			CSBR	384	----
00 000 0000	Stephen Coonrod			HCHR	188	----
00 000 1802	Mrs. Thomas Cotterell[Dishon]			CJRI	824	----
11 Jul 1802	Hon.James T. Cunningham	Wright & Nancy(Taylor)	Ky/Ky	PBCO	281	1843
00 000 0000	James T. Cunningham			PBCO	440	1836
00 000 1819	James Daughtery			CSER	382	----
30 Sep 1817	Isom David			CMCD	596	1848
00 000 0000	John V. Elden	James & Sarah(Van Meter)	Ky/x	HFUL	753	1839
03 Jan 1838	Nancy J[Elliott]			HMAC	271	1854
00 000 0000	Charles B. Fletcher			CJRI	744	----
13 Apr 1832	W. Friend			CELW	355	----
00 000 1822	David S. Gilmore	Alexander & Millie(Mudd)	Vac.1805/Va.	PBMO	B106	----
21 Jul 1824	Edie J. Glassco[Brown]			PBCO	212	----
00 000 0000	Madison Glassco	Enoch & Rachel		PBCO	303	----
00 000 0000	Clement Goar			PBCO	394	----
00 000 0000	Elijah Graham			HCHR	265	----
27 Oct 1804	Harrison Graham			HCHR	265	----
06 Aug 1823	Maria J. Graham[McQuality]			HCHR	265	----
00 000 0000	Jacob Greenawalt			HSAN	789	1830
17 Mar 1840	Silas J. Grigsby			HMCD	889	1844
00 000 0000	B.D. Gristy			CSBR	392	1830
00 000 0000	Benjamin D. Hamblen			COLE	652	1852
04 Mar 1827	Martha M. Hampton[Waters]			HMAC	274	1830
05 Sep 1824	Elizabeth Hart[Goar]	Jacob & Matilda(Goar)	Ky/Ky	PBCO	394	----
20 Jan 1824	Martha Hart[Leckard]	Miles H & Catherine C(Yocum)	NC96/Ky	COLE	406	----
23 Aug 1814	Thomas Hart			COLE	652	----
	Rev. James J. Haycraft	John & Hannah(Parker)	Ky/Va	PBMA	451	----
	Hiram Heavenrill	George & Sally		HLAS	B453	1829

BIRTHDATE	NAME OF BIOGRAPHEE	PARENTS/BIRTHPLACE/BIRTHDATE	SOURCE/PAGE	DATE
00 000 1816	Charles Hill		GWCD 598	1830
10 Mar 1839	Robert Hodgen	Robert & Frances(Gibson) Va/Boyle	PBDP 978	----
24 Oct 1823	Samuel Huddleston	John Ky/x	HMAC 163	----
23 Jan 1822	Oliver R. Jackson	John & Sarah(Price)	CJRI 539	----
00 000 1836	M.W. Jones	Jesse P & Magdalen(George)	PBWA 666	----
12 May 1823	Atharine Keeling	Lewis & Lydia(Haney) Ky/Ky	HFUL 687	----
00 000 0000	Sarah A. Keith[Lucas]	Ky/Ky	CSBR 392	1835
00 000 0000	Mary E. Kendall[Midgett]		CELW 354	1849
31 May 1810	Charles Kennedy	Peter & Rachel(Colvin)	BCSB 426	----
07 Mar 1828	W.W. Kermicle	Samuel & Mary J(Trainer) Ky/Va	CJRI 829	----
27 Mar 1823	Dr. Andrew H. Kimbrough	Richard C & Jane(Morrison) SC/Ky	PVED 228	----
27 Mar 1823	Dr. Andrew H. Kimbrough	Richard C & Jane(Morrison) NC/x	PPVE 292	----
26 Oct 1817	James Kinkade	**/x	BRCM 480	----
22 Oct 1845	James M. Kinkade	James & Martha A(Veach) 1817***?***1816	BRCM 478	1850
16 Aug 1807	Elisha Lender	Isaac & Nancy(Richardson) Vt/x	PBCO 494	----
16 Aug 1807	Elisha Linder		COLE 550	1829
00 000 0000	Melissa Linder[McCartan]		MACL 297	1856
26 Nov 1808	Hugh McDonald	John & Mary(Larue)	HMCH 454	1832
31 Oct 1807	James McMurtry		PBKN 234	----
02 Oct 1794	John Miles		PBWA 497	1806
00 000 0000	Col. D.A. Morrison	James & Mary(McWilliams) NJ/x	PBKN 234	----
27 Aug 1805	William Nichols	George & Mary(Beard) Ga/Md	HSTC 341	----
00 000 0000	George Parker		HMAC 271	1848
00 000 0000	Mary Peebles[Kuster]		CJRI 758	----
00 000 0000	William Peebles		HMAC 273	1839
14 Nov 1836	Rachel Quinn[McMaster]	Thomas & Nancy(Kennedy) Va/**	BCSB 230	1837
17 Mar 1829	William J. Reed	John & Julia(Merrifield) Ma/x	HMCH 456	----
20 Nov 1809	Eliza Rice[McMurtry]		PBKN 234	----
19 Aug 1821	H.H. Riley	Ky/Ky	KNOX 702	----
00 000 0000	A. Ritty[Roberts]		HMAC 272	1864
00 000 0000	William R, Roberts		HMAC 272	1864
23 Jul 1823	Miles Rogers		HEDG 713	----

BIRTHDATE	NAME OF BIOGRAPHEE	PARENTS	BIRTHPLACE	SOURCE	PAGE	DATE
13 Dec 1839	William W. Sardidge	Joshua & Mary		HMCD	1155	----
00 000 0000	William Shaw			HMCH	564	----
08 Jun 1797	Benjamin Shep_ar		Va/x	HMOR	596	1828
00 000 0000	Catherine Smoot[Snain]			HMCH	564	----
03 Feb 1825	Arxina Southgate[Stice]			PPWA	271	1829
23 May 1814	James R. Spencer	Elisha & Nancy(Hupp)		HGJR	979	----
05 Sep 1846	George W. Standiford	Archibald B & Eliz J(Courtright)		BRCM	444	1836
00 Dec 1814	Irverson L. Twyman			HMCD	308	----
28 Aug 1828	Horace Van Me_er	William & Elizabeth(Goodin)	Pa/**00	PERJ	747	1839
16 Mar 1830	John B. Varble	Philip & Edna(Spellman)	Ky/Ky	PBWO	381	----
10 Sep 1827	Elizabeth Veech[Kermicle]	John & Mary(Kinkade)	Ky/Ky	BRCM	441	1852
06 May 1821	Daniel H. Vertrees	John & Nancy(Haycraft)	**/**	HMOR	600	----
22 Jan 1824	Mary A Vertrees[Furbey]	John & Nancy	Pa/Pa	HMOR	595	1829
08 Oct 1826	George W. Waggoner	Adam & Mary A(Terry)	Ky/Ky	PEMO	B268	----
00 000 0000	Jackson Walker	John	NC/x	PHCC	102	----
19 Dec 1856	Hardin B. Wal_ers	Jacob W & Lydia(Funk)	Ly1817/Ky1823	BLOG	433	1875
03 Jun 1789	Edward Williams			HSAN	913	1826
00 000 1819	R.J. Wiseheart	John & Elizabeth(Miller)	Ky/Ky	HGSH	587	----
25 Feb 1847	William N. Wood	N.H & Elizabeth(Lyon)	Ky/Ky	PBSM	273	1852
12 Jan 1816	Singleton G. Wright			BCSB	491	----

H A R L A N   C O U N T Y

BIRTHDATE	NAME OF BIOGRAPHEE	PARENTS/BIRTHPLACE/BIRTHDATE		SOURCE/PAGE	DATE
00 000 1805	George W. Lowder	William & Margaret(Harris)		HSAN 1033	----

H A R R I S O N   C O U N T Y

BIRTHDATE	NAME OF BIOGRAPHEE	PARENTS/BIRTHPLACE/BIRTHDATE		SOURCE/PAGE	DATE
13 Sep 1818	Peter Adams	Angelo & Elizabeth(Killen)	Md/Md	PBDP 258	----

BIRTHDATE	NAME OF BIOGRAPHEE	PARENTS/BIRTHPLACE/BIRTHDATE	SOURCE/PAGE	DATE
00 000 0000	Samuel Adams	William	PPVE 842	1825
24 Jun 1825	Alfred Allison	Otha	PPVE 1145	----
00 000 0000	E.J[Bell]		HCHA 179	1855
00 000 0000	J.W. Bell		HCHA 179	1855
00 000 0000	M.F. Bell[Michaels]	John	LOGA 839	----
00 000 0000	Nancy J. Bell[Parker]	John & Fanny(Minton) Va/Va	PBDP 433	----
08 Jun 1797	Col.Joseph M. Blackburn	William & Elizabeth(McClanahan)	HEDG 648	----
12 Oct 1805	John Boyd	Arthur George	PBCO 230	1817
00 000 0000	Elizabeth Bridges[Brownell]		HSAN 760	----
00 000 0000	Robert Brownfield		HCHA 179	1832
00 000 0000	A.J. Burns		HCHA 180	1871
30 Mar 1807	John M. Campbell	James & Jane(Campbell) Scott/Scott	BCSB 313	----
00 000 0000	Hannah Chambers[Monroe]	James & Sally	COLE 527	1851
20 Mar 1838	Mary E. Chambers	James **/x	PBCO 333	----
00 000 0000	Sarah Campbell[Gosnell]	John & Nancy(Townsend)	CJRI 495	----
22 Jan 1816	Thomas G. Chambers	James & Sallie(Rankin)	PBCO 243	----
22 Jan 1816	Thomas G. Chambers	James & Sally	COLE 517	1838
11 Apr 1814	Dr. William M. Chambers	James & Sallie(Rankin) Pa/Ky	PBCO 294	----
05 Sep 1821	William Chandler	John & Polly(Jones)	PVED 746	1828
01 Jan 1812	Nelson W. Corrington	Stephen & Rachel B(Veach) NJ1769/Ky65	HGJR 886	----
00 000 0000	S.A. Craig[Hersman]		CSBR 386	1834
04 Sep 1838	Amanda[Compton]		PBCO 310	----
00 000 0000	D.W. Cummings		HCHA 183	1870
25 Dec 1805	John Cummins		PVED 787	----
25 Dec 1807	John Cummins	Joseph & Lydia Pa/x	HEDG 698	----
00 000 0000	Robert Cummins		CJRI 533	----
27 Feb 1828	Joseph Cunningham	William & Mary(Humes) Pa1778/Pa	PPVE 41	----
24 Aug 1812	M.M. Dill		HEDG 570	1833
00 000 0000	S.K. Dunn		HCHA 179	----
10 Dec 1821	S.W. Dunn	Elijah & Sarah(Foster) Va/Ky	HSAN 893	----
23 Nov 1794	Irvine Foster		HSAN 893	----
08 Dec 1821	Mary J. Foster[Dunn]	Evans & Margaret(McKee)	HSAN 893	1829

Date	Name	Parents	Birthplace	Ref	No.	Year
07 Aug 1807	James B. Frazier			HADM	803	1827
11 Sep 1818	Lafayette H. Frazer George			GHHA	566	1827
18 Feb 1811	Lemuel G. Frazer			HADM	803	1827
00 000 0000	G.W. Fry			CSBR	386	1836
00 000 1827	George K. Gosnell			CJRI	495	----
16 Oct 1822	Martha A. Gruelle[Threlkeld]			COLE	655	1834
08 Feb 1817	J.T. Hagerty			HMGD	1140	1830
08 Feb 1817	John T. Hagerty			CMGD	597	1830
16 Jun 1797	John C. Hamilton			HMOR	697	----
00 000 0000	Elizabeth Harrison[Stipp]			BRBM	180	----
00 000 1811	John T. Hendricks	John & Cynthia(Wilson)	**/**	PBCO	280	----
29 Aug 1816	George Hersham	Henry & Elizabeth(Fry)	Va/Ky	CSBR	265	1834
00 000 0000	America Hersman[Means]			CSBR	387	1850
14 May 1829	George Hersman			CSBR	386	1834
01 Oct 1818	George D. Huffman	Daniel P & Elizabeth(Switzer)	Va/Md	PVED	754	----
10 Feb 1811	Frederick A. Jackson William		Ky/x	PBWA	198	----
00 000 0000	Isaac N. Jacquess	Isaac & Elizabeth(Johnson)	NJ1786/x	CELW	253	----
00 000 0000	Adam James			PBAD	565	1831
00 000 0000	Gerhard Jansen			CELW	354	1836
24 Feb 1796	David Jennings			CSBR	385	1828
12 Aug 1808	William Jones			PVED	210	----
14 Aug 1808	William D. Jones	John D & Sarah(Blackburn)		PBCO	352	----
27 Jan 1810	William R. Jones			COLE	654	1834
00 000 1812	Elizabeth Leonard_Young]			PVBD	555	----
00 000 0000	Joseph Lilly			PBSM	541	----
28 Sep 1854	Julia A[Longstore]			HHBN	296	----
20 Mar 1839	Dr. B.T. McClain	George & Sarah	Ky/Ky	PPPI	144	----
00 000 1806	William E. McCrory	James		COLE	525	----
01 Apr 1818	Lewis McFarland			HADM	765	----
24 Jan 1796	Robert N. McFerland William		**/x	BCSM	324	----
31 Jul 1858	Margaret McKee[Foster]			HSAN	893	----
00 000 0000	Dr. William T. McLean	Chambers A & Lucy A(Taylor)	Ky/Ky	PBWC	407	----
02 Apr 1825	Eliza Makenson [Campbell]			PPVE	602	----
00 000 0000	Hiram Makenson	Andrew & Hannah	Ky/Ky	PVED	718	1828
00 000 0000	Christiana W. Martin[Phillips]	Edward W & Sarah A(Phillips)	Ky/Oh	PBWL	579	1828
00 000 0000	Nancy Martin[Adams]			PPVE	842	----

BIRTHDATE	NAME OF BIOGRAPHEE	PARENTS/BIRTHPLACE/BIRTHDATE	SOURCE/PAGE	DATE
25 Aug 1810	Rebecca Maze[Boyd]		PBCO	230	----
00 000 0000	Sarah M. Morrow[LeQuatte]		PBRI	340	----
01 Apr 1812	Emelia Nesbitt[Fraizer]		HADM	803	----
00 000 0000	Rebecca Newell[LeNeve] William		PPVE	556	----
02 Jul 1823	WilliamC. Parker George M & Ann(Jones) Va/Ky	PBDP	433	----
00 000 0000	C. Ann R. Porter[Chambers]		COLE	516	----
00 000 0000	Edith Price[Cummins]		CJRI	533	----
30 Nov 1806	Amberry A. Rankin		HMEM	725	1828
15 Sep 1816	William L. Rankin James & Anna(Dills)	HMEM	725	1833
08 Jun 1833	Sophronia A. Rankin[Walker] James S & Sarah(Laughlin) Ky/Ky	GHHA	780	----
00 000 1800	Mary Richards[James]		PBAD	565	----
00 000 0000	Zachariah Robertson		PVED	599	----
18 Aug 1814	Dancy P. Seckman James & Katie(Bishop) Md/Md	BCSB	264	1832
07 Aug 0000	Harvey Shawhan David		PSTC	146	----
07 Aug 1828	Dr. John W. Slade Lemuel W & Ann x/Clark	PBAD	247	----
00 000 0000	Martha E. Smith[Dora]		COLE	544	----
12 Dec 1815	Henry Summers		HADM	785	----
12 May 1818	Richard Summers		HADM	733	1835
31 Jan 1808	Lilburn Swinford SC/Va	COLE	645	----
04 Oct 1825	S.C. Swinford		COLE	577	----
07 Feb 1816	Matthew P. Threlkeld		COLE	655	1830
04 Sep 1838	Amanda[Turney]		PBCO	310	----
02 Jun 1819	Benjamin D. Turney John & Sarah(Jones)	PBCO	309	----
18 Jun 1834	John B. Turney John & Sarah(Jones) Bourbon1795/**1800	PBCO	344	----
18 Jan 1829	Sophia O. Van Doren Joseph	COLE	527	1835
03 Mar 1840	Elizabeth Vaughn[Brownell]		HSAN	760	----
00 000 1824	Saphrona Washburn[Trimble]		HADM	798	----
28 Sep 1830	John S. Webber		HCHA	142	----
00 000 0000	John S. Webber		HCHA	181	1864
00 000 0000	M.A[Wheat]		CSBR	387	1836
00 000 0000	Amelia B. Whittaker[Moore]		PBDP	581	----
14 Aug 1836	Thomas C. Williams James C & Mary(Lindsey) Ky/Ky	HENR	B179	----
08 Sep 1824	Christian Zumalt		BHIQ	B191	1828

BIRTHDATE	NAME OF BIOGRAPHEE	PARENTS/BIRTHPLACE/BIRTHDATE	SOURCE/PAGE	DATE
00 000 0000	Sinai F. Aldeson[Blunt]		HMEM	843	----
08 Oct 1824	John B. Ames	Erasmus & Mary	HMGD	996	----
00 000 0000	J.B. Amos		MACL	302	1832
26 Jul 1839	Hon. William H. Barlow		PHEF	B4	1851
00 000 0000	Mary E[Barrick]		HMAC	274	1857
15 Dec 1846	Charles W. Bishop		COLE	649	1869
21 Feb 1831	Aaron A. Blunt		HMEM	843	1833
09 Nov 1821	Presley T. Brooks	Miles & Lucy(Pullian) Va1781/Va1784	PBML	380	----
09 Nov 1821	Presley T. Brooks		HMCL	1009	----
00 000 0000	Sarepta Brooks[Darnall]	Miles & Lucy	PBML	720	----
00 Apr 1843	James T. Brown	Patrick H & Louisa(Enlow) Va/Ky	LOGA	665	1856
00 000 0000	Martha A. Brown[Edgar]	Armsted & Sarah(Ferguson)Ky08/Ky03	PHKX	B109	----
31 Jul 1834	Abram Cotterell		CJRI	824	----
24 Jan 1812	Jefferson M. Dawdy	James & Margaret(Morse) SC76/SC75	PBKN	201	----
11 Oct 1825	Thomas D. DeHart	William & Jane(Houston)	CSBR	349	1830
00 000 0000	Thomas D. DeHart		CSBR	391	1833
10 Jan 1826	W.E. Durham		VTBU	349	1834
19 Nov 1827	Lowry J. Edgar	James & Sarah(Trowbridge) NC81/NJ87	PHKX	B198	----
00 000 0000	Lowry J. Edgar	James & Sarah(Trowbridge) NC81/NJ87	PBKN	712	----
00 000 0000	Mary A. Ferguson[Brown]		KNOX	658	----
00 000 0000	Martha Furgason[Goff]		KNOX	677	----
00 000 0000	James Goff		KNOX	677	----
05 Apr 1844	William H. Jackson	Andrew J & Fanny G(Crane) Ky/Ky	BEFF	791	----
21 Jul 1820	Moses A. Jones	Alexander & Susan(Woosley) Ky/Ky	HSAN	769	1821
00 000 0000	Mary Kelly[Taylor]		HSAN	1045	----
00 000 1831	Mary E. Johnsey[Logsdon] George B & Jane(Simms)		PBMO	B197	----
27 Mar 1825	John Kesinger	Lynn & Betsy(Peebles) x/SC	HMAC	138	----
00 000 0000	John Kesinger		HMAC	274	1846
00 000 1853	John W. Logsdon	Robert & Mary E(Johnson) **/**	PBMO	B197	----
00 000 1828	Robert Logsdon	William K & Maria(Remus) **/NCO8	PBMO	B197	----
00 000 0000	Marsham Lucas		PBWA	217	----
00 000 0000	Sarah McDowell[Kermicle]		CJRI	829	----

BIRTHDATE	NAME OF BIOGRAPHEE		PARENTS/BIRTHPLACE/BIRTHDATE	SOURCE/PAGE	DATE
30 Jul 1816	Oliver H.P. Maxey	Philip		MACL 227	1831
00 000 0000	Lydia A. Montgomery[Watkins]			BCSB 224	---
00 000 0000	Emeline Peebles[Adams]			HMAC 270	1837
23 Jan 1833	Lewis M. Peebles		Bird & Nancy(Brooks) NC/Larue	PBWA 427	---
16 May 1849	Dr. Z.T. Smith			HCAS 271	---
09 Feb 1807	Isaac Taylor			HSAN 1045	1828
00 000 0000	Cynthia A Whitman[Lucas]			PBWA 217	---
05 Jan 1844	Joseph S. Wiltberger		Joseph & Amelia(Finley) Pa/x	GPPD B578	---
08 Dec 1835	W.H. Wiltberger		Joseph W & Amelia(Finley) Pa94/Ky05	PEDK 417	1846
00 000 0000	Preston Wright			HMAC 274	1840
00 000 0000	Susan[Wright]			HMAC 274	1840

H E N D E R S O N   C O U N T Y

BIRTHDATE	NAME OF BIOGRAPHEE	PARENTS/BIRTHPLACE/BIRTHDATE	Tn/Tn	SOURCE/PAGE	DATE
27 Oct 1825	William W. Anderson	George H & Nancy(Mann)		BGHR 835	---
27 Oct 1825	William W. Anderson	George H.		PCHR 199	---
00 000 0000	W.W. Anderson			HCHR 260	1851
15 Sep 1825	Samuel H. Book	Henry & Sarah(Miller)	Va/x	HWCL B86	---
00 000 1830	John Boyle	John & Sarah(Green)	Ire/Va	TAZE 654	1837
14 Feb 1807	James Camron	Thomas	Ire/x	HFUL 513	---
00 000 1836	Dr. S.L. Chearny	Henry M & Martha(Hazelwood)	Va02/Vall	HGSH 604	---
01 May 1826	James H.L. Crumbaugh	Henry & Sarah(Baldock)	Md89/Ky	PBML 387	---
01 May 1826	James H.L. Crumbaugh	Henry & Sarah(Baldock)	Md89/x	HMCL 878	1828
01 May 1826	James H.L. Crumbaugh	Henry & Sarah(Baldock)	Md1789/Scott02	BRML 337	---
01 Mar 1826	James H.L. Crumbaugh	Henry & Sarah(Baldock)	Md/Ky	BNCL 990	---
01 Mar 1826	James H.L. Crumbaugh	Henry & Sarah(Baldock)	Md1789/Scott02	BNCL 991	---
00 000 0000	Martha A. Grant[Jarrett]	Joel		CJRI 556	---
00 000 1862	Prof.James J. Hassett	James & Frances(Church)	Irel812/**35	HGSH 706	---
00 000 0000	Julia A. Hudson[Hensley]			MACL 295	---
27 Jan 1818	Henry L. Legate			HGJR 408	---
00 000 0000	W.H. Lynn			CELW 354	1879
14 Jul 1815	Young E. McClendon	John & Sarah(Pratt)		PBRI 533	---
26 Aug 1829	Abner R. Moore	Haywood & Nancy(Russell)	1805/**05	HGSH 729	---

BIRTHDATE	NAME OF BIOGRAPHEE	PARENTS/BIRTHPLACE/BIRTHDATE		SOURCE/PAGE		DATE
23 Jan 1818	William H. Newton			PBML	551	----
00 000 0000	John North			MACL	299	1866
22 Feb 1814	Alexander Perkins			COLE	530	----
00 000 0000	A.M. Powell			HMAD	581	1863
17 Jul 1817	William D. Price	William D	Va/x	BCSB	240	1833
31 Aug 1810	Willis Pruitt			PPWA	292	1848
31 Aug 1810	Willis Pruitt	Doakes & Milly(Hanks)	NC/NC	PBWA	201	----
01 Feb 1809	N.A. Rankin			PPWA	220	1834
01 Feb 1809	Nathaniel A. Rankin	Dr. Adam & ---(Speed)	Pa/x	PBWA	215	----
00 000 0000	J.M. Rutledge			AMEN	23	1839
09 Oct 1832	Ann M. Talbot[Farrar]			COLE	635	----

H E N R Y   C O U N T Y

BIRTHDATE	NAME OF BIOGRAPHEE	PARENTS/BIRTHPLACE/BIRTHDATE		SOURCE/PAGE		DATE
00 000 0000	Austin Adams	Horatio		PBWA	674	----
00 000 0000	J. Adams			HMAC	270	1830
22 Nov 1823	Jefferson Adams	Horatio & Sytha	**/x	HMAC	261	----
00 000 0000	Aaron M. Aten			CJRI	527	----
00 000 0000	Samuel T. Bartlett			PBMO	B95	1835
00 000 0000	Samuel T. Bartlett	Samuel & Elizabeth(Owens)	Va/Va	PBMO	B282	----
10 Sep 1833	Isaac Callender			PHKX	B217	----
00 000 0000	Sarah J. Carr[Rawlings]			CELW	350	1865
00 000 0000	A.J[Churchill]			HCHA	181	1863
00 000 0000	Lucinda Churchill[Crim]	George		HGSH	773	----
00 000 0000	William T. Conner			HDEW	345	1836
05 Jan 1807	Jonathan & Eleanor(English)		Md/x	HGJR	472	----
00 000 0000	Margaret Demott[Aten]			CJRI	527	----
00 000 0000	Lewis Dillman			ACLY	50	1852
00 000 0000	S. Dillman			ACLY	50	1834

Date	Name	Parents / Origin	Code	No.	Year
00 000 1836	T.O. Eddy		HADM	619	----
00 000 1805	Elizabeth Elston[Sims]		LOGA	735	1825
00 000 0000	Martha Elston[Bunting]		CELW	346	1840
00 000 0000	James H. Gillespie		HWCL	B194	----
26 Sep 1817	Edward Gregory	Peter	Va/x	PBSM	600	1803
00 Jul 1832	James W. Heaton	John & Sarah(Malin)	Pa/**	BRJM	442	----
00 000 1854	John C.B.Heaton	James W.		BRJM	417	----
08 Nov 1814	Dr. A.M. Henry	Joseph & Mary(White)	Pa/Va	PBCO	562	----
00 000 0000	Emily H. Hill		HDEW	344	1836
20 Apr 1834	Rodney P. Hill		PBDP	678	----
00 000 1840	James H. Jenkins		HEDG	670	1856
00 000 0000	Eliza[Kesinger]		HMAC	274	1832
00 000 0000	Rebecca A. Knox[Harsman]		CSBR	386	1838
00 000 0000	Elijah A. Lawson		CELW	350	1827
00 000 0000	Mary Lemaster[Hatfield]		CSBR	378	1826
00 000 0000	Sarah Malin[Heaton] Rev.		BRJM	442	----
16 Mar 1833	Eliza J. Manfort[Farris]	David & Mary J.	Ky1824/Ky	COLE	586	----
07 Nov 1847	Dr. Charles W. Martinie	David & Mary	Ky/Ky	CHAM	980	----
07 Nov 1847	Charles W. Martinie	David & Mary		PVED	797	----
04 Apr 1815	Andrew J. Mead	William & Mary(Scott)		BCSB	200	1840
00 000 0000	Richard H. Mead		CSBR	382	1840
00 000 0000	Mary Mitchell[Howk]		CSBR	384	1851
11 May 1812	I.J. Monfort		PBCO	363	1836
02 Sep 1811	George S. Moore		PPWA	240	1835
01 Sep 1836	Dr. Lewis Perry	William A & Caroline B.	Ky/Oh	LOGA	333	----
30 Aug 1808	John Reed	John O & Margaret(Eweng)	Pa/Va	PHCC	205	----
15 Sep 1822	R.S.D. Roberts		PBMO	B86	----
15 Sep 1822	R.S.D. Roberts	Nelson/x	PBMB	328	----
15 Sep 1822	Richard S.D. Roberts	---- & Sarah(Simmons)Nelson80/Henry	PBMB	328	----
00 000 1836	J.L. Scott		COLE	555	----
03 Jul 1832	John R. Shaw	Stephen & Milcah(Nutall) Va1810/Vac12	PHCC	370	1846
00 000 0000	Sarah Simmons[Roberts]		PBMB	331	----
00 000 0000	R.N. Smith		ACLY	50	1838
00 000 0000	James P. Stark		HCHR	262	1870
26 Jun 1824	James E. Suddeth	Henry & Pamelia		HGJR	406	----
05 Mar 1852	Dr. W.L. Suggett	Dr. James M & Caroline M.		HWCL	B208	----
22 Oct 1812	T.J. Taylor		PPWA	306	1835

00 000 1832	Peter Troutman	Michael	Scotland/x	PEMC	722	1848
28 Dec 1818	Samuel Truitt			PEMB	385	----
22 Oct 1816	Elisha Varble	Philip & Sarah(Barrett)		HGJR	870	----
07 Feb 1809	Nancy Wigginton[Whitaker]			LOGA	545	1827
05 Sep 1847	Madison Willan		Eng/Ky	HMCL	956	----

H I C K M A N   C O U N T Y

BIRTHDATE	NAME OF BIOGRAPHEE	PARENTS/BIRTHPLACE/BIRTHDATE		SOURCE/PAGE	DATE
00 000 0000	Edwin R. Houchin	Alexander	Ky/x	BRJM 468	----

H O P K I N S   C O U N T Y

BIRTHDATE	NAME OF BIOGRAPHEE	PARENTS/BIRTHPLACE/BIRTHDATE		SOURCE/PAGE	DATE
15 Jun 1808	Margaret Cannaday[Pray]	John		BRML	310	----
00 000 1821	Ira B. Carey	John & Frances(Stokes) Ky1791/Ky1799		HGSH	684	----
00 000 0000	John Clark			AWOO	3	1836
00 000 0000	R.E. Dance			ACLY	49	1859
00 000 1823	Bailum Ezell			HGSH	616	1859
07 Aug 1810	John Fike	Abel & Rachel(Crownover) Va1777/NJ1785		HSTC	277	----
00 000 0000	Lucinda Gatlen[Roberts]			BRJM	581	1845
13 Jun 1834	Ambrose G. Gaunt	Thomas & Maria(Mott)	Va/Va	PAUP	B305	----
23 May 1827	Joseph W. Gaunt	Thomas & Maria(Mott)	Va/Va	PAUP	B304	----
00 000 1838	James Gore	James & Regina(Tevler) Va1788/SC1798		HGSH	621	----
15 Aug 1825	Wiley Gray	Russell & Martha(Phelps)	**/**	PBRJ	252	1827
00 000 0000	Elizabeth Henderson[Hayes]			HDEW	344	1859
04 Mar 1819	Joseph Henry	Joseph & Lucy(Shumacke)	Ire/Va	PBCW	456	----
13 Jun 1814	Emilla Hensley[Black]			PBMB	316	----

BIRTHDATE	NAME OF BIOGRAPHEE	PARENTS/BIRTHPLACE/BIRTHDATE	SOURCE/PAGE	DATE
00 000 1817	Andrew Herrin	David	HGSH 898	1819
00 000 0000	John W. Killough		CELW 349	1866
00 000 0000	Thomas J. Killough		CELW 345	1862
00 000 0000	William Killough		CELW 349	----
00 000 1827	Nancy E. Littlepage		HGSH 616	----
15 Mar 1831	Franklin McLain	Samuel & Lurania(Warson) SC/x	HGSH 562	1835
00 000 0000	J.L. Metcalf		HMAC 276	1835
00 000 0000	R.J. Metcalf		HMAC 276	----
01 Aug 1817	Richard J. Metcalf	William & Elizabeth(Jones) NC1774/Va80	HMAC 159	----
31 Mar 1820	James L. Metcalf	William & Elizabeth(Jones) NC1774/Va80	HMAC 160	----
10 Nov 1828	Thomas M. Metcalf	William & Huldah A(Davis) Ky/Ky	HMAC 106	----
10 Nov 1828	Rev.Thomas M. Metcalf William	Christian09/x	PBMA 845	----
26 Jul 1819	John H. Smith John	Va/Va	HMCD 651	1829
00 000 0000	Corilla Thomas[Adkisson]		HDEW 341	1857
05 Dec 1837	William B. Todd	John & Angelina(Brown) Tn/Tn	BRJM 268	----
00 000 0000	Elizabeth A. Vawter[Fruit]		HMAD 584	1854
00 000 0000	Robert B. Willis		CELW 346	1837
13 Oct 1813	W.R. Willis		PPWO 531	1834

J A C K S O N   C O U N T Y

BIRTHDATE	NAME OF BIOGRAPHEE	PARENTS/BIRTHPLACE/BIRTHDATE	SOURCE/PAGE	DATE
00 000 0000	Lizzie Harris[Scott]		CSBR 384	1857
00 000 0000	O.H. Rose		MACL 293	1881

J E F F E R S O N   C O U N T Y

BIRTHDATE	NAME OF BIOGRAPHEE	PARENTS/BIRTHPLACE/BIRTHDATE	SOURCE/PAGE	DATE
00 000 0000	A.J. Allen		HCHA 176	1854
15 Jan 1842	Dr. George W. Allen	Stephen & Elizabeth(Jackson)	HCHA 123	----
00 000 0000	Col. C.P.J. Astor		BHDP B46	----

BIRTHDATE	NAME OF BIOGRAPHEE	PARENTS/BIRTHPLACE/BIRTHDATE	SOURCE/PAGE	DATE
21 Nov 1839	J.W. Atherburn		HEDG 611	----
28 Feb 1804	John Atherburn		HEDG 610	----
05 Dec 1829	John Atherburn	John & Huldah	HEDG 610	----
15 Mar 1828	F.R. Augustus		HEDG 556	1831
13 Nov 1822	John D. Augustus		HEDG 638	1847
15 Jul 1830	S.O. Augustus		HEDG 554	1831
00 000 1835	Ed Baldwin		PPDM 236	----
00 000 0000	Frances A. Barnes[Roby]		CELW 350	1858
07 Jun 1848	Dr. Christopher Bates	William C & Eliza J. Ky/Va	PVED 852	----
00 000 0000	W.T. Bean		HDEW 342	1861
00 000 0000	Hannah Biggane		HMAD 562	1852
00 000 0000	Kate Birmingham[Churchill]		CELW 345	1857
00 000 0000	W. Read Blair		HMAC 273	1866
00 0c 1824	Elizabeth Boulton[Redmond]		PPVE 899	----
14 Feb 1832	Allen Briscoe	Henry & Catherine(Brooks) Va/Va	PHCC 9	----
27 Jan 1825	Dr. William T. Briscoe		BCLA 706	1835
00 000 0000	John Brookie		BRBM 349	----
00 000 0000	Rebecca K. Brown[Hitt]		HJOD 772	----
00 Jan 1832	Hon. William R. Brown	William Md/x	BRJM 560	1870
00 000 0000	Mary Burgess[Taylor]		CELW 348	1832
15 Jul 1826	James H. Butler	Hezekiah & Margaret(Payne) Md/Va	HMCH 478	1832
16 Apr 1842	W.F. Butler		PPRI 271	1866
21 Aug 1832	George D. Carpenter	Daniel & Esther(Dunlap)	HMCH 506	1848
00 000 0000	L. Carpenter		HGHA 176	1863
22 Jul 1825	John S. Cornwell	Va/Ky	HEDG 616	1851
19 Sep 1807	Edward Craig		HMOR 660	1829
24 Jul 1824	Capt. B.S. Crane	William & Hannah(Johnson) Va/Va	PAUP B246	----
08 May 1825	Benjamin A. Curry	Thomas & Malinda(Murphy) 1802/x	PBAD 548	----
09 Nov 1836	Christopher S. Curry	Thomas & Malinda(Murphy) Ky/Ky	HADM 738	----
00 000 0000	James J. Dickey		AHEN 18	----
00 000 0000	P.H. Dorsey		HMAC 270	----
08 Nov 1833	Plutarch H. Dorsey	Elias & Martha(Booker) Md1796/x	BRMA 225	----

Date	Name	Parents	Notes	Code	No.	Year
11 Oct 1823	W. Montjoy Dorsey	Elias	Md/x	PBMA	801	---
08 Oct 1823	William M. Dorsey	Elias		BRMA	297	---
00 000 1814	Thomas Dunn			PBDP	785	---
03 Oct 1826	Charles A. Easum	William & Catherine(Tyler)	Md/**	HADM	759	1836
00 000 0000	W.S. Eaton			ACLY	49	1854
00 000 0000	Dr. W.W. Elliott			MACL	305	1876
00 000 0000	Amelia Emig[Gaffner]			MACL	299	1860
00 000 0000	Adam Emig			MACL	299	1860
08 Jun 1856	Adam Emig	Peter & Catharina		MACL	215	1860
00 000 0000	Elizabeth Emig[Leonard]			MACL	300	1863
00 000 1819	Elizabeth Evinger[Wilholt]			PHCC	159	---
00 000 0000	James Faith			HMAC	275	1871
01 Jan 1855	William Ferguson			BMCH	235	1876
30 Nov 1790	Daniel Field			EFAY	607	1818
22 Sep 1841	P.C. Glasman	Peter & Mary(Bean)	Ger/Ger	HWCL	B131	1847
00 000 0000	Martha Green[Montgomery]			HMAD	579	1847
09 Jun 1803	Joseph Hanley	Samuel & Mary(Ripple)	Ire/x	PBCO	448	---
03 May 1827	Dr. Martin H. Head	Benjamin & Margaret N(Brengman)Va81/05		BRMA	214	---
00 000 0000	Dr. M.H. Head			HMAC	267	1851
00 000 0000	William Hessey			PPVE	853	---
00 000 0000	George Hett	Joseph & Susanna(Lehen)	Ger/Ger	BROG	229	---
13 Jun 1849	Alfred M. Hewlett			HENR	B258	---
00 000 0000	Mary Hill[Perry]			HSAN	808	---
09 Jan 1827	Alexander Hitch			COLE	647	1828
13 Apr 1809	Charles L. Hollingsworth	Joseph & Margaret(Beeler)Va71/Va		PHCC	207	---
20 Jan 1810	Albert Hughes			HADM	804	1836
28 Feb 1837	Samuel Jacobs			HADM	828	1849
24 Dec 1827	James G. Johnson	George & Eleanor(Guthrie)	**/**	BHAN	326	---
24 Dec 1827	James G. Johnson	George & Eleanor(Guthrie)		HMCH	127	---
19 Mar 1820	Catherine Jones[Birch]	William		COLE	514	1831
20 Nov 1817	John Kelley	John & Elizabeth(Miller)		BCLA	777	1811
00 000 0000	June R. Kinder[Holliday]			HMAD	557	---
00 000 0000	Rosy Kinkead			HDEW	345	---
00 000 0000	Kate Krauskopf[Zimmerman]			MACL	300	1869
00 000 0000	William H. Kron			HMAD	556	1850
00 000 0000	Marie C. Krome[Lange]			HMAD	582	1850
00 Jul 1842	Hon. William H. Krone			HMAD	194	---

JEFFERSON COUNTY (CONT.)

BIRTHDATE	NAME OF BIOGRAPHEE	PARENTS/BIRTHPLACE/BIRTHDATE		SOURCE/PAGE	DATE
00 000 1858	Paul S. Leitz	Theodore L & Matilda(Scheidemantle)Ger/		PEPE 499	----
00 000 0000	S.W. Leonard			MACL 294	1857
00 000 0000	Paul S. Lietz	Thomas L & Matilda(Scheidemantle)Ger/x		PEPE 809	----
00 000 0000	William D. Linton			MACL 297	1866
00 000 0000	John M. Little			HSTC 377	----
10 May 1802	D. Lively			HPIK 864	----
26 Jan 1837	George M. Luken	Samuel S & Mary B(Bills)	Pa/Tn	BROC 211	----
10 Dec 1855	S. Rupert Leicester	Elon W & Lucy B(Sargent)	Va/Ma	PBML 1087	----
10 Jul 1844	Dr. W.S. McBurnie	Prof. James V.		HSAN 648	----
26 Oct 1833	N.L. McCauley	Daniel & Mary A(Jeffrey)	**/x	CURI 809	----
00 000 1829	Samuel McClure	William & Nancy(Wheeler)	Fayette/x	PPPI 350	----
29 Mar 1825	David Martin	Wesley B & Lydia(Snyder)	Va1792/x	PBCO 488	1847
20 Nov 1827	George H. Mason	George & Elizabeth		LOGA 586	1835
22 May 1819	Elizabeth Miller[Keller]			BCIA 778	----
13 Jul 1816	William F. Musgrove			CURI 826	----
10 May 1818	Abram K. Netherton	Abram & Amy(Ashbaugh)	Va/x	HMAC 200	----
02 Feb 1832	Welch Newman	John & Charity		GHHA 875	----
05 Sep 1828	Daniel Omer	Jacob & Priscilla(Curry)		HADM 767	----
00 000 0000	Nimrod Ott		Ger/Ger	PPME 284	----
00 000 0000	J.D. Perine			HFAY 96	----
00 000 0000	Nancy[Perine]			HFAY 96	----
00 000 0000	Horatio Perry			HSAN 808	----
00 000 0000	Eliza Peter[Metcalf]			HMAC 276	1848
00 000 0000	John Poulter			PBCO 346	1830
00 000 0000	Sallie Rice[Stevens]		Ky/x	PEPE 219	----
23 Jul 1824	Miles Rogers	Elias & Parmilia(Holden)	Vt/NY	PVED 897	----
04 Jul 1830	James A. Roseberry			BHAN 634	----
01 May 1827	J.O. Rudy			COLE 554	1830
00 000 1822	P.O. Rudy			HEDG 596	----
08 Jul 1824	W.H. Rudy			HEDG 682	1830
00 000 0000	Edward Samoniel			CELW 354	1857
00 000 0000	Edward Samoniel			CELW 257	1857
00 000 0000	Samuel Samoniel			CELW 257	1857
00 000 0000	William Samoniel			CELW 354	1859

BIRTHDATE	NAME OF BIOGRAPHEE	PARENTS	BIRTHPLACE/BIRTHDATE	SOURCE	PAGE	DATE
13 Sep 1840	James R. Scott			PHEF	B172	---
00 000 0000	William Shafer	Joseph F & Elizabeth(Evinger)	Ger/Ky	PBCO	505	---
18 Jan 1796	Ninevah Shaw	Joseph	1773/x	PHCC	46	---
00 000 0000	Trimble Shaw	Jesse	Ky/x	PVED	707	---
00 000 0000	Martha S[Simrson]			HGHR	264	1861
31 May 1821	Alexander M. Smith	George & Isabel(Carmichael)	Ky/Pa	HADM	927	1832
09 Aug 1828	Silas G. Slaughter	John W & Elizabeth	Pa/Pa	HMOR	597	---
00 000 0000	James Snider			MACL	294	1842
00 000 0000	Margaret Spargle=[Crum]			BCSB	436	---
19 Mar 1844	William M. Stivers	Felix & Edna(Frederick)	**/**	PCHR	305	---
00 000 0000	H.C. Stevenson			ACLY	50	1854
00 000 0000	G.J. Stramer			HMAD	556	1879
00 000 0000	Mary Tierney[Hunt]			PBMC	397	---
04 Jan 1859	J.R. Troendle	Joseph F & Louise(Smith)	Fr/Fr	CBKA	791	---
04 Mar 1827	Murray F. Tuley			EFAY	529	---
00 000 0000	Prof.Martin T.Van Cleve			BRJM	175	---
00 000 0000	George Waggerer	James	Va/Va	GHHA	858	---
27 Jun 1828	Benjamin F. Whips			HADM	810	1842
00 000 0000	Emeline Whips[Fisher]			HADM	625	---
00 000 0000	Mary A. Wallace[Hutcheson]			HADM	851	---
16 Apr 1817	George C. Waggener	James & Elizabeth(O'Neil)	Va/x	HMCH	392	---
25 Jun 1811	James G. Welsh	Robert & Mary(Guthrie)	Pa/Ky	HADM	771	1835
08 Jan 1820	Moses Welsh	Robert & Mary(Guthrie)	Pa/Ky	HADM	771	---
16 Feb 1810	Neely Withrow	William		PBHE	544	1828
00 000 0000	Louisa J[Wright]			HMAC	274	1867
00 000 0000	Belle[Yancey]			HMAC	270	1867
00 000 0000	Mary Yann[Buchanan]			HMAD	579	1871
00 000 0000	John Yann			HMAD	580	1871
00 Nov 1815	Hon. William T. Yeargin			HADM	907	---

J E S S A M I N E   C O U N T Y

BIRTHDATE	NAME OF BIOGRAPHEE	PARENTS/BIRTHPLACE/BIRTHDATE		SOURCE/PAGE	DATE
00 Nov 1829	John W. Allsman	Aaron & Elizabeth(Logan)	Ky/x	HGHR 216	---

JESSAMINE COUNTY (CONT.)

BIRTHDATE	NAME OF BIOGRAPHEE	PARENTS/BIRTHPLACE/BIRTHDATE	SOURCE/PAGE	DATE
00 000 0000	Elizabeth Arnold[Smalley]		HMAC 275	1850
00 000 0000	Sophronia Arnold[Smalley]		HMAC 275	1856
30 Apr 1828	B.F. Ballard Henry	Va1792/x	HMCL 990	1856
07 Apr 1849	Love E. Ballard[Crigler] Dr. James		PBML 1192	----
00 000 1823	Mary S. Benedict[Rafferty]		PHCC 317	----
19 Oct 1853	John R. Burns		HSAN 808	----
11 Jan 1823	Moses H. Cawby		HMCL 921	----
22 Feb 1825	G.W. Chowning		HLOG 347	1855
00 000 1849	Thomas B. Corman Abraham		HMCL 773	----
05 Mar 1816	Martin Dickerson Lewis & Catherine(Rice)		PBWA 573	----
00 000 0000	Dr. H.L. Harris		HCHA 182	1874
29 Aug 1846	Dr. Harvey L. Harris Harvey L.	**/x	HCHA 153	----
16 Nov 1842	W.H. Hicks Argus & Sallie(Myers)		PAUP B327	----
00 000 0000	Katie Hogan[Ballard] William		BRML 644	----
12 May 1849	Allen R. Hollis Berly & Elizabeth(Woods)	Va/x	BRML 387	1857
30 Aug 1832	Harrison Horine John & Margaret(Bash)	**/**	PBML 192	----
00 000 0000	Sarah Horine[Houser] Henry		BRML 562	----
00 000 0000	Elizabeth Houser[Hoover]		PBML 804	----
15 Sep 1830	Harrison Houser Peter & Sarah(Horine)	x/**08	PBML 803	----
15 Sep 1830	Harrison Houser Peter & Sarah(Horine)	Ky1799/**	BRML 561	----
27 Jun 1840	Jesse Hudson		COLE 624	1851
24 Mar 1833	Sophia Hunter[Tudor]		PBML 521	----
00 000 0000	Mary E. Level[Horine] Littleton & Mary(Goss)	Va/Va	PBML 193	----
00 000 1832	Milton McClure James & Frances(Dickerson)	Va/Ky	PBWA 783	----
22 Oct 1832	Milton McClure James A & Frances(Dickerson)Va/Ky		HMAC 108	----
20 Apr 1840	Margaret E. Mahan[Shields] Elijah & Jane(Scott)Woodf02/**02		HMCL 1007	----
13 Oct 1801	Solomon Mason		HMCL 970	----
15 Mar 1830	Henry M. Miller William		PBML 515	----
04 Sep 1840	William Miner John Pa1775/x		HFUL 664	----
00 000 1835	Julia[Moore]		HMAC 276	----
16 Jan 1819	M.I. Overstreet Robert D & Jane(Lowrey)		PBKN 776	----
24 Aug 1824	William B. Payne Fleming & Susan(Hightower)		HCAS 216	----

BIRTHDATE	NAME OF BIOGRAPHEE	PARENTS/BIRTHPLACE/BIRTHDATE		SOURCE/PAGE	DATE
13 Nov 1825	John Perry	John & Charity(Hayes)		HMCL 1040	1836
24 Apr 1834	Samuel Perry	John & Charity		HMCL 1040	1836
29 May 1832	Louisa Perry[McWhorter]	John & Charity		PBML 451	---
29 May 1832	Louisa Perry[Wilson]	John & Charity		PBML 451	1836
24 Sep 1817	Nathaniel Perry	John & Charity(Pew)	Pa1790/NC1800	HMCL 1012	---
24 Apr 1834	Samuel Perry	John & Charity(Pew)	Ky/Ky	PBML 1042	---
15 Jan 1827	Zerelda Perry[Munsell]	John & Charity(Pugh)	Ma1792/x	PBML 1034	---
25 Aug 1861	Naomi Pierce[Collins]	James & Mary J(Gibney)	Ky/Ky	PBMC 445	---
24 Mar 1856	Joseph Sageser			HMCL 884	---
17 Dec 1830	Lavina Sageser[Howard]			HMCL 884	---
17 Dec 1830	Lavina Sageser[Howard]	Henry & Nancy(Woodard)	**/**	PBML 291	---
17 Sep 1816	James Shields	James & Mary(Paul)	Irel781/83	HMCL 1007	---
00 000 0000	Jacob T. Smith			PBML 575	---
13 Feb 1808	J. Springer			COLE 645	---
22 Jan 1828	W.R. Welch	John & Elizabeth(Rice)	Ky/Ky	HMAC 101	---
22 Jan 1828	William R. Welch			EFAY 582	1864
00 000 0000	A. Withers			HMCL 829	1834

JOHNSON COUNTY

17 Feb 1821	John Stafford	John & Polly(Davis)	Va/Va	PVED 944	---

KENTON COUNTY

BIRTHDATE	NAME OF BIOGRAPHEE	PARENTS/BIRTHPLACE/BIRTHDATE		SOURCE/PAGE	DATE
01 Feb 1858	Samuel S. Davis	John B & Anna E(Sharpe) Mason/Mason		BROC 363	---
01 Feb 1858	Samuel S. Davis	John B & Anna E(Sharpe)		BRKI 1094	---
15 Mar 1850	Winfield S. Gardner	Louis W & Electa R(Richmond) 1812/In17		BRKI 1151	---
01 Mar 1836	Douglas Glasgow	Adam & Mary A(Stevenson)		HMCD 568	1842
00 000 0000	Mary Gleason[Small]	John & Mary		HLOG 376	---

BIRTHDATE	NAME OF BIOGRAPHEE	PARENTS/BIRTHPLACE/BIRTHDATE	SOURCE/PAGE	DATE
30 Jul 1815	A.J. Grizzel	Solomon & Nancy	HJAC	115	----
30 Jul 1815	Andrew J. Grizzell	Solomon & Nancy(Coyle) Va/Va	PBRJ	810	----
03 Nov 1859	Dr. Charles C.Grizzell	Andrew J & Catherine(Stephens)**/x	PBRJ	810	----
00 000 0000	W.H. Grizzell		HJAC	129	1861
00 000 1833	Thomas Jordan	Richard & Mary(Jones)	HLaS	B620	----
00 000 1827	Lafayette Lancaster		KANE	838	----
12 Mar 1847	Abigail E.S. McMurtry	Matthew & Elizabeth(Smyth) Ire07/Ire04	PEMO	B204	----
17 Aug 1837	Ezekial J. McMurtry	Matthew & Elizabeth(Smyth) Ire07/Ire04	PEMO	B203	----
20 Apr 1843	James M. McMurtry	Matthew & Elizabeth(Smyth) Ire07/Ire04	PEMO	B204	----
13 Nov 1838	Jane E. McMurtry	Matthew & Elizabeth(Smyth) Ire07/Ire04	PEMO	B204	----
26 Dec 1834	Mary McMurtry	Matthew & Elizabeth(Smyth) Ire07/Ire04	PEMO	B203	----
10 Feb 1841	Susanna E. McMurtry	Matthew & Elizabeth(Smyth) Ire07/Ire04	PEMO	B204	----
00 000 0000	Margaret McCaffrey[Milligen]		HGHR	266	----
00 000 0000	J.M. Mardis		AGLY	49	1876
00 000 0000	I.N. Martin		CJRI	813	1853
00 000 0000	Jesse Morgan		HJAC	131	1850
00 000 0000	Maria Morgan		HJAC	131	1850
00 000 1826	Dr. A.G. Pickett		COLE	553	----
00 000 1800	Hiram Powell	Oner R. Va1771/x	PPVE	1070	----
00 000 0000	Virginia R. Powell[Martin]		CJRI	813	----
00 000 1810	M.C. Rafferty		PHCC	317	----
00 000 0000	Roswell Richmond		BRKI	1381	1855
00 000 1826	E. Rucker	William M & Julie A(Loyd) Ky/Ky	GHHA	746	----
00 000 1834	Emma Salmon[Bacon]	Jacob	PVED	934	----
15 Nov 1822	R.R. Scott	Elmore Va1790/x	PHCC	100	----
00 000 0000	Catherine Stephens[Grizzel]		HJAC	115	----
10 Dec 1835	John W. Wayland	Stanton & Catharine Va/x	HJAC	83	----
04 May 1841	Dr. Joseph P. Wayland	Joseph & Nancy(Massey) Va1778/Va92	BRDK	54	----
23 Mar 1827	Robert Yelton		CJRI	298	----

K N O T T   C O U N T Y   (N O N E)

KNOX COUNTY

BIRTHDATE	NAME OF BIOGRAPHEE	PARENTS/BIRTHPLACE/BIRTHDATE	SOURCE/PAGE		DATE
00 000 0000	J.J. Ballinger		HMAC	272	1867
00 000 0000	Maria[Brines]		CELW	357	1816
05 Jan 1812	S.W. Carpenter	Benjamin & Melee(Shook)	PJEF	B80	----
00 000 0000	Elizabeth Deweese		AWOO	3	1832
00 000 1830	Sarah Faris[Early]		HSTE	676	----
18 Aug 1826	Dudley Hopper		COLE	647	1837
18 Aug 1826	Dudley Hopper	Jacob & Lovina(Garland) Tn/Va	PBCO	456	----
08 Dec 1804	Andrew Jackson	John	BREM	60	----
01 Apr 1827	William Johnson	John & Charlotte NC/NC	GRUN	B138	----
00 000 0000	Nannie J[McElvain]		HMAC	272	1866
00 000 1830	L.H. Moore	J. L & Leminah(Kitchen) Ky/Ky	HFUL	453	----
00 000 0000	Henry C. Pemberton	Thomas & Deborah(Moore) Tn/**	CSER	383	1836
00 000 0000	Louisiana Pemberton[Hill]		CSER	382	1836
08 May 1814	Sidney Rochester		HWEM	817	1835
25 May 1810	Susan Sexton[Scott]		KNOX	704	----
00 000 0000	Eliza J. Steward[Carr]		BCLA	714	----
00 000 0000	Martha Tinsley[Clark]		CELW	352	1862

LARUE COUNTY

BIRTHDATE	NAME OF BIOGRAPHEE	PARENTS/BIRTHPLACE/BIRTHDATE	SOURCE/PAGE		DATE
04 Aug 1810	Mary Bradley[Creenawalt]		HSAN	789	1830
06 Feb 1851	Dr. Henry B. Brown	Patrick & Louisa(Enlows) Va1800/Va1813	BLOG	343	----
28 May 1830	Peter Kermicle	Samuel & Mary(Trainor) Md/Va1800	BRCM	441	----
17 Dec 1846	John T. Kermicle	Samuel & Mary(Trainor) Md/Va1800	BRCM	459	----
00 000 1805	Charles Morgan		HADM	887	1847

LAUREL COUNTY

BIRTHDATE	NAME OF BIOGRAPHEE	PARENTS/BIRTHPLACE/BIRTHDATE	SOURCE/PAGE	DATE
24 Nov 1828	Henry L. Jackson	H.T & Adaline(Pearl)	BRML 763	----
00 000 0000	Adaline Pearl[Jackson]	John	BRML 763	----
00 000 0000	Elizabeth Penfold[Woods]	**1806/** Va/x	CELW 345	1819
30 Oct 1846	Thomas Williams	Campbell & Mary(Box)	PPME 352	1869

LAWRENCE COUNTY

BIRTHDATE	NAME OF BIOGRAPHEE	PARENTS/BIRTHPLACE/BIRTHDATE	SOURCE/PAGE	DATE
00 000 0000	Mary M. Brumfield[Shafer]		CELW 359	1841
06 Aug 1829	Rev. Thomas Cox	John & Polly(Markham) **1799/**1817	PVED 324	1829
00 000 0000	John Strahan		CELW 355	1864
00 000 1825	John Strahan	William NC/x	CELW 342	----

LEE COUNTY (NONE)

LESLIE COUNTY (NONE)

LETCHER COUNTY (NONE)

-110-
a

BIRTHDATE	NAME OF BIOGRAPHEE	PARENTS/BIRTHPLACE/BIRTHDATE	SOURCE/PAGE	DATE
00 000 0000	Mary E[Abbott]		HGHA 179	1849
12 Oct 1834	M.T. Bagby	Willis & Mary(Thompson) Ky1800/Ky99	PAUP B311	----
11 Oct 1816	William Bagby	Robert & Frances Va/Va	BHAN 567	----
08 Mar 1817	Hillary Ball	Richard C & Katie(Clary) Md/Md	PBWL 491	----
12 Mar 1837	William Beckett	William & Delilah(May)	HFUL 507	1852
08 Sep 1825	Isaac N. Bassett		HMER 832	1862
00 000 0000	Amanda J. Bell[DePugh]		HMAD 563	1834
00 000 0000	Charles Bilderback		CSBR 379	
00 000 0000	Martha A. Boggs[Parker]		CSBR 390	1878
00 000 0000	Nannie Boggs[Cwens]		CSBR 386	1878
00 000 0000	S.G. Boyd		AHEN 5	1859
23 Apr 1815	Samuel G. Boyd		HHEN 285	1819
00 000 0000	Melinda Brown[Tolle]		HDEW 345	1852
00 Oct 1833	David F. Campbell	Edward & Mary(Lewis) Va/**	PBGW 576	----
00 000 0000	Sarah L. Crawford[Bilderback]		CSBR 379	1857
10 Dec 1826	A.W. Davis	Solomon Ky/x	HFUL 794	----
00 000 0000	Rebecca Davis[Lewis]		HMCL 984	----
13 Dec 1806	David Dickson	Robert & Phebe(Means) Md/Pa	PVED 593	----
10 Oct 1843	Richard Fetters	Daniel & Sarah(Gillman) Pa/Pa	BCLA 739	----
00 000 0000	Rev. James Harper		CSBR 386	1835
15 Jul 1832	Barton L. Harrison	James & Sarah C(Lee)	HFUL 831	1855
09 Aug 1828	Francis M. Harrison	James & Sarah C(Lee)	HFUL 831	1848
00 000 0000	Martin M. Harry		HCHA 177	1849
00 000 0000	J.M. Hasson	Theophilus N & Margaret(Riley)	HFUL 487	1834
20 Oct 1819	A.R. Hayden	Jonathan & Rebecca(Taylor) Pa/NJ	PBHE 209	----
30 Oct 1821	Jerome B. Henderson	William P & Elizabeth(Hendrickson)Pa/NJ	PBWL 500	92/84
11 Feb 1847	Katie O. Henderson[Abrogast]		HMCL 952	----
00 000 0000	Sarah P. Henderson[Rea]		ECHA 141	1849
20 Oct 1809	James H. Kelley	Henry & Catherine(Buchanan) Va/x	HFUL 492	----
03 Jun 1819	John H. Kelley	William & Anna(Hannahs) Ky/x	HFUL 492	----
03 Jun 1812	John H. Kelly	Henry & Catherine(Buchanan) Va/Ky	HFUL 556	1835

Date	Name	Parents / Other	Origin	Code	No.	Year
00 000 0000	Margaret Lai d[Calliher]			HADM	868	----
12 Nov 1823	John S. Lee			HFUL	803	1846
11 Dec 1833	George M. Lewis George M.		**/x	HMCL	984	1849
00 000 0000	Eliza Luman[Lanterman]			HMAD	577	1828
00 000 0000	Eliza Luman[Lanterman]	John & Polly		HMAD	489	1828
10 Apr 1831	Samuel Lyons William D.		Md/x	BCHA	577	----
09 Apr 1819	Augustus Maples	David & Mary(Buchanan)		PBKN	535	----
09 Oct 1803	Hannah Maples[Conrad]			HMCL	878	----
01 Jan 1828	Elizabeth Means[McDannald] Major John		**/x	BCSB	247	1858
00 000 0000	George W. Means			CSBR	387	1829
22 Mar 1825	J.R. Means			HMCL	920	----
00 000 0000	Major John Means John		Pa/x	BCSB	247	----
00 000 0000	Mary E. Means[McDannold]			CSBR	392	1835
21 Sep 1831	Owen A. Means Robert & Sarah(Rumsey)		Pa1785/Pa	----	----	----
00 000 0000	D.W. Owens			CSBR	386	1878
16 Aug 1845	Dr. D.W. Owens Lewis & Dorotha(Hathaway)		**/x	BCSB	394	----
04 Jan 1806	Nancy Pitts[Riggs]			PBML	561	----
31 Jan 1830	Joseph G. Putnam Daniel K & Anna(Grover)		Va/Md	HFUL	837	1854
00 000 0000	Daniel J. Rankin			HCHA	178	1831
00 000 0000	John J. Rea			ECHA	141	1849
05 Dec 1842	Matilda J. Rigdon[Grayson] Eli T & Dicie(Hurst)		Ky/Ky	PBML	522	----
07 Jan 1817	Sarah Sexton[Strode]			HFUL	692	----
00 000 0000	Thomas P. Smith			HCHR	261	1870
00 000 0000	Brunett Spragg[Snyder]			CSBR	381	1862
00 000 0000	E.W. Swearingen			HDEW	345	1830
00 000 0000	John L. Swearingen			HDEW	345	1830
13 Jan 1823	Johnson A. Swearingen Bartley & Jane(Rankin)			CHAM	1037	1848
00 000 0000	J.I. Taylor			VTBU	208	1848
00 000 0000	H.C. Trent			PPRI	414	1850
22 Sep 1830	Henry C. Trent German N & Eliza(Doyal)		Ky/Ky	PBRI	302	----
00 000 0000	R.M. Turhune[Ellis]			HDEW	341	1849
00 000 0000	Emily J. Walker[Lee]			HFUL	803	----
06 Oct 1831	Joshua G. Walker Hugh			HFUL	895	1835
30 Aug 1825	James Waring			HADM	876	1835

BIRTHDATE	NAME OF BIOGRAPHEE	PARENTS/BIRTHPLACE/BIRTHDATE		SOURCE/PAGE	DATE
			Md/x		
00 000 0000	Lucy Aldridge[Skeeters]			PVED 960	----
00 000 0000	Ann O. Black[Weyl]			CELW 350	1855
25 Sep 1832	Reuben G. Bright	Henry & Maria(Gentry)	**/**	PBML 226	----
23 Oct 1835	William M. Bright	John & Elizabeth(Morrison)	Ky/Ky	PBML 234	----
23 Oct 1835	William M. Bright	John & Elizabeth(Morrison)		BRML 521	----
23 Oct 1835	William M. Bright	John & Elizabeth(Morrison)		BMCL 950	----
26 Sep 1797	James Clarke	John & Ann(Whitten)		CWCD 334	1829
26 Sep 1797	James Clarke	John & Ann(Whitten)		HMCD 297	----
00 000 0000	Susan Clements[Briggs]			CASS 858	----
00 000 0000	John B. Culbertson			HWCL B148	----
00 000 0000	Lockie B. Daniels[Flint]			PPVE 413	----
00 000 0000	Maria W. Davidson[Jennings]			MACL 294	1820
00 000 0000	Nancy Davidson[Carrigan]			MACL 297	1820
00 000 0000	William Davidson			MACL 294	1820
22 Mar 1845	Martha A. Delanay[Meredith]			PPWA 256	----
00 000 0000	G.W. Denton			AMEN 22	1830
00 000 0000	Benjamin Douglas			HSTC 378	----
00 000 1828	W.E. Eastham			HMAC 191	----
00 000 0000	Lucy E. Edwards[King]			HMAC 271	1858
10 May 1862	W.A. Flint			PPVE 411	----
00 000 0000	Thomas H. Foley			CSBR 383	1865
00 000 0000	Margaret Goodnight[Moore]			CSBR 361	----
12 Jan 1835	John B. Guest			PBCO 260	----
17 Sep 1807	Reuben Leach			PHCC 348	----
04 Oct 1830	Samuel F. Logan	Allen & Martha(Givens)	**1790/**	PBCO 380	----
00 000 1801	James McCollum			HWCL B152	----
02 Nov 1801	John McKinney	George & Ann(Riley)		HMER 824	----
23 Oct 1823	W.L. Magill	William	Va1788/x	PHCC 310	----
03 Jun 1816	L. Murphy	Thomas	**1788/x	PHCC 66	----
09 Nov 1788	Thomas Murphy	John	Ire/x	PHCC 66	----
27 Jan 1822	William J. Oliver	David & Jemina(Frith)		HADM 766	----
00 000 0000	Anna M. Owsley[Sims]	Harry & Mary(Finley)	NC/Va	HLOG 376	----
00 000 0000	E.A[Paine]			HCHA 181	1856

BIRTHDATE	NAME OF BIOGRAPHEE	PARENTS/BIRTHPLACE/BIRTHDATE		SOURCE/PAGE	DATE
25 Aug 1790	Milton Rayburn			LOGA 657	1831
00 000 1796	Jesse Renfro	James		HMAD 439	1810
12 Aug 1829	John Sandidge	Daniel & Parmelia(Tate)Va1804/Casey		HMCD 792	1832
00 000 1812	Joshua Sandidge	John & Patience		HMCD 803	----
00 000 0000	B.S. Shackelford			HCHA 180	1856
00 000 0000	C[Shackelford]			HCHA 180	----
26 Dec 1822	W.T. Spires	John		HMQR 583	1831
14 May 1826	J.H. Suduth			HEDG 601	----
09 Jan 1789	Joseph G. Williams	John & Amelia(Gill)	Va1764/NC	GHHA 785	----
24 Mar 1792	Wesley Williams	John & Amelia(Gill)	Va1764/NC	GHHA 785	----
00 000 1850	David Wilson	William D.		HMCL 913	1855
00 000 0000	John M. Yowell			HMAC 271	1850

L I V I N G S T O N   C O U N T Y

BIRTHDATE	NAME OF BIOGRAPHEE	PARENTS/BIRTHPLACE/BIRTHDATE		SOURCE/PAGE	DATE
19 Mar 1851	Alexander H. Covington	George W.	Tn/x	BRJM 424	----
00 000 0000	Robert H. Davis			KNOX 669	----
18 Oct 1823	Sarah M[Dukes]			PBMO B188	----
00 000 0000	David Heath	Samuel	NJ/x	PBDP 592	----
00 000 0000	William E. Hill			HMAD 562	1831
11 Jan 1807	William E. Hill	David	NC/x	HMAD 528	----
00 000 1814	William C. Parrant			HCHR 32	c1820
03 Jan 1845	William M. Stringer	William & Mary		PAUP B334	----
00 000 0000	J.C. Thompson			HJAC 131	1847
00 000 0000	Lucy A. Vance			GSBR 378	1829
00 000 0000	John J. Williamson			BRJM 498	----
00 000 0000	Martha Wilson			HMAD 562	----

BIRTHDATE	NAME OF BIOGRAPHEE	PARENTS/BIRTHPLACE/BIRTHDATE	SOURCE/PAGE	DATE
00 000 0000	W.T. Adams		CSBR 386	1833
07 Mar 1831	William T. Adams	Benjamin & Sarah(Bell) Md/x	BGSB 244	1830
04 Jan 1843	W.L. Appling		PLAS 645	1854
00 000 1817	John O. Bernard	Jesse B & Mildred A(Crewdson) Va/Va	PBAD 293	----
23 Jan 1798	Alfred M. Balch		COLE 584	----
17 Dec 1824	Daniel Biddlecome	John & Elizabeth(Cawhy) Vt/Tn	CASS 851	----
21 Nov 1813	James C. Boyles	John NC/x	HWCL B172	----
00 000 0000	J.W. Branom		HMAC 275	1877
05 Nov 1819	Daniel P. Bryan	Archibald & Sidney	LOGA 698	----
00 000 0000	Samuel B.F. Caldwell	Samuel	PRDP 285	----
27 Jun 1813	Alexander Campbell	Owens & Mary(Clark) NC/x	CSBR 279	1840
00 000 0000	William O.F.Campbell	Owen NC/x	BGSB 220	----
06 Feb 1823	Abner A. Clark	Abner & Nancy(Gozum) NC/Ky	BGSB 323	1835
25 Oct 1824	Edward B. Clark	Howard & Eliza J(Wilson) Warren/Ky	HMAC 228	----
11 Sep 1820	Francis A. Clark	Abner & Nancy(Gozam)	BGSB 439	1835
00 000 0000	H.M. Clark		CSBR 384	1834
15 Feb 1811	Harrison Clark	Abner	BCSB 206	----
07 Mar 1822	John J. Clark	Samuel & Melvina(Huddleston) Ky/Ky	BRWA 535	1829
04 Dec 1825	Joseph F. Clark	Samuel B.	PBWA 356	----
00 000 0000	Mary E. Clark[Rigg]		CSBR 391	1837
00 000 0000	Purlina Clark[Rigg]		CSBR 391	1835
00 000 0000	R.B. Clark		HMAC 277	1830
16 Feb 1811	William A. Clark	Thomas & Mary(Anthony) NC1770/x	BCSB 316	1839
16 Feb 1811	William A. Clark	Thomas NC1770/x	CSBR 278	----
00 000 0000	Rosena M. Collins[Schmalhausen]		CELW 351	----
15 Apr 1849	Sirilla M. Crain[Ewing]		HMCL 936	----
20 Jul 1841	Wesley T. Crain	William & Amanda(McMillan) **/**	PBML 274	----
21 Sep 1819	William D. Crain	Amsted & Sarah	LOGA 571	----
00 000 0000	Mary A. Crane[Huff]		MACL 296	1839
00 000 0000	Mary S. Dillon[Capps]	William	PBWA 441	----
01 Sep 1808	A.P.H. Doyle	John	HFAY 55	----
00 000 0000	E.M. Doyle	John Va/x	PSTC 243	----
15 Oct 1848	Clark Duncan		HSAN 741	----
00 000 1839	Elmer E. Ewing		BRML 347	----
00 000 0000	John H. Farmer		TAZE 399	----

Date	Name	Parents/Spouse	Origin	Code	No.	Year
00 000 0000	Lucinda Fletcher[Newton]	C & Mary		HGSH	923	----
00 000 0000	George Farthing			BRCM	253	c1855
00 000 0000	Henrietta Furr[Glass]			MACL	302	1866
00 000 0000	Patrick H. Gordon			CELW	353	1834
17 Aug 1823	John R. Grinter	Francis & Susan	Va/Va	LOGA	575	----
00 000 0000	John Harris	Rev. William		PEMO	B63	----
00 000 0000	A.E[Holland]			HFAY	98	1864
00 000 0000	Mary E[House]			HWAS	85	1864
00 000 0000	Mary Hurt[Rigg]			CELW	356	1827
00 000 0000	David P. Hunter			CELW	347	1827
05 Jan 1844	John W. Hutcheson			HADM	851	1847
00 000 0000	Wesley M. King			HMAC	275	1835
00 000 0000	Mary A[Lawrence]			HMAD	577	1859
01 Aug 1815	William McAdams			HADM	805	1835
00 000 0000	Margery A[McBride]			HMAC	272	----
25 Jul 1824	Polly A. McCann[Chowning]			COLE	585	----
17 Dec 1809	Finis McCutchen	Hugh & Elizabeth(McCombs)	Va1773/NC	HFUL	560	----
00 000 0000	Thomas McGown			BRJM	157	----
00 000 0000	Henry C. McPherson			HMAD	577	1859
00 000 0000	James McPherson			HMAD	577	1859
00 000 1820	Matilda Madole[Turner]	William & Patsey		HGSH	950	----
00c 1820	S.O. Maxcy	Joel & Betsy A(Brown)	Va/Va.	HSAN	935	----
00 000 0000	F. Meriwether			MACL	294	1862
17 Nov 1817	J.R. Miles	Alexander & Mary(Irvin)	NC1788/Ga	HMAC	169	----
16 Jun 1818	George H. Miller	George & Mary(Owent)	Va/Fayette	HSAN	859	1829
27 Feb 1813	Anna B. Mitchell[Filcher]			HJOD	753	1830
00 000 0000	Minery[Mitchell]			HFAY	98	1833
00 000 0000	R.B. Mitchell			HFAY	98	1837
00 000 0000	Mary A[Norvell]			HMAC	271	1849
00 000 0000	A.J. Pell[Fer..ey]			GSER	392	----
13 May 1832	Hester E. Poor[Adkirs]	Col. D.W.		HMCL	934	1854
16 Aug 1820	William W. Redman	Solomon & Rebecca(Williams)	Ky/Ky00	HCAS	309	----
00 000 0000	C.M. Robertson			AMEM	22	1850
10 Jun 1821	C.M. Robertson	Martin & Sarah(Morton)		HMEM	716	1827
00 000 0000	James H. Rohrer	Jacob & Artemisia(Ashbaugh)	Ma/x	PEWA	559	----
08 Apr 1814	David Rotramel	Henry & Keziah(Simpson)		PJEF	B127	----
00 000 0000	Margaret Rotramel[Ccad]			CELW	347	1830
00 000 0000	Ashur Shelton			HWAS	85	1852
00 000 0000	Mallory Shelton			HWAS	85	1852

L O G A N   C O U N T Y   (C O N T.)

BIRTHDATE	NAME OF BIOGRAPHEE	PARENTS/BIRTHPLACE/BIRTHDATE	SOURCE/PAGE	DATE
25 May 1814	P.B. Solomon	Lewis & Sarah(Bowden) NC/x	HMAC 183	----
00 000 0000	Thomas Stephenson		PPPI 136	----
13 Jan 1821	I.M. Stribling	Benjamin & Nancy(Washburn)	ACAS 29	1827
07 Sep 1854	Francis A. Swenner	Richardson NC1814/x	BRJM 331	----
00 000 0000	Hugh Tinnon		CSBR 386	1830
01 Mar 1825	Edward Trabue	Aaron	HGJR 420	1837
29 May 1820	Eliza J. Trabue[Boggess] Haskens	Va1790/x	PBWA 461	----
08 May 1799	Edmund C. Vancil		PBWA 829	----
02 Dec 1839	George M. Walker		HADW 810	----
00 000 0000	Nancy M. Walker[Thacker]		HMAC 272	1842
26 Aug 1821	Samuel Weller		HMOR 564	1852
12 Oct 1812	William White	John & Catherine(Simons) Va1785/x	HWCL B101	1824
00 000 0000	Judith F. Willson[Fruit]		HMAD 584	1832
00 000 0000	Agnes E. Wimpey[Holland]		HFAY 50	----
17 Aug 1841	J. William Young	John H & Margaret(Ewing) Va1816/**	BRML 722	----

L Y O N   C O U N T Y

BIRTHDATE	NAME OF BIOGRAPHEE	PARENTS/BIRTHPLACE/BIRTHDATE	SOURCE/PAGE	DATE
00 000 0000	Cora Holloway[Duncan]	J.N.	BCLA 734	----
00 000 0000	Eliza Y. Long[Ball]	Griffin	PRJD 221	----
00 000 0000	Elizabeth A. Lyon[Roe]		OGLE 856	----
11 Jun 1805	Elizabeth Lyon[Roe]		BOGL 1005	----
00 000 0000	Mary J. Sanders[Smith]		BCHR 989	----
11 Jun 1828	William C.H. Smith	Thomas & Sarah(Hall) NC1809/x	PBWD 507	----

McC R A C K E N   C O U N T Y

BIRTHDATE	NAME OF BIOGRAPHEE	PARENTS/BIRTHPLACE/BIRTHDATE	SOURCE/PAGE	DATE

BIRTHDATE	NAME OF BIOGRAPHEE	PARENTS/BIRTHPLACE/BIRTHDATE	SOURCE/PAGE	DATE
00 000 1835	Columbus C. Briggs	Elijah & Mary(Brown) Ky c1800/Ky c1808	HGSH 761	----
24 Aug 1833	Jasper Culley	M.M & Huldah J(Moore) Ma/x	PAUP B243	----
20 Feb 1865	James L. Glass	T.V & Kittie(Nolan) Christian/**	BRJM 548	----
00 000 0000	Dr. Malcolm Graham		HJAC 129	1876
00 000 1835	Semiramis Kemble	Collins & Elizabeth(Harlow) Ky/Ky	PEPE 439	----
00 Jan 1848	Mary E. Murphy_McCoy]	James H & Rachel J(Butler)	PAUP B271	----
00 000 0000	Mary E. Murphy_McCoy]	James H & Rachel J(Butler)	PAUP B271	----
00 000 0000	William Southard		HWAD 573	1865
12 Aug 1832	Capt.John White	William & Martha	PAUP B235	----

McCREARY COUNTY (NONE)

McLEAN COUNTY

BIRTHDATE	NAME OF BIOGRAPHEE	PARENTS/BIRTHPLACE/BIRTHDATE	SOURCE/PAGE	DATE
00 000 0000	James I. Brydon	Benjamin F & Emily A(Oldham) Ky/Ky	BCLA 709	----
00 000 0000	Alice Patterson[Skinner]	John & Elizabeth	BMCL 1295	----

MADISON COUNTY

BIRTHDATE	NAME OF BIOGRAPHEE	PARENTS/BIRTHPLACE/BIRTHDATE	SOURCE/PAGE	DATE
00 000 0000	L.M. Alverson		PCHR 379	----
05 Jul 1800	J.A. Ball	John & Nancy(Adams) Va/NC	HSAN 794	1829
05 Jul 1800	Japhet A. Ball		HSAN 1060	1825
10 Nov 1800	Hon.Charles Ballance	Willis & Rejoice(Green) Va/Va	PEPE 217	----
00 000 1825	E.D. Ballard	James A & Pauline(Davis)	HSAN 819	----
25 May 1826	Dr. James L. Ballard	Dr. W.J. Va/x	BRML 644	----

BIRTHDATE	NAME OF BIOGRAPHEE	PARENTS/BIRTHPLACE/BIRTHDATE	SOURCE/PAGE	DATE
18 May 1832	Elzira Barclay[Quinn]		PBWL	----
18 May 1832	Elzira F. Barclay[Quinn]	Peter & Elizabeth(Park) **/**	BMCL	----
04 Jan 1850	Jesse E. Barclay	William F & Mary J(Roberts) **/x	BRML	1855
05 Oct 1830	A.J. Barnes	James & Mary(Roberts)	HMCL	----
00 000 0000	Rachel A. Barnes	Turner	HMCL	----
11 Jan 1810	Curtis Batterson	Abraham & Susan(Henline)	PBWL	----
29 Sep 1807	Martin Batterton	Abraham & Susan(Hainline) Va1775/**	PBWL	----
29 Sep 1807	Martin Batterton	Abraham & Susanna	HMCL	----
12 Mar 1833	Preston W. Bentley	William F & Mahala(Bentley)	BMCL	----
17 Mar 1846	Mary E. Boatman[Carver]		HCAS	----
00 000 0000	May J. Boulware		PBWL	----
26 Mar 1847	Taylor Boulware		BMCL	----
04 Dec 1829	Thomas H. Brasfield		PPME	----
04 Dec 1829	T.H. Brasfield	James E & Tabitha(Moberly) Va/SC	HMEM	1834
00 000 0000	Nancy Brawner[Thompson]		PBPE	----
25 Nov 1816	Gideon Carver	Pleasant M & Catherine(Shryock)Va83/FavHFUL	----
00 Oct 1802	William Champ		HMCD	811	1834
15 Sep 1822	Charles H. Chitty		PPWO	494	1832
00 000 0000	Curtis F. Columbia	George	BCHA	54	----
00 000 0000	Eliza Colyer		CELW	346	1838
19 May 1863	Abraham L. Coyle	William & Lydia(Hudson)	BMCL	985	----
18 Jan 1860	Cassius M. Coyle	William & Lydia(Hudson) **1824/**1828	BMCL	985	----
04 Oct 1869	John W. Coyle	William & Lydia(Hudson)	BMCL	986	----
01 Aug 1824	William Coyle	Isaac	BMCL	985	----
00 000 0000	Martin Dunbar		CSBR	389	1854
21 Jul 1822	Dr. Benjamin I. Dunn Nathiel A & Sophia W(Irvin) Ky/Va	HMCD	414	----
00 00c 1776	Joseph Durbin		HSAN	974	1829
00 000 0000	Margaret Eads[Hoffman]		CSBR	388	1856
00 00c 1800	Green Epperson		COLE	596	----
17 Nov 1827	William D. Epperson		PBKN	820	----
17 Nov 1827	William D. Epperson P.W & Elizabeth(Dalton) Va/Va	KNOX	673	1828
00 000 0000	Serilda Evans[Wilson]		BMCL	1296	----
00 000 0000	Lucy Farthine[Wells] William & Sarah	PJEF	B142	----

-118-

Birth Date	Name	Parents / Notes	Origin	Code	No.	Year
00 000 1800	Eli Fletcher			LOGA	539	----
00 000 1823	Thomas C. Fletcher	Zachariah & Margaret(Campbell) Ky/1798		LOGA	540	----
30 Oct 1826	Charlotte P. Fox[Smith]			BWCL	1296	----
20 Sep 1822	Thales H. Givens	James & Martha(Miller)		PBKN	238	----
25 Sep 1820	Thales H. Givens	James & Martha(Miller)	Va/Va	KNOX	677	----
04 Apr 1837	James F. Golden			HMCL	1024	----
01 Mar 1829	Julia A. Golden[Stagner]			HMCL	1026	1852
00 000 0000	Julia A. Golden[Stagner]			PBML	423	----
00 000 0000	W.F. Guess			CELW	353	1858
06 Jun 1796	George Henline			HMCL	1021	1828
07 Mar 1816	Enoch Hieronymous	William & Alvira(Darnell)	Va1788/x	TAZE	489	1828
17 Oct 1826	William Hieronymous	William & Alvira(Darnell)	Va1788/x	TAZE	490	1828
04 Dec 1816	William Hiett			PPWA	278	1836
01 Jan 1832	John W. Hill	Isaac & Maria(Porter)	NC/Pa	HCHA	78	----
00 000 1810	William L. Hill			HMCL	927	----
00 000 0000	Lydia A. Hooten[Miller] Nicholas			PBML	516	----
15 Jun 1827	R.S. Howard			HMCL	884	----
15 Jun 1827	Robert S. Howard	Ignatius	Ky/x	PBML	288	----
27 Sep 1815	Thomas Hubbard	John & Elizabeth(Parks)	Ky/x	HMOR	548	1831
04 Apr 1828	Lydia Hudson[Coyle]	John & Fannie(Brochman)	NY/Pa	BWCL	985	----
14 Oct 1827	Ephraim Jarvis	William & Mary(Hale)		HMCD	583	1836
01 Aug 1812	James Jarvis	William & Mary(Hale)		HMCD	582	1829
01 Aug 1812	James Jarvis			CMCD	598	1829
25 Dec 1809	John Jarvis			COLE	636	1832
28 Dec 1858	W.C. Johnson	R.H & Susan(Goodloe)	In/Franklin	PPVE	1011	----
00 000 1791	Charles Jones			PBDF	898	----
10 Apr 1829	Elisha S. Kearby	Jesse & Patsy(Burnham)	Ky/Ky	BWCL	1127	----
10 Apr 1829	Elisha S. Kearby	Jesse & Martha B(Burnham)Woodford/**		HMCL	1010	05/11
28 Jan 1833	Matilda Keen[Noble]	James & Frances(Cobb)	NC/Va	PBML	852	----
14 Mar 1836	Dr. J.S. Lackey			HMCL	837	1857
00 000 1832	Isaiah Lain			BRML	640	----
11 Sep 1829	Isham G. Lain	John & Sallie(Baker)		PBML	272	----
28 May 1827	William B. Lain	John & Sallie(Baker)	Va1795/Md	PBML	277	1856
07 May 1821	Aaron Logsdon	George & Sally(McKenzie)		BCSB	476	1824
00 000 1780	Joseph Logsdon			HSAN	788	----
06 Sep 1809	Joseph Logsdon	William & Elizabeth(Beheimer) x/**		BCSB	531	----
00 000 0000	Malinda Logsdon[Dunbar]			CSBR	389	1854
05 Jan 1838	Squire Logsdon			HMCD	831	----

BIRTHDATE	NAME OF BIOGRAPHEE	PARENTS/BIRTHPLACE/BIRTHDATE		SOURCE/PAGE	DATE
00 000 0000	Perry Logsdon			GSBR	384	1865
08 Jul 1842	Hon. Perry Logsdon	Joseph & Lucy(Parker)		BCSB	203	----
28 May 1831	James Loman	Isaac & Phebe(Davenport)	Ky/Ky	PJEF	B141	----
10 Mar 1815	---McBride[Gragg]	James & Elizabeth		HSAN	1043	----
00 000 0000	Lizzie McCosland[Guess]			CELW	353	1858
21 Jan 1814	James McGlothin			PPWA	291	----
00 000 0000	Mary Martin[Hoxsey]			HMAD	574	1819
00 000 0000	Mary Mason[Wallace]			PBAD	330	----
02 Feb 1818	Sarah J. Millen[Ware]	Frederick		PBML	1095	----
16 Feb 1814	William Moore			HPIK	733	----
12 Jun 1822	Abner L. Noble	William & Eleanor(Ransom)	Fayette/Va	BCSB	342	1834
04 Jul 1834	Thomas J. Noble	David & Rebecca(Portwood)	**/**	PBML	851	----
00 000 0000	Emily J. Olive[Webb]			GSBR	393	1851
00 000 0000	Emily J. Oliver[Webb]			GSBR	361	1851
00 000 0000	Emily Orchard[Cox]	John		GSBR	327	----
07 Feb 1779	James Pantier			PPME	462	----
14 Jul 1815	Elder John Park	Eli & Winnifred(Dillingham)	NC/x	PBML	241	----
14 Jul 1815	Jonathan Park	Eli	NC/x	HMCL	1030	1853
00 000 1839	Sidney Q. Park	Rev. John & Berthana(Quinn)	Ky/Ky	BWCL	1229	----
01 May 1815	Lucy Parker[Logsdon]	Jonathan & Patsey(Everson)	**/**	BCSB	531	1844
00 000 0000	Absalom Parks			GSBR	390	1837
08 May 1830	Absalom A. Parks	Daniel & Minerva(Adams)		GSBR	326	1836
00 000 1867	Louisa[Pembrooke]			HMAC	276	----
26 Jan 1801	Capt. Charles D.Phelps	Jarrot & Millie(Duncan)	Va/Va	COLE	602	1830
12 Feb 1803	Elizabeth Phelps[Turner]	Jarrot & Millie		COLE	605	----
00 000 0000	A. Pitcher			HEDG	681	----
11 Dec 1832	John W. Pitman			HMEM	773	1842
00 000 0000	Catherine Porter[Butler]			PVED	226	1834
03 Sep 1820	Benjamin M. Quinn	Hiram & Elizabeth		PBML	1104	----
08 Jan 1825	Hiram W. Quinn	Hiram & Elizabeth(Moberly)	**/**	PBML	1107	----
08 Jan 1825	Hiram W. Quinn	Hiram & Elizabeth(Moberly)	1786/1796	BWCL	1247	Va/**
10 May 1827	James W. Quinn	Hiram & Elizabeth(Moberly)		BWCL	1248	----
10 May 1827	James W. Quinn	Hiram & Elizabeth(Moberly)		PBML	466	----

BIRTHDATE	NAME OF BIOGRAPHEE	PARENTS/BIRTHPLACE/BIRTHDATE	SOURCE	PAGE	DATE
09 Aug 1802	Polly Ray[Jarvis]		COLE	636	1832
10 Oct 1825	John W. Richards		HADM	808	---
10 Oct 1825	John W. Richards	Reason	PBAD	582	---
14 Jan 1820	John R. Smith	Md1789/x	BMCL	1296	1852
01 Mar 1829	Rev. John S. Stagner	Pa/Ky	HMCL	1026	---
00 000 0000	Rev. John S. Stagner		PBML	423	---
08 Jan 1820	James M. Stevens		HADM	874	1831
04 Jul 1828	Thomas H. Tudor		PBML	521	---
03 Feb 1795	Fountain Turner	Thomas & Anna SC/Va	COLE	605	---
07 May 1817	Rev.John T. Warren	John & Tabetha(Vincent)	CJRI	550	1869
00 000 0000	Emily J. Watt[Rigg]		CSBR	382	1858
00 000 0000	Mourning A. Watts[McHatton]		CSBR	382	1851
00 000 0000	Allen Webb		CSBR	393	1851
25 Jul 1820	Allen Webb	Joshua & Letty(Howard)	CSBR	361	1851
00 000 1814	Perry Wells	Richard & Mary Pa/Ky	HPIK	737	1851
00 000 0000	J.W. Wilkerson		CSBR	389	1831
28 Mar 1816	Capt.J.B. Williams	Levi & Polly(Reid) Ky/Ky	GHHA	669	---
22 Aug 1819	Jesse C. Williams	Richard G & Catherine(Folder)Va/Ky1797	HMCH	136	---
22 Aug 1819	Jesse C. Williams	Richard & Catherine(Holder)Va86/Clark97	BHAN	333	---
00 000 1819	J.C. Williams	Richard G & Catherine(Folden)	GHHA	767	---
28 Mar 1816	John R. Williams	Levi & Mary(Reid)	BHAN	641	1831
16 Oct 1813	Judge Samuel Wood	Richard Va/x	HMOR	654	1826
28 Nov 1808	William Wood		COLE	606	1834
19 Apr 1817	Matilda Woods[Honn]		COLE	599	1835
17 Apr 1817	Matilda Woods[Honn]	Ky/Ky	PBCO	478	---
06 Dec 1807	Thirza Woods[Epperson]	Adam & Mary(Kerby)	COLE	596	1834

M A G O F F I N   C O U N T Y   (N O N E)

M A R I O N   C O U N T Y

BIRTHDATE	NAME OF BIOGRAPHEE	PARENTS/BIRTHPLACE/BIRTHDATE	SOURCE/PAGE	DATE
08 Jul 1825	Sarah A. Allen[Wilson]		HLOG 476	1866

BIRTHDATE	NAME OF BIOGRAPHEE	PARENTS/BIRTHPLACE/BIRTHDATE	SOURCE/PAGE	DATE
00 000 0000	Martha Bland[Liston]		HMAC	107	----
22 Jun 1838	John Buckler		COLE	560	----
22 Jun 1838	John T. Buckler		PBCO	190	----
00 000 1851	James W. Collins	James E & Lavisa(Bledsoe) Va/Va	BLOG	342	1871
17 Mar 1830	James W. Crune		COLE	585	----
00 000 1851	Robert L. Cunningham	Samuel & Emeline(Cooper)	HGJR	954	1852
16 Feb 1818	Samuel Cunningham	Robert & Nancy Pa/Ky	HGJR	950	----
29 Jan 1834	William P. Graham	William & Elizabeth(Jackson)**/Hardin	PEPE	930	1836
19 Apr 1834	Dr. Benjamin J. Hall	Joseph A & Mary A(Mudd) Ky/Ky	HGJR	732	----
07 Nov 1813	Thomas Holmes	Nathan & Mary(Miller) Ky/Ky	HFUL	919	1833
00 000 1823	William J. Leonard	James	PPVE	996	----
00 000 0000	Joseph Liston		HMAC	107	----
25 Sep 1803	Joseph Liston	George Va/x	PBMA	797	----
05 Jun 1828	Dr. Milburn McCarty		PPWO	553	----
00 000 0000	Micajah C.Malone	Micajah & Susan(Batsell) Ky/x	ERMA	371	----
00 000 0000	Thomas C. Malone		HMAC	272	1859
29 Aug 1830	Dr. John H. Norris	Moses	BRJM	372	----
00 000 1825	James M. Rigg	Richard & Margaret(Louderback)Ky/x	BLOG	379	1837
08 Aug 1814	Richard Scott	Richard & Jane(Smith) Ky/Ky	HMCD	646	----
02 Jun 1840	John L. Spaulding		EFAY	493	----
19 Mar 1827	Anthony Thornton	Harrison P & Elizabeth(Chamberlain)Ky/Va	HMCD	312	1858
00 000 0000	Edward E. Trovillion	James Y. Va/x	BRJM	188	----

M A R S H A L L   C O U N T Y

BIRTHDATE	NAME OF BIOGRAPHEE	PARENTS/BIRTHPLACE/BIRTHDATE	SOURCE/PAGE	DATE
00 000 1840	M.J. Brewer	Ambrose & Rebecca(Gowen) NC1818/Tn1822	HGSH	856	----
27 Jun 1858	John H. Duncan	Samuel & Ruhamah(Frizzell) Tn/Tn	HGSH	879	----
00 000 0000	John G. Fleenor	George NC1801/x	BRJM	252	----

22 Sep 1829   Elias Ford   Boze & Susan(Averitte)   Ky/Ky   PBMC 356 ----
13 Jan 1827   Aaron C. Ford   Boze & Susan   SC1804/Ky   HSAN 924 1851
00 000 1843   Gilford Pippers   Gilford & Sarah(Mosely)   BRJM 254 ----

MARTIN COUNTY (NONE)

MASON COUNTY

BIRTHDATE	NAME OF BIOGRAPHEE	PARENTS/BIRTHPLACE/BIRTHDATE	SOURCE/PAGE		DATE
00 000 0000	James Altig		AMEN	26	1836
00 000 1821	James Altig		HMEM	747	1836
19 Jan 1818	J.C. Anderson	William C & Catherine(Cook)	BHIQ	B96	1830
00 000 1796	Joseph Artus		HADM	594	----
09 Mar 1828	John R. Baldwin	George & Rebecca(Downing) Vac1803/Ky	PVED	208	----
10 Sep 1824	C.E. Barclay	Stephen & Nancy(Downing) Oh1800/Ky1800	HMCL	957	1835
00 000 1801	Elizabeth Batman[Summers] Owen	Wales/x	BRML	256	----
00 000 1817	Jesse A. Boulton		PBMB	185	----
00 00c 1823	W.J. Boyd	J & L.C(Bailey) Ky1794/Md1796	HGSH	527	----
00 000 0000	Fanny Biggars[Dye]		BRML	709	1869
00 000 0000	Elias Bramel		HCHR	265	1852
17 Mar 1826	Elias Bramel	Elisha & Rebecca(Morse) Md/Md	HCHR	257	1828
00 000 0000	Asahel Bruir		HCHA	176	----
00 000 0000	Martha Churchill[Fletcher] John		PPDM	881	----
00 000 0000	Matilda A. Coburn[Garrard]		CELW	350	1856
30 Nov 1825	Robert I. Coley William & Elizabeth(McClain)		PBCO	334	1831
00 000 0000	Elizabeth Collins[Bredwell]		CELW	357	1848
00 000 0000	Susan Collins[Bredwell]		CELW	357	1858
00 000 0000	Joseph Conway		HMAD	334	1812
00 000 1790	Joseph Conway		PBRI	611	----
00 000 0000	Henry B. Cummings		HCAS	233	1840

BIRTHDATE	NAME OF BIOGRAPHEE	PARENTS/BIRTHPLACE/BIRTHDATE		SOURCE/PAGE	DATE
20 Jan 1856	Thomas B. Davis	John B & Anna E(Sharpe)		BRKI 1094	----
00 000 0000	Benjamin Delaplain			HMAD 563	1807
00 000 0000	Henry De Pugh			HMAD 563	1867
21 Mar 1838	Charles L. Downing	Robert & Susan(Haw)	Ky/Oh	PVED 569	----
22 May 1823	James E. Downing	Reason	Ky/x	PBDP 533	----
19 May 1819	Azael Downtain			HMOR 734	1837
03 Feb 1839	Ross P. Dye			BRML 709	1869
00 000 0000	Almirna Dyhouse[Grafton]			MACL 302	1877
00 000 0000	James Ellis	Elijah & Phoebe(Payton)	Va/Va	BCSB 304	1831
00 000 0000	Mary Ellis			HDEW 345	1840
04 Jan 1822	Ann[Farrell]			HADM 721	1852
22 Mar 1826	George W. Gibson	John & Elizabeth C(Yates)	Pa/Pa	BGLS 281	----
22 Mar 1826	G.W. Gibson	John & Elizabeth(Yates)	Pa/Pa	HLAS B575	----
04 May 1800	James Gordon			HEDG 573	----
00 000 0000	Henry P. Grover	Joseph & Sarah(Putnam)		BCSB 530	1835
00 000 0000	Mahala Grover[Harper]			CSBR 386	----
17 Dec 1830	Mary A. Greene[Evans]			HADM 791	----
15 Aug 1807	Rachel Grinard[Dimmitt]			HFUL 700	----
17 Nov 1799	James Hanson	Samuel		HMCD 283	----
00 000 1841	J.B. Harl	John & Mary		HPIK 729	----
00 000 0000	A.E. [Henninger]			HFAY 98	1848
00 000 0000	M.I. [Henninger]			HFAY 98	1845
10 May 1806	Archibald P. Hensley			HCHA 120	----
14 Oct 1817	Catherine D. Houghton[Purkipile]	Chas. P & Elizab(Vandeventer]		HMEM 751	1824
00 000 0000	William C. Houghton			AMEN 22	1824
27 Aug 1842	Nathan Hudson	George W & Sarah A(Fisher)		HMEM 751	1871
16 Dec 1811	John E. Jackson			CMCD 598	1837
08 Jan 1802	Charles W. Jennings	Isreal & Mary(Waters)	Mdc1774/x	BRCM 514	c1818
00 000 0000	J.D. Johnson	James & Clemency(Donovan)	Va/Md	HCHA 177	1850
19 Nov 1820	J.D. Johnson			HCHA 102	----
00 000 0000	John Johnston	David H		PVED 626	----

Date	Name	Parents/Spouse	Code	No.	Year
00 000 0000	Nathaniel Kent	John	PBML	562	1843
03 Nov 1817	Joseph Killgore		PVED	969	----
24 Aug 1843	George Kirk	Benedict & Ellen(Curtis) Md/**	PBML	1121	----
21 Mar 1803	William Knott		HPEO	826	----
13 Apr 1813	John Lamb		HMOR	720	----
02 Nov 1828	James B. Leach	Thomas & Docia A(Davis) Va/Ky	BHAN	458	----
06 Feb 1864	Hon. John S. Lee	James A & Elizabeth A(Wood)	HPEO	668	----
20 Aug 1823	W.H.H. McArty		HEDG	591	1833
00 000 0000	Keziah McAtee[Jones]		PPWO	601	----
29 Jun 1806	Robert R. McKinley		PPWA	269	1843
14 Jul 1821	Dr. W.H. McNary	John & Sallie(Tennis) Va1768/Pa1778	PHCC	120	1840
00 000 0000	Sidney S. Mannen		PJEF	B147	c1844
23 Dec 1833	John Mayhugh	Fielding & Jane(Dixon) Va/x	PPVE	977	1877
09 Mar 1806	Jacob Merrell	Andrew & Elizabeth(Stout)	HMEM	699	1832
10 Apr 1851	H.L. Miller	Robert & Abarilla(Barnes)	PBPE	413	----
09 Mar 1853	J.R.R. Morford	Isaac & Martha(Mackey) NJ/Pa	HMCH	546	----
06 Jul 1800	Isaiah Nichols	Thomas & Dulcibela(Berry)	PHEF	B203	----
00 000 0000	David T. Nicholson		LOGA	671	----
00 000 0000	Olando M. Parker		CSBR	391	1835
00 000 1835	William Parker		PBWH	230	----
06 Nov 1835	William Parker		PLAS	487	----
09 May 1822	Andrew M. Peddicord	Andrew & Della(Eaton) **/Harrison	BRCM	506	1851
08 Jan 1841	Thomas J. Pepper	James S & Lydia(Worthington)**00/**05	PBCO	496	----
00 000 0000	Clara D. Perrine[Foulton]		PBMB	185	----
03 Oct 1835	Alvin Pollitt		HFUL	835	----
00 000 0000	John Putnam		GSER	387	1837
00 000 0000	Malinda Rankin	Hiram & Jane(Swearingen)	ECHA	150	1828
00 000 1827	William A.Rariden	Jesse & Ruth(Applegate) Pa/x	HFUL	755	1848
25 Jun 1840	A.G. Rees	Albert G & Caroline(Helns) Ky1801/Ky	PLAS	578	----
21 Jan 1831	William P. Rees	William	BGLS	337	----
09 Jul 1829	John Redden		PPVE	76	----
14 Sep 1808	M.O. Reeves	Austin & Elizabeth(Dill) Va/Md	HSAN	704	1834
16 Apr 1813	Lewis G. Reid	Lewis E & Elizabeth(Peyton) Va/Va	HMCD	282	1835
00 000 0000	Emily Rice[Walton]		BHAN	353	----
00 000 1813	Thomas J. Richards	Jacob Md/x	CHAM	1012	----
01 Apr 1818	Caroline Ricketts[Lamb]		HMOR	720	----

M A S O N   C O U N T Y   (C O N T.)

BIRTHDATE	NAME OF BIOGRAPHEE	PARENTS/BIRTHPLACE/BIRTHDATE	SOURCE/PAGE	DATE
07 Dec 1793	John Ross		HSAN 870	----
00 000 0000	Mary A. Roland[Scott]		HWCL B33	----
25 Apr 1831	Dr. T.H. Runyon	Daniel & Ruth(Robinson) Ky1788/Ky1788	PPVE 608	----
07 Jun 1829	Richard H. Schultz	Christian & Charlotte(Lee) Pa/Ky	PBWA 254	----
16 May 1819	Thomas Senteney	**1794/Va	PBCO 470	----
04 Oct 1840	Charles Shackleford	Joab & Elizabeth(Doing)	HWCL 821	1824
00 000 0000	Henry B. Shipley		AMEN 26	----
08 Feb 1844	John W. Showalter		EFAY 479	1881
00 000 0000	J.L. Simcox		HMAD 556	----
00 000 0000	Mary J. Singleton[Rigg]	William P & Susan(Ensor)	CSBR 278	1856
00 000 0000	Alvira[Skillman]		HWAS 86	----
10 May 1844	Robert A. Sommerville		HEDG 666	----
15 Feb 1858	Jennie Spencer[Pepper]	Va/Ky	PBCO 496	1833
00 000 0000	David B. Stayton	Thomas & Betty	HGHA 178	1830
03 Jun 1818	David B. Stayton		HCHA 114	1830
03 Jun 1818	David B. Stayton	Joseph	ECHA 22	----
27 Feb 1831	Mary A. Summers[Maddux]	Elijah & Elizabeth(Batman)**/**1801	BRML 256	----
13 Aug 1818	James Thompson		PVED 613	c1850
18 Dec 1842	James Trisler	Joseph & Elizabeth(Wells) Oh/Ky	PVED 545	----
11 Apr 1813	Rev. Peter Wallace		EFAY 548	----
11 Apr 1813	Rev. Peter Wallace	Thomas & Catharine	PBWL 880	----
11 Apr 1813	Rev. Peter Wallace	Thomas & Catherine	GHHA 667	----
00 000 0000	Thomas M. Wallace		CSBR 386	1866
09 Jan 1809	Frederick M. Walton	William & Barbara	BHAN 353	1835
09 Jan 1809	Frederick M. Walton	William & Barbara Ky/Ky	GHHA 527	1835
00 000 0000	Eliza A. Walton[Mannen]		PJEF B147	c1844
00 000 1818	Simeon B. Walton	William & Barbara Va/Va	HMCH 336	1840
15 Feb 1804	Henry West		BRML 766	----
15 Feb 1804	Henry West		EWCL 1340	----
00 000 0000	John Wheeler	Benjamin	HWAC 274	1834
06 Sep 1806	John Wheeler	Benjamin Va1782/x	PBWA 429	----
16 Sep 1806	John Wheeler	Ky/x	HWAC 140	----

BIRTHDATE	NAME OF BIOGRAPHEE	PARENTS/BIRTHPLACE/BIRTHDATE		SOURCE/PAGE		DATE
00 000 0000	Mary[Wheeler]			HMAC	274	1834
24 Feb 1819	Joseph Wherry	James & Catherine(Downing)	Pa/Pa	PVED	712	----
10 Mar 1807	Thomas M.Whitaker	James & Cordelia(Field)	Md/Md	HMCL	896	----
00 000 0000	Dr. Matthias Winans			HWCL	B156	----
08 Jul 1826	John S. Winter	John & Margaret(Livingston)	Md/Md	HFUL	818	----
18 Jul 1827	John W. Wood	William	Ky/x	PBKN	409	----
00 000 1805	Lydia Worthington-on[Pepper]	Thomas	Md/x	PBCO	496	----
14 Aug 1851	Dr.Richard R.Worthington	Samuel	1808/c1820	PVED	630	----
15 Aug 1851	Dr.R.R. Worthington	Gen. & Sally(Runyon)	Ky/Ky	PPVE	1142	----
12 Jun 1837	Peter Williamsen	Mahlon & Margaret(Stout)	NJ1799/**1800	BCHA	553	----
00 000 1813	Dr. S.R. Youngman	Jesse & Amy(Dicks)	Va/Pa	CJRI	583	----

M E A D E   C O U N T Y

BIRTHDATE	NAME OF BIOGRAPHEE	PARENTS/BIRTHPLACE/BIRTHDATE		SOURCE/PAGE		DATE
14 Jun 1814	Benjamin Allen	Benjamin & Mary	Pa/x	HEDG	648	----
15 Nov 1828	Abraham Bennett			COLE	610	----
10 May 1815	Joshua Brown	Samuel & Henrietta(Hobbs)	Pa/Ky	PBKN	619	----
05 Jan 1831	Jane Chism[Bennett]	John		COLE	610	----
09 Dec 1837	Capt.Henry A. Denton			PHEF	B14	----
09 Feb 1826	John Gray			HMCL	1061	----
27 Jun 1842	William M. Greenwell	George & Amanda(Renfro)	Ky1816/Ky1813	BCSM	170	----
00 000 0000	William M. Greenwell			GSBR	389	1845
01 Mar 1837	Captain Samuel Jarrett Wilson	& Catherine(Dowell)	Va/Ky	CJRI	556	----
26 Oct 1830	William M. Murphey	Davis & Lucinda(Conn)	Ky1809/Ky1810	HWCL	B26	----
26 Jul 1832	Joseph Partridge			PHEF	B61	1845
08 Dec 1862	Harlen A. Payne	James & Harriet(Buckler)		BCHR	957	----
07 Nov 1815	Lytle R. Wiley		Ky/Ky	PBML	608	----
00 Oct 1852	William S. Wilson	William S.		PBRJ	570	----

M E N I F E E   C O U N T Y   (N O N E)

BIRTHDATE	NAME OF BIOGRAPHEE	PARENTS/BIRTHPLACE/BIRTHDATE	SOURCE/PAGE	DATE
25 Sep 1788	John Armstrong		PPWO 558	1819
00 000 0000	William H. Armstrong		AWOO 3	1834
15 Sep 1806	Albert J. Banta		PPWO 493	1833
03 Jul 1809	Cornelius D. Banta	Jacob & Mary(Banta) NJ/x	PBWO 269	----
00 000 0000	C.D. Banta		AWOO 3	1855
03 Jul 1809	C.D. Banta		PPWO 493	1833
00 000 0000	David Banta		AWOO 3	1849
00 000 0000	Rachel Banta		AWOO 3	1833
22 Dec 1815	Rachel B[Banta]		PPWO 493	1833
26 Aug 1831	James H. Bogart		HADM 831	1871
00 000 0000	Elizabeth I. Bone[Dickey]		HCHR 261	----
27 Oct 1788	William C. Bramwell	Milton	PBWL 366	1811
05 Apr 1806	Cary Burford		HDEW 233	----
00 000 0000	David Campbell		HADM 884	----
00 000 0000	Sarah Cardwell[Adams]		MACL 216	----
06 Oct 1828	F.T. Carver	Elijah & Sophia(Haff) Ky/Ky	HCAS 348	----
15 Feb 1826	Henry H. Cecil	Samuel W & Kasiah(Bryan) Md/Va	PBCO 447	1830
19 Jul 1826	Henry G. Conder	Thomas M & Nancy(Whittinghill)Ky/Ky	HCHR 153	----
00 000 0000	George Debaun		HMAD 507	1816
09 Aug 1855	Malinda B. Demaree[Scott] Haldman & Martha J.	**/**	BCSB 139	1857
21 May 1812	J.M. Driskell		HEDG 570	1828
28 Apr 1813	Martha Dunlap[Ruddell]		HADM 808	----
28 Aug 1806	George T. Dunn		HEDG 669	----
00 000 0000	Ludwell H. Demaree		BCSB 381	1857
07 Dec 1836	Dr.Jeremiah D. Donovan		PBSM 626	----
15 Feb 1826	Henry Cecil		COLE 585	----
00 000 0000	David Cosat		PPVE 775	----
00 000 0000	James M. Curry		GSER 386	1835
07 Jan 1807	Joseph T. Eccles	Henry & Polly(Gaunt) Va1781/**1783	PBMO B103	----
13 Jun 1813	William H. Franklin		CMCD 596	1839
13 Jun 1813	William H. Franklin	James & Nancy(Whitten)	HMCD 1148	----

BIRTHDATE	NAME OF BIOGRAPHEE	PARENTS/BIRTHPLACE/BIRTHDATE	SOURCE/PAGE	DATE
30 May 1833	Elder James S. Gash	John J & Thomas(Jackson) Ky/Ky **07/**06	HMCH 299	1835
19 Jan 1832	Laban Gritten	John R & Nancy(Atkinson)	PVED 231	1842
06 Jan 1793	Solomon Hart	David	BRMA 419	----
00 000 0000	Amanda J. Harris[Murray]		EFAY 789	1833
28 Sep 0000	Jesse Henry		HMOR 664	----
00 000 0000	Aquilla Huff	Va/Va	PBSM 465	----
16 Apr 1821	William Johnson	John & Charity(Ryerson) Pa/Ky	KNOX 685	1831
00 000 0000	George Jones		HEDG 670	1840
00 May 1815	Catherine Kennady[McAllister]	Philip & Sarah	HMOR 667	----
00 000 0000	Eliza J. McBride[Bloomfield]	Charles	CJRI 301	1826
00 000 0000	David McGinnis		HSAN 931	----
00 000 1797	John McMurtry		HMER 811	----
20 Feb 1801	Hon.William McMurtry		PBKN 321	----
00 000 0000	Juretta Marrs[Dunn]		HEDG 669	----
21 Feb 1821	George W. Montague	James & Elizabeth(Edmondson) Va/Va	LOGA 498	1834
00 000 0000	T.D. Moore		HMAC 276	----
00 000 0000	Martha Nourse[Irwin]	William Eng/x	BCSB 441	----
00 000 1805	Hiram Paire		HGJR 967	----
20 Apr 1819	William H. Phelps		CMCD 599	1836
00 000 0000	James Pogue	William Ire/x	PBSM 420	1805
04 Feb 1817	David Pyle	Ralph & Rachel	HPIK 421	----
00 000 0000	Peter Rigg		CSBR 391	1830
00 000 0000	John Sprenge		HMAD 485	1810
08 Jan 1784	John Springer	John	PBRJ 827	----
08 Jan 1784	Henry C. Taylor	Jesse & Elizabeth(Colliers) Ky/Ky	BCHR 995	1844
13 Nov 1860	Sarah J. Titef[Litherland]		CELW 356	----
00 000 0000	James H. Van Arsdale	Peter	HGJR 898	----
28 Jun 1816	Joseph H. Vandever		CELW 348	1858
00 000 0000	W.G. Vandyke		AWOO 3	1855
00 000 0000	Judy A. White[Yager]		HMAD 574	1834

M E T C A L F E   C O U N T Y

BIRTHDATE	NAME OF BIOGRAPHEE	PARENTS/BIRTHPLACE/BIRTHDATE	SOURCE/PAGE	DATE
03 Sep 1831	Moses Harbison	Abram B & Hannah(Rhea) Va97/Barren1808	HCAS 284	----
27 Nov 1834	James J. Hundley		HMEM 806	----

BIRTHDATE	NAME OF BIOGRAPHEE	PARENTS/BIRTHPLACE/BIRTHDATE	SOURCE/PAGE	DATE
00 000 1851	Edward Bybee	George W & Rhoda C.	HPIK 727	----
13 Jun 1822	W.B. Carter	William	HFUL 424	1829
00 000 0000	Sarah Emmeronment		HDEW 346	1848
15 Mar 1829	Charles W. Greenup	John & Elizabeth(Harland) **1797/**1800	HMCD 753	----
00 000 1829	Charles Greenup		CMCD 597	1836
00 000 1835	S.F. Greenup		CMCD 597	1836
29 Dec 1827	George T. Harlan	Wesley & Nancy(Greenup)	HMCD 923	1834
29 Dec 1827	George T. Harlan	Wesley & Nancy(Greenup)	CMCD 373	1834
19 Mar 1812	Rev. Lebin L.Harlan	Rev.George B & Mary A(Kelly)Metc/Monroe	PBMA 629	x/Va
18 Feb 1847	Milford E. Huffman	William A & Clarissa C(Harland) Ky/Ky	BCHR 907	----
00 000 0000	Elizabeth Jones[Ventres]		GSBR 381	1834
00 000 0000	J.S. Jones		GSBR 380	1836
00 000 0000	Samuel M. Jones		HWAS 84	1875
11 Jan 1836	Capt.Henry W. Kerr	Abraham NC/x	PBMA 317	----
00 000 0000	Jemima Lane[McCraw]		HDEW 340	1830
00 000 0000	Mary Lane[McCord]		HDEW 342	1830
14 Oct 1823	Tillmon Lane	Ezekiel & Talitha.	HDEW 325	1827
14 Oct 1823	Tillmon Lane	Ezekiel & Talitha(Guest) Tn/Ky	PBDP 799	----
00 000 0000	Tilman Lane		HDEW 346	1835
30 Jan 1822	Charles S. Lisenbey	Benjamin G & Margaret(Simpson)	HDEW 329	1828
00 000 0000	James Lisenby		HDEW 340	1829
00 000 1802	William Moore		CMCD 599	1835
01 Jan 1831	Joseph P. Page	Robert & Mary(Park) Va/x	HMOR 611	----
18 Mar 1823	Jesse Pennington	Jesse & Elizabeth(Penley) SC/SC	HWCL B106	----
00 000 1814	Richard Pennington		CMCD 599	1830
15 Mar 1810	Thomas J. Pennington		CMCD 599	1830
00 000 1818	Robert Peck		CMCD 599	1830
00 000 0000	Elizabet J.Lisenby		HDEW 346	1848
16 Jan 1856	George E. Quimby	James B & Elizabeth(Hogan) Tn/Ky	HWCL B70	----
22 Oct 1837	Demetrius Sims		HEDG 644	1858
00 000 0000	William T.Sims		HEDG 673	----
00 000 0000	Elizabeth Thompson		HDEW 346	1836

M O N T G O M E R Y   C O U N T Y

BIRTHPLACE	NAME OF BIOGRAPHEE	PARENTS/BIRTHPLACE/BIRTHDATE	SOURCE/PAGE	DATE
21 Feb 1821	Isom Adams	Ellington & Elizabeth(Gorden) Ky/**	HCHR 182	----
21 Feb 1831	Isom Adams	Allerton & Elizabeth(Gorden) Ky/Ky	PCHR 387	1833
00 000 0000	Joseph Adams		HCHR 265	----
17 Jan 1833	Hon.Joseph Adams	Ellington & Elizabeth(Gordon) **/x	PCHR 335	----
17 Jan 1823	Joseph Adams	Ellington & Elizabeth(Gorden)**04/**09	HCHR 178	----
00 000 0000	N.C. Bradley[Reynolds]		HCHR 265	----
21 Jan 1811	Tobias S. Bradley	Judge William & Rebecca(Smith)	PEPE 193	----
03 May 1799	Joseph Campbell	Alexander & Jane(Anderson) Va/Va	HSAN 795	1817
00 000 0000	Dr. Richard T. Colliver Samuel		CJRI 250	1852
25 Sep 1810	Isaac N. Craig		COLE 517	1828
25 Sep 1810	Isaac N. Craig	Robert & Elizabeth(Nickel) Va1781/Va	PBCO 466	----
07 Aug 1817	R.O. Crawford	Alexander B & Charlotte(Riggs) Md/Va	PBDP 970	----
01 Jun 1818	Benjamin F. Dooley	Obed & Elizabeth Va/Va	PBDP 763	----
15 Dec 1812	Robert Downs		HEDG 669	1829
11 Dec 1825	Lorenzo D. Evans	John & Ann(Beecraft) Wales/Md	PBSM 293	----
00 000 1825	Martha J. Flooc[Carlin]	William J & Jane(Anderson)	GHHA 697	----
00 000 1798	William Garrett		PBSM 641	----
00 000 0000	H.R. George		HCHR 265	----
26 Feb 1798	James Gill	Captain NJ1757/x	CJRI 351	----
17 Sep 1823	William H. Gillaspie	Simon & Juliette(Halloway) WV/WV	KNOX 676	----
18 Dec 1821	Randel R. Gorden	Randall & Rachel(Baker) Va1784/x	HCHR 183	----
17 Apr 1850	Thomas J. Gorden	William & Lydia E(Ribelin) Ky/Ky	BCHR 890	----
03 Jun 1825	George W. Hainline	George & Flora(Cockerel)	HMCD 639	1838
00 000 1789	Jacob Hainline		HMCD 627	----
14 Mar 1796	John Hainline		HMCD 930	----
07 Sep 1816	John D. Hainlire	George & Flora(Cockerel) Fayette/Tn	HMCD 674	----
07 Sep 1817	John D. Hainlire	George & Flora(Cockerel) Fayette/Tn	CMCD 357	----
30 May 1823	William G. Hairline	George & Flora(Cockerel) Clark/Tn91	CMCD 369	1838
00 000 1842	John W. Hall	Leonard & Angeline(Hammond) Ky/x	BMCL 1069	----
30 Apr 1807	William Hanks		HEDG 670	1828
15 Oct 1844	J.A. Hensley	Evan S & Amis(Anderson) Ky/Ky	PHKX B801	1864
21 Nov 1836	Dr. J.W. Hensley	Evan S & Anis(Anderson) Va/Va	PBKN 515	----
20 Jan 1801	John Hutton		COLE 615	1816

MONTGOMERY COUNTY (CONT.)

BIRTHDATE	NAME OF BIOGRAPHEE	PARENTS/BIRTHPLACE/BIRTHDATE		SOURCE/PAGE		DATE
00 000 0000	James T. Jones			HMAD	582	1875
00 000 0000	Gabriel Keath	Uriah	Va/x	PBAD	361	----
18 Jan 1814	John M. Lockridge	John & Margie(Killough)	Ky/Ky	HSAN	772	----
00 000 1817	W.L. McClintick			HADM	658	1830
00 000 1797	John McDannold	Reuben	Va1750/x	BCSB	246	----
00 000 0000	Thomas I.McDannold	John	Va/x	BCSB	194	----
12 Oct 1825	James Miller			HEDG	588	1834
00 000 1810	G. Morton			PHEF	B249	----
23 Sep 1815	Robert Mosley		Va/x	HEDG	641	----
25 Oct 1834	Susan J. Nelson[Dooley]			HMCL	1001	----
00 000 0000	Susan Nelson[Dooley]	William & Annie(Smith)	Ky/Ky	PBML	1101	----
11 Sep 1813	Elder A.D. Northcutt			HCHR	36	----
11 Sep 1812	Elder Andrew D. Northcutt	William	Va/x	HCHR	183	----
10 Jul 1801	Michael O'Hair			HEDG	672	----
10 Jul 1801	Michael O'Hair			PBCO	542	----
04 Oct 1814	Thomas Payne			HADM	726	1835
12 Jul 1821	John Peugh			HHEN	411	1828
13 Jun 1805	Jesse A. Pickrell			HSAN	1044	----
28 Apr 1838	Marcus F. Pleak	Joseph R & Sarah J(Riblin)	Ky/Ky	PBSM	599	----
09 Oct 1819	Gilbert Pritchett	Lewis & Elizabeth(Grooms)	Va/Va	HWCL	B166	----
24 Dec 1823	James Raffurty	James & Nancy(Booth)		HMAC	214	----
00 000 0000	James Raffurty			HMAC	271	----
18 Oct 1822	W.R. Rayburn			PPWA	337	1823
18 Oct 1822	William R. Rayburn	George	Ky/x	PBWA	309	----
00 000 1801	Polly Reid[Garrett]	Joseph		PBSM	641	----
18 Feb 1817	Parmelia Ribelin[Schulz]			HADM	809	----
22 Apr 1810	Henry Schulz			HADM	809	1839
11 Dec 1822	Shadrach Scott	William L & Africa(Lee)	x/Va	PEPE	400	1828
22 Oct 1830	Judge Andrew Simpson	Thomas & Caroline(Badger)	Ky/Ky	PCHR	364	----
11 Mar 1841	James W. Stevens	Jacob		HFUL	671	----
00 Apr 1810	Matilda[Swain]			HSAN	929	----
22 Apr 1812	George Trimble			HSAN	895	1835

BIRTHDATE	NAME OF BIOGRAPHEE	PARENTS/BIRTHPLACE/BIRTHDATE	SOURCE	PAGE	DATE
00 000 0000	Charles Turley	James	LOGA	814	1829
11 Dec 1822	Charles Turley	Charles	LOGA	643	1823
00 000 1816	Hamilton Turley		HLOG	420	1839
15 Feb 1827	Rebecca J. Wagle[Caldwell]	Asa & Cassandra Ky/Ky	CJRI	567	----
28 Jan 1821	Mary Wheeler[Hancock]		PBDP	695	----
10 Jun 1801	Hon. Archibald Williams		HADM	415	----
10 Jun 1801	Archibald Williams		EFAY	590	----
15 Nov 1795	John A. Williams	John & Amelia(Gill) Va1764/NC	GHHA	785	----
14 Apr 1829	Robert E. Williams	Robert P & Christina A(Urquhart)Ky/Ky	BCSB	500	1850
05 Oct 1837	Robert T. Williams	Col. John & Carolina(Morrow)	PPDM	602	----
29 May 1810	William T. Williams	John Va/x	PJEF	843	----
30 Aug 1854	William Wymore	Dr. Peter	BRJM	507	----
17 Feb 1800	Maj. Stephen Yocum	George & Rebecca(Powell) Va/Va	CMCD	523	----
19 Mar 1829	Samuel N. Young	Thomas R & Mary(McCann)	PHEF	B123	----
19 Mar 1829	Samuel N. Young	Thomas R & Sarah(McCann)	BEFF	893	1845

M O R G A N   C O U N T Y

BIRTHDATE	NAME OF BIOGRAPHEE	PARENTS/BIRTHPLACE/BIRTHDATE	SOURCE/PAGE		DATE
27 Aug 1851	Bedford Cash	James & Sally(Cree) Ky/Kyc06	PSTC	342	----
00 000 0000	F.G. Cockrell		MACL	295	1837
00 000 0000	Elizabeth Craig[Cockrell]		MACL	295	1837
25 Sep 1810	Isaac Craig		PBCO	276	----
10 Dec 1824	James Elledge		HEDG	269	1828
30 Apr 1827	James L. Gillmore	Jeremiah & Mary[Lansaw] A11802/ky1806	PHEF	B210	----
07 Nov 1826	Hon.William Gillmore	Jeremiah & Mary[Landsaw]	BEFF	763	1832
07 Sep 1827	James Hanks	William	PVED	911	1828
24 Feb 1842	R.M. Johnson	John P & Mary(Day) Va/Ky	PAUP	B317	----
04 Apr 1827	J.G. Lycan	NC/x	HEDG	671	----
28 Jan 1820	J.V. Lycan	NC/x	HEDG	672	----
00 000 0000	Hannah Morgan[Moore]	1815/x	PVED	909	----
00 000 1818	Miles Murphy		PBCO	326	----
00 000 1792	William Murphy		PBCO	326	----

BIRTHDATE	NAME OF BIOGRAPHEE	PARENTS/BIRTHPLACE/BIRTHDATE		SOURCE/PAGE		DATE
00 000 0000	Lydia Ogden[Lycan]	Jesse & Nancy(O'Hair)	Va/x	PVED	777	----
22 Jan 1818	Stephen Ogden			HEDG	673	1834
22 Feb 1829	Michael O'Hair	John & Eliza(Hardwick)	Ky/Ky	PBCO	404	----
22 Aug 1822	James S.O'Hair			PBCO	365	----
22 Feb 1829	M.E. O'Hair			COLE	643	1842
14 Nov 1849	Sarah J. Powers[Murphy]	Louis & Emily J(Cox)	Ky/Ky	PBCO	326	----
08 Jan 1833	Ella J. Swango[O'Hair]	Abram		PBCO	542	----
09 Jan 1831	Jesse Swango			HEDG	674	1853

M U H L E N B E R G   C O U N T Y

BIRTHDATE	NAME OF BIOGRAPHEE	PARENTS/BIRTHPLACE/BIRTHDATE		SOURCE/PAGE		DATE
25 Sep 1820	William P. Allensworth			TAZE	710	1830
18 Jun 1825	Rev. John Altic	Abraham & Elizabeth	Pa/Pa	LOGA	888	1829
16 May 1816	B.J. Beard	John & Mary M(Unsel)	Va/Md	PHCC	161	----
19 Apr 1804	Mary F. Bell[Williams]			HADM	799	----
10 Dec 1807	Elizabeth Black[Ashmore]	John		COLE	292	1811
00 000 1803	Alfred Biggerstaff			HGSH	677	----
16 Jun 1826	James Campbell	David M & Jane	Ky/Ky	HADM	736	1830
15 Dec 1825	William C. Davis	Amos & Elizabeth(Coin)	Kyc1800/Ky	HGSH	692	----
18 Feb 1812	Amos Dick	Peter & Christina(Shut)	NC/Pa	PBDP	900	----
18 Feb 1812	Amos Dick	Peter & Christina(Shut)	NC/Pa	HDEW	201	1829
17 Jan 1807	Andrew Gates	Michael & Catherine(Groves)	Pa/NC	HSAN	765	1830
00 000 0000	Frank W. Gates			HMAC	272	1865
23 Dec 1838	Frank W. Gates	Henry	**/x	PBWA	421	----
25 Apr 1815	Sampson Groves	Solomon & Elizabeth(Dukes)		PBWA	831	----
08 Nov 1830	Dr. W.T. Ingram	James	Va1808/x	PRBJ	767	1840
08 Nov 1830	Dr. William T.Ingram	James & Nancy A(Reno)	Va/x	HJAC	73	1840
00 000 1838	D.R. Johnston			HMAC	271	----
00 000 1839	Nancy[Johnston]			HMAC	271	----
13 Dec 1826	J.H. McPherson			PBWO	B197	----
01 Oct 1827	Jonathan Patterson	David & Polly(Harbaugh)	Tn1806/x	PBSM	259	1828

BIRTHDATE	NAME OF BIOGRAPHEE	PARENTS/BIRTHPLACE/BIRTHDATE		SOURCE	PAGE	DATE
25 Apr 1828	Jacob L. Plain	David		PBWA	456	---
25 Apr 1828	Jacob L. Plain	David & ---(Landis)	Md/Va	HMAC	121	---
14 Aug 1825	Andrew Rauch	Jacob & Pauline		HSAN	776	1829
28 Dec 1827	Charles Rauch	Jacob & Pauline(Poley)		HSAN	775	1829
00 000 0000	A.M. Solomon			HMAC	276	1835
04 Oct 1821	Arial M. Solomon	Henry	1799/x	PBWA	553	---
00 000 0000	D.N. Solomon			HMAC	275	1829
11 Jan 1821	Dempsey N.Solomon	Judge Lewis & Sarah(Bowden)	NC/NC	HMAC	224	---
01 Apr 1812	Lewis Solomon			PBWA	761	---
01 Apr 1812	Lewis Solomon			HMAC	271	1827
01 Apr 1812	Judge Lewis Solomon	Lewis		PBWA	761	---
01 Apr 1812	Lewis Solomon	Lewis	NC1780/x	HMAC	219	---
22 Jun 1821	Major W.H. Sumners	David & Mary A(Cash)	NC/NC	PJEF	B33	---
28 May 1845	James Turner			HMEM	857	1854
28 Jan 1842	William C. Turner			HMEM	857	1854
00 000 0000	J.E. Wilkinson			MACL	295	1866
05 Mar 1843	Joseph C. Williams	Samuel	NC1791/x	BRJM	230	---
11 Sep 1833	Samuel H. Welch	Jesse & Sarah(Landers)	Ky/x	PBWB	424	---

N E L S O N   C O U N T Y

BIRTHDATE	NAME OF BIOGRAPHEE	PARENTS/BIRTHPLACE/BIRTHDATE		SOURCE	PAGE	DATE
30 Apr 1834	Charles Blanford			HEDG	692	1837
00 000 0000	Sanford Bond			GSBR	392	1849
08 Jul 1821	John N. Bowlds	John & Jane(Fulkerson)		HWCL	B94	1831
07 Apr 1810	Benjamin F. Brown	Samuel & Henrietta(Hobbs)		HMER	809	1831
17 Mar 1808	Harrison Brown	Samuel & Henrietta,		HMER	637	1834
20 Dec 1803	Harmon G. Brown	Samuel & Henrietta(Hobbs)	Pa/Ky	KNOX	657	1837
22 Dec 1826	Richard Brown			COLE	633	1854
08 Feb 1806	Sarah Brown[Frans]	Simeon & Henrietta(Hobbs)		PBKN	548	---
15 Nov 1815	Joshua G. Burch	John H & Nancy(Greenwell)	Md1782/Md	PBRJ	813	---
00 000 0000	Artemisia Burkhead			HPIK	483	---
09 Jul 1801	James H. Chenoweth	William & Mary(Van Meter)	Va/x	HPIK	483	1832
00 000 0000	Eliza Chrisman[Patrick]	Nathaniel	**/x	PVED	1010	---
02 Oct 1794	Jonah Combs			HMEM	750	---
00 000 0000	Robert Cotton			PVED	485	1822

BIRTHDATE	NAME OF BIOGRAPHEE	PARENTS/BIRTHPLACE/BIRTHDATE		SOURCE/PAGE		DATE
00 000 0000	Elizabeth Crawford[Roby]			CELW	348	1856
00 000 0000	Huldah J[Dorman]			HMAC	271	1848
10 Dec 1829	Dr. W.W. Duncan	James & Editha(McKay)	SC/**	HWCL	B216	----
00 000 0000	Thomas Gant	William & Jane(Holt)	Eng/Eng	PERJ	442	1831
22 Apr 1826	Allen R. Gearheart	Thomas & Ellen	Va/Ky	KNOX	676	----
16 Feb 1818	George H. Hagan	Leonard & Elizabeth(Cook)		KNOX	678	1850
23 Oct 1802	Stephen D. Hambaugh	Henry & Rebecca(Morris)		GSBR	304	1823
00 000 0000	Dr. C. Harris	Edward & Sarah(Wells)	Ky/Ky	CJRI	578	----
24 Jan 1811	Rebecca L. Heady[Lycan]	Stillwell & Susanna(Stonebreaker)		PHCC	208	Ky/Pa
26 Apr 1811	Martial Heavenhill	George		HLAS	B453	1829
00 000 0000	Hannah Howard[Cotton]			PVED	485	----
03 May 1823	Dr. Samuel A.Humphrey	Samuel & Margaret	**/**	PPVE	750	1844
05 Oct 1815	Rev. Thomas W. Hynes	William R & Barbara(Chenault)	Md71/Va93	PBMO	841	----
00 000 0000	William H. Jenkins			HMAC	270	1854
28 Feb 1824	John H. Kendall	Benjamin & Matilda	**1797/x	HSAN	927	1853
00 000 0000	Nathaniel Langley			PVED	697	----
20 Jun 1817	James H. Langsford	Nicholas & Sallie(Tichinor)	Eng/x	HMCD	981	1838
06 May 1795	Major Thomas Long	James	Va/x	HCHR	134	----
00 000 0000	Sarah McCormick[Amis]	Andrew		PVED	407	----
21 Oct 1816	Jonathan McCown	James		HEDG	664	1831
00 Apr 1788	Margaret Neal[Williams]			HSAN	913	1826
00 000 0000	Thomas O'Neal			PPVE	377	1821
00 000 0000	Thomas O'Neal	John		PVED	435	----
21 Jun 1825	George Patrick			HEDG	713	----
00 000 0000	Ruth M. Patrick[Bradley]		Ire/Ire	PVED	931	----
00 000 0000	R.R. Phillips			CELW	352	1851
17 Aug 1838	Capt.William T.Prunty	Robert M & Ann(Heavenhill)	Ky/Ky	CJRI	767	1857
12 Mar 1832	Chilton Rogers	Greenberry & Elizabeth(Shelton)	**/Md	PHCC	293	70/78
16 Dec 1806	Elizabeth Rogers[Clapp]			PBDP	880	----
00 Oc 1848	James P. Slaughter			HEDG	719	1859
23 Jan 1826	Isaac T. Thomas	James & Abigail(Langsford)	Ky/x	HMCH	523	----
00 000 0000	J.T. Thomas	James & Abigail		GHHA	890	----
20 Dec 1819	James M. Thomas	Eleazor & Annie(Garrett)	Ky/Ky	HMCH	417	----

N I C H O L A S   C O U N T Y

BIRTHDATE	NAME OF BIOGRAPHEE	PARENTS/BIRTHPLACE/BIRTHDATE	SOURCE/PAGE	DATE
16 Aug 1832	Martha A Dooley[Young]	William	HMCL 1008	1851
23 Nov 1804	James E. Doughty	John & Jane(Ellis)	GHHA 629	----
00 000 1794	David Foster	James	PBWA 269	----
00 000 0000	J.L. Foster		HMAC 272	1864
20 Jan 1812	Aris Galbreath		COLE 623	----
17 Aug 1809	William H. Galbreath	William H & Phebe(Foreman) Pa/Spencer	PBCO 253	----
15 Jul 1816	Elizabeth A. Hamilton[Morgan]		HMCL 1011	----
00 000 0000	-- Hardin		AMEN 19	1854
26 Oct 1844	Lewis W. Hardin	William & Patsy(Fleming) Va/Ky	BGHR 896	----
12 Feb 1852	Andrew A. Honn	Absalom & Miranda(Moler) Bourbon/Bourbn	PBCO 347	1858
04 Oct 1822	Daniel A. Honn	Daniel & Annie(Erverman) Ky/Ky	PBCO 199	----
09 May 1826	Martha J. Honn[Shulse]	David & Anna	COLE 604	1859
22 Jul 1814	Peter K. Honn	David & Annie(Ebberman) Pa/Ky	PBCO 478	1835
22 Jul 1814	Elder Peter K.Honn	Daniel & Anna	COLE 599	1835
05 Jan 1819	S.D. Honn		HEDG 618	----
00 000 0000	Nancy E. Hook[Honn]	Mathias & Matilda(Huddleston) Ky/Ky	PBCO 199	----
15 Feb 1832	B.F. Howes	Reuben & Catherine Md/Ky	GHHA 631	1850
00 000 1836	Elizabeth J. Huddleston[Crawford]		HMOR 718	----
22 Dec 1829	William W. James	Alexander C & Mary A(Robinson)Md/De	PBSM 639	1831
08 Jun 1806	Mary Kennedy[Yates]	Thomas Pa/x	PHEF B122	----
14 Nov 1852	James B. Lewis	O.M & Elizabeth(Mann) Ky1824/**	BRCM 57	----
14 Nov 1853	James B. Lewis	Orin M & Elizabeth F(Hibler)NY26/**33	PBCW 269	----
07 Jun 1819	Nancy A. Kincade[McLaughlin]		HADM 805	----
22 Jan 1854	Edmund C. King	Rev. Clark & Margaret F(Martin)	HADM 829	----
05 Apr 1817	Eleanor K. Lockridge[Wilson]		HLOG 477	1866
00 000 0000	William McClintock		HSTC 374	----
25 Jul 1791	James McCoy	John & Mary(Eberman)	HSAN 1006	----
25 Jul 1791	James McCoy		HSAN 987	1818
00 00c 1816	James McCune		PBWC 476	1826
08 May 1830	Sarah J. McCune[Nichols]		HADM 806	----
15 Jun 1830	Robert W. McMahan	Andrew & Mary	GHHA 632	1831
20 Oct 1826	T. Jefferson McMahill		PPWA 325	1838
16 Apr 1819	--- McWilson		PPWA 325	1838

Date	Name	Parentage / Spouse	Code	No.	Year
00 000 0000	Malinda Martin[Dehart]		CSBR	391	1864
16 May 1806	Gerard Morgan		HMCL	1011	----
00 000 1813	William E. Morgan		CHAM	995	----
19 Apr 1813	William F. Morgan	Gerrard & Sarah(Sanderson) Va1772/Va77	BCHA	624	----
18 Jan 1804	Woodson Morgan		HCHA	133	----
04 Oct 1824	Sally Munson[Turney]		PBCO	310	----
04 Jul 1808	J.B. Nickel		HMCD	304	----
00 000 1814	Thomas M. Powell		PVED	820	1834
00 000 0000	H. Rayburn		ACLY	49	1851
00 000 0000	T.H. Riley		CHAM	1012	----
23 Nov 1843	B.H. Shankland	A.G & Judith(Stoops) **/**	HCAS	299	1853
17 Oct 1827	A.J. Shulse	Henry & Winnifred Ky/Va	COLE	604	1859
21 Sep 1821	Daniel Smith	Nathan & Mary(Killam) Md/**	PBSM	291	----
20 Feb 1831	Lawson H. Smith	William & Elizabeth(Henderson)Ky/Ky	HSAN	1009	----
22 Apr 1831	Samuel Stoops		BMCL	1306	----
00 000 0000	Maria Tarr[Spicer]		PBAD	281	----
05 Jul 1822	Margaret Taylor[Holliday]		HMOR	718	----
17 Jan 1816	Rev. Prestor W Thomson James H.	Pa/x	HMCD	714	----
04 Oct 1854	George B. Tucker		PVED	954	----
08 Jun 1830	William H. Victor	Ambrose D & Eliza(Sturgis) Ky/Ky	PBML	943	----
00 000 0000	Aaron Wells		BKAN	656	----
00 000 0000	James Walls		HEDG	691	----
00 000 1820	Judge Richard B.Warfield	Richard & Sarah(Wadkins)Md73/Md83	HGSH	664	----
00 000 1805	Aaron Wells		BKAN	656	----
30 Apr 1828	William W. Wes-	Elijah & Elizabeth(Henderson) De/Md	HSAN	781	----
24 Dec 1830	Ann E. White[Gayle]		LOGA	874	1830
19 Jan 1826	Joseph W. Whor-on	Ky1796/x	HWOR	751	----
00 000 0000	Sarah J. Wood[Victor] Nimrod		PBML	943	----
19 Nov 1807	Joab Yates		PHEF	B122	----
13 May 1838	Joseph Yates	Joab & Mary(Kennedy) **1807/**1806	PHEF	B121	----

THIS IS THE THIRD VOLUME IN THE KENTUCKIANS IN . . . SERIES. PREVIOUS VOLUMES COVERED THE STATES OF MISSOURI, OHIO AND INDIANA.

BIRTHDATE	NAME OF BIOGRAPHEE	PARENTS/BIRTHPLACE/BIRTHDATE	SOURCE/PAGE	DATE
14 Sep 1825	A.B. Allen	Asa & Abigail(Campbell) Tn/Ky	HPIK 612	1844
00 000 0000	William T. Barnard	Garrett & Martha A(Morton) Ky/Ky	LOGA 630	----
21 Mar 1833	James N. Barnett		PPWO 548	1850
16 Sep 1830	Lilburn D. Bennett	Asa & Delilah(Woodward) Md/Md	HWCL B7	----
28 Mar 1825	J.R. Carter	William Va1790/x	HWCL B45	----
00 000 0000	Sarah C. Carter[Walser]		CELW 357	1872
00 000 0000	A.S. Cox		HJAC 128	1840
00 000 0000	David Cox		HJAC 131	1845
00 000 0000	G.W. Cox		HJAC 128	1857
00 000 0000	Alfred Davis		HJAC 128	1840
00 000 0000	Philip R. Davis		HJAC 128	1840
00 000 0000	Rev. Philip Davis	Gideon Md/x	PBRJ 736	----
23 Jan 1830	Edwin Hedrick	Samuel & Sarah(Lucas) Oh/SC	BRCM 373	1841
19 Jan 1817	Asahel Hinman	George W & Nancy(Stewart) Bullitt91/Ky	HPIK 493	----
00 000 1845	Dr. C.O. Kelly	Rev. C.J & Plina H(Haynes) **1818/**23	HGSH 794	----
00 000 0000	Jane M[Lawler]		HFAY 96	1837
15 Jun 1838	Richard P. Nall	Larkin & Juliet(Griffin) Ky/Va	LOGA 854	----
15 Jun 1838	Richard P. Nall	Larcan & Julia(Griffin) Ky/Va	BLOG 248	----
00 000 0000	Alexander Peck		HFAY 97	1838
15 Aug 1830	Thomas M. Rogers	Samuel R & Sarah(Morgan)	HWCL B33	----
12 Dec 1809	Elizabeth Sumner[Hammett]		HPEO 728	----
15 Sep 1816	Judge Samuel J.R.Wilson	Thomas M & Rachel(Fulkerson)	HWCL B16	1822

O L D H A M   C O U N T Y

BIRTHDATE	NAME OF BIOGRAPHEE	PARENTS/BIRTHPLACE/BIRTHDATE	SOURCE/PAGE	DATE
00 000 0000	R.H. Barrick		HMAC 274	1836
31 Mar 1810	Reuben P. Bell	Robert F & Mary(Pemberton) Pa/Ky	PBWO 353	----
19 Jan 1805	J.F. Boyer		HEDG 613	----
18 Oct 1820	John K. Boyer	Frederick & Naomi(Kester) Pa/**	PVED 779	----

OWEN COUNTY

Birthdate	Name of Biographee	Parents/Birthplace/Birthdate	Source	Page	Date
27 Nov 1810	Allen Clore	Benjamin & Ann(Christopher) Va/Va	PBSM	667	----
09 Jun 1819	William M. Curry	Daniel & Susan(Stafford) Jefferson/Jeff	HADM	738	1837
00 000 1823	O.T. Ellis		HADM	620	----
17 Mar 1845	George T. Feathergill William	Ky/x	PBAD	220	----
27 Nov 1834	Capt. James H. Glore Milburn & Sarah(Clark)	**/**	PPDM	682	----
00 000 0000	Cornelia E. Gurton[Walden]		CJRI	280	----
30 Mar 1828	Western R. Humphrey	John M & Frances(Nay) Ky/Ky	CJRI	237	1829
27 Dec 1824	James M. Jett		PBMO	B74	----
27 Dec 1824	James W. Jett	William B & Clarissa(Parker) Va/In	PBMB	484	----
16 Dec 1827	Dr. Abram L. Kellar	Abraham H & Rebecca(Netherton)Tn/Tn	PBSM	653	----
10 Oct 1825	Thomas Lacy	Jesse & Lucy(Willhite) Va/Va	CJRI	331	c1834
25 Jul 1824	Richard J. Oglasby		PBWA	163	----
00 000 1833	John W. Mars		HADM	725	1842
14 Jan 1824	William Nay	Sanford & Nancy(Bennett) Va/Ky	PVED	1010	----
25 Jul 1824	Richard J. Oglasby		PBWA	183	----
00 000 0000	William S. Outhouse		MACL	299	1830
14 Jan 1821	A.J. Pinnell	Edward	HEDG	621	----
14 Jan 1821	A.J. Pinnell	Edward & Nancy(Ross) Va1795/**	PBCO	345	----
03 Apr 1826	J.J. Pinnell	Joseph	HEDG	623	----
14 Nov 1828	W.J.S.Pinnell	Abraham	HEDG	622	----
14 Nov 1828	William Pinnell	Abraham & Frances M(Estes)	PVED	952	----
24 Jan 1824	Willis O. Pinnell	George & Lucy(Christopher) Va/Va	PVED	1105	----
16 Nov 1816	Sarah Roney[Tyler]	James & Mary(Aiken) Va/Va	PBWC	530	----
02 Jul 1818	Harrison Shroder		HEDG	645	1828
22 May 1822	Jefferson Shroder		HEDG	644	1836
00 000 0000	E.F. Taylor		AMOU	8	----
18 Jul 1821	Samuel Walden		CJRI	280	----
07 Dec 1828	Capt. A.T. Welman	Andrew A & Elizabeth(Williams)Va/Ky	CJRI	340	1845
00 000 1816	Mary J. Wright[Lilly]		PBSM	541	----

BIRTHDATE	NAME OF BIOGRAPHEE	PARENTS/BIRTHPLACE/BIRTHDATE	SOURCE/PAGE		DATE
00 000 0000	Paulina Bowen[Johnson]		CELW	351	1874

OWEN COUNTY (CONT.)

BIRTHDATE	NAME OF BIOGRAPHEE	PARENTS/BIRTHPLACE/BIRTHDATE	SOURCE/PAGE	DATE
22 Feb 1820	S.S. Chandler	Scott/x	HEDG	668	1852
27 Aug 1825	Samuel Garvey	Samuel & Maria(Elliston)	HSAN	959	1830
22 Aug 1829	William F. Garvey	Samuel	HSAN	927	----
00 000 0000	Sarah Hughes[McClain]		PPPI	144	----
00 000 0000	James M. Johnston		HCHA	180	1855
11 Nov 1823	Triplett L. Jones	Shelton & Elizabeth(Squires) Ky/Ky	PEDP	386	----
30 Jan 1827	Frederick Razor		HMCL	977	----
11 Feb 1835	Dr. John H. Shelton	Austin & Emily(Callender) Va/Va	PBSM	674	1879
17 May 1819	Julia G. Stafford[Tandy]		HADM	809	----
00 000 1807	John F. Swegert		HCHR	267	----
00 000 0000	Rachel[Turpin]		HSAN	929	----
08 May 1842	Elizabeth Wilhoit[Barclay] Willis C & Marie(Hancock)		HMCL	958	1852
30 Oct 1845	Irene R. Wilhoite	Alexander & Sarah(Gossett) **/**	PBML	894	----
24 Apr 1829	Lewis J. Wilhoite	Lewis & Patsey(Taylor) **/Ky	PBML	1002	----

OWSLEY COUNTY

BIRTHDATE	NAME OF BIOGRAPHEE	PARENTS/BIRTHPLACE/BIRTHDATE	SOURCE/PAGE	DATE
00 000 1808	Nicholas Darnall		BRML	584	1828
00 000 1808	Nicholas Darnall		PBML	720	----
08 Nov 1814	John M. Little	Henry & Elizabeth(Jackson)	HSTC	260	1850
24 Nov 1823	George W. Pleasants		PPRI	301	1853
23 Nov 1823	Judge George W. Pleasants		BRKI	1360	----

PENDLETON COUNTY

BIRTHDATE	NAME OF BIOGRAPHEE	PARENTS/BIRTHPLACE/BIRTHDATE	SOURCE/PAGE	DATE

20 May 1825	Hadassah Best[Feagan]	Thomas & Elizabeth		Ky/Ky	PBCO	219	----
00 000 0000	Nancy[Brownfie-d]				HCHA	179	1833
01 Sep 1822	J.M. Bryan	Luke & Mary(Sanders)		NC/NC	HWCL	B225	----
15 Feb 1825	James R. Chambers				PBMC	413	----
20 Apr 1823	Laban Chambers	James & Nancy(Buoy)	**1791/Va	PBMC	596	----
15 May 1826	Thomas Chambers	James	1791/x	PBMC	517	----
24 Feb 1815	David P. Colvin			HADM	801	----
24 Feb 1815	D.P. Colvin	George & Nancy(Davis)	Va1784/89	PBAD	229	----
00 000 0000	Dr.Prometheus E.Duvall	James W & Melinda W(Colvin)	Va/Va	PBCO	564	----
26 Sep 1800	Mary[Forsyth]			HADM	802	----
00 000 1853	M.M. Fox	B.S & Sarah(McChesney) Hopk24/Caldw32	HGSH	616	----
19 Dec 1809	Francis Hendricks[Swinford]			COLE	645	----
17 Aug 1797	Frederick Hendricks			HMCD	658	----
27 Feb 1867	Charles Huddlestor	George R & Melinda(Pribble)	BRCM	583	----
22 Aug 1855	Dr. William J. Jayne			BEFF	633	----
22 Aug 1855	Dr. William J. Jayne	Alexander & Sophrona(Highfill)Ky19/Ky25	PHEF	B130	----
15 Oct 1818	John McNay			PBAD	564	----
12 Apr 1825	Dr.George W. Marshall	Stephen & Hannah(Sinks)	Md/x	PBAD	433	----
00 000 1811	John Nicholson			PBAD	191	----
06 Mar 1829	Agnes E. Rawlings[Tindall]			HADM	809	----
04 Jun 1841	James H. Record	William S & Susannah(Said)	PPDM	580	----
16 Dec 1847	S.H. Record	William S & Martha(Said)	Tn/Oh	PBCO	371	1857
00 000 0000	Ebenezer Riddle			HADM	796	1829
00 000 1822	George D. Riddle	George D.	Ky/x	PBAD	179	----
30 Apr 1828	P.M. Riley[Tucker]			HEDG	715	----
09 Jan 1819	William P. Smith	William & Martha(Johnson)	Va/Va	PEPE	802	----
03 Dec 1824	William CW.Sterne	John W & Elizabeth(Duncan)Va1792/**01	PBAD	431	----
08 Dec 1824	William C.W. Sterne	John W & Elizabeth(Duncan) Va1792/01	HADM	732	1829
26 Mar 1821	Joel F. Watson	John W	Md/x	PJEF	B39	----
15 Aug 1854	Sarah E. Watson[Duvall]	Joseph M & Hannah W	PBCO	564	----
14 May 1804	Joel G. Williams			HADM	799	----

P E R R Y   C O U N T Y   (N O N E)

BIRTHDATE	NAME OF BIOGRAPHEE	PARENTS/BIRTHPLACE/BIRTHDATE	SOURCE/PAGE	DATE
07 Apr 1824	L.J. Adkins	Elijah	HMCL 934	1854

P O W E L L C O U N T Y (N O N E)

P U L A S K I C O U N T Y

BIRTHDATE	NAME OF BIOGRAPHEE	PARENTS/BIRTHPLACE/BIRTHDATE	SOURCE/PAGE	DATE
15 Dec 1819	Rhoda Adams[Allen]	James & Elizabeth	HMCD 970	----
18 Feb 1843	James Allen	Thompson & Rhoda(Adams) Ky1819/x	HMCH 565	----
29 Aug 1819	Rufus T. Allen	David & Patsey(Harris) SC/Va	HMCD 970	----
00 000 1822	Robert Barber		CMCD 595	1829
15 Dec 1871	Dr.Brent L.Barker	William M & Malenda(Sievers)**36/Ger	PPPI 332	----
01 Dec 1836	William M. Barker	James I & Canada(Simpson) Va1795/x	PPPI 339	----
07 Jan 1826	William Bray	Nathan & Catherine(Ranard) NC/Ky	GHHA 845	----
00 000 1844	Green Burgess		HPEO 812	----
11 May 1818	Reuben R. Debord		HPEO 814	1839
14 May 1810	James Eoff		PHCC 340	1849
00 000 1851	William S. Freeman	Stephen F.	HPIK 728	----
17 Dec 1852	James M. Gooch	Stephen C & Mary(Eoff) Ky/x	PHCC 85	----
28 Jan 1810	George Hammer		VTBU 223	1849
00 000 0000	John Hart	Benjamin & Nancy(Blankinship) Ky/Ky	HGJR 307	----
00 000 0000	O.D. Jasper	Thomas & Elizabeth(Dunham) Ky/Ky	HMOR 642	1841
00 000 1812	Thomas Jasper		HADM 643	1837
09 Nov 1815	David B. Jones	Joshua & Elizabeth(Barrow) Va/NC	HGJR 1071	----
11 Apr 1811	William L. King		HADM 804	1830
03 Jun 1820	Charles Lee		HCHA 163	----
03 Feb 1847	James H. Lee	Squire & Elizabeth A(James)**1820/**21	BCHA 570	----

BIRTHDATE	NAME OF BIOGRAPHEE	PARENTS/BIRTHPLACE/BIRTHDATE	SOURCE/PAGE	DATE
11 Aug 1804	Henry B. Meek	Bazel & Ellen(Roberts) Va1763/NC1777	PPWO 542	----
00 000 0000	H.H. Meek		AWOO 5	1830
00 000 0000	Mary[Phillips]		HCHA 181	1867
00 000 1820	George W. Ratekin	Va/Va	KNOX 701	----
17 Apr 1813	G.W. Smith	Joseph & Hannah	COLE 619	1823
00 000 0000	Letha Thomas[Conover]		HCHR 263	1873
29 Jul 1829	Washington H. Wade		HADM 855	1829
06 Jul 1844	John H. Weddle	Samuel & Anna(Spencer)	PBDP 780	----
00 000 0000	Sarah A[Young]		HMAC 276	1877

R O B E R T S O N   C O U N T Y   (N O N E)

R O C K C A S T L E   C O U N T Y

BIRTHDATE	NAME OF BIOGRAPHEE	PARENTS/BIRTHPLACE/BIRTHDATE	SOURCE/PAGE	DATE
26 Feb 1808	J.C. Bethuram		PPRI 465	----
00 Mar 1836	James B. Crawford	Harrison & Alice(Thompson) Ky/Ky	GHHA 699	1850
00 000 0000	James Laswell		AGLY 50	1852
02 Feb 1822	S.W. Pope		HEDG 665	----
00 000 0000	Ann Quinn[Six]		CSBR 387	1851
00 000 0000	L.W. Roberts		AMEN 26	1862
26 Apr 1809	Benjamin Stewart		HPIK 466	----
00 000 0000	Elitha Tate[Notes]		BHAN 215	----
25 Nov 1835	William Wilson	James Va/x	HMGH 340	----

R O W A N   C O U N T Y   (N O N E)

BIRTHDATE	NAME OF BIOGRAPHEE	PARENTS/BIRTHPLACE/BIRTHDATE	SOURCE/PAGE	DATE
19 Aug 1826	Hardin Elmore	Hiram & Sarah(Walker) NC/Ky	PEMB 510	----
00 000 0000	M.M. Elmore		HFAY 98	1833
14 Oct 1831	Dr. J.S. Garner		COLE 615	----
14 Oct 1831	Dr. J.S. Garner	Paris & Sarah L(Pierce) NC1801/1806	PECO 355	----
20 Mar 1851	Edgar M. Heafer	Napoleon B & Elizabeth C(Clark)WV/**	PEML 213	----
01 Oct 1834	J.E. Lane	Gholson & Mary(James) Ky/Ky	HMCH 312	----
01 Oct 1834	John E. Lane	Gholson & Mary(Jones)	HMCD 1146	1836
01 Oct 1834	John E. Lane	Ghalson & Mary(Jones) Ky/Ky	HMCD 325	1836
14 Nov 1825	Martha Sheppard[Grider]	Elder Thornton NC1796/x	HGJR 980	----

BIRTHDATE	NAME OF BIOGRAPHEE	PARENTS/BIRTHPLACE/BIRTHDATE	SOURCE/PAGE	DATE
02 Mar 1812	Jacob T. Adams		HEDG 668	1825
08 Feb 1822	David S. Allen	Joseph & Katherine(Skilman) Va/x	PPDM 822	----
08 Feb 1822	David S. Allen	Joseph & Catherine(Skillman)	PEMC 588	----
00 000 0000	G.W. Bates		CSBR 387	1852
10 Dec 1800	William Burt		TAZE 489	1827
02 Sep 1838	James P. Butler	William H & Hattie J(Spicer) Ky/Ky	BRML 139	----
10 Feb 1857	William K. Crockett	Col.William D & Eliza(Ware) c1819/x	BROC 179	----
10 Feb 1856	William K. Crockett	William D & Eliza(Ware)	BRKI 1084	----
00 000 0000	Samuel Cummings		HMAC 277	1825
21 Dec 1813	Capt.Samuel Cummings	John Va1763/x	HMAC 256	----
00 000 0000	F.M. Curry		CSBR 385	1830
00 000 0000	Harriet P. Curry[Taylor]		CSBR 387	1830
00 000 0000	Robert N. Curry		CSBR 385	1830
12 Feb 1802	Robert N. Curry	Alexander & Elizabeth(Nutter)Mq70/De76	HMAC 256	----
00 000 0000	Joseph W. Ewing		HLOG 411	1856
05 Jun 1809	John P. Gano		HEDG 639	----

Date	Name	Parents / Notes	Origin	Code	No.	Year
27 Aug 1827	George F. Hackett			COLE	568	1834
00 000 0000	Levi Hackett			COLE	522	1835
00 000 0000	Adaline Johnson[Scott]			BCSB	197	1831
00 000 0000	Peter B. Karnes			HMAC	273	----
00 000 0000	Dr. B.C. Keene			HEDG	581	----
00 000 0000	Stout Kendrick			CSBR	387	1835
10 Sep 1813	William H. Kendrick			CMCD	598	1839
30 Sep 1846	Victor M. Kenny	Joseph B & Lavina(Lander)	Bourb06/Bour08	HSAN	1032	----
00 000 1810	John P. Kinkade			HMCD	729	----
14 Jun 1842	Reuben Lancaster	Lewis & Jane(Mallory)	**/**	BCSB	352	1866
01 Oct 1808	Stewart Lindsey	Robert	Va/Woodford	HPIK	435	----
00 000 0000	Elijah Lucas			PVED	504	----
21 Mar 1813	J.H. Lurton			HMOR	698	1832
00 000 0000	Nancy A. Mabee[Course]			HMAD	583	1835
00 000 0000	Bancy A. Mabee[Kinder]			HMAD	583	1835
00 000 0000	Nancy A. Mabee[Wood]			HMAD	583	1835
12 Feb 1817	Alexander MacHetton	Samuel & Sarah	1783/1795	PHCC	332	----
09 Nov 1807	William H. McMiller			HMOR	668	1833
00 000 1814	B.F. Martin			HMCD	1077	----
00 0c 1825	Lewis Massey	William & Nancy	**/**	HMOR	623	1836
30 May 1812	Jesse Moore	Jesse & Margaret(Hedger)	Va/Va	PVED	908	----
00 000 0000	Daniel Morris			PBDP	689	1839
00 000 0000	George W. Morris			HEDG	672	----
18 Aug 1821	J.C. Mulberry	James & Judy Ann(LaForce)	Va/Ky	HGJR	877	----
13 Sep 1817	John McAuley Palmer			BRMA	133	----
13 Sep 1817	John M. Palmer			PEMA	166	----
18 Jul 1847	Mary E.D. Parker	Fielding & Phebe(Hughes)		PBCO	458	----
00 000 0000	Martha Patterson[Threlkeld]	Mathew & Margaret(McHatten)		PBCO	280	Pa/Pa
00 000 0000	Amanda Price[Curry]			CSBR	257	----
00 000 0000	Amanda M. Price[Curry]			CSBR	385	1831
00 000 0000	James R. Price			AMEN	23	1865
00 000 0000	Sophia Price[Brockman]			BCSB	131	----
29 Dec 1829	Amanda Risk[Allen]	John & Anna(Dougherty)	Va/Va	PEMC	588	----
00 000 0000	Nancy B. Ritchey	--- & Catherine(Bronson)	Va/Va	PEML	672	----
00 000 0000	Isaac Roberts	Azariah & Lucy(Smith)		PBCO	431	1828
31 Aug 1818	Dr. Samuel R. Saltonstall			TAZE	658	----

BIRTHDATE	NAME OF BIOGRAPHEE	PARENTS/BIRTHPLACE/BIRTHDATE	SOURCE/PAGE	DATE
15 Mar 1837	Jesse W. Scott	Thomas & Elizabeth	TAZE 647	1843
18 Apr 1848	Dr. Thomas W.Scott	Thomas W & Catherine(Fitzgerald)	BCSB 188	----
11 Aug 1832	Edward L. Shepherd	William & Evaline(Ball) Va/Va	PBSM 659	1846
00 000 1819	William R. Shirley		BLOG 468	----
17 Oct 1815	John Short	Pennell & Jane(Butler) De/In	HGJR 836	1831
04 Apr 1804	William K. Smith		HPIK 439	1839
00 Dec 1815	George Stevens		HSAN 739	----
12 Nov 1842	Wilbur F. Stevenson	Evan Va1???/Va.	PBDP 233	----
25 Dec 1813	William Stevenson	James & Mary(Elliott)	HCAS 328	1829
02 Dec 1813	William Stevenson	James & Mary(Elliott) Oh/Ky	BCSB 373	----
02 Apr 1838	Benjamin F. Stodgell		BCHR 994	----
30 Jan 1816	Elihu Stout	Philemon & Penelope(Anderson)	HSAN 777	1836
19 Apr 1822	Philemon Stout	Philemon & Penelope(Anderson) NJ/NJ	HSAN 801	1836
29 Jan 1823	F.M. Stout	Isaac & Lydia(Baxter) **/Ky	CSBR 328	----
00 000 0000	Francis M. Stout	Isaac & Lydia(Baxter) **/Ky	CSBR 390	1844
29 Jan 1822	Francis M. Stout		BCSB 350	1844
08 Jan 1830	John Thompson	John & Mary Va/x	HMOR 675	----
01 Oct 1852	John C. Thomas	James Q & Mary(West) Ky/Ky	ECHA 62	----
00 000 0000	Rev. Thomas Threlkeld	Jesse & Lucinda(Campbell) Va/Va.	PBCO 280	----
00 000 1813	Maj. Harrison Tyner		PHEF B178	----
04 Dec 1800	Jacob Ward		CASS 976	1829
26 Jun 1822	William W. Ward	William A & Nancy(Wirt) Ky/Va	BCSB 393	1844
05 Nov 1834	Thomas W. Watts	Simeon & Hannah D. **/x	BCSB 463	1838
05 Dec 1830	John C. White		COLE 591	1849
25 Sep 1826	Henry J. Williams	Thompson	HPIK 466	----
08 Apr 1820	Jane Williams[Stewart]	Thompson & Sarah A(Smith)	HPIK 466	----
05 Jun 1808	William Wright	James & Frances(Finnie) Va/Va.	HMOR 586	1829

SHELBY COUNTY

BIRTHDATE	NAME OF BIOGRAPHEE	PARENTS/BIRTHPLACE/BIRTHDATE	SOURCE/PAGE	DATE

Date	Name	Parents/Spouse	Origin	Code	No.	Year
14 Nov 1832	Andrew J. Aller	Stephen & Elizabeth(Jackson)	**/**	HCHA	101	----
29 Jan 1822	Hon.James C. Allen	Benjamin & Margaret(Youel)	Va/Va	CJRI	724	----
29 Jan 1822	Hon.James C. Allen	Benjamin & Margaret(Youel)	Va/Va	BRCM	84	1834
00 000 0000	Paula E. Atchison[Eskew]			HDEW	346	----
10 Jul 1817	Damaris[Barnsback]			HMAD	535	----
02 Jan 1827	Dr. William F. Bayne	William & Barabara(Blankenbaker)	Va/Bour	HMCH	331	1831
26 Sep 1825	Emily Booth	Stephen		HADM	801	----
00 000 0000	Stephen Boyd			HCHA	176	----
17 Dec 1804	Stephen Boyd	William & Elizabeth(Wiley)		ECHA	67	----
00 May 1839	Cornelius G. Bradshaw			HMCL	768	----
00 000 0000	George Bristow	Gideon		HWCL	B129	1848
00 000 0000	A. Busey		Va/x	HCHA	176	1829
06 Jul 1798	Fontain J. Busey	Samuel		HCHA	180	----
00 000 0000	Matthew W. Busey	Samuel	SC/x	BCHA	615	----
29 Apr 1825	Matthew W. Busey	Samuel & Catherine(Seigler)	NC1768/Va76	CHAM	884	----
00 000 0000	Nancy D. Busey[Staney]			HCHA	120	----
20 Mar 1801	R.R. Busey	Matthew & Sarah(Fibel)	Ger/Ger	BCHA	418	1831
10 Sep 1825	Elizabeth Bush[Busey]			BCHA	615	----
15 May 1798	Elizabeth Bush[Busey]			CHAM	885	----
24 Feb 1850	James Boyd	Stephen & Jemina(Kitson)	**/Ky	ECHA	30	1869
30 Sep 1842	Col. Matthew W. Busey	Samuel & Catherine(Seigler)		ECHA	35	1827
00 000 0000	F.W. Chrisman			HMCL	771	----
27 Mar 1834	C.S. Churchill	George & Sarah(Arnold)	Va/Va	HSAN	855	----
00 000 0000	Elizabeth Collings[Bristow]	William		HWCL	B129	1835
00 000 0000	Dr. W.H. Cook	Fielding B & Meekee(Rosebery)	**/**	PEMB	272	----
00 000 0000	John Coots			HMAC	271	----
17 Jan 1826	Jesse Crim	John	Va/x	HGSH	773	1877
00 000 0000	E.C. Dedman			HCHA	179	1830
00 000 0000	Moses Deere	Larkin & Elizabeth(Constantine)	Va/Ky	BCHA	291	1847
00 000 0000	Amelia Duncan[Wightman]			MACL	298	----
00 000 0000	Mary E. Featheringill[Walker]			HADM	810	1830
00 000 0000	Nancy A. Fink[Solomon]			HMAC	271	----
05 Jun 1814	John N. Fullinwider	Henry & Harriet(Neil)	Pa/Va	HSAN	959	----
01 May 1829	Zachariah Gill			ECHA	44	1852
01 May 1829	Zachariah E. Gill	Bede & Eliza(Edlin)	Va/x	BCHA	60	1853

BIRTHDATE	NAME OF BIOGRAPHEE	PARENTS/BIRTHPLACE/BIRTHDATE	SOURCE/PAGE	DATE
00 000 1803	Scott R. Graham	John S.	HLOG 430	1854
00 000 0000	Tevis Greathouse		HFAY 52	----
00 000 1805	William Green	James Eng/x	HEDG 669	----
00 000 1831	Dr. Benjamin M. Griffith		HSAN 670	----
12 Jun 1841	Willson D. Grow		HMCL 915	----
11 Mar 1832	O.H. Hall	Benjamin L & Evaline(Pickrell)	HSAN 960	1823
12 Apr 1828	Gilbert B. Hankins	Gilbert & Rebecca(Caress) Va/Ky	PCHR 342	----
05 Apr 1818	Baxter D. Harbison	David Jr. & Martha. D(Venable) x/Va	BCHA 44	----
17 Sep 1845	Warren M. Hill	William F & Mary(Maxwell) Me/Me	BCHA 261	----
28 Sep 1829	Jesse Hinkle	--- & Jessie(Oglesby) **1802/Ky97	PAUP B21	----
00 000 0000	Lydia A. Holden		HCHR --	----
13 Sep 1819	Dr. Robert J. Hornsby Joseph		PBWA 206	----
10 Aug 1811	Claybourn Jones	William & Elizabeth(Sutherland)Va/Ky	PBMC 707	----
13 Jul 1817	Damaris[Judy]		HMAD 535	----
23 Mar 1881	Louis E. Jordan	Rev. Henry F & Sue L(Beard)**1840/x	BCHR 916	----
09 Oct 1876	Winfield B. Jordan	Rev. Henry F & Sue L(Beard)**1840/x	BCHR 916	----
24 Mar 1814	F.S. Kester		HEDG 582	----
00 000 0000	Dr. William T. Kirk	Allen T & Frances E	HLOG 434	----
22 Feb 1799	David Locke		HGJR 1026	----
17 May 1815	Harrison D. Lyon	Henson & Nancy(McCoun) Va1790/Clark95	HSAN 1025	----
00 000 1825	Lorrin McClure[Thompson]	Greenup & Mary(Marcumpsey)	HMCD 703	----
00 000 0000	William H. McClair		BCHR 938	----
00 000 0000	Nancy A. McMullen[Ross]		HMAC 270	1836
11 Oct 1813	Mahala A. Marston		PBCO 363	1836
23 Jul 1811	John A. Metcalfe		HEDG 664	1828
27 Jan 1827	Jeremiah Miller	Dabner & Elizabeth	LOGA 587	1829
28 Dec 1821	Rebecca Miller[Jones]	Reuben & Nancy(Sturgeon) Ky/Ky	PBPE 198	----
07 Aug 1810	Matthias Mount		TAZE 457	1833
00 000 0000	Octavia Mount[Longmate]		HDEW 342	1861
13 Sep 1817	John McAuley Palmer	Louis D & Ann(Hansford) Va/Va	HMAC 89	----
22 Feb 1822	V.A. Payne		HEDG 594	1843
17 May 1807	W.K. Payne	John & Elizabeth(Wright) Ky/Ky	COLE 603	1822

Date	Name	Parents / Notes	Origin	Code	No.	Year
04 Oct 1828	Robert Plunkett			PHCC	316	---
18 Dec 1815	Samuel Pulliam	James & Susan(Greer)	Va/Va	HMCD	639	---
00 000 1806	Nancy Ratcliff[McLean]	Joseph & Mary(Bryant)	Va1781/Va82	PBAD	376	---
00 000 0000	Benjamin P. Reid			HWCL	B134	---
22 Nov 1834	Seaton S. Rice	Strother G & Hannah(Underwood)	**/**	PVED	869	1832
02 Oct 1827	Andrew J. Richey	Robert & Elizabeth(Biggs)	Ky/Ky	PPPI	176	---
02 Oct 1827	Andrew J. Richey	Robert & Elizabeth(Biggs)	Ky/Ky	PBSM	618	1832
00 000 0000	James N. Rigg			CSBR	382	1869
00 000 0000	George L. Ritter			HMAC	271	1872
23 Jul 1827	Hannah E. Robinson			COLE	585	---
00 000 0000	Lawrence Roby			CELW	350	1858
00 000 0000	Meekee Roseberry[Cook]	Charles	Va/x	PBMB	272	---
09 Mar 1829	Caroline M. Rucker[Suggett]			HWCL	B208	---
30 Jul 1823	Posey Rush	Abraham & Mary(Mattox)	Pa1800/Va1802	PHCC	294	---
00 000 0000	Francis S. Scott			HDEW	345	1840
03 Mar 1832	James R. Scott		Ky/x	HGHA	78	---
00 000 0000	Mary A. Scott[Warner]			MACL	294	1857
00 000 0000	Isham Scroggar			CSBR	393	1840
07 Feb 1813	William Shannon	Hugh & Sarah(Kendall)	Ire/x	PBML	672	---
00 000 0000	James M. Sharp			CELW	357	1825
00 000 0000	Nancy Sharpe[Talbot]	Benjamin	Md/x	PBCO	530	---
10 Aug 1820	John D. Street	David & Catherine(Duncan)		PBMO	B267	---
00 000 0000	William S. Street			HMAC	272	1831
10 Mar 1819	Alfred F. Swope	Michael & Jane(Ringo)		HADM	751	1839
00 000 1807	Isham Scoggan	William D.		BCSB	172	---
12 Sep 1840	May A. Shelburn[McClair]		1810/1812	BCHR	938	---
00 000 0000	James W. Summers			HMOR	611	1859
00 000 0000	Jacob Smith			HGHA	177	1831
10 Mar 1819	Alfred F. Swope	Michael & Jane(Ringold)	Va/Va	PBAD	268	---
06 Apr 1812	F. Taggart	Samuel	Ire/Ire	HMAC	95	---
00 000 0000	Preston Talbot	Ezekiah	Ky/x	PBCO	530	---
00 000 0000	E.A. Taylor	George & Polly E.		HMOR	675	---
00 000 0000	Ives A. Taylor			PVED	432	---
00 000 0000	Maximillis Taylor[Swigert]			HCHR	267	---
17 Oct 1814	Sarah A. Taylor[Hughes]			HADM	804	---
00 000 1805	Thomas A.Taylor			PPVE	654	---

BIRTHDATE	NAME OF BIOGRAPHEE	PARENTS/BIRTHPLACE/BIRTHDATE	SOURCE/PAGE	DATE
06 Oct 1814	Joel C. Traylor	James & Nancy(Cardwell) Va/Va	PBWO B297	---
00 000 0000	M.A.M. Truman		HCHA 177	1830
00 000 0000	Tarlton L. Truman		HCHA 177	1833
00 000 0000	Isaac Veech		PBMC 604	1831
00 000 0000	H.M. Watts		HCHR 267	---
06 May 1799	Richard Webb	Va/Va	PHPI 629	1833
03 Sep 1830	George G. Webber	William T. Va1785/Va1789	CHAM 1049	1833
03 Sep 1830	George G. Webber	William & Nancy(Basket) Va1785/Va06	BCHA 260	---
00 000 1830	George G. Webber	William T & Nancy(Baskett)	ECHA 75	---
00 Oct 1807	Thomas R. Webber		CHDI 180	---
06 Oct 1807	Thomas R. Webber		ECHA 45	---
00 000 0000	Thomas R. Webber	W.T & Nancy(Basket) Va/Va	HCHA 108	---
06 Oct 1807	Thomas R. Webber		CHAM 1050	1833
30 Nov 1803	Bland B. Whitaker		LOGA 545	1827
00 000 0000	Mary E. Wight[Van Pelt]		HMCL 840	---
00 000 1831	Barnett Williams		HMOR 584	1834

BIRTHDATE	NAME OF BIOGRAPHEE	PARENTS/BIRTHPLACE/BIRTHDATE	SOURCE/PAGE	DATE
00 000 0000	F.O. Albright		HJAC 128	1871
01 May 1856	Samuel Anderson		PBSM 556	---
04 Nov 1811	John R. Chaney	Payton & Anna(Logan) Allen1822/x	HMEM 754	1837
00 000 0000	Elizabeth[Chickman]	Moses & Elizabeth Va/Ky	HFAY 98	1817
00 000 0000	Thomas Chickman		HFAY 98	1817
18 May 1817	David F. Coffey	Nathan	HPIK 530	1829
00 000 1842	James F. Compton	William S & Mary M(Mayfield) Ky/NC	CJRI 577	---
00 000 0000	Amos Dick		HDEW 340	1865
17 Feb 1815	Levi Dick	Peter & Christina(Shutt)	BGSB 216	1829
19 Feb 1834	Dr. C.H. Doss		HPIK 679	---

BIRTHDATE	NAME OF BIOGRAPHEE	PARENTS/BIRTHPLACE/BIRTHDATE		SOURCE/PAGE		DATE
15 Sep 1827	John R. Fletcher	James & Jane(McElvain)		HSAN	764	1828
08 Mar 1816	Nathan Fletcher	James & Jane(McElvain)		HSAN	764	1828
19 Sep 1841	Dr. Isaac G. Gee	William & Malinda(Billingsby)	Ky/x	PBCW	495	1852
19 Sep 1815	Dr. I.G. Gee	William & Melinda(Billingsly)	Barr/WarrmPJEF	B140		---
12 Jul 1815	Margaret Gilliland[Moore]			HPIK	733	---
19 Feb 1826	Dr. L.B. Gregory	Benjamin	NC/x	PJEF	B136	---
24 Oct 1822	Samuel Logan	Elder John		HMCD	625	---
19 Apr 1818	William S. Hall			CMCD	597	1836
08 Mar 1816	John M. Hart			HSAN	768	---
24 Oct 1822	Samuel Logan	Elder John	SC/SC	HMCD	625	---
00 000 0000	Jason N. McElvain			HMAC	272	1851
19 Mar 1826	Jason N. McElvain	William	Va/Pa	HMAC	212	---
17 May 1818	James N. McElvain	William & Jane(Neely)	Pa1783/NY	PBMO	B156	---
19 Mar 1826	Jason N. McElvin	William & Jane(Neely)	Va1783/x	BRMA	324	1851
00 000 0000	Elizabeth C. Newell[Solomon]			HMAC	275	1840
00 000 0000	Susan C. Newell[Taylor]	James & Ann(Solomon)	Ky1800/x	BRMA	240	1840
00 000 0000	Thomas S. Pope			MACL	301	1843
18 Nov 1822	Mary S. Reed[Arnold]			PPWA	287	1827

S P E N C E R   C O U N T Y

BIRTHDATE	NAME OF BIOGRAPHEE	PARENTS/BIRTHPLACE/BIRTHDATE		SOURCE/PAGE		DATE
02 Mar 1832	Levi Coffman			BLOG	408	---
20 Feb 1815	Thomas Collins	Benjamin & Phoebe(Browdie)	Ky/Ky	PBAD	440	---
00 000 0000	J.W. Frazier			PBCO	404	---
00 000 0000	Elizabeth Goff[Pulliam]			HMCD	639	---
14 Jan 1834	John Gore	Robert & Amanda(Graff)	Ky1809/Ky	HGAS	203	1841
07 Aug 1837	William R. Jewell			PPVE	950	1830
18 Oct 1820	William C. Junior	Joshua & Elizabeth(Romine)	Tn/Ky	CLRI	568	---
22 Jul 1812	William Kester			HEDG	619	---
29 Aug 1814	James M. Miller	John H & Jane	Va/Pa	COLE	526	1838
29 Dec 1827	Willis C. Pierson	Willis		PBDP	600	---
01 Dec 1818	Caleb Reed	Thomas & Anna(Kirkham)	Pa/Ky	COLE	603	1829
09 Oct 1817	Jane Reed[Galbreath]			COLE	623	---

BIRTHDATE	NAME OF BIOGRAPHEE	PARENTS/BIRTHPLACE/BIRTHDATE		SOURCE/PAGE		DATE
04 Jul 1855	Alice J. Rucker[Suggett]	George W & Julia(Bennett)		HWCL	208	----
00 000 0000	Susan M. Searcy[Alford]			HMAC	270	1850
00 000 1828	Mary J. Swope[Randall]			HGAS	310	----
11 Mar 1822	Angeline E. Taylor[Welsh]			HADM	771	----
27 Nov 1819	John J. Womack			PEWA	313	----
00 000 0000	John J. Womack			HMAC	277	1835

T A Y L O R   C O U N T Y

BIRTHDATE	NAME OF BIOGRAPHEE	PARENTS/BIRTHPLACE/BIRTHDATE		SOURCE/PAGE		DATE
20 Feb 1832	Eliza Feather[Gebhart]	John & Polly(Harp)	NC/NC	PHKX	B421	----
25 Feb 1862	Mary Feather[Gebhart]	Albert & Diema(Wilson)	Ky/Ky	PHKX	B421	----
00 000 0000	M.A. Horton[Bacon]			HMAC	270	1875
29 Jan 1869	William C. Mardis	Carter	Ky1847/Ky	BRKI	1270	----
13 May 1812	Jasper Rice	Edwin & Elizabeth(Bayley)	Va/Va	HMAC	221	----
26 Jan 1824	John R. Wilson			HLOG	476	1866

T O D D   C O U N T Y

BIRTHDATE	NAME OF BIOGRAPHEE	PARENTS/BIRTHPLACE/BIRTHDATE		SOURCE/PAGE		DATE
00 000 0000	Dr. D.H. Alvis			AHEN	8	1871
00 000 1840	Dr. H.H. Black	James		GHHA	594	----
00 000 0000	P.F[Carson]			HWAS	85	1861
00 000 0000	R.H. Carson			HWAS	85	1849
24 Dec 1828	W.S. Britt	Jefferson		LOGA	696	----
07 Feb 1824	Benjamin B. Butler	Collier & Nancy(Hale)	Va/x	HMCH	327	----
20 Oct 1825	Capt.James Cunningham	John	Ire/x	PBGW	311	----

24 May 1835	Benjamin F. Duvall	Moses & Martha(Butler)	Va/Ky	GHHA	867	1855
18 Aug 1814	George Dycus	Andrew & Margaret	NC/NC	HFAY	70	1832
00 000 1802	Charles W. Floyd	John W & Betsy(Johnson)	Ky/In	PEMO	B14	---
05 Jun 1833	Dr. T. Warren Floyd	John & Elizabeth(Johnson)		HMAC	201	---
15 Jan 1811	Capt. Ephraim M. Filmore			PEMO	B144	---
12 Apr 1821	David Graham	Matthew & Janette	SC/SC	PBWA	668	---
00 000 1824	W.C. Graves			HADM	631	1826
15 Feb 1825	Robert B. Haggard	Buckner & Ellen(Paden)	SC/SC1788	PBMB	369	---
25 Mar 1833	F.M. Hall	Young		HMGL	1038	1835
25 Mar 1833	Francis M. Hall	Young & Rachel F(Hay)	Ky/Ky	PBML	704	1835
00 000 0000	C.C. Hatcher			HMAD	573	1856
18 Sep 1814	George F. Hay	Peter & Elizabeth(Finley)	Ma1770/Va	PBML	397	---
01 May 1848	John B. Hester	Benjamin R & Margaret H(Henry)	NC/x	PBCW	474	1864
00 000 0000	N.W. Holland			AWOO	98	---
02 Dec 1811	John H. Johnson			HADM	793	---
09 Nov 1825	James Jones	William & Chrissie(Gibson)	Tn/Tn	PJEF	B105	---
09 Nov 1825	James Jones	William & Crissy(Gibson)	Tn/Tn	PBCW	479	---
15 Nov 1827	William Law	Fielding & Betsey(Vaughn)	NC/Ky	PBMB	474	---
04 Sep 1813	Archibald McDowell	William & Mollie N(Thompson)	WV/WV	PVED	477	---
00 000 0000	E.B. Meriwether			HMAC	272	1844
29 May 1817	David G. Moore	David & Elizabeth	Va/SC	PPWO	603	---
01 Nov 1839	Hon. William M. Moore	David & Ann(Ellison)		TAZE	540	1846
00 000 0000	D.G. Moore			AWOO	3	1846
00 000 0000	Maria J[Paden]			HMAC	272	1851
00 000 1830	Robert N.Pader	James	SC1777/x	PBMO	B163	1835
26 Feb 1826	John J. Reeder			HADM	783	1830
28 Mar 1843	J.P. Robertson	Jesse B & Harriet(Key)	Va/Tn	PHEF	B204	1878
00 000 0000	Permelia[Shelton]			HWAS	85	1858
00 000 0000	Dr. J.B. Sims			HLOG	376	---
00 000 0000	Elizabeth R. Smith			HMAC	275	1844
05 Jan 1818	Hon. James H. Stewart	Rev.William K & Lucretia P(Moore)	NC/SC	PBWA	399	1830
15 Aug 1820	William W. Stewart			CMCD	600	1830
15 Aug 1819	William W. Stewart	William K & Lucretia(Moore)	NC/SC	HMCD	1022	1829
00 000 0000	Iverson Stokes			HGHR	264	1829
00 000 0000	Dr. J.J. Troutt			HWAS	84	1863
22 Oct 1844	Dr. James J. Troutt			HWAS	56	1863

T O D D   C O U N T Y   (C O N T.)

BIRTHDATE	NAME OF BIOGRAPHEE	PARENTS/BIRTHPLACE/BIRTHDATE		SOURCE/PAGE		DATE
00 000 1818	Andrew Vance			BRML	489	----
20 Aug 1843	Thomas I. Walker	T.I & Eliza(Wagoner)	Ky/Ky	BHAN	46	----
26 Mar 1824	Barrett White	Daniel & Eliza(Anderson)	Va/Va	HPEO	702	1835
00 000 0000	Douncey A. White			HDEW	342	1880

T R I G G   C O U N T Y

BIRTHDATE	NAME OF BIOGRAPHEE	PARENTS/BIRTHPLACE/BIRTHDATE		SOURCE/PAGE		DATE
00 000 0000	Abram Allen			HMAD	583	----
04 Jan 1826	William H. Brewer	William & Delilah(Hough) NC1803/Va1807		PBMO	B98	----
04 Jan 1826	William H. Brewer	Hon.William & Della(Hough) NC/Va1807		PBMB	155	1834
00 000 0000	W.Y. Crosthwait			HCHR	265	----
22 Mar 1826	William Y. Crosthwait	Samuel T.	Tn/x	HCHR	240	----
00 000 0000	Capt.Thomas M. Davis	Jonathan & Margaret(McLean)	Va/Pa	PBMO	B72	1817
00 000 0000	William Davis	Rev. John T.		PBMO	B82	----
09 Aug 1825	John Gore	John & Sophia	Ky/Ky	PCHR	220	----
31 Oct 1828	William F. Gore	John	NC/x	HCHR	168	1830
31 Oct 1828	William F. Gore	John & Sophia(Barten)	SC/x	PCHR	230	----
06 Apr 1852	Rev. John T. Hoye	Henry & Elizabeth		HMER	621	1857
08 Nov 1830	James B. Hutchison			PBMO	B148	1848
19 May 1823	William B. Hundley	J.B & Uriah(Dorsey) Ky1794/1801		HCHR	131	----
00 000 1808	Milly Kennedy[Murray]			HPIK	865	1830
05 Jan 1840	J.B. Mathis	William & Cynthia(Scott) **1814/**1818		PAUP	B271	----
05 Apr 1827	David Gore	Michael & Elizabeth(Mitchell)	SC/Ky	BRMA	80	1833
01 Jan 1823	Elizabeth Hargrove[Cox]	Willis & Rachel		BRMA	358	----
18 Jan 1836	Robert D. Mathis	William		BRJM	282	1849
23 Jan 1818	W.H. Newton		**/x	HMCL	1025	1833

BIRTHDATE	NAME OF BIOGRAPHEE	PARENTS/BIRTHPLACE/BIRTHDATE	SOURCE/PAGE	DATE
00 000 0000	Jesse Olive		HMAC 269	1847
00 000 0000	Joel H. Olive		HMAD 574	1828
00 000 0000	John B. Ricks		HCHR 260	1836
00 000 0000	Frances E. Roper[Davenport]	Henry C & Nancy(Lewis) Va/Va	PBMO B196	---
00 000 0000	Jane Scott[Davis]	Samuel	PBMO B72	---
00 000 0000	Jane Scott[Smith]	Samuel	PBMO B72	---
00 000 0000	Henrietta Wimberley[Drennon]		HCHR 265	1856
00 000 0000	Leander B. Young		HCHR 263	---

T R I M B L E   C O U N T Y

BIRTHDATE	NAME OF BIOGRAPHEE	PARENTS/BIRTHPLACE/BIRTHDATE	SOURCE/PAGE	DATE
27 Mar 1810	Mary C. Duncan[Gardner]		HSAN 913	1833
00 000 0000	Joseph Faro	Joseph & Hannah	HSAN 742	---
21 Jun 1805	John Gardner		HSAN 913	1833
00 000 1835	Simpson Johnson		CJRI 499	---
28 Mar 1844	Tifflin P. Logan		COLE 551	1858
09 Jan 1829	J.L.F. Miller		COLE 589	---
13 Mar 1825	John W. Miller		COLE 589	1837
00 000 0000	J.A. Pinnell		AHEN 15	1848
05 Nov 1823	Joseph A. Pinnell		HHEN 239	1843
28 Feb 1842	Hon.J.M. Truitt	Samuel & Cynthia A(Carr) Henry18/Inl18	PBMB 333	---
02 Nov 1839	Mayfield Truitt	Samuel & Cynthia A(Volbert) Ky18/Ky18	PBMB 344	---
00 000 0000	Elkanah Trout	David Pa/x	PBMA 757	---

U N I O N   C O U N T Y

BIRTHDATE	NAME OF BIOGRAPHEE	PARENTS/BIRTHPLACE/BIRTHDATE	SOURCE/PAGE	DATE
00 000 1812	Edmund Anderson	John Vac1781/x	HGSH 671	---
20 Jun 1813	Ann E. Barker[Mason]	Thomas & Sarah(Lay) Va/Va	BHBU 581	---

BIRTHDATE	NAME OF BIOGRAPHEE	PARENTS/BIRTHPLACE/BIRTHDATE		SOURCE/PAGE	DATE
22 Dec 1832	Thomas Blackwell	John & Margaret(Pullam)		PBDP 530	----
00 000 0000	Susannah Brady[Henson] James			PBRJ 714	----
00 000 1824	W.T. Brooking			CMCD 595	1834
00 000 1831	T.W.M. Burroughs	George & Martha(Coleman) Md1793/c1796		HGSH 529	----
00 Aug 1821	Dr. E.C. Colvard	Alexander & Sarah(Johnson)Va1767/Va86		HGSH 531	----
00 000 0000	Margaret Dills[Blackwell]			PBDP 530	----
00 000 0000	Lizzie G. Everton[Baker]			HGSH 592	----
05 Nov 1822	William K. Gittings	William H.	Md/x	HMCH 511	----
00 000 1799	John Hall			HGSH 702	c1818
00 000 1831	William M. Hardey	John & Mary A(Riley)	Md/Ky1804	GHHA 830	----
21 Jun 1818	Robert B. Latham			HSAN 687	----
28 Jan 1820	L.A. McKlearnan	Joseph & Julia A(Smith)		KNOX 694	----
01 Jan 1829	Thomas McMurray	George & Eliza(Waller)	Ky/Ky	HMCH 526	1829
01 Jan 1809	Marshal Mason			BHBU 581	----
17 Aug 1813	Ebenezer B. Mitchel	Peyton & Elizabeth(Briggs) Va1791/1795		PBWL 970	----
08 Sep 1855	Hon. Joseph H. Mulligan			HENR B170	1856
08 Mar 1848	James T. Omer	Lewis S & Susan H(Taylor)	Ky/Ky	HADM 767	1866
00 000 1809	Orval Pool	John	Va/x	HGSH 568	1816
00 000 0000	Dr. W.H. Shirley	S.P & Clarissa(Sigler) Caldwellc26/x		HWCL B167	----
27 Oct 1800	John E. Washington	Joseph H & Sallie Ann(Offutt)		CASS 977	----
00 000 1818	James M. Wathem	Joseph	Md/x	HGSH 585	1819
00 000 0000	Jonathan Wilson			AGRU 10	1849
00 000 0000	Jonathan Wilson			HGRU 926	----
00 000 1809	Jonathan Wilson	Thornton	Ky/x	BGLS 573	----

W A R R E N   C O U N T Y

BIRTHDATE	NAME OF BIOGRAPHEE	PARENTS/BIRTHPLACE/BIRTHDATE	SOURCE/PAGE	DATE
01 Feb 1828	Wyett Adams	Jesse & Elizabeth(Goodman)	HMCL 957	1830
01 Feb 1828	Wyett Adams	Jesse & Elizabeth(Goodman)	PBWL 1051	1830

Date	Name	Parents/Spouse	Origin	Ref	No.	Year
11 Nov 1803	Gen. Moses K. Anderson		NC/SC	HSAN	636	---
00 000 1803	John Armstrong	Aaron & Mary(Landers)		PBSM	487	1825
00 000 0000	Morris M. Armstrong			HMAD	440	1816
00 000 0000	Morris M. Armstrong			HMAD	566	1816
16 Feb 1816	Sarah Barnett[Brittin]			HMCL	875	---
11 May 1836	Nathaniel H. Beckham	Nathaniel & Elizabeth(Low)**1802/**03		HMCL	919	---
11 May 1836	Nathaniel Beckham	Nathaniel & Elizabeth(Low)	Ky/**	PBML	1042	---
16 Mar 1794	Maj. Nathaniel Blackford			HWCL	B61	---
00 000 0000	Hugh H. Boyles			HWCL	B146	---
03 Jul 1836	Dr. J.M. Bramson	Hezekiah & Emeline(Baily)	Va/Ky	HWCL	B128	---
22 Jan 1804	Charles L. Briggs			HLOG	451	---
14 Mar 1832	Charlotte Briggs			HLOG	451	---
25 Sep 1829	Elisha Butler			PBDP	749	---
02 Oct 1826	James W. Butler	Peter		KNOX	659	1829
00 000 0000	Elizabeth[Case]			HFAY	98	1835
00 000 0000	John Casey			HFAY	98	1832
00 000 1824	Nancy T. Clarke[Webb]			HGSH	838	---
18 Sep 1828	John W. Crawford		Va/x	HHEN	312	1851
18 Sep 1828	John W. Crawford	John & Elizabeth(Howard)		PBHE	556	1833
15 Feb 1797	Nancy Davis[Grimes]			HPIK	901	1836
04 Feb 1850	Dr. Euclid M. Duncan			BCLA	734	---
00 Sep 1817	William Ellsworth			HMCL	966	1823
23 Aug 1843	V.M. Foley	Leroy M & Caroline(Ellis) **1822/Va		PAUP	B126	---
00 000 1818	Sarah A[Fulks]			MACL	196	---
06 Oct 1815	Preston L. Funkhouser	John & Elizabeth(Newman)	Ky/x	HWCL	B108	1816
27 Mar 1821	Dr. Samuel D. Gardner	Asa B & Amelia(Bowles)	Va/Va	PBCO	347	---
00 00c 1828	William J. Gatewood			HGSH	541	---
21 Nov 1834	Martha F. Gilmore[Wright]			HMCL	896	---
09 Apr 1815	P.R. Gilmore			HMCL	900	---
18 Nov 1814	Thomas D. Gilmore	Andrew H.	NC/x	HMCL	882	1836
00 000 0000	Enoch Greathouse			CELW	348	1821
00 000 1787	John Greene	George & Lucy(Jones)		HGJR	670	---
00 000 0000	Mary Ground[Huffman]			CELW	348	1835
07 Sep 1811	Virgil Grubb	Jacob & Sallie(Rice)	Va1775/x	PBCW	240	---
14 Jun 1803	John Hammett	William & Anna(Oliphant)		HPEO	728	---
06 Apr 1846	Mary E, Harris[Deal]	Alexander C & Mary(Northfleete)Ky06/PulPBML		PBML	566	/819
16 Mar 1825	Betsey Hood[Maxwell]			PBML	462	---

BIRTHDATE	NAME OF BIOGRAPHEE	PARENTS/BIRTHPLACE/BIRTHDATE	SOURCE/PAGE	DATE
00 000 1827	Sarah Hunt[Prater]	John & Elizabeth(Wright)	PBMO B86	----
24 Aug 1813	Elliott T. Isbell		HJOD 712	1832
20 May 1853	Dr. N.H. Jackson	C.C & Sarah(Hendrick) Va1820/**1830	PBMO B21	----
04 Mar 1832	William A. Jenkins		HADM 804	1842
00 000 0000	Robert B. Johnson		PBJD 197	----
00 000 0000	Dr. R.H. Jones		AGLY 50	1867
00 000 0000	Sarah E. Kelsey[Over]		CELW 347	1852
22 May 1829	R.W. Lair		PPWA 313	1832
08 May 1809	Sarah[Lair]		PPWA 291	1833
31 May 1831	T.A. Lair		PPWA 291	1832
03 Apr 1797	William M. Lair	Ger/NC	PPWA 492	----
09 Sep 1812	John Latham		HSAN 687	----
25 Jan 1804	Philip C. Latham		HSAN 686	1819
23 Dec 1798	Richard Latham	James & Mary(Briggs) Va1768/Va72	HSAN 687	----
00 000 0000	Mary P. Lewis[Jones]	James A & Margaret	BLOG 227	----
15 Oct 1815	E.H. Lomax	E.H & Rachel(Hiat) SC/Va	KNOX 691	----
26 Sep 1799	George McHenry	William	PBHE 280	1810
00 000 1833	William J. Martin	Benjamin & Sarah(Armstrong) Va/Ky	HGSH 916	----
01 May 1811	John Masters		VTBU 325	1826
00 000 1819	Martha Maxey[Bartlett]		PBMO B95	----
18 Dec 1823	Lemuel C. Meadows	Elijah J & Jane(Cobb) Ky/Ky	KNOX 695	----
05 Oct 1835	Gen. G.M. Mitchell	Bedford	COLE 523	1851
00 000 0000	Sarah D[Nave]		HFAY 98	1831
00 000 0000	Mary S[Prater]		HFAY 98	1832
08 Oct 1841	Thomas W. Potter		HPIK 773	1860
13 Nov 1834	Erasmus W. Pendleton	Samuel C & Eliza(Covington) Va/Ky1808	HWCL B28	----
03 Oct 1816	George W. Price	James B & Mary(Wall) NC1792/x	HMCL 810	1833
29 May 1830	Peter B. Price		HMCL 977	----
27 Nov 1815	James H. Randall	William & Mary(Beadles) NY/Va	HFUL 809	----
16 Apr 1798	James Rawlins	James & Lydia(Green) NC/NC	HGJR 1120	----
20 May 1818	Samuel H. Reid		HSAN 1026	----
29 Aug 1825	Isom Robertson		PHKX B675	----
00 000 0000	O.P. Robertson		HMCL 978	----

BIRTHDATE	NAME OF BIOGRAPHEE	PARENTS/BIRTHPLACE/BIRTHDATE		SOURCE/PAGE		DATE
07 Jul 1809	John Scroggin			HLOG	419	1812
00 000 0000	Levi Sears		NC/NC	HFAY	81	----
00 000 0000	Levi Sears			HFAY	98	1828
02 Sep 1816	Andrew W. Simmons	James & Sarah(Stice)	Ky1795/Ky1798	PBWA	482	----
10 Aug 1809	James Simmons	William & Esther(Stice)	Va1775/SC1779	PBWA	413	----
19 Aug 1825	Dr. Jesse H. Smith	David & Jane		HSAN	847	1865
26 Nov 1816	Jeremiah Taylor			BJEF	B34	----
19 Jul 1854	Newton Tibbs			BCLA	843	----
27 Apr 1816	Jemima R. Wallace[Gardner]	William & Nancy(Smith)		PBWA	482	----
00 000 0000	Sarah R. Wallace[Wallace]	William & Nancy(Smith)		PBWA	492	----
09 Dec 1814	Henry H. Warren		Va/x	HMOR	601	----
00 000 0000	Caroline Watt[Barnsback] F.N.			CJRI	556	----
00 000 0000	N.S. Watt[Barnsback]			HMAD	584	1817
00 000 1844	William T. Watt	Fideler N & Henrietta	Ky/Ky	CJRI	524	----
31 Aug 1815	William L. West	David L & Mary(Armstrong)		HGJR	394	1817
22 May 1827	Easton Whitten			PBMO	B308	----
00 000 0000	John Wood			CELW	355	1809

W A S H I N G T O N   C O U N T Y

BIRTHDATE	NAME OF BIOGRAPHEE	PARENTS/BIRTHPLACE/BIRTHDATE		SOURCE/PAGE		DATE
07 Apr 1827	Emeline[Atkinson]			CMCD	595	1830
00 Mar 1855	A.W. Bascom			HMCL	935	1865
00 000 0000	Hettie[Brants]			HJAC	128	1868
00 000 1798	Ira Briscoe		Va/Ire	HPIK	717	1834
00 000 0000	William Cannon	Edward & Peggy		CMCD	596	1833
00 000 1829	John Charter			CMCD	596	1833
28 Sep 1799	David Clarke	John & Ann(Whitten)		CMCD	335	1829
31 Mar 1819	William B. Clarke			CMCD	596	1829
31 Mar 1819	William B. Clarke	James & Polly(Lewis)	x/NC	HMCD	956	1829
01 Apr 1818	Nathan W. Farris			HMCD	632	----
26 Jun 1806	Benjamin Fowler			HMCD	893	1847
28 Nov 1830	Bloomer Fowler	Benjamin & Mary(Gordon)		HPIK	762	----
00 000 0000	William H. Gittings	Kinsey & Mary(Clemmons)		GHHA	920	----

W A S H I N G T O N   C O U N T Y   (C O N T.)

BIRTHDATE	NAME OF BIOGRAPHEE	PARENTS/BIRTHPLACE/BIRTHDATE		SOURCE/PAGE	DATE
08 Jul 1827	Henry W. Green	James & Nancy(Warren)	Md/Ky	CJRI 232	1852
16 Feb 1862	Dr. William E. Grigsby Redman		Va/x	HMCH 184	----
00 000 1812	Victor M. Hardin			CMCD 597	1834
00 000 1808	Jefferson Hayes			HMCD 630	1832
00 000 0000	Nancy Hayden[Yeager]			EHAN 354	----
00 000 1802	William H. Hays			HMCD 624	----
00 000 0000	Harrison Head			HMCD 931	1832
00 000 1812	John H. Head			CMCD 598	1831
00 000 0000	Maria J. Head[Hayes]			HMCD 630	----
16 Feb 1816	William T. Head			HMCD 317	----
00 000 0000	William Hooper	Fountain		PPDM 811	----
15 Sep 1807	Adonijah Hungate			HMCH 173	1833
28 Feb 1810	Harrison Hungate	John & Mary(Coffman)		HMCD 863	1830
07 Apr 1827	Charles C. Hungate			CMCD 598	1848
00 000 0000	M. Hurst			AMEN 19	1849
05 Sep 1844	Stith T. Hurst	James	Ky/SC	HMEM 732	----
00 000 0000	Elizabeth Ingraham[Silvers]			PBCO 490	----
00 000 0000	Fanny M. Jones[Bascom]			HMCL 935	----
17 Nov 1791	John Kirk	James		HMCD 554	1836
00 000 0000	William Lambert			CSBR 380	1836
21 Jan 1832	William J. Lambert	William & Catherine(Dennis)	**/Mercer	BGSB 534	1828
15 Mar 1813	Azariah Lewis	William & Elizabeth(Burns)	Va/x	BGSB 222	----
17 Nov 1796	Temperance Lockhart[Roberts]			HSAN 928	----
09 Aug 1794	Peter Long			PBMO 842	1824
22 Jun 1817	Shelton J. Mattingly			HMOR 736	1835
08 Feb 1799	B.J. Montgomery	Elisha & Margaret	Ky/Ky	TAZE 481	----
18 Nov 1797	David Morgan			COLE 627	1872
15 Jul 1801	Hon. Matthew Robb	Thomas & Lydia(Waller)	Irel769/Wales95	ERML 694	1830
00 000 0000	James T. Rogers			HMAD 561	1830
00 000 1805	David Seybold			CMCD 600	1818
00 000 1816	James Seybold			CMCD 600	
00 000 0000	Bletcher Silvers	John & Nancy(Springer)	Ky/Ky	PBCO 490	

BIRTHDATE	NAME OF BIOGRAPHEE	PARENTS/BIRTHPLACE/BIRTHDATE	SOURCE/PAGE	DATE
04 Sep 1816	William F. Tucker	Truman & Esther(Fitzgerald) Md/Md	PBWO 551	----
00 000 0000	John M. Tinney	Nathaniel & Caroline(Marshall)Va/Va	BCSB 368	----
00 000 1828	Horace Ward		CMCD 601	1833
00 000 1823	James R. Ward		CMCD 600	1833
00 000 1827	Z.T. Webster	Ky/Ky	HPIK 797	1835
18 Sep 1811	James Williams	James & Ada	CMCD 601	1834
07 Apr 1827	Caroline Willis[Hunter]		CMCD 598	1830
06 Feb 1822	Cynthia A. Willis[Hall]		CMCD 597	1830
16 May 1816	Mary Willis[Russell]		CMCD 600	
00 000 1822	Thomas F. Wilson		CMCD 601	1832
00 000 1820	William S. Wilson		CMCD 601	1833
00 000 0000	William Wilson		PBRJ 267	----

W A Y N E   C O U N T Y

BIRTHDATE	NAME OF BIOGRAPHEE	PARENTS/BIRTHPLACE/BIRTHDATE	SOURCE/PAGE	DATE
00 000 0000	William D. Anderson		PBMA 545	----
11 Oct 1814	James Barrow	John & Emma Lee NC/NC	HJAC 102	1818
03 Oct 1829	John L. Bryan		HHEN 286	1854
00 000 0000	Dr.John L. Bryan	Dr.Edward & Lettice(Pierce)	PBHE 228	----
14 Jul 1829	James F. Carpenter	William	HMOR 618	1839
00 000 0000	Maria Chance[Emsminger]		HMAD 568	1833
26 Nov 1846	John M. Chrisman	Charles S.	BRJM 332	1860
23 Aug 1843	Albert S. Coomer	James M & Peggy(Taylor) Tn/**	BMCL 980	----
22 Nov 1829	Shelby M. Cullom		PBMA 174	----
00 000 0000	William N. Dodson		PBML 791	----
16 Apr 1866	Dr. Coleman Eads	Jacob H & Nancy(Tuttle) **1829/x	HMCH 446	1830
21 Nov 1825	Rigdon S. Fletcher		HPEO 648	1830
00 000 0000	Elizabeth D[Fo-ey]		CSBR 383	1865
00 000 0000	Celia Herrin[Leech]		CELW 352	1860
09 Jun 1814	Israel Huffaker		VTBU 231	1856
20 Nov 1822	Rufus F.G. Moore	George W & Margaret(Gholson) In/x	BMCL 1203	----
28 Dec 1818	Isaac N. Pevehouse		HADM 897	1835
00 000 0000	J.J. Pevehouse		CSBR 392	1833
00 000 0000	Susana[Pevehouse]		CSBR 392	1832
00 000 1816	John Price	Richard & Mary(Johnson) Va/Va	PBCO B198	----

WAYNE COUNTY (CONT.)

BIRTHDATE	NAME OF BIOGRAPHEE	PARENTS/BIRTHPLACE/BIRTHDATE		SOURCE/PAGE		DATE
00 000 0000	Minnie E. Roberts[Garner]	Squire & Penelope	Ky/Ky	PBCO	356	----
22 May 1809	Thomas Scott			HMOR	626	----
15 Dec 1800	Isiah Turney			HMOR	561	1819
11 Nov 1802	N.B. Van Winkle			HMOR	627	----
00 000 0000	Catherine J. Van Winkle[Devore]			HMOR	482	----

WEBSTER COUNTY

BIRTHDATE	NAME OF BIOGRAPHEE	PARENTS/BIRTHPLACE/BIRTHDATE		SOURCE/PAGE		DATE
27 Jul 1850	Dr. Joseph R. Baker	Freeman & Hannah(Bridges)	Ky1814/Tn	HGSH	595	----
00 000 0000	Caroline O'Neal[Killough]			CELW	349	1866

WHITLEY COUNTY

BIRTHDATE	NAME OF BIOGRAPHEE	PARENTS/BIRTHPLACE/BIRTHDATE		SOURCE/PAGE		DATE
01 Feb 1835	Francis F. Beames	William	**/x	BRJM	388	----
00 000 0000	Elizabeth Beems[Cooper]	James & Nancy	Va/Va	HSTE	734	----
23 Apr 1813	T.L. Early			HSTE	676	1837
08 Apr 1820	Martha J[McDonald]			VTBU	379	1827

WOLFE COUNTY

BIRTHDATE	NAME OF BIOGRAPHEE	PARENTS/BIRTHPLACE/BIRTHDATE	SOURCE/PAGE	DATE

BIRTHDATE	NAME OF BIOGRAPHEE	PARENTS/BIRTHPLACE/BIRTHDATE	SOURCE/PAGE		DATE
10 Aug 1844	Michael A. Murphy	Miles & Sibble(O'Hair)	PBCO	326	1856
09 Jun 1811	Rosanna O'Hair[Perisho]		COLE	644	---
09 Jun 1811	Rosanna O'Hair[Wells]		COLE	644	---

WOODFORD COUNTY

BIRTHDATE	NAME OF BIOGRAPHEE	PARENTS/BIRTHPLACE/BIRTHDATE	SOURCE/PAGE		DATE
04 Aug 1804	Dr. H. Alexander		PHCC	295	---
12 Jul 1818	Garrett Armstrong	John A.	PPWO	653	---
00 000 0000	Eliza J. Arnold[Scoggan]		GSBR	393	1840
08 Jan 1806	John Arnold		PPWO	558	1819
00 000 0000	John Baker		GJRI	727	---
00 000 0000	Susan E. Binee[Stewart]		GELW	351	1855
21 Apr 1832	James M. Buford		PPRI	270	1839
27 Jul 1803	Thomas Bullock	Thomas & Lucy(Redd)	PPWO	595	1835
12 May 1827	William S. Bullock	Thomas & Agnes(Ware) **/Franklin	PBWO	329	1835
00 000 0000	Elizabeth Carr[Brawley]		PBHE	433	---
12 Oct 1804	Rev. James Conover		HMOR	741	---
00 000 1812	Walter W. Elbli		HADM	620	---
16 Jun 1809	Eliza Ellis		PPWO	558	1821
26 Jun 1823	Nelson Graves	Richard	PBMC	344	1828
00 000 0000	Mary A. Green[Banciusky] James **/x		PVED	494	---
25 Oct 1805	John Griffith	Alexander & Elizabeth(Edwards) Pa/SC	PBRI	421	---
20 Nov 1844	Campbell S. Hearn	Warren & Jane(Alexander) Owen/**	PBAD	198	---
22 Dec 1826	Isaiah E. Huffman	Alexander & Mildred(Eddine)Va00/Va97	HCAS	350	---
00 000 0000	Benjamin Johnson		GELW	351	1874
00 000 0000	Mary Jones[Martin]		HWCL	B227	---
00 000 0000	Isaac McCuddy		HDEW	344	1838
00 000 1792	James Malone		PHCC	311	---
00 000 0000	William Martin		HWCL	B227	1833
10 Mar 1807	John Musick	Jesse & Hannah Va/Va	LOGA	503	---
00 000 0000	Charles H. Nall		GSBR	383	1836
01 Oct 1800	Rev. George O'Bannon		PBCO	515	---

BIRTHDATE	NAME OF BIOGRAPHEE	PARENTS/BIRTHPLACE/BIRTHDATE	SOURCE/PAGE	DATE
00 000 0000	Mrs. A.[Pilcher]		HFAY 95	1829
07 Apr 1846	Dr.J.F. Price	Jacob F & Mariah R(Miles) Ky/Ky	HSAN 702	1861
00 000 0000	A.B. Ratcliff		GSBR 392	1837
23 Jan 1808	Isaac N. Reding	E.W & Catherine(Conover) Pa/x	PPME 434	----
24 Dec 1812	Martha J. Reding[Conover]		HMOR 741	----
06 Jan 1817	Rev. James C. Rucker Rev. Ahmed & Nellie Va/x		HDEW 191	----
11 Oct 1853	Rev. James W. Skinner Thomas & Jane(Biggar) Scotland/Scotld		BRWS 31	----
13 Apr 1804	James T.B. Stapp		EFAY 502	1816
15 Nov 1818	George C. Stewart	Ralph	CHAM 1033	----
00 000 0000	George L. Thompson	William & Elizabeth Pa/Scotland	HPIK 415	----
00 000 0000	Elizabeth Trabue[Gill]		HMAD 579	1835
00 000 0000	Col. Dudley Wickersham		HSAN 727	----
22 Nov 1819	Col. Dudley Wickersham		EFAY 587	1843
13 Sep 1791	Martha M. Yates		HSAN 930	----
16 Sep 1809	Charles S. Young	James & Lucinda(Baldwin) **/Va	PVED 555	----

C O U N T Y   N O T   G I V E N

BIRTHDATE	NAME OF BIOGRAPHEE	PARENTS/BIRTHPLACE/BIRTHDATE	SOURCE/PAGE	DATE
00 000 0000	Serelda Abshire[Cline]		HGSH 868	----
00 000 0000	Martha A. Adair[Richards]		PBAD 582	----
00 000 0000	E.A. Adams		MACL 295	1828
00 000 0000	E.S. Adams		AMOU 6	1855
00 000 0000	Amanda Adams[Makemson] Samuel & Nancy Ky/Ky		PVED 583	----
00 000 0000	Eli Adams	William	PHCG 326	1810
00 000 0000	Ellington Adams		HCHR 37	1836
00 000 0000	Isom Adams		HCHR 265	----
00 000 1802	John Adams		PBMO B7	----
00 000 0000	Jacob Adams		PRDP 345	----
00 000 1805	Joseph Adams		HMOR 321	1830
00 000 1818	Peter Adams		PHPI 468	----
00 000 0000	Elizabeth[Adar]		ACAS 22	1852

Date	Name	Parents/Spouse	Origin	Code	No.	Year
30 Dec 1814	Sarah Adkins[Hackett] James			PBCO	576	1835
00 000 1836	S. Adkinson			ACLA	71	1878
00 000 0000	Sarah Adkinson Stem] Pleasant & Fanny			PBWA	287	----
00 000 0000	Sarah A. Adkinson[Sullivan]			HMCD	747	1816
00 000 0000	Joseph Albin			CJRI	322	----
09 Jul 1795	Sinai F. Alderson[Blunt]			HMEM	813	----
03 Oct 1814	David Alexander			HSAN	834	1854
00 000 1839	E.R. Alexander			ACLA	71	----
00 000 0000	Joseph Alexander			PBKN	257	1841
00 000 0000	J.W. Allaman			HCHR	262	----
00 000 0000	Dr. J.G. Allan			BEFF	666	----
00 000 0000	G.W. Allen			HCHA	178	1863
00 000 1834	Henry Allen			OCHA	89	1858
00 000 0000	J.M. Allen			HPIK	630	----
00 000 1829	Joseph Allen			OCHA	89	1860
00 000 0000	Josiah Allen			PBKN	473	----
00 000 0000	Robert N. Allan			PHCC	225	----
00 000 0000	Sally Allen[Garrison]			HPIK	455	1826
00 000 0000	Sarah Allen Archibald			BREM	209	1852
00 000 0000	Leonard Alkire			HMEM	358	----
00 000 0000	John Allison			CJRI	510	----
00 000 0000	Aaron Allman Andrew		Ger/x	HCHR	216	----
13 Sep 1830	George W. Allpin Reuben & Susan(Brumbeck)		Ky/x	BCSB	133	1835
14 Feb 1850	George T. Allslip William P.			BRJM	377	----
00 000 0000	David Alsop			HLOG	491	----
00 000 0000	William Alvey			HSAN	957	----
00 000 0000	C.F. Anderson			HCHA	176	1857
00 000 0000	Elizabeth Anderson[George]			HCHR	262	1850
00 Sep 1798	George Anderson			HWCL	240	----
00 000 0000	H.B[Anderson]			HWAS	84	----
00 000 1810	James S. Anderson			HMOR	321	1830
00 000 0000	John Anderson			HLOG	505	----
00 000 1815	John G. Anderson			HFUL	418	1835
00 000 1810	Joseph C. Anderson John & Elizabeth(Conaway)		Md/Ky	GHHA	594	----
00 000 0000	Lydia A. Anderson[Haines]			HCHR	262	----
00 000 0000	Mary A. Anderson[Waggener]		Va/Va	GHHA	858	----
00 000 0000	William Anderson			HLOG	343	----
00 000 0000	William Anderson			HLOG	505	----
00 000 1815	James Antel			HMOR	321	1820
00 000 0000	Christopher Anthory			HMOR	657	----

BIRTHDATE	NAME OF BIOGRAPHEE	PARENTS/BIRTHPLACE/BIRTHDATE		SOURCE/PAGE	DATE
00 000 0000	Charles K. Archer			PHCC 185	----
25 Dec 1812	James C. Archer			HMCD 698	----
15 Aug 1799	Lewis Armstrong			CELW 298	----
00 000 1800	Maurice Armstrong	John & Elizabeth(Martin)	Ire/1760	HMAC 192	----
00 000 0000	Maurice Armstrong	Joshua	Pa/x	BRMA 471	----
00 000 0000	Nancy Armstrong[Jones]	Joshua & Sarah(Morris)	Pa/Va	HMOR 574	----
00 000 0000	Nancy Armstrong[Pitts]			PEWL 1179	----
00 000 0000	Martha [Andrews]			HMAC 269	1832
00 000 0000	Ann E[Armour]			HMAC 272	1828
00 000 0000	John Armour			HMAC 272	1828
00 000 0000	Mary Arnold[Ham]			PEWL 1112	----
00 000 0000	John Arrowsmith			BMCL 923	----
00 000 0000	Dr. George N. Arteburn			HLOG 519	----
00 000 0000	Mary Arthurburn[Poulter]			PVED 1046	----
00 000 0000	A.L. Asbury			HJAC 129	1832
00 000 0000	Henry Asbury			HADW 401	1834
00 000 0000	James Ash			LOGA 564	----
09 Feb 1830	Rebecca J. Ash[McPherson] Jesse		Ky/Ky	PEWO B198	----
30 Sep 1802	Hezekiah J. Ashomre			COLE 511	1830
30 Sep 1802	Hezekiah J. Ashmore	Samuel & Letitia(Guthrie)		COLE 592	----
00 000 0000	James J. Ashurst			HLOG 405	----
04 Jun 1834	George W. Atchison	Isam & Mary	Va/Ky	LOGA 825	1834
00 000 0000	Aaron Atherton			PAUP B239	----
00 000 0000	Elizabeth Atherton[Atherton]			PAUP B239	----
00 000 0000	John F. Averitt	Nathan	Ky/x	PBDP 375	----
00 000 0000	Emiline Baily[Bramson] David & Martha			HWCL B128	----
00 000 0000	Joseph Baird			PVED 474	----
00 000 0000	Lavina[Baird]			HJAC 130	1863
00 000 0000	Permelia C[Baird]			HMAC 272	1830
00 000 0000	Samuel Baird			HMAC 272	1845
00 000 0000	G. Baker			HSAN 442	1828
00 000 0000	Thomas J. Bagwell			HWCL 177	----
00 000 1817	George Baker			HGSH 594	----
00 000 0000	Jacob Baker			HSAN 441	1828
00 000 1803	Sarah A. Baker[Barger]			TAZE 496	----
00 000 0000	V.A. Baker			HCHR 263	1855
00 000 0000	David Baldwin			HLOG 491	----

Date	Name	Parents/Spouse	Origin	Code	No.	Year
00 000 0000	Elizabeth[Baldwin]			HWAS	83	1830
00 000 0000	Elizabeth Baldwin[Baird]			PPVE	719	----
00 000 0000	Elizabeth Baldwin[Labertew]			PBML	877	----
00 000 0000	Jeremiah Baldwin			HLOG	491	1838
00 000 0000	L.B. Baldwin			HWAS	83	1830
00 000 0000	Harden Bale	William		AMEN	23	----
00 000 0000	John Ball	William		PBJD	221	----
00 000 0000	Dr. J.L. Ballard			PBML	890	----
00 000 0000	Fanny Ballinger[Kelly]			BHAN	362	----
00 000 0000	Isaac Banta			HLOG	543	----
00 000 0000	Jacob Banta			AWOO	5	1849
00 000 0000	John Barbee			PHCC	146	----
25 Sep 1798	Eli Barbre			HSAN	887	----
00 000 0000	John D. Barber			HMCD	590	1830
00 000 1825	Nathan Barber			HMCD	590	1830
00 000 0000	James Barker			HCHR	33	1828
17 Sep 1836	William T. Barnard			HLOG	459	----
00 000 1832	Dr. A.T. Barnes	Craven & Mary(Howard)	Ky/Ky	PBML	1198	----
00 000 0000	John Barnes			HMEM	636	----
00 000 0000	John Barnes			TAZE	638	----
00 000 1844	Reece Barnes			HMCD	644	----
00 000 0000	John F. Barlow	Elias & Polly(Gilland)		PHPI	537	1872
00 000 1806	Robert E. Barnett	George		PVED	748	c.1829
00 000 0000	J.R. Barnett			HLOG	505	----
00 000 0000	John R. Barnett			HLOG	471	----
19 Mar 1797	Jane Barnett[Rayburn]			LOGA	657	1831
00 000 0000	S.A. Barnett			HLOG	505	----
21 Apr 1808	Jacob Barnsback	George F.J & Mary(Minter) Ger1781/x		HMAD	449	1809
00 000 0000	Sarah Barr[Clarcomb]			GHHA	899	----
00 000 0000	John Barritt			PHPI	411	----
00 000 0000	John M. Barrera			HFUL	580	----
00 Sep 1839	Daniel T. Barret			BCHR	841	----
00 000 0000	George W. Barnett			PEMB	270	----
00 000 0000	Samuel Barlow			PHKX	B807	----
00 000 0000	T.S. Barrow			HMAC	270	1830
00 000 0000	Granville Barry			VTBU	275	----
07 Jun 1825	Isaac Barton	William & Mary(Brewer)	Tn/Tn	HPIK	784	----
00 000 1809	Thomas Barton	David	Md/x	BCSB	406	----

C O U N T Y   N O T   G I V E N

BIRTHDATE	NAME OF BIOGRAPHEE	PARENTS/BIRTHPLACE/BIRTHDATE	SOURCE/PAGE	DATE
00 000 0000	W.T. Bashaw		HSAN	441	1829
00 000 0000	William G. Bates	John Pa/x	PVED	852	----
00 000 0000	E.G. Batterton		AMEN	19	1818
00 000 0000	J.H. Batterton		ACAS	19	1849
14 Dec 1801	William Batterton	Amos & Nancy Va1781/NC1784	HSAN	1014	----
00 000 0000	Samuel Bayless		PVED	557	----
00 000 0000	Gertie Bayne[Grundon]		CELW	354	1882
00 000 0000	Becky Bays[Zimmerly]		PVED	773	----
00 000 0000	Elvira Beach[Carter]		HWCL	48	----
00 000 0000	J.B. Beadle		ACIA	71	1845
00 000 1812	Asa Beall		PRPE	584	1833
00 000 0000	Catherine A[Beals]		CJRI	299	----
00 000 1807	Garrett Bean		GHHA	551	----
04 Aug 1827	Thomas Bean	Thomas & Elizabeth(Martin) Tn/Tn	BRJM	342	----
08 Feb 1822	William Beeler	William **1796/x	PBWL	1156	1806
00 000 0000	Benjamin Bell		HLOG	481	----
00 000 0000	M.A. Bell[Payne]		HCHR	262	1850
00 000 0000	Mary Bell[Dickerson]	Robert	PCHR	317	----
00 000 0000	Thomas Bell		HLOG	481	----
00 000 0000	Ladon Beghtol	Peter	BCSB	543	c1840
00 000 0000	John Bellamy		HMAC	274	1852
00 000 0000	William Benn		HPIK	590	1826
00 000 0000	Eliza Bennett[Adams]		HFUL	814	----
00 000 1802	Isaac R. Bennett		HMOR	322	1829
00 000 0000	Lucy Bennett[Latham]		HSAN	687	----
00 Oct 1796	Lucy Bennett[Redman]		PBCO	374	----
00 000 0000	Nathaniel Bennett		TAZE	515	----
00 000 0000	James Benson		PBWL	756	----
00 000 0000	E. Bentley		VTBU	314	----
00 000 1831	P.W. Bentley		PBWL	348	----
00 000 1827	G. Berkshire		OCHA	89	1857
00 000 0000	Nancy J. Berkshire[Talkington]		CELW	350	----
00 000 0000	J.O. Bernard		HADM	400	1834

Date	Name		Parents	Origin	Code	No.	Year
00 000 0000	John Bever	Michael			PPVE	904	---
00 000 0000	Thomas Billings				HLOG	406	---
00 000 0000	John H. Bilyeu	Peter			PCHR	445	---
00 000 0000	Amelia Bird[Campbell]				CELW	226	---
00 000 0000	Mary Bishop[Marks]				PBKN	193	1835
24 Jan 1818	Carter T. Black		Thomas & Edith	SC1768/Ky	HSAN	760	1819
17 Sep 1798	David Black		Thomas & Edith	SC1768/Ky	HSAN	760	1819
06 Mar 1803	Elizabeth Black		Thomas & Edith	SC1768/Ky	HSAN	760	1819
00 000 0000	Elizabeth Black[Walton]				BRBW	483	---
13 Dec 1807	Isaac Black		John & Nancy(Lewis)	Va/Va	PPWO	596	---
00 000 0000	James Black		John	Pa/x	PPVE	270	---
08 Aug 1809	John Black		Thomas & Edith	SC1768/Ky	HSAN	760	1819
04 Aug 1806	Nancy Black		Thomas & Edith	SC1768/Ky	HSAN	760	1819
00 000 0000	R.K. Black				MACL	296	1827
03 Jul 1796	Sarah Black		Thomas & Edith	SC1768/Ky	HSAN	760	1819
03 Sep 1813	Thomas Black		Thomas & Edith	SC1768/Ky	HSAN	760	1819
21 Feb 1828	Thomas G. Black		James B & Mary G(McCaslin)Ky1799/93		PBMO	B282	---
00 000 0000	Thomas Blackwell				PHPI	412	---
00 000 0000	Emily Blackwell[Hornback]				HPIK	764	---
00 000 0000	Henry Blagg				GPFD	B528	---
00 000 0000	Robert Blair				ACLA	71	1882
06 Feb 1797	William G. Blair				PVED	595	---
00 000 0000	William M. Blair				HPIK	807	1828
26 Jun 1847	J.H. Blanford				HKDG	692	---
00 000 0000	John Blevins				PBCO	204	1819
00 000 0000	Isabella A[Blodgett]				HMAC	269	1840
00 000 0000	Laban Blunt				HMEW	658	---
00 000 0000	Richard Blunt				HMEW	658	---
00 000 0000	Samuel Blunt				HMEW	658	---
00 000 0000	Thomas F. Blurt				HMEW	658	---
13 Jun 1769	Elijah Boatman				HCAS	348	---
18 Nov 1772	Estella Boatman				HCAS	348	---
12 Apr 1768	Ida M. Boatman				HCAS	348	---
00 000 0000	Harrison Boggess				PBRI	627	1836
00 000 0000	Nancy Boggs[Ward]				PPVE	245	---

BIRTHDATE	NAME OF BIOGRAPHEE	PARENTS/BIRTHPLACE/BIRTHDATE	SOURCE/PAGE	DATE
09 Oct 1825	William Bolding	Thomas & Sally(Wayman) Ky/NY	KNOX 655	----
00 000 0000	John Boling		HHEN 311	----
00 000 0000	Elizabeth Bond		HADM 401	1827
00 000 0000	Granville Bond		HADM 401	1827
00 000 1783	George Boon		BREM 69	1815
00 000 0000	Isaiah Boone		PHPI 537	1872
08 Dec 1808	Levi D. Boone	Rev.Daniel & Anna(Grubbs) x/Va	BCHI 273	----
00 000 0000	Armilda Booth[Hedges]	Stephen & Mary(Congleton) Va/Bourbon	PBAD 168	1833
00 000 0000	Christopher C. Booth	Stephen & Mary(Congleton) Va/Bourbon	PBAD 168	1833
00 000 0000	Clarinda Booth[Hedges]	Stephen & Mary(Congleton)Va/Bourbon	PBAD 168	1833
00 000 0000	Elizabeth Booth[Corwin]	Stephen & Mary(Congleton)Va/Bourbon	PBAD 168	1833
00 000 0000	Emily Booth[Turner]	Stephen & Mary(Congleton) Va/Bourbon	PBAD 168	1833
00 000 0000	Judith Booth[Johnson]	Stephen & Mary(Congleton) Va/Bourbon	PBAD 168	1833
00 000 0000	Mary Booth[Duncan]	Stephen & Mary(Congleton) Va/Bourbon	PBAD 168	1833
00 000 0000	Sarah Booth[Sibley]	Stephen & Mary(Congleton) Va/Bourbon	PBAD 168	1833
00 000 0000	William A. Booth	Stephen & Mary(Congleton) Va/Bourbon	PBAD 168	1833
00 000 1799	Nancy Bostick[Rutledge]		HMCL 978	----
00 000 1831	Dr. William Booz	Richard & Frances A(McCallister)Ky10/12	GHHA 677	1837
27 Feb 1832	John H. Boston	George & Mahala(Southerlin) Ky/Ky	GHHA 595	----
00 000 0000	Reuben J. Boston		BHAN 224	----
00 000 0000	Rebecca Boswell[Webb]		PBGW 380	----
00 000 0000	George W. Botts		AMEN 19	1870
00 000 1782	John Boucher		HWAS 54	----
00 000 0000	Nancy[Boulware]		HMOR 616	----
00 000 0000	S.A. Boulware[Quinn]		PBWL 294	----
31 Aug 1827	P.G. Bourland	Miles	HMOR 631	1830
06 Jan 1824	William W. Bourland	William & Rachel(Slaten) Al/x	HGSH 599	----
00 000 0000	Elijah Bourn	Elijah Eng/x	PBWO 237	----
00 000 0000	Jeremiah Bowen		AGAS 22	1830
00 000 0000	John M. Bowen		HCHR 264	1865

Date	Name	Origin	Code	No.	Year
00 000 0000	M.A[Bowen]		HCHR	264	1865
03 Apr 1804	Nancy J. Bowen[Van Sandt]		PHEF	B249	----
00 000 0000	Jane E[Bowers]		HWAS	85	1854
00 000 0000	David Bowles		HLOG	531	----
00 000 0000	Mourning Bowles[Nichols]		PBAD	332	----
00 000 1825	David Bowles		OPLO	85	1849
00 000 0000	A.C. Boyd		HLOG	345	----
00 000 0000	Mary Boyd[Johnson]		HGJR	991	1829
00 000 0000	Mary E. Boyd[Bridges]		CHAM	872	----
00 000 1837	W.P. Boyd		OCHA	89	1864
00 000 1823	J.H. Boyer		HMOR	322	1830
00 000 0000	Nancy Boyle[Ashlock]		HGJR	871	----
00 000 1800	Willis Bagby Robert	Va/x	PAUP	B311	----
00 000 0000	Matthew Braber		HMEM	358	----
00 000 0000	Eliza Bracken[Montgomery]		PPME	497	1826
00 000 0000	Elizabeth Bracken[Kays]		KNOX	685	----
00 000 1810	Elizabeth Bracken[Kays]		PBKN	194	----
00 000 0000	Sarah E. Brackett[Stanley]		PPPI	124	----
17 Apr 1798	Christian Braden[Blair]		PVED	595	----
08 Mar 1832	J.F. Bradshaw		PBWA	286	----
00 000 0000	Nancy Bradshaw[Huston]		HMCD	276	----
00 000 0000	Ann Brake[Briggs]		HADM	736	----
00 000 0000	Samuel Brandenburg		PHPI	471	1864
00 000 0000	Alzena B. Brannan[Costley]		PBDP	935	----
18 Dec 1811	Thomas Brannan Dudley & Mary		HGJR	877	1824
00 000 0000	T.H. Brassfield		AMEN	19	1834
00 000 0000	W.R. Brassfield		HSAN	442	1832
00 000 0000	Archer Bratton	Ire/x	PPVE	430	----
00 000 0000	Preston Breckinridge		HSAN	441	1834
07 Feb 1815	Rev. William Breeden		HMCH	295	----
00 000 1812	Samuel Brents		BCHR	851	----
16 Apr 1814	William G. Brentz		PCHR	272	----
00 000 0000	Mary L. Bretz[Westenberger]	Ger/Ky	HSAN	726	----
00 000 1817	W.T. Brewer		HMOR	322	1823
00 000 0000	James I. Bridges		BCHR	852	----

BIRTHDATE	NAME OF BIOGRAPHEE	PARENTS/BIRTHPLACE/BIRTHDATE	SOURCE/PAGE	DATE
00 000 1817	J.S. Briscoe		ACLA 71	1835
28 Jul 1817	John B. Briscoe	Henry Md1762/x	PHCC 146	----
00 000 0000	William Britt		HLOG 491	----
00 000 1828	William S. Britt		OPLO 85	1859
00 000 0000	Leah Brockett[Middletown]		HLOG 472	1835
00 000 0000	James Brockman		CSBR 260	1836
00 000 0000	Dr. James Brockman		BGSB 131	1835
26 Feb 1829	Alexander V. Brookings	Thomas A & Mary L(Threshley)	CMCD 321	1835
25 Feb 1829	Alexander V. Brooking	Thomas A & Martha(Threshley)Na95/Ky	HMCD 682	----
22 Feb 1842	Darvel E. Brooks	John & Susan(Clingen) Ky/x	PBMC 521	----
00 000 0000	John T. Brooks		AMEN 23	1838
00 000 0000	Mary Brooks[Capps]		PBWA 224	----
00 000 0000	Nancy Brooks[Breckenridge]		PBHE 626	----
00 000 0000	Serepta Brooks[Darnall]		BRML 584	1829
00 000 0000	Thompson Brooks		PBWA 205	----
00 000 0000	Alzema B. Brown[Costley]		HDEW 331	1828
00 000 1799	Bedford Brown		HMOR 322	----
00 000 0000	Eliza Brown[Bacon]		PVED 953	----
00 000 1823	George S. Brown		HMOR 322	1828
00 000 1823	George S. Brown	Bedford Ky1804/x	BRMA 332	1828
00 000 0000	Harrison Brown		PHKX B1083	1834
00 000 0000	Dr. Henry B. Brown		HLOG 346	----
00 000 0000	J.A. Brown		AMOU 6	1866
16 May 1811	James M. Brown		PBRJ 668	----
00 000 1818	Lemuel M. Brown		PBRJ 403	1840
00 000 1824	L.W. Brown		HMOR 322	1833
00 000 0000	Maggie Brown[Carter]		PAUP B256	----
00 000 0000	Martha[Brown]		PHKX B1083	1834
00 000 0000	Martha P[Brown]		HMAC 272	1862
00 000 0000	Mary Brown[McClelland]		HSAN 1055	----
00 000 0000	Mary Brown[Clare]		HPIK 673	----
00 000 0000	Mary A. Brown[Smallwood]		HDEW 341	----

00 000 0000	Reuben Brown		BRMA	333	1828
00 000 0000	Robert Brown		PBWL	1110	---
00 000 0000	S. Brown		HLOG	481	---
00 000 1782	Samuel Brown	John & Elizabeth(Crossly) NJ/NJ	HMER	811	---
00 000 0000	Rev. William Brown		TAZE	537	1830
00 000 0000	William B. Brown		HSAN	122	1832
00 000 1831	Thomas Brownfield		OCHA	89	1832
00 000 1821	D. Browning		PFAY	85	1830
00 000 0000	Franklin Browning		PHPI	412	1856
00 000 0000	Hon. O.H. Browning		HADM	413	1831
00 000 0000	Thomas Broyles		PBDP	224	---
23 Aug 1831	James Brunington		PPWA	301	1840
00 000 0000	Elisha Bryant		PBCO	405	---
20 Dec 1803	Harmon G. Brown		PBKX	275	---
00 000 1810	Benjamin Brunington	George & Mary Md1776/Md82	KNOX	658	---
00 000 0000	Jordan Bruner	David & Nancy	LOGA	697	---
00 000 0000	Mary A. Brunet[Hawes]		LOGA	577	1836
20 Jul 1843	Rhoda Bryant[Hart]	Moses	PHKX	B499	---
00 000 0000	Jacob C. Bruner		HWAD	403	---
00 000 0000	Peter Bruner		HLOG	491	---
00 000 1829	J.T. Brunk	Jesse & Naomi Ky/Md	HMOR	633	1831
00 000 0000	David P. Bryar		HLOG	491	---
00 000 1860	J.L. Brydon		ACLA	71	1891
00 000 0000	George Buchanan		HLOG	406	---
16 Sep 1845	James B. Buckler		HEDG	707	---
00 000 0000	Abraham Buckles		HMCL	960	---
00 000 0000	J.W. Budd		AMOU	8	1851
00 000 0000	M.R. Bullock		AWOO	5	1834
00 000 0000	W.H. Bullock		AWOO	8	1835
00 000 0000	Thomas Burbridge		HFUL	684	1847
21 Jan 1841	L. Burchett		HLOG	553	---
00 000 1841	P.E. Burke		OCHA	89	1878
06 Feb 1817	William Burke	John & Catherine(Barlow) Va1785/x	PBMO	B187	---
00 000 0000	Artemisa Burkhead[Chenoweth]		HPIK	482	---
00 000 1861	John A. Burkshire		OCHA	89	1862
00 000 0000	Rebecca Burnes		HSAN	442	1830

BIRTHDATE	NAME OF BIOGRAPHEE	PARENTS/BIRTHPLACE/BIRTHDATE	SOURCE/PAGE	DATE
00 000 1806	Isham Burnett	Rolland & Polly Va/Va	HMOR	616	----
00 000 0000	Richard Burnett	Rolland & Polly Va/Va	HMOR	616	----
00 000 0000	John R. Burns		HSAN	1053	c1828
00 000 0000	Mary J. Burns[Cass]		HSAN	809	----
29 May 1821	Mary Burnside[Dunseth]		COLE	565	----
00 000 0000	A. Burress		VTBU	221	----
00 000 0000	J.B. Burress		VTBU	221	----
00 000 1827	Seth Burris	Job & Sarah(Hendricks)	HGJR	303	----
00 000 0000	Jane Burroughs[Scobee]		PBWL	1086	----
17 May 1803	Jesse Burroughs		PVED	c385	----
00 Sep 1840	Polly Burt[Quisenberry]		BLOG	437	----
00 000 1817	F.J. Busey		OCHA	89	1826
00 000 1834	J.S. Busey		OCHA	89	1853
00 000 0000	Nancy Bush[Floyd]		PBJR	344	c1841
00 000 0000	Isabel Bushong[Adams]		BHBU	439	----
00 000 0000	Elizabeth Butler[Robinson]		HGSH	740	----
00 000 0000	Mary Butler[Atteberry]		HWCL	44	----
00 000 0000	Dr. Noah Butler		GHHA	898	----
00 000 0000	William M. Buzley		HSAN	871	----
00 000 1804	Isabel Bushong[Adams]		BRBM	566	----
00 000 0000	Mary Byars[Vancil]		BRMA	384	1808
00 000 0000	Benjamin Byers		CJRI	553	----
00 000 0000	Will Byers		CSBR	383	1847
00 000 0000	Delilah Caldwell[Sears]		BROC	217	----
21 Jan 1807	J.G. Caldwell	William & Nancy(Robards) Va1779/Va	HSAN	442	1841
00 000 0000	John Caldwell		HSAN	888	----
00 000 0000	Maria Caldwell[Robinson]		HLAS	B373	----
00 000 1828	Robert L. Caldwell		HMOR	322	1830
24 Jun 0000	Thomas Caldwell		CMCD	595	1832
00 000 0000	Elizabeth Callahan[Todd]		BRCM	442	----
00 000 0000	John Callahan		GHHA	696	----
00 000 0000	M.S. Calvin		HLOG	515	----
00 000 0000	A. Campbell		HPIK	482	----

Date	Name	Parents	Place	Ref	No.	Year
00 000 0000	A.E. Campbell			HCHR	261	1874
00 000 0000	Adeline Campbell[Lawler] Hugh		1812/x	PCHR	212	---
00 000 0000	Alexander Campbell Alexander		Ire/x	CELW	226	---
00 000 1824	David Campbell		Ky/Ky	PBAD	283	---
00 000 1829	Edward Campbell	Joseph & Joanna	Ky/Ky	PBAD	283	1830
00 000 1826	James Campbell	Joseph & Joanna	Ky/Ky	PBAD	283	---
00 000 0000	James Campbell	Joseph & Joanna		HADM	401	---
00 000 0000	Mary Campbell[McClure]			PPWO	543	---
00 000 0000	Mary G. Campbell[McClure]			PBWO	408	1827
00 000 1820	Thomas Campbell	Joseph & Joanna	Ky/Ky	PBAD	283	---
00 000 1808	William Campbell			HADM	884	1830
22 Oct 1808	Mary Camerer[Wheeler]			HMAC	140	---
00 000 0000	Ira A.A. Camfield			AMOU	6	---
03 Mar 1833	Rachel Cannon[Dreman]		Va/x	HSAN	795	---
12 Oct 1812	Maria Cantebury[Primm]			AMEN	38	---
00 000 0000	Martha B. Canthorn[Kimbrough]			GHHA	601	---
02 Oct 1792	Fannie[Cantrall]			HSAN	923	---
22 Feb 1808	John M. Cantrall	Zebulon G.	1773/x	PBDP	290	---
00 000 0000	Asa Capps			PBWA	224	---
00 000 0000	Elizabeth Carr[Kester]			PHCC	211	---
00 000 1807	Lucy Carr[Miller]			PBWA	563	1865
00 000 1819	John H. Carrell			GJRI	303	1851
00 000 0000	John R. Carrington			PHPI	539	---
00 000 0000	K.S. Carson			HWAS	83	---
00 000 0000	Elizabeth Carter[Norris]			PVED	561	1829
00 000 0000	Julia Carter[Givers]			PHKX	B863	1849
00 000 1809	Nancy Carter[Crews]			HWCL	B48	---
00 000 0000	Polly Carter[Jackson]			HGAS	319	---
11 Oct 1827	Rutherford G. Carter			HFUL	424	1822
00 000 0000	W.W. Carter			ACAS	19	---
00 000 1832	Rachel Cary[Paill]			HFUL	861	---
00 000 0000	Jonathan Cartmell			BRML	393	---
00 000 1803	George Carts			HMOR	323	---
00 000 0000	Anna Case			VTBU	213	---
26 Nov 1825	John Casey			PBMO	B301	---
00 000 0000	Lee Cason[Horrell]			HMCD	699	---
00 000 0000	John R. Cass			HSAN	809	---

BIRTHDATE	NAME OF BIOGRAPHEE	PARENTS/BIRTHPLACE/BIRTHDATE	SOURCE/PAGE	DATE
13 Oct 1833	Margaret E. Cassity[Rauch] Alexander		HSAN 776	----
07 Dec 1799	Aquilla Cast Ezekiel		PVED 227	1803
00 000 0000	Nancy A. Castator[Chittenden]		CJRI 511	----
00 000 0000	C.L. Castello		HLOG 506	----
00 000 1853	C.L. Castello		OPLO 85	1873
00 000 0000	William H. Castello		HLOG 506	----
20 Aug 1819	J.R. Catterton Diler & Sarah Ann		KNOX 661	----
00 000 1835	J.S. Causey		AWOO 8	----
00 000 0000	M.B. Cave[Vanarsdale]		HCHR 262	1876
00 000 0000	W.D. Cayoe		HWAS 85	1863
00 000 0000	Huldah Caywood[Swain]		PBRI 527	----
00 000 0000	Susan Cecil[Manlove]		GHHA 538	----
00 000 0000	Ellen Ceders[Trabue]		PHPI 397	----
00 000 1811	Rachel Centony		PBSM 310	----
00 000 1827	James N. Chaille John & Jane	Md/x	CJRI 795	----
00 000 0000	Eliza J. Chamberlain[Swope]		CJRI 523	----
00 000 0000	James I. Chambers	Ky/Ky	PHPI 472	----
00 000 0000	Paschal H. Chambers		HWCL 10	----
00 000 1830	Andrew Champ William & Frances(Maupin)	Ky1802/x	HMCD 811	----
00 000 0000	Elizabeth Champion[Mansfield]		KNOX 692	----
00 000 0000	Ruth Champion[McMurtry]		PBKN 321	----
00 000 0000	Ruth Champion[McMurtry]		PHKX B462	----
00 000 0000	Martha[Chandler]		HFAY 97	1823
00 000 0000	Susan Chandler[Barnes]		TAZE 638	----
00 000 0000	Emily J. Chapman[Smith]		BLOG 291	----
00 000 1813	Elizabeth A.[Chappell]		HMOR 322	1827
00 000 1822	Rev. James A. Chase		LOGA 458	1864
00 000 0000	Abraham Chenoweth		HPIK 408	1832
29 Oct 1819	H.J. Chenoweth Abraham & Rachel	Ky/Ky	HPIK 482	----
00 000 0000	James Chenoweth Richard		PBMC 483	----
00 000 0000	James H. Chenoweth		HPIK 482	----
00 000 0000	John C. Chenoweth Thomas	Ky/x	PBDP 427	----
00 000 0000	Rachel[Chenoweth]		HPIK 408	1832

Date	Name	Parents / Notes	Code	No.	Year
00 000 0000	Sanford Cherry		HLOG	499	---
00 Jan 1816	John A. Chesnu-	James & Elizabeth(Stevenson) SC/NC	HSAN	137	1826
00 000 1826	R.I. Chitty		HCAR	470	1848
00 000 0000	Catherine Chorn[Hobson]		HGJR	1014	---
00 000 0000	B. Chowning		HLOG	492	---
08 Feb 1829	Ruth Chowning	Charles & Mary(Owens)	PBCO	440	---
00 000 0000	Joel Churchill		PHPI	538	1833
00 000 0000	Burchard H. Churchill		HMCD	321	1828
23 Oct 1811	C.S. Churchill-		HSAN	442	---
00 000 1817	Moses F. Clare		HPIK	674	---
00 000 0000	Alfred Clark		PHPI	414	---
00 000 0000	Benjamin Clark		PBCO	538	1833
00 000 1798	Benjamin Clark		COLE	621	---
30 Sep 1809	David W. Clark	John W & Ann(Isgrig) NJ/Md	HLOG	506	---
00 000 0000	E.B. Clark		HMAC	268	1830
00 000 0000	H.C. Clark		HMAC	269	1852
00 000 0000	Joseph F. Clark		HMAC	268	1832
00 000 0000	Nancy[Clark]		HMAC	268	1830
03 Sep 1822	Rebecca Clark[Parker]		COLE	573	1828
00 000 0000	Y.B. Clark		HCHR	262	1839
00 000 0000	David Clarke		PBWA	501	---
20 Nov 1829	Rebecca J. Clarke[Chapman] David & Eliza S(Russell)Ky99/Ky05		HFUL	426	---
29 Sep 1822	Samuel L. Clarke	James & Mary(Lewis)	HMCD	665	---
00 000 0000	Elvira[Clarkson]		PVED	242	---
00 000 0000	George Clarkson		PVED	242	---
00 000 0000	Mildred J. Clarkson[Williams] Dr J.M.		PBAD	280	---
00 000 0000	Mary Claston[Woodard]		BEFF	886	---
04 Feb 1828	George W. Claycomb		PPWA	300	1835
00 000 0000	Francis Clayton		HMOR	557	---
00 000 0000	Phoebe[Clayton]		HMOR	557	---
00 000 1819	Rosan[Claypool]		HJOD	662	1847
00 000 0000	Moses Clayton		BRMA	535	---
23 Apr 1818	E.R. Clemens	David Va/x	GHHA	659	1843
29 Jan 1850	Martha G. Clements[Duncan]		CHAM	920	---
00 000 0000	Mary A. Clements[Cirry]		CSBR	385	1834
00 000 0000	Nancy Clements[Lewis]		PPVE	555	---

BIRTHDATE	NAME OF BIOGRAPHEE	PARENTS/BIRTHPLACE/BIRTHDATE	SOURCE/PAGE	DATE
00 000 0000	Henry Clifton		HWCL 148	----
00 000 0000	William C. Cloud		HGSH 685	1832
00 000 0000	Thomas Cloyd		HSAN 442	1824
00 Feb 1807	George Coats		HGJR 883	1832
00 000 0000	Mary Coats[Doyle]		PEMO B202	1832
00 000 0000	Mary Coats[Doyle]	John & Rachel(Richardson)	HGJR 951	----
00 000 1844	L.B. Cocran		BHAN 184	----
00 000 0000	Celia Cockerel[Hainline]		HMCD 627	----
00 000 0000	William M. Coe		HCHR 266	----
00 000 0000	K.C. Coffee[Campbell]		HPIK 482	----
00 000 0000	Henry T. Coffey		AMEN 19	1868
06 Sep 1799	Mary Coffey[Meadows]		PBWA 661	----
00 000 1838	Eliza A. Coffman[Darnall]		BMCL 995	----
00 000 0000	Isaac Coffman		HLOG 492	----
00 000 0000	Levi Coffman		HLOG 492	----
16 Sep 1812	Isaac Cogdal	Joseph & Lucy(Southern)	HMEM 749	1823
00 000 0000	Nancy Cogdall[Miller]		HMEM 850	----
00 000 0000	Capt. Joseph B. Coghlan		EFAY 605	----
00 000 0000	Jacob Y. Coil		BCSB 488	----
00 000 0000	Sarah S[Cole]		HMOR 323	1828
00 000 1829	Albert Coley	William H & Elizabeth(McClane) Va/Ky	HPIK 674	1853
00 000 0000	Rebecca Collings[Darr]		PPVE 763	----
00 000 0000	J.W. Collins		HLOG 348	----
00 000 0000	Millie Collins[Dunbar]		PHKX B484	1826
00 000 1823	C.F. Columbia		OCHA 90	1842
00 000 0000	John A. Colvin		HLOG 506	----
00 000 1821	Luther K. Colvin		HHEN 257	1856
00 000 0000	L.K. Colvin		AHEN 14	1851
00 000 1831	Turner Colvin		ACLA 71	1866
22 Feb 1806	Jonathan Combs		HGSH 531	c1825
00 000 0000	Mary A. Combs		HADM 401	1829
00 000 0000	Thomas Combs		CASS 926	----

Date	Name	Parents / Origin	Code	No.	Year
00 000 0000	Andrew Comstock		HLOG	348	---
00 000 0000	John W. Comstock		HLOG	428	---
00 000 0000	H.D. Conder		HCHR	261	1864
00 000 0000	Isaac Conkright		HPIK	632	---
00 000 0000	Lizzie[Conlee]		HWAS	83	---
00 000 0000	Whitfield Conlee George		BRMA	546	---
00 000 0000	C. Conover		HMEM	568	---
00 000 0000	John G. Conover		HMEM	568	---
00 000 0000	William Conover		HMEM	568	---
00 000 0000	Elizabeth Constant[Elkin]		PBMC	315	---
00 000 0000	Nathan E. Constant		HSAN	1051	---
00 000 0000	Bartlett Conyers		AMEN	26	1828
00 000 0000	Jane Cooledge[Eranson]		PPME	404	---
00 000 0000	Catherine E[Cock]		HMAC	273	1848
14 May 1824	L.P. Cook Joseph & Parmelia(Morse)	Va/Carolina	HWCL	B103	---
00 000 1828	George Coombs		ACLA	71	1842
00 000 0000	Stephen Coonrod		BCHR	865	---
00 000 1812	A.B. Cooper Jacob & Sarah(Kenner)		HMCD	781	1854
15 Mar 1819	Isabella A. Cooper[Van Sandt] Murdock & Elizabeth(Parker)		PBMO	B255	Ky/Ky
00 000 0000	William K. Cooper	Va/Va	HMCH	477	---
25 Sep 1826	William T. Cooper Edmund L & Mary(Perry)	Va/Va	HGJR	952	---
27 Feb 1832	Hardan W. Corman		BMCL	981	---
00 000 0000	S.T. Corn		HMAC	267	1866
11 May 1857	Matilda Cornwell[Redman] Hiram & Lucy(Toler) Ky1812/Va1820		PBCO	375	---
00 000 0000	Thomas Correll		HSAN	441	1830
00 000 0000	Susan M. Corwin[Priett]		PAUP	B323	---
00 000 0000	B.F. Corwine		HLOG	451	---
00 000 0000	Richard Corwire		HLOG	451	---
25 Dec 1813	Nathaniel Cosby William & Frances	Eng/Ger	BLOG	592	1836
00 000 0000	David Cossairt Albert	Ky/x	PPVE	414	---
15 Oct 1801	Maj. William Costley William & Margarette		HGJR	786	---
23 Nov 1816	John J. Cottingham		COLE	612	---
00 000 0000	John Cottrell		CJRI	512	---
00 000 1822	B.F. Couchman		HMOR	322	1827
00 000 1819	E.R. Couchman		HMOR	322	1827
07 Feb 1808	Lucinda Council[McHenry]		PBCO	280	---

BIRTHDATE	NAME OF BIOGRAPHEE	PARENTS/BIRTHPLACE/BIRTHDATE	SOURCE/PAGE	DATE
00 000 0000	Michael Cowger		CJRI 531	----
00 000 0000	Charles Cox		HADM 737	1829
00 000 1821	Charles Cox		HMOR 322	1852
00 000 1850	George H. Cox		OPLO 85	----
26 Dec 1846	Dr. George W. Cox	Ky/x	PBRJ 663	----
00 000 0000	John W. Cox		PBHE 384	----
00 000 1834	N.C. Cox	Samuel & Jane(Hampton)	HMCD 770	----
00 000 0000	Nancy[Cox]		HMOR 570	1834
00 000 0000	William F. Cox	Joseph	CSBR 328	----
00 000 0000	Garrett Cozine		HFUL 794	----
00 000 0000	Jonathan Crabb		HHEN 350	----
00 000 0000	Stephen Crabtree		HLOG 472	----
00 000 0000	Priscilla Crafton[Craig]		HADM 738	1829
00 000 0000	Clarinda Craig[Davis]		PBCO 273	----
00 000 1807	Edward Craig		HMOR 323	1830
00 000 0000	Isaac N. Craig	Robert Va/x	PBCO 285	----
00 000 1817	J. Perry Craig		HMOR 323	1834
00 000 1807	James Craig		HMOR 323	1830
10 Aug 0000	John Craig		HADM 874	1830
00 000 0000	John Craig		HADM 738	1829
00 000 0000	Jonathan Craig		HADM 400	1829
00 000 1848	M.M. Craig		PFAY 85	1861
00 000 1815	Maria S[Craig]		HMOR 323	1827
00 000 0000	Mary Craig[Baston]		MACL 298	----
00 000 1811	Mary A[Craig]		HMOR 323	1832
00 000 0000	Rachel Craig[Cox]	John & Lulu(Crampton) Ky/x	PBAD 159	----
00 000 0000	Rachel N. Craig[Cox]	Robert & Elizabeth(Nichol) Va/Va	BCSB 165	----
00 Oct 1804	William Craig	William Ky/x	PBCO 531	----
12 Sep 1812	James J. Craill		HFUL 911	----
00 Dec 1818	Eliza Crain[Stevens]		HADM 874	----
07 Sep 1854	Emma A. Crane[Verry]		HMCL 941	----
00 000 0000	Lafayette Crane		HPIK 575	----
00 000 0000	Mary A. Crane[Huff]	William Va/x	BRCM 181	----

Date	Name	Notes		Source	Page	Year
00 000 0000	Y.B. Cravens	Elijah		HWCL	108	----
00 000 0000	Mary A. Crawford[Cockern]			HMCH	154	----
00 000 0000	Elizabeth R[Crews]			CJRI	567	----
17 Apr 1807	Hooper Crews			BCHI	531	----
00 Oc 1804	Jesse Crews			HWCL	B48	----
00 000 1818	William Crews	Matthew		HWCL	B11	1822
00 000 0000	Rachel[Cromwell]			PPVE	1058	----
00 000 0000	George W. Crooke			HMAC	276	1850
00 000 0000	Sylvenie[Crooke]			HMAC	276	1870
00 0c 1800	Alvin Cross			HSAN	878	----
00 000 0000	Solomon Cross			PBDP	751	----
24 Jan 1812	W.D. Crow			HSAN	795	1823
00 000 0000	Caroline Crowder[Foster]			HMAD	583	1829
03 Oct 1827	Mary E. Crumbaugh	Daniel & Martha(Robinson)		HMCL	878	1828
00 000 0000	Martha A. Crutchfield[Lawson]			CELW	350	1864
00 000 0000	Permelia Cullom[Brown]			TAZE	537	1830
00 000 0000	J. Cummings			CAOG	94	1849
10 Feb 1845	Capt. Robert S. Cummins	Moses & Rebecca A(Scott)	Ky/Ky	CJRI	534	----
00 000 0000	James Cunningham			PPVE	45	----
00 000 0000	Margaret Cunningham[Rainey]			BRGW	153	1824
00 000 0000	Matthew J. Cunningham			PJEF	B83	----
00 000 0000	William Cunningham			BGSB	513	1837
00 000 0000	David Cure			HADM	401	1823
17 Feb 1824	Elizabeth Curl[Curry]			HADM	738	1828
00 000 0000	H.P. Curry			AMEN	23	----
00 000 0000	Mary Curry[Smith]			HADM	750	----
22 Jan 1830	Richard S. Curry	Thomas & Malinda(Murphy)	Ky/Ky	HADM	738	1837
00 000 0000	Susan E.P[Cushing]			HGHR	266	----
00 000 0000	Sarah Curry[Davis]			HSAN	933	----
00 000 0000	Sam Dabbs			GHHA	275	----
00 000 0000	Mary Dailey[Standerfer]			HGSH	740	----
00 000 0000	John Dale			HGSH	690	----
00 000 0000	Francis A. Dallam			GHHA	659	----
00 000 0000	Frank A. Dallam			HMCH	162	----
00 000 0000	B.F. Dalzell			HLOG	429	----
00 000 0000	Charles Damron	Wilson	Va/x	BRJM	465	----

BIRTHDATE	NAME OF BIOGRAPHEE	PARENTS/BIRTHPLACE/BIRTHDATE		SOURCE/PAGE	DATE
00 000 0000	F. Dancy			VTBU 349	----
00 000 0000	Rev. J.A. Daniels			HMEM 568	----
00 000 0000	Aaron Darnall			PVED 522	----
00 000 1799	James M. Daugherty			HMOR 324	1830
00 000 0000	John Daugherty			PHCC 298	----
00 000 0000	John Daugherty	Thomas & Mary	Ky/Ky	BGLS 277	----
00 000 0000	Thomas Daugherty	John		BGLS 240	----
00 0oc 1802	Lucy Davenport[Major]			PBWO 283	1834
07 Mar 1834	Merrill C. Davenport	Ephraim & Sallie	NC/NC	HMOR 636	1868
00 000 1822	Milton C. Davenport			HMOR 323	1825
05 Sep 1826	Hezekiah Davidson			PPDM 556	1829
08 Jan 1815	Daniel Davis	John & Elizabeth(Green)		HGJR 307	----
00 000 0000	David B. Davis			HLOG 520	----
22 Mar 1820	Edward Davis			HGAS 340	----
00 000 0000	Edward Davis			AGAS 22	1835
00 000 0000	Elijah Davis			CASS 876	----
31 Dec 1813	James Davis	James	Bourbon/x	PBMC 473	----
00 000 1796	James Davis			HGAS 340	----
00 000 0000	Jerome Davis			HSAN 933	----
00 000 0000	John H. Davis			AGAS 23	1835
00 000 0000	Joseph Davis		Va/x	FBMC 727	1828
23 Dec 0000	Juliann Davis[Davis]			HGAN 340	----
17 Feb 1815	Levi Davis	Peter & Christina(Shutt)	NC/x	HGAS 330	----
00 000 0000	Lucinda[Davis]			KNOX 669	----
00 000 0000	Lydia Davis[Kizer]			PPPI 490	----
00 000 1821	Nancy Davis[Hodges]			PBWO B203	----
14 Apr 1826	Richard L. Davis	James B & Elizabeth(Hawkins)	Va/Va	HGAS 340	----
00 000 0000	Richard Davis			CASS 876	----
00 000 1870	S.J. Davis			OCHA 90	1884
00 000 0000	Solomon Davis			KNOX 669	----
00 000 0000	Sophia Davis[Poplett]			PHKX B759	1834
00 000 0000	Thomas Davis			PBCO 273	----
30 Dec 1817	Thomas Davis			PBCO 190	----

	Name		Code	No.	Year
00 000 0000	Minerva Davidson[Stokes]		PAUP	B195	--
00 000 0000	Howell Dawdy		PBKN	256	--
24 Jan 1812	Jefferson M. Lawdy James & Margaret(Morse)	NC/SC	KNOX	669	--
00 000 1798	John Dawdy		PBWA	644	--
00 000 0000	Robert P. Dawes		HLOG	492	--
00 000 0000	Arminta Dawson[Tomlinson]		BLOG	624	1841
00 000 1819	Creed H. Dawson		BLOG	404	--
00 000 0000	Mary E[Dawson]		HWAS	85	1864
00 000 0000	Nancy Dawson[McPherson]		HCHR	261	1870
00 000 0000	Robert W. Dear.		PBRJ	212	--
00 Jan 1809	Margaret Deane[Arnett] James	Ky/x	HFUL	828	--
00 000 1826	Mary A. Deator.		HMOR	323	1831
00 000 0000	J.F. Deboe		HCHR	266	--
00 000 0000	W.B. Dedman		AMOU	8	1868
00 000 0000	Harrison Deering		ACAS	19	1849
00 000 1850	J.A. Demonbrun		PFAY	85	1880
00 000 0000	Aaron Denning		HGSH	944	1818
00 000 1805	Benjamin Delaplain Samuel	Fr/x	HMAD	508	1807
00 000 0000	Louisa J[Dennis]		HWAS	84	1873
00 000 0000	Celia J. Densmore[Clawson]		HCHR	263	1854
00 000 1831	Noel B. Devol		ACLA	71	1852
00 000 1819	A.B. Devore		HMOR	324	1831
18 Oct 1819	John Devore		PBWH	342	--
00 000 0000	Letitia D. Devore[Fry] John		HMOR	638	--
00 000 1805	Uriah J. Devore		HMOR	324	1831
00 000 0000	William M. Dewees Nimrod		PHPI	541	--
27 Oct 1822	William M. Dewees		PBDP	324	1831
04 Jul 1838	--- Dewitt John & Mary(Spurling)	Va/Va	PHCC	298	--
00 000 1815	Levi Dick		HMOR	324	1831
00 000 0000	E.A. Dickerson		HSAN	442	1831
00 000 0000	John Dickerson		PCHR	317	--
00 000 0000	John H. Dickerson		HCHR	164	--
00 000 0000	Martin M. Dickerson		BRMA	187	--
00 000 0000	Mary E. Dickerson[Hunter]		BCHR	946	--
00 000 0000	Michael Dickerson		PBML	1057	--

BIRTHDATE	NAME OF BIOGRAPHEE	PARENTS/BIRTHPLACE/BIRTHDATE	SOURCE/PAGE	DATE
00 000 0000	John Dickey		PBMC 413	----
05 Mar 1843	Samuel H. Dickey		PBHE 602	1851
00 000 0000	Thomas H. Dickey		HMAC 273	1867
00 000 0000	William Dickey		PPDM 222	----
00 000 0000	Thomas J. Dickirson		CELW 351	1828
00 000 0000	John Dickison		PBPE 500	----
00 000 0000	Polly Dickison[White]		PBPE 500	----
00 000 0000	John Dickson		PPVE 812	----
00 000 0000	Louis Dillman	Vachel & Harriett B(Smith) Ky/Tn	BRGM 41	----
00 000 0000	Margaret Dills[Blackwell]		PHPI 412	----
00 000 0000	Mary Dills[Gum]		PPME 456	----
00 000 0000	Thomas Dinwiddie		HGAS 321	----
00 000 0000	Vizilla[Dinwiddie]		HCAS 321	----
00 000 0000	Solomon Dixon		HLOG 532	----
17 Dec 1839	Thomas J. Doak		HMGD 1144	----
00 000 0000	Nancy R. Dickerson[Boggess]		HMAC 274	1835
00 000 0000	Elizabeth Dobson[Davis]		HCAS 236	----
00 000 0000	Gilbert Dodds		HSAN 657	----
00 000 0000	Martha Dodson[Moore]		PBWL 809	----
00 000 0000	Sarah[Dodson]		HMAC 270	1848
00 000 0000	William M. Dodson		PBWL 663	1847
00 000 0000	Mary Doke[Darnall]		PVED 522	----
24 Apr 1823	John L. Donalson	James & Sarah(Klines) Ky/Ky	TAZE 501	1873
00 000 0000	Elizabeth Donnellsen[Linville]		PBSM 551	----
00 000 0000	Sarah Donner		HSAN 442	1830
00 000 1816	J.P. Donovan		ACLA 71	1845
00 000 0000	Archibald Dorothy		GHHA 701	1836
17 Sep 1851	James W. Dooley		HMGL 965	1852
00 000 0000	Samuel L. Dorsey		HMAD 573	1834
00 000 1814	Samuel L. Dorsey	Nimrod & Matilda(Dorsey) Md1789/x	HMAD 491	1834
00 000 0000	Daniel Doty		CJRI 513	----
00 000 0000	Thomas Doty		PHEF B228	----
00 000 0000	Josiah Douglas		HADM 400	1835
00 000 0000	William Douglas		HMEM 358	----

Date	Name	Note	Code	No.	Year
00 00c 1828	Minerva Douglass[Srodgrass]		CJRI	318	---
00 000 0000	S.S. Douglass		AHEN	18	1854
00 000 0000	William S. Douglass		ACAS	19	1850
00 000 0000	Rev. Nathan H. Dowring	Va/x	HCAS	198	1842
00 000 1810	Andrew Downs	Thomas	HGJR	976	c1833
00 000 0000	Hugh Doyal		CJRI	304	---
00 000 0000	Elizabeth Doyle[Lickson]		PPVE	812	---
00 000 0000	Mary[Doyle]		PPVE	812	---
15 Jan 1809	Thomas Doyle	Samuel & Mahala(Lovelace)	HGJR	951	---
00 000 0000	Thomas Doyle		PBMO	B202	1832
00 000 1816	S.R. Drake		ACLA	71	1837
00 000 0000	Robert M. Drury		HMAC	268	1852
00 000 0000	Andrew M. Duff		BRML	254	---
00 000 0000	George Dunbar		PHKX	B484	1826
00 000 1822	Washington Dunbar		HHEN	481	c1835
02 Dec 1813	Darius Duncan	James	PPVE	436	1833
00 000 0000	Eliza W. Duncan	Pa/x	HADM	400	1820
00 000 0000	James T. Duncan		HSAN	1014	---
00 000 0000	N.A[Duncan]		HJAC	129	1870
00 000 1810	S.S. Duncan		HMOR	323	1822
00 000 1806	William Duncan	Henry	HGSH	880	---
00 000 0000	John M. Duning		PBML	800	---
00 000 0000	Andrew Dunlap		HMCD	982	1841
22 Mar 1811	E.P. Dunlap		PBKN	536	---
00 000 0000	Elijah T. Dunn		HLOG	499	---
00 000 0000	Margaret Dunn[Peters]		CJRI	333	---
00 000 1831	N.L. Dunn		PFAY	85	1836
00 000 0000	Thomas Dunn		PHPI	365	---
00 000 1831	Z.M. Dunn		OCHA	90	1834
18 Apr 1831	Z.M. Dunn	Zephaniah	HCHA	115	1833
00 000 0000	Joseph P. Durben		HCHR	33	---
00 000 0000	William Duvall		HGSH	537	---
00 000 0000	Alice Dye[Mayrugh]		PPVE	978	---
00 000 0000	Martha A[Dyer]		HLOG	411	---
00 000 0000	Nancy Dyer[Salisbury]		HFUL	961	---
00 000 1815	Mary A. Dyke		CHAM	940	---
02 Feb 1834	J.A. Eads		HMOR	324	1835
			HEDG	572	---

BIRTHDATE	NAME OF BIOGRAPHEE	PARENTS/BIRTHPLACE/BIRTHDATE	SOURCE/PAGE		DATE
00 000 0000	Joseph S. Eakins		ACAS	22	1864
00 000 0000	Jane Earl[Robeson]		PPWO	447	----
00 000 0000	James Easley		HSAN	796	1829
03 Jul 1824	Mary F. Easley	Ambrose & Elizabeth(Haggard)	HSAN	796	----
00 000 0000	W.W. Easley		ACAS	22	1864
00 000 0000	Annie O[Eastham]		HMAC	276	1859
00 000 0000	George A. Eastham		HMAC	276	1850
00 000 0000	W.E. Eastham		HMAC	276	1851
00 000 1807	Daniel Easton		PBCO	233	----
00 000 0000	George S. Eaton		ACAS	19	1854
00 000 0000	Martha J. Eaton[Sisson]		HGJR	285	----
16 Apr 1827	Martha Jane Eaton[Sisson]		LOGA	881	----
00 000 0000	Catherine Eberhardt		AMOU	8	1873
00 000 0000	J.E. Eden		AMOU	6	1853
00 000 0000	John Eden		AMOU	6	1853
00 000 1819	G.W. Edgar		OPLO	85	1835
00 000 0000	Mattie Edie[Lafferty]		HMER	639	----
00 000 0000	D.E. Edrington		COAG	98	1838
00 000 0000	Ambrose Edwards		HMEM	680	----
00 000 0000	C.S. Edwards		AMOU	8	1872
00 000 0000	James L. Edwards		VTBU	350	----
00 000 0000	Penelope Edwards[Shaw]		BRBM	386	1828
00 000 0000	William Edwards		HWCL	185	----
00 000 1816	Cynthia Elder[Baker]		HGSH	594	----
00 000 0000	Annie Elkin[England]		HMEM	758	----
00 000 1826	Minerva A. Ellidge[O'Hair]		PBCO	365	1852
00 000 0000	David Ellis		GHHA	519	1828
00 000 0000	Minerva J[Ellis]		HJAC	130	----
13 Oct 1833	Permelia Ellis[Hitch]		COLE	647	----
00 000 0000	Mary A. Ellison[Moore] Reuben		PPWO	603	----
00 000 0000	Rachel Ellsberry[McKee]		PVED	887	----
22 Feb 1820	Ira F. Elrod	Michael & Ruth(Evans)	HFUL	---	1831
30 Sep 1819	Francis M. Emerson	William & Polly(Tuggle)	EMCL	1019	----
00 000 1805	Charles D. Emmons		PHCC	299	----

	Name		Code	No.	Year
00 000 0000	Lodama England[Lawson]		CELW	350	1820
00 000 0000	John Engle		BRCM	341	---
00 000 0000	William Engle		HMEM	358	1823
00 000 0000	John N. English		HGJR	345	---
00 000 1817	F.B. Ennis		ACLA	71	1833
00 000 1824	Harry M. Ennis		HMOR	324	1834
00 000 0000	James H. Epperson		CMCD	353	---
00 000 0000	Eliza Esqueridge George & Elizabeth(Robison)		HWGL	59	---
00 000 0000	Joseph Essex		PAUP	B286	---
00 000 0000	Susan Estey[Messer]		PBML	887	---
00 000 0000	James W. Estill		AMEN	23	1823
00 000 0000	Elizabeth Estill[Cantrell]		HMEM	119	---
00 000 1837	Marietta Enochs[Graham]		PHKX	B431	---
00 000 0000	J.C. Evans		PHPI	367	1832
00 000 0000	Richard Evans	Ger/x	HPIK	761	---
00 000 0000	Jacob Evinger John G.		PHCC	156	---
00 000 1784	Sophia Evinger[Snider]		PHCC	158	---
00 000 0000	E.S. Ewing		HLOG	493	---
00 000 0000	John C. Ewing		GHHA	775	1847
00 000 0000	John H. Ewing		HLOG	500	---
00 000 0000	Robert W. Ewing		AMEN	19	1857
00 000 1841	John H. Ewing Nathan & Nancy(Young)	Ky/Ky	BMCL	1021	---
00 000 0000	Squire William Ewing		COLE	546	---
00 000 0000	Williamson Ewing		HLOG	481	---
00 000 0000	Catherine Eye[Cowger]		CJRI	531	---
00 000 0000	Hannah Fair[Smith]		HGJR	881	---
00 000 0000	Margaret Falkner[Breeze]		BRCM	574	---
00 000 0000	H.B. Farmer		HLOG	532	---
00 000 0000	Jennie W[Farmer]		HWAS	84	1833
00 000 0000	Marion Farmer		HMAD	572	1852
00 000 1848	A.P. Farthing		PFAY	86	1884
00 000 0000	Marcus G. Faulkner		HWAS	83	1831
00 000 1834	Virginia Feathermgill[Wright]		PBAD	457	---
28 Aug 1827	Amanda J. Fenton[Moyer]		HLOG	390	---
00 000 0000	Highland Ferguson[Martin]		PPME	308	---
00 000 1818	Richard Ferris		OPLO	85	1836

BIRTHDATE	NAME OF BIOGRAPHEE	PARENTS/BIRTHPLACE/BIRTHDATE	SOURCE/PAGE		DATE
00 000 1807	O.B. Ficklin		PHCC	22	1828
00 000 0000	Orlando B. Ficklin		BRCM	448	----
16 Dec 1808	Orlando B. Ficklin		PHEF	A143	----
00 000 0000	Orlando B. Ficklin	William & Elizabeth K(Williams) Va/Va	PBCO	187	----
16 Dec 1808	Orlando B. Ficklin	William & Elizabeth K(Williams) Va/Va	COLE	519	----
00 000 0000	Alexander P. Field		HMAD	184	----
00 000 0000	Joseph Field		HGJR	1118	----
00 000 0000	Lewis Field	Lewis	BRJM	146	1810
00 000 0000	Andy Finley		HCHR	34	1829
00 000 0000	David Finley		PVED	442	----
00 000 0000	John Finley		HCHR	34	1829
00 000 0000	David Finley		PPVE	650	----
00 000 1833	Elizabeth T. Fisher[Ellis]		GHHA	519	----
00 000 0000	John R. Fisher		PBSM	331	----
00 000 0000	Sarah Fisher[Field]		BRJM	146	----
00 000 0000	Jesse Flatt	Edward & Rosa. Va/Va	HGJR	828	----
15 Sep 1815	John Flatt	Edward & Rosa(Garrison) Barren/NC	HGJR	828	----
00 000 0000	G.J. Fletcher		HSAN	441	1830
00 000 1823	T.C. Fletcher		OPLO	85	1834
00 000 0000	Zachariah Fletcher		LOGA	540	1834
00 000 1801	Alexander B. Florer		PBCO	254	----
00 000 0000	Anna E[Floyd]		HMAC	277	1859
00 000 0000	Nathaniel W. Floyd		PBRJ	344	c1841
00 000 0000	T. Warren Floyd		HMAC	277	1859
00 000 0000	J.M. Foley		AMOU	8	1849
00 000 1800	Leah Foley[Reynolds]		HGSH	651	----
02 Jun 1802	Margaret Forbes[Cross]		HSAN	878	----
00 000 0000	Jacob Foreman		HPIK	454	----
00 000 0000	Augustine E. Foster		HMEM	730	----
00 000 0000	Harrison Foster		PBML	679	1851
11 May 1815	John P. Foster		HHEN	226	1838
00 000 1827	John T. Foster	David	HGJR	889	1835

Date	Name	Parents / Notes	Origin	Code	No.	Year
00 000 0000	Letta Foster[Fowe]			BGLA	767	c1836
00 000 0000	Permelia[Foster]			HMEM	730	---
00 000 1806	John Foutch	John		HFUL	718	1827
10 Jun 1837	John B. Fowler		Va/x	BRKI	1140	---
00 000 0000	William Francis	Charles & Nancy	Ky/Ky	HADM	739	---
24 Feb 1847	Virginius Frayser	P.G.	Va/x	BRJM	355	---
00 000 1818	Lafayette H. Frazer			BHAN	374	1826
00 000 0000	Jane Frazier[Lowry]			HGHR	261	1856
00 000 0000	Nancy Frazier[Dawdy]			PBMO	B11	---
00 000 0000	Thomas Frazier			PBCO	365	---
02 Dec 1826	Dr. William Friend	Ephraim & Rachel(Murphy)	Ky/Ky	CELW	310	---
00 000 0000	Nancy Frost[George]			HGHR	265	---
00 000 0000	James Fruit			LOGA	702	---
11 Sep 1803	Milton Fry			HMOR	638	---
14 Jun 1844	Thomas Fry			HSAN	743	---
00 000 1808	J.F. Fulkerson			BRJM	531	---
00 000 0000	J.H. Fullenwider			HSAN	441	1834
00 000 0000	J.N. Fullenwider			HSAN	441	1834
00 000 0000	William S. Fullenwider			BMCL	1040	---
00 000 0000	Isaac Fulton			AMEN	19	1830
00 000 0000	John B. Fulton			PBSM	314	---
00 000 0000	Isaac Funk			HMCL	784	---
17 Nov 1797	Isaac Funk	Adam & Nancy(Moore)	Pa/Pa	PBML	1160	---
00 000 1835	G.F. Fuqua			ACLA	72	1876
00 000 0000	Coleman Gaines			HLOG	352	---
00 000 0000	H.P. Gaines			AMEN	19	1856
00 000 0000	Henry P. Gaines			HLOG	473	---
00 000 0000	Anna Galloway[Harbert]			HPML	813	---
25 Jun 1782	Joseph Galloway	David & Mary(Johnson) Scott36/1739		PBMC	214	---
20 Jan 1804	Leah Gannis[McClure]			PBML	876	---
00 000 0000	Thomas G. Gardner			HLOG	352	---
05 Oct 1831	William M. Gardner			PPWA	301	1848
00 000 0000	B.J. Garrett			AMOU	8	1850
00 000 0000	W.D. Garrett			AMOU	8	1851
30 Nov 1807	Clarissa Garrison[Wall]	Aaron & Lucy(McColun)	SC/Oh	PBML	581	---
00 000 0000	Elijah Garrison			HPIK	455	1826
00 000 1823	J.R. Garwood			ACLA	72	1827
00 000 0000	Sarah Garwood[Spain]			CJRI	780	---

BIRTHDATE	NAME OF BIOGRAPHEE	PARENTS/BIRTHPLACE/BIRTHDATE	SOURCE/PAGE	DATE
00 000 0000	John J. Gash	John & Ann(Wood)	HMCH 299	----
00 000 0000	Peter Gasaway		BCLA 752	----
00 000 1815	Peter Gasaway		PHCC 113	----
00 000 0000	Wilson G. Gaskins		PCHR 218	----
25 Mar 1835	Elvira Gates[Foster]	John & Lucinda	HSAN 764	----
00 000 0000	Joseph T. Gates		HLOG 412	----
00 000 0000	Joseph Gattan		HSAN 981	----
00 000 0000	Z.W. Gatton		ACAS 22	1824
00 000 1812	Zachariah W. Gatton		HMOR 324	1824
13 Nov 1812	Zachariah W. Gatton		HCAS 204	----
00 000 0000	Major B.H. Gatton		HMEM 568	----
00 000 0000	H.P. Gatton		HMEM 568	----
00 000 0000	James M. Gaunt	Thomas Va/x	PAUP B305	----
00 0Oc 1826	Allen Gebhart	Thomas & Nellie(Robbins) Va/Taylor	PHKX B421	----
00 000 0000	Mary E. George[Shake]		HCHR 262	1851
00 000 0000	R.W. George		HCHR 262	1850
00 000 0000	James German		HFUL 700	----
08 May 1803	James Gilbert		BRJM 482	----
00 000 0000	Simon Gilbert		COLE 615	----
00 000 1855	P.M. Gilbert		OPLO 85	1857
00 000 1832	John Gillham		BHAN 156	----
00 000 0000	John W. Gilliland		HLOG 483	----
00 000 1805	William P. Gilliland	Robert	PBAD 260	----
28 Oct 1828	S.G. Gillaspie		PPWA 349	1864
24 Feb 1824	Polly Gillum[Cowden]		HMCL 999	----
10 Sep 1814	D.H. Gilmer		HPIK 681	----
00 000 0000	Alexander Gilmore		HMEM 346	----
00 000 0000	James L. Gilmore		BEFF 762	----
00 000 0000	Lucinda Gilmore[Jacobs]		PBAD 372	----
00 000 0000	Elizabeth Gimlin[Burleson]		HMAC 268	1830
00 000 0000	Julia[Givens]		KNOX ---	----
00 000 0000	T.H. Givens		KNOX ---	----
00 000 0000	Thales H. Givens	James	PHKX B863	----
00 000 0000	Lydia[Givens]		HMOR 545	----

Date	Name	Parents / Spouse	Place	Code	No.	Year
00 000 0000	J.P. Glasscock			AMOU	8	1869
00 000 0000	G.W. Glenn			AMEN	22	1856
00 000 0000	Isaac D. Glenn	Samuel & Elizabeth		BRBM	693	----
00 000 1800	Isaac D. Glenn			BRBM	258	----
00 000 0000	Jacob Glenn			HHEN	315	----
08 Nov 1809	Jacob Glenn	James & Sarah(Shoafanstall)		PBHE	269	1871
00 000 0000	Kate B[Glenny]			HMAC	344	----
00 000 0000	Matilda Glove[Adam]		Ky/x	HSTC	948	----
00 000 0000	Dr. Abbott Goddard	--- & Prudence		PBML	19	1825
00 000 0000	E.M. Goff			AMEN	362	----
00 000 0000	Iredell Goff			PHCC	483	----
00 000 0000	John R. Goff			HLOG	19	1825
00 000 0000	William Goff			AMEN	439	----
00 000 0000	William Goff			PPME	450	1818
19 Aug 1822	Capt. Caleb Gonterman	Jacob		HMAD	B63	----
00 000 0000	Nancy Goodman[Harris]	William & Sarah(Maxey)		PBMO	86	1854
00 000 0000	Thomas Goodman			PFAY	324	1835
00 000 1835	R.A. Goodrick			HMOR	449	----
00 000 0000	Nancy Goodson[Harris]	William & Sarah(Maxey)	Va/Va	PBMB	230	----
00 000 0000	J.C. Goodwin			CJRI	893	----
00 000 0000	Mary Gordon[Fowler]			HMGD	766	1825
00 000 0000	William Gordon			HSAN	260	1831
00 000 0000	John Gore			HCHR	267	1847
00 000 0000	Michael Gore			HMAC	267	----
00 000 0000	W.F. Gore			HCHR	143	----
00 000 0000	Walton Gore	John		BRJM	538	----
00 000 0000	Virginia C. Gorin	Sanford P.		PPWO	275	1868
00 000 0000	Mary Gosins[Clardy]			HMAC	266	----
00 000 0000	Mary E. Gosney[Tobias]			HCHR	306	----
00 000 0000	James Gossett			VTBU	324	----
00 000 0000	George Graff			HMOR	724	1834
22 Feb 1826	Washington Graff			HSAN	1043	1834
10 Jun 1818	William Gragg					
00 000 0000	Margaret Graham[Armstrong]			PBSM	559	----
00 000 0000	Sarah E. Graham[Wright]	Fergus & Martha(Tyree)		BCSB	491	----
00 000 0000	Ezekiel Grantham			PBMO	B285	----
15 Nov 1857	L. Kate Graves[Talbott]			GHHA	590	----
00 000 0000	Richard Graves			HCAS	203	1828

BIRTHDATE	NAME OF BIOGRAPHEE	PARENTS/BIRTHPLACE/BIRTHDATE	SOURCE/PAGE	DATE
00 000 1803	Mary Gray[Jackson]	John	BRBM 60	----
00 000 0000	Robert W. Gray		AWOO 5	1857
00 000 1833	Thomas Grayham	John & Susan	HPIK 409	1855
00 000 0000	America Greathouse[Hoover]		HPIK 457	1825
00 000 0000	Mahala Greathouse[Hoover]		HPIK 458	1820
00 000 0000	Elizabeth S. Green[Clark]		HCHR 262	1839
00 000 0000	John Greene		HGJR 802	----
00 000 1843	Eliza A. Greenwood[Fitzjarrel]		PBMO B219	----
00 000 1823	James Gregory		OCHA 90	1861
00 000 1854	Samuel M. Gregory		OCHA 90	1865
00 000 1834	Alfred W. Greer		HMCH 255	1856
00 000 0000	Nancy Gregson[Sander]		PPVE 883	----
00 000 0000	Frances Griffin[Ary]		TAZE 528	----
00 000 1816	W.H. Griffith		ACLA 72	1849
26 May 1841	John D. Grigg	Joseph W & Delila(McCullough)Va02/Va06	PBWA 294	----
20 Apr 1820	L.B. Grigsby	Aaron Va/x	HSTE 706	----
00 000 0000	William Grigsby		HFUL 871	----
00 000 0000	William H. Grigsby		HMCD 882	----
00 000 0000	Sarah Grimsley[Broadhead]		HMCD 656	----
00 000 1828	David Grubb		ACLA 72	1835
00 000 1827	M.J. Grissom		PFAY 86	1860
00 000 0000	Simeon Guinn		EFAY 755	----
00 000 0000	Emily Gulley[Clevinger]		BMCL 969	----
00 000 0000	Jemina Gum		AMEN 23	1830
00 000 0000	Jesse Gum		PPME 456	----
00 000 0000	Jesse Gum		HMEM 695	----
14 Dec 1813	Thomas D. Gum		PPME 420	----
00 000 0000	William Gum	John & Sarah(Johnston)	AMEN 23	1830
00 000 1835	J.J. Guthrie		GHHA 554	----
00 Jan 1790	Mary Guthrie[Garrett]		PBAD 209	----
00 000 0000	William L. Guthrie	John P. Va/x	HMCH 263	----
27 Nov 1835	Benjamin F. Guy		HMCD 670	----
02 Sep 1808	George G. Guy	Benjamin & Rebecca(Flo₂rs)	HMCD 669	----

14 Nov 1812	Levi Hackett	Peter		PBCO	576	1835
29 Jul 1829	Virginia F. Halen			BMCL	1062	---
00 000 0000	William Hadley			HJAC	130	1864
00 000 1806	William Hadley	John & ---- (Guthrie)	Md1776/x	HMAD	455	1817
00 000 0000	John Hagaman			HMAC	276	1856
00 000 0000	A.T. Hagan			VTBU	243	---
00 000 0000	George H. Hagan			PHKX	B804	1841
00 000 0000	Amy Hagden[Fulton]			PBSM	314	---
00 000 0000	Dr. J.R. Haggard			DUPA	230	1840
00 000 0000	Martha Haggard[Newton]			PBML	660	1836
00 000 0000	Dr. J.W. Haghey			HLOG	555	---
00 000 0000	Fletcher Haines			HCHR	262	1854
00 000 1816	Green Hainline	Henry	Ky/x	BLOG	443	---
00 000 0000	James V. Hale			PAUP	B69	---
00 000 0000	Susan[Hale]			PAUP	B69	---
00 000 0000	Joseph A. Haley			HCHR	37	1837
00 000 0000	Nancy A. Haley			HADM	401	1834
00 000 0000	David T. Hall			HMAC	273	1840
14 Apr 1814	E.C. Hall			VTBU	243	1834
00 000 0000	George Hall	Micajah & Mary(Sellers)		BMCL	1068	---
05 Apr 1838	J.D. Hall			PPWA	302	1846
30 Apr 1837	M.W. Hall			PPWA	302	1846
00 000 0000	Nancy Hall[Dale]			HGSH	690	---
00 000 0000	Phineas C. Hall			PJAC	131	1806
15 Oct 1819	Andrew J. Hamilton			HMCD	688	---
00 000 0000	E.H. Hamilton			HADM	400	1833
00 000 0000	George A. Ham	Martin & Mary A	Ky/Il	HMOR	546	---
00 000 0000	Hezekiah Ham			PBML	1112	---
00 000 0000	James Ham	Moses	Ky/x	PJEF	B51	---
15 Oct 1819	Andrew J. Hamilton			HMCD	688	---
00 000 0000	E.H. Hamilton			HADM	400	1833
00 000 1815	Elijah Hamilton	Allen & Saline		HPIK	490	1820
00 000 0000	Dr. J,M. Hamilton			HJAC	72	1822
00 000 1797	Rev. John C. Hamilton			HMOR	325	1834
00 000 0000	Lloyd F. Hamilton			HSAN	127	---
00 000 1838	Richard M. Hamilton			BMCL	1072	---

BIRTHDATE	NAME OF BIOGRAPHEE	PARENTS/BIRTHPLACE/BIRTHDATE		SOURCE/PAGE	DATE
00 000 0000	J.W. Hambrick			HWAS	85	1867
00 000 0000	Addison W. Hammer	Frederick		PCHR	251	1827
00 000 0000	Mary J. Hammer			HCHR	265	----
02 Nov 1817	William L. Hammer			HCHR	-	1827
00 000 1803	John Hammett			PBPE	531	----
00 000 0000	Sarah Hammonds[Clark]			PBCO	538	1831
00 000 0000	Amanda Hampton[Haynes]			PPWO	539	1852
00 000 0000	John J. Hampton			HLOG	507	----
00 000 0000	John L. Hampton			HLOG	507	----
00 000 0000	Elizabeth Hancock[Anderson]			PBWA	545	----
00 000 0000	Elizabeth B. Hancock[Kinsall]		Va/Va	HGSH	551	----
00 000 1823	Levi E. Hancock			PHPI	448	----
07 Feb 1845	Martin A. Hankins	Cheston	Ky/x	BRJM	214	1857
00 000 0000	William Hanks	John		PHPI	292	----
00 000 1797	Jane Hanna[Council]			HSAN	1052	----
00 000 1810	Rev. Philip K. Hanna			PBHE	369	1835
00 000 0000	Elizabeth Harbaugh[Davidson]			PPPI	481	----
00 000 0000	Joseph B. Harbest			PBWL	813	----
00 000 0000	Moses Harbison			ACAS	22	1840
00 000 0000	George W. Hardin			HCHR	267	----
00 000 0000	Paschal Harding			ACAS	19	1826
00 000 1810	Rev. P.K. Hanna			HHEN	246	1835
00 000 1854	A.J. Hamilton			PFAY	86	1855
00 000 1817	Peyton Harding			HMOR	325	1826
00 000 0000	J.V.M. Hardisty			HMCH	306	c1830
16 Nov 1825	Jerome Hardisty			PPWA	232	1839
00 000 0000	William Hargise			HCHR	37	1838
00 000 1862	E.W. Harlan			HMAC	273	----
00 000 0000	Elizabeth[Harlan]			HMAC	273	----
00 000 1840	Rev. L.L. Harlan			HMAC	273	----
00 000 1864	Lucinda C[Harlan]			HMAC	273	----
00 000 1834	Sallie M[Harlan]			HMAC	273	----
00 000 0000	Wesley Harlan			HMCD	731	1834

Date	Name	Parents / Notes	Origin	Code	No.	Year
00 000 1800	John Harmon			PBCO	470	----
00 000 0000	William Hanks	John	Ky/x	PHPI	292	----
00 000 0000	Isaac Harness			BMCL	1075	----
00 000 0000	James Harney			HMOR	546	----
00 000 0000	Jacob Harp			HLOG	555	----
03 Aug 1834	Millard Harp			HLOG	555	----
00 Jan 1813	C.W[Harper]			WIWI	839	----
00 000 0000	Stephen Harper			GSBR	266	1820
00 000 0000	Edward F. Harmel			HMAC	270	1869
00 000 0000	Chatham H.D. Harr-s Rev.William & Nancy	Va1767/Va1770		PBML	467	1857
00 000 0000	Cyilene Harris[Himshaw] William & Harriet(Paseley)	Ky/Ky		BMCL	1097	----
00 000 1827	Dr. D.M. Harris			GHHA	971	----
00 000 0000	John Harris Rev. William & Nancy(Hismith)Va/Va			PBWB	449	----
00 000 0000	Amanda J. Harris[Murray]			BLOG	408	----
04 Jul 1846	R.E. Harris Dr. R.			HMCD	1105	----
00 000 1807	W.P. Harris			HMOR	325	1829
00 000 1830	Ann E. Harrison[Terhune]			PPME	408	----
00 000 0000	Ann E. Harrison[Terhune]			PPME	483	----
00 000 0000	Elizabeth Harrison[Stipp]			HFUL	815	----
00 000 0000	Elvira Harrison[Wight]			HCHR	261	1867
00 000 0000	Julia A. Harrison[Jewell]			PBWA	436	----
24 May 1830	William C. Harrison James & Sarah			HFUL	798	----
00 000 1802	David Hart			HMOR	325	1828
00 000 0000	Elizabeth Hart[Lester]			HADM	745	----
00 000 0000	James Hart			PHPI	286	----
00 000 1829	John Hart Joseph	NC/x		FSTE	64	1835
00 000 1839	Mary Hart[Roge-]	Ky/Ky		HMCL	1031	----
00 000 0000	Milligan Hart			HSAN	767	----
00 000 0000	Mary Hartsock[Threlkeld]			HGSH	831	1857
00 000 0000	James Hartley Thomas	Va/x		PPDM	694	----
00 000 0000	James Hartley Thomas	Va/x		PBMC	419	----
00 000 0000	Hannah M. Hascall[Brown]			PBKN	275	----
00 000 0000	Emma[Haskell]			HMOR	325	1830
00 000 0000	J.H. Hatche			VTBU	190	----
00 000 0000	Sarah Hatfield[Howard]			PBDP	266	----
00 000 0000	Herman C. Hauss			HSTC	375	----
00 000 0000	James M. Hawes			LOGA	577	1835
00 000 0000	Nancy Hawes[Howser]	Ky/x		BLOG	651	----
00 000 0000	William Hawkins Crosby	Ire/x		PPVE	751	----
00 000 0000	William Hawkins			HCHR	267	----

BIRTHDATE	NAME OF BIOGRAPHEE	PARENTS/BIRTHPLACE/BIRTHDATE	SOURCE/PAGE		DATE
00 000 0000	Elisha Hayden		HPIK	456	1833
00 000 0000	Nancy Hayden[Tracy]		PBHE	221	----
28 Feb 1868	Ulysses G. Hayden	Robert W & Jennie(Reeves) Ky/Ky	HPPB	563	----
00 000 0000	George W. Hayes		BCSB	579	----
00 000 0000	S.H. Haynes		HJAC	130	1874
00 000 0000	Henry Hays		PBML	884	----
00 000 0000	John Hart	Thomas	FUST	B429	1836
00 000 1855	Thomas W. Hart		PFAY	86	1861
00 000 0000	Benjamin Head		BCHR	900	----
00 000 0000	Temperance Headington[Williams] Laban Ky/x		PBAD	280	----
00 000 0000	W.B. Headley		HCHR	260	----
00 000 0000	Benjamin Heady		CJRI	562	----
20 Jul 1825	John C. Hearn	James & Nancy(Dix)	PBKN	227	----
00 000 0000	David Heath		PHPI	577	1845
00 000 0000	Nancy[Heaton]		HMAC	275	1853
00 000 0000	Mary Heinline[Bulson]		PHKX	B591	----
00 000 0000	John Heltsley		AMOU	8	1873
00 000 1810	D. Pat Henderson		HMOR	325	1831
00 000 0000	Elizabeth P[Henderson]		HHEN	355	----
00 000 0000	Henderson Henderson		HMAC	268	1833
00 000 0000	John P. Henderson	Rev. John	HGJR	714	----
00 000 0000	John P. Henderson		HMAC	274	1853
00 000 0000	John W. Henderson		HDEW	344	----
08 Jul 1791	Patsie D. Henderson[Anderson]		HWCL	B224	----
28 Mar 1799	Jonathan Hendrick		HMEM	722	----
02 Jun 1833	Ellen Hendricks[Luckett]		HSAN	811	----
00 000 0000	Europe Hendricks		AMOU	8	1831
00 000 0000	Lorley Hendricks		AMOU	8	1831
13 Aug 1833	Lovicy G. Hendricks[Roberts]		PBSM	634	----
00 000 0000	Samuel Hendricks		PBSM	254	----
00 000 0000	Thomas Hendricks		HPIK	411	----
31 Jan 1851	Dr. W.S. Hendricks		GHHA	587	1852

	Name	Parents/Note		Code	No.	Year
00 000 0000	James Hendron			AWOO	8	1864
00 000 0000	China Henline[Burt]			LOGA	696	1828
00 000 0000	George Henline			PBML	785	---
00 000 0000	Byers Hensley	Nathan & Mary(Mosier)	Ky/Tn	GHHA	830	---
00 000 0000	Evan S. Hensley	Elijah		PHKX	B801	---
00 000 0000	John A. Hensley			HFUL	701	1853
00 000 0000	Emily Henly[Mcrris]			HPIK	501	---
00 000 0000	Catherine Henson[Craig]			PBCO	466	---
00 000 0000	Elizabeth Henson[Guinn]			EFAY	755	---
00 000 0000 1821	Elijah Henry			HMOR	325	1830
00 000 0000 1800	John Henry			HMOR	325	1828
00 000 0000 1816	America A. Herbert[Florer]			PBCO	254	---
00 000 0000	Elizabeth Herell[Camron]			HFUL	513	1843
00 000 0000 1841	Richard F. Herndon	Richard		HSAN	675	1833
00 000 0000	James Herron			HSAN	441	1851
00 000 0000	J.W. Herrott			OCHA	91	---
00 000 0000 1836	L.W. Hess			HLOG	483	---
00 000 0000	George T. Hickman			HSAN	1053	---
00 000 0000	James Hieronymous			TAZE	490	---
00 000 0000	James Hieronymous			TAZE	602	---
00 000 0000	James Hieronymous	William	1788/x	LOGA	704	1828
17 May 1814	William Hieronymous			PBML	1191	---
24 Apr 1820	Hiram S. Higgins	James		HFUL	531	1836
00 000 0000	James Higgins			HSAN	676	1818
00 000 0000 1815	Marvin Hilbert			ACLA	72	1852
00 000 0000	John Hildreth			HEDG	661	1835
00 000 0000	Charles Hill			BCHA	152	---
00 000 0000	Isaac Hill			COLE	635	---
00 000 0000	J.H. Hill			CAOG	96	1864
00 000 0000	John T. Hill			HCHR	262	---
00 000 0000	Mary A. Hill[Ielgi]			HCHR	227	1827
00 000 0000	R.E. Hill			HCHR	262	1865
00 000 0000	Samuel Hill			PHCC	305	---
00 000 0000	William Hill	Henry		PBSM	423	---
00 000 0000	William E. Hill			HMAD	527	1830
00 000 0000	William Hinch	George		HMAD	550	---

BIRTHDATE	NAME OF BIOGRAPHEE	PARENTS/BIRTHPLACE/BIRTHDATE	SOURCE/PAGE		DATE
00 000 0000	Charity Hinds[Watwood]	Joseph	HFAY	69	1817
00 000 0000	Lewis Hinton		PBSM	524	----
25 Mar 1821	Frances B. Hise[Leach]	George & Nancy	LOGA	708	----
00 000 0000	J.T. Hite	John S.	HEDG	617	----
00 000 0000	Julia Hitt[Holmes]	Jesse	HMOR	690	----
25 Nov 1825	George Hix	William & Martha	BHIQ	B166	----
01 May 1821	Gerrit Hix	William & Martha	BHIQ	B165	----
00 000 0000	Henson Hobbs		HPIK	411	----
00 000 1814	Hinson S. Hobbs	Solomon & Mary L(Young) Oh/Ky	HPIK	494	----
09 May 1835	Vienna Hockensmith[Foster]	Andrew J & Mary(Parks)Ky1802/Ky08	HGJR	889	----
00 000 0000	Catherine Hogan[Ballard]		PBML	890	----
00 000 0000	Mary E. Hogan[Anderson]		BRMA	21	1835
00 000 0000	John Hoke	George Pa/x	HWAS	64	----
28 Nov 1814	John A. Hoke	Leonard & Barbara Pa/Pa	HADM	742	1844
00 000 0000	P.E. Hoke		AMOU	6	1836
00 000 0000	A.S. Holden		HCHR	260	1856
00 000 0000	Henry Holland		BLOG	458	----
00 000 0000	James Holland		HMEM	568	----
08 Feb 1803	Julia A. Holland		HMEM	722	----
04 Apr 1828	N.W. Holland	Jeremiah & Ann(Shemwell) Va/NC	HFAY	50	----
00 000 1820	Charles L. Holliday		HMOR	325	1831
14 Nov 1821	Nancy H. Holliday[Robertson]	Rev. Charles	HMAC	102	----
03 Nov 1832	Lemira Holloway[Greenawalt]	George W & Harriet(Tade)Ky/Ky	PBMO	B221	----
00 000 1829	Robert Holloway		PPWA	214	1851
00 000 0000	B.F. Holman		AMEN	19	1854
00 000 0000	Mary[Holmes]		HMOR	690	----
00 000 0000	Thomas Holmes		HFUL	658	----
00 000 0000	William Holmes		PBML	718	----
00 000 0000	William Holmes		HLOG	413	----
00 000 0000	D.S. Holstlaw		MACL	297	1830
00 000 0000	Daniel S. Holstlaw		MACL	266	c1830
00 000 0000	David S. Holstlaw		BRCM	590	c1830
00 000 0000	Rebecca Homes[Wrigley]		HMCD	704	----

Date	Name	Parents/Notes		Birthplace	Code	No.	Year
00 000 1819	Samuel D. Honn				PBCO	391	---
00 000 0000	Lida[Hooper]				HPIK	638	---
00 000 0000	John Hopkins				HWCL	131	---
00 Jan 1808	Solomon Hornback				HPIK	765	1829
03 Jul 1810	Solomon Hornback				HPIK	764	1836
00 000 0000	W.H. Horn				VTBU	372	---
00 000 0000	James L. Horrell				HWCD	699	1827
00 000 0000	Lowry Hoskins				PBCO	324	---
00 000 0000	John Hostetler				PPDM	244	---
00 000 1799	Elizabeth G[Houchin]				LOGA	835	---
00 000 0000	Peter Houser	Abraham		Md/x	BRML	562	---
00 000 0000	David Housh				PBKN	547	---
00 000 0000	Caleb Houston				AMOU	6	1863
00 000 0000	C.J. Houts				BRJM	477	---
00 000 1851	Alonso J. Hover			Tn/x	BMCL	1104	---
00 000 0000	Ellen Howard[Rawlings] Ignatius				PBML	1170	---
05 Dec 1821	M.M. Howard				PJEF	B121	---
00 000 0000	Joseph Howe				BCLA	767	c1836
00 000 0000	A.D. Howell				BRJM	219	---
00 000 0000	John Howser				HLOG	357	---
27 May 1832	Mildonetta Howser_Metcalf]				HLOG	390	---
00 000 0000	Christopher Hoxey				BRMA	359	---
17 Feb 1839	James W. Huddleston	Barnett G & Susan(Winter)		Va/Va	CJRI	555	---
00 000 0000	Robert Hudgen				PHPI	484	1848
00 000 1813	Isaac Hudson				HMOR	324	1827
00 000 1807	James E. Hudson				HGSH	624	---
00 000 0000	Ben J. Huff	George N & Elizabeth		Ky/Ky	PHKX	B531	---
24 Feb 1841	John W. Huffman				HLOG	462	---
00 000 0000	I.E. Huffman				ACAS	22	1827
00 000 1803	Eliza A. Huffcrd[Fouts] George				HFUL	484	---
00 000 0000	John A. Hughes				HMOR	325	1823
08 Jun 1807	Richard T. Hughes				CJRI	236	1852
00 000 0000	Robert Hughes	Robert		Va/x	HWAS	69	---
21 Jan 1818	Robert Hughes				HWAS	83	1807
00 000 0000	W.C. Hughes				HLOG	483	c1845
00 000 0000	E.F. Hulbertson[Hilliar]				HMAC	268	1857
00 000 0000	Anna Hulet[Swihart]				CSBR	394	1857

BIRTHDATE	NAME OF BIOGRAPHEE	PARENTS/BIRTHPLACE/BIRTHDATE	SOURCE/PAGE	DATE
00 000 0000	Martha J. Hull[Devol]		BCLA	730	----
00 000 1806	Samuel Hull	John NJ/x	BRCM	32	----
00 000 1818	Otho Hulse		HADM	815	1847
00 000 1816	Thomas Hulse		HADM	815	1859
00 000 0000	Margaret[Hume]		HPIK	411	1828
00 000 0000	W.A. Hume		HPIK	411	1828
00 000 1811	B.N. Humphrey		HMOR	325	1829
00 000 0000	F.G. Humphrey		VTBU	215	----
02 Oct 1809	John Humphrey		HSAN	915	----
02 Oct 1806	Mary[Humphrey]		HSAN	915	----
00 000 1817	William D. Humphrey		HMOR	325	1828
00 000 0000	Adonijah Hungate		GHHA	904	1833
19 Sep 1824	Joseph Hunt	John R & Hannah(Daivis) Ky/Ky	BCSB	197	----
00 000 0000	A.C. Hunter		HLOG	500	----
00 000 0000	Benjamin A. Hunter		EFAY	763	----
00 000 0000	Elizabeth Hunter[Donner]		BCHR	876	----
00 000 0000	G.D. Hunter		HLOG	483	----
00 000 0000	James A. Hunter		HLOG	500	----
00 000 0000	James B. Hunter		PPDM	269	----
00 000 0000	Mary B[Hunter]		HLOG	500	----
00 000 0000	William Hunter		BCHR	946	----
00 000 0000	Nancy Hupp[Spencer]		HGJR	978	----
00 000 1827	H.M. Hurst		**ACLA**	72	1830
00 000 1818	N. Hurst		**ACLA**	72	1818
00 000 1800	William S. Hurst		HMOR	325	1829
00 000 0000	James Hurt		VTBU	351	----
00 000 1841	William Hurt	John W. Ky/x	HMCL	1062	----
15 Aug 1841	William Hurt		BMCL	1106	----
01 Oct 1814	Elizabeth Husband	Hamm & Sarah NC1791/SC1790	HSAN	769	1820
01 Apr 1813	Evalina Husband	Hamm & Sarah NC 1791/SC 1790	HSAN	769	1820
18 Jul 1818	Jane Husband	Hamm & Sarah NC 1791/SC 1790	HSAN	769	1820
22 Jan 1820	Martha Husband	Hamm & Sarah NC 1791/SC 1790	HSAN	769	1820
18 Nov 1816	Polly Husband	Hamm & Sarah NC 1791/SC 1790	HSAN	769	1820

Date	Name	Parents/Spouse	Origin	Code	No.	Year
00 000 0000	Ann Hutchison[Wilson]			CJRI	343	---
28 Mar 1796	Elijah Iles	Thomas	Pa65/x	HSAN	580	---
28 Oct 1809	Hancil Ingram			HLOG	398	---
00 000 0000	Col. W.T. Ingram			HJAC	128	1865
00 000 1840	Mary B.F. Ingels[Chambers]			COLE	516	1880
00 000 1828	H. Inman			OCHA	91	1865
00 000 0000	Henry Inman			HADM	844	1834
00 000 0000	Gracie Irving[Woolburn]			GHHA	768	---
00 000 0000	Mary F. Irwin[Dyson]			GSBR	377	---
00 000 0000	Abraham Isaacs			HMAC	277	1839
00 000 1778	Hannah Isgrigg[Pattison]			BLOG	579	---
00 000 0000	Amanda[Jackson]			HLOG	462	---
00 000 0000	Elizabeth Jackson[Kelley]			BRML	546	1829
00 000 1815	F.J. Jackson	Vincent & Jane(Shearer)	Md/Pa	HPIK	846	---
00 000 1810	James Jackson			HCAS	319	---
00 000 0000	Jeannetta Jackson[Tyler]			HGJR	829	1820
00 000 1820	Milton Jackson			PFAY	86	1830
00 000 0000	Permelia Jackson[Rodgers]			HMAD	579	1834
00 000 1822	H.S. Jacobs	John & Nancy(Gwinn)	Va/x	HFUL	920	---
00 000 0000	Mary Jacobs[Calvin]			CJRI	562	---
00 000 1820	Jesse Janes	Walter & Ardra(Crook)		HMCD	730	1834
00 000 1828	John Janes	Walter & Ardia(Crook)		HMCD	730	1834
00 000 0000	Alsey K. Jared[Watt]			CJRI	524	---
00 000 0000	Louisa J. Jasper[Lester]			HMOR	686	---
00 000 0000	Benjamin Jenkins			PBCO	363	---
00 000 1800	James Jenkins	Shadrack	NC/x	PBRJ	501	---
00 000 0000	Charles Jennings	Israel		PBCW	212	---
00 000 1849	Levi Jewell			ACLA	72	1877
25 May 1805	John Johns	George W.	Ky/x	PPVE	530	1833
00 000 1822	Alexander Johnson			HMOR	326	---
00 000 0000	Belle F. Johnson[Duff]			BRML	254	---
00 000 0000	Benjamin Johnson			HSTC	372	---
17 Aug 1820	C.P. Johnson	Benjamin	Va/x	HMOR	666	1830
00 000 1832	Daniel Johnson			OCHA	91	1856
29 Jul 1818	Dicy Johnson[Covey]	James & Catherine		BRML	275	---
00 000 1831	Elnor Johnson			HADM	401	1831

BIRTHDATE	NAME OF BIOGRAPHEE	PARENTS/BIRTHPLACE/BIRTHDATE		SOURCE/PAGE	DATE
00 000 0000	Eleanor Johnson[Hopkins]			PBWH	361	----
00 000 0000	Evalina Johnson[Goodwin]			CJRI	230	----
00 000 1814	George W. Johnson Robert			HGSH	710	1821
00 000 0000	J.D. Johnson			VTBU	215	----
00 000 1849	J.H. Johnson			OCHA	91	1874
00 000 1827	J.W. Johnson			ACLA	72	1856
00 000 1858	J.W. Johnson			OCHA	91	1862
00 000 1808	James R. Johnson			HMCL	969	1830
00 000 0000	Jane Johnson[Blue]			PBML	1059	----
00 000 1780	John Johnson			PHCC	308	----
00 000 0000	Mary Johnson[Rhodes]			PBML	246	----
00 000 0000	Matilda Johnson[Hall]			PBCO	465	----
00 000 0000	Rachel Johnson[Selby]			CJRI	521	----
00 000 0000	Reuben Johnson			PHKX	B893	----
00 000 0000	Thomas Johnson			HADM	828	----
00 000 0000	William Johnson			PBCW	491	----
01 Apr 1827	William K. Johnson John & Charlotte(Hart)		Ky/NC	HGRU	843	----
06 Feb 1826	David Johnston John & Sarah(Matheny)		Ky/Oh	PPVE	539	1834
00 000 0000	John H. Jolley			HMAC	268	----
31 Aug 1812	Benjamin L. Jones			PBML	394	----
00 000 0000	Carter T. Jones			BHAN	158	----
00 000 0000	Clara Jones[Wilson]			PHPI	495	----
00 000 0000	Clementine Jones[Thropp]			HMEM	717	----
12 Sep 1830	John Johnston Isaac B & Elizabeth(King)			ERMA	88	1836
00 000 0000	Susanna[Johnston]			BRKI	1221	----
01 Apr 1827	William K. Johnston John & Charlotte(Hart)		Ky/NC	HGRU	843	----
00 000 0000	Eliza Jones[Ward]			HMAD	564	----
00 000 1849	J.S. Jones			OPLO	86	1866
18 Aug 1828	John W. Jones Joseph		Ky/x	BRKI	1214	----
00 000 0000	Jonas Jones			PHPI	297	1853
00 000 0000	Lucy Jones			HSAN	442	1836
18 Nov 1819	M.R. Jones			PPWA	303	1839

00 000 0000	Mary A. Jones [Alexander]			GSBR	386	1849
00 000 0000	Nancy Jones[Ackin]			PHPI	252	----
00 000 0000	S.G. Jones			HSAN	442	1836
00 000 0000	Tabitha[Jones]			HMAC	268	1834
00 000 0000	W.T. Jones			HSAN	442	1834
10 Nov 1810	William P. Jones	Elijah & Sarah(Hamrock)	Va/Va77	PBWA	365	1866
00 000 0000	William B. Jones			LOGA	313	1851
00 000 0000	James W. Judy			AMEN	23	----
00 000 0000	James Junken			PBCO	300	----
00 Aug 1829	Dr. James Kay			HMCD	417	----
00 000 0000	William Kays			KNOX	685	----
09 Apr 1804	William Kays			PBKN	194	----
00 000 0000	Lucy Keelen[Lumsden]			BCHA	156	----
00 000 0000	Richard Keer			HPIK	728	----
15 Jan 1824	Peyton A. Keith Peyton R			BGSB	486	1837
00 000 0000	Mary H. Keiser[Baker]			HCHR	263	1854
00 000 0000	H.V. Kellar			AMOU	8	1832
00 000 0000	Cinderella Keller[Gore]			BRMA	80	----
00 000 0000	Sarah J. Keller[Wayne]			HMAC	277	1844
00 000 0000	Amos Kelley			BRML	546	1829
00 000 0000	Joseph Kelley			GHHA	538	----
00 000 0000	Mary Kelley[Taylor]			HSAN	1057	----
00 000 0000	Sarah Kelley[Lewis]			HADM	745	----
00 000 0000	John M. Kelly			AMOU	6	1861
00 000 0000	Nancy E. Kelly[Byars]			CJRI	553	----
00 000 0000	William Kelly			CJRI	330	1805
00 000 1806	James Kelsey			PBWA	414	1834
00 000 1805	James Kelsey			PBWA	255	----
00 000 0000	Andrew Keltner			HSAN	1017	----
00 000 0000	Catherine Kemper[Carson]			HMAC	273	1842
00 000 0000	Sarah Kemper[Miller]			BGSB	592	----
00 000 0000	Levi Kennedy			HGJR	287	----
00 000 0000	Nancy Kennedy[Miller]			CJRI	517	----
00 000 1823	John Kessinger Lynn & Betsy(Peebles)		Ky/x	BRMA	32	1842
00 000 1825	Solomon Kessinger			HPIK	469	1825

BIRTHDATE	NAME OF BIOGRAPHEE	PARENTS/BIRTHPLACE/BIRTHDATE	SOURCE/PAGE	DATE
00 000 0000	Daniel Kester		PHCC 211	----
00 000 0000	Benjamin C. Kilburn		CJRI 541	----
00 000 0000	Nancy Killen[Smith]		HSAN 717	1831
00 000 0000	George W. Killman		BCHR 851	----
00 000 0000	William Kimbrough		GHHA 601	----
00 000 0000	Andrew Kincaid		PBDP 609	----
00 000 0000	James Kincaid		PBHE 239	1836
26 Jul 1847	Robert F. Kincaid	Asa & Margaret(House) Ky/Ky	PPDM 283	----
00 000 1858	E.G. King		OPLO 86	1889
00 000 0000	Jacob King		CJRI 364	----
00 000 0000	John King		HGJR 851	----
00 000 1805	Silas King	Peter	BRBM 256	----
00 000 0000	Thomas A. King		HSAN 442	1831
00 000 1811	William King		PBAD 191	1830
00 000 0000	Gay Kinkead		HCHR 266	----
00 000 1858	R.A. Kinlin		ACLA 72	1874
00 000 0000	Margaret Kinton[Barlow]		PHKX B807	----
00 000 0000	Cyrus Kirby		PPME 463	1809
00 000 0000	Cyrus Kirby		AMEN 31	1811
00 000 0000	Kissiah[Kirby]		AMEN 31	----
00 000 0000	A.S. Kirk		AMEN 19	1836
24 Aug 1842	George Kirk		HMCL 1017	1874
00 000 0000	Samuel Kirkpatrick		AWOO 8	1831
00 000 0000	Charles Kissick		VTBU 253	----
00 000 0000	Sarah Kittinger[Messick] Martin Pa/x		HSTC 316	----
00 000 0000	Sarah E. Kittenger[Messick] NC/x		PSTC 657	----
00 000 0000	Emily Knight[Spire] Albert		PAUP B84	----
00 000 0000	Felix Koons		PBKN 445	1835
00 000 0000	Ann Kreyliel[Powell] Eng/x		PPVE 1070	----
00 000 1802	Henry Lackey		HMOR 326	1830
00 000 1807	Mary Lackey		HMOR 326	1830
00 000 0000	Nancy C. Ladd[Madeira]		HCHR 266	----

Date	Name	Parents	Origin	Source	No.	Year
09 Apr 1799	William Lair			PPWA	291	---
00 000 0000	James L. Lamb			HCHR	267	---
00 000 0000	John Lamb			PSTE	351	---
00 000 0000	Joel Lambert	Benjamin	Va/x	BGLS	710	---
00 000 0000	Martin Lambert			KNOX	687	---
00 000 0000	Josiah Lamboro			LOGA	299	---
19 Apr 1818	William J. Laner	Joseph & Elizabeth		PAUP	B161	---
00 000 0000	Rebecca Lancaster[Rogers]			HMEM	745	---
00 000 0000	Evaline Land	Philip & Elizabeth(Fike)	Va1785/x	HSTC	277	---
15 Jan 1832	John T. Land	William F & Jane C(Warren)		CJRI	542	1836
00 000 0000	Lucinda Land[Yount]			BMCL	970	---
00 000 0000	Moses Land	Philip & Elizabeth(Fike)	Va1785/x	HSTC	277	---
00 000 0000	Rebecca Land	Philip & Elizabeth(Fike)	Va1785/x	HSTC	277	---
00 000 0000	Henry Landers			PBMO	B301	---
00 000 0000	E.D. Langford			HWAS	83	1877
00 000 0000	Mary A. Langdon[Henry]			BHAN	249	---
00 000 1848	Dr. William O. Langdon	Dr. William S.		HGJR	722	---
00 000 1786	James Langley			HMOR	326	1829
18 Apr 1796	Jesse Langley			HCHR	33	1828
00 000 0000	Rebecca A. Langley[Hammer]			PCHR	251	---
00 000 0000	W.F. Langley			HCHR	260	1830
00 000 0000	B.S. Lanham			HLOG	484	---
00 000 1806	Dolly A[Lanterman]			HLOG	484	1830
00 000 1771	Priscella[Larinore]	Thomas		HMOR	326	---
25 Nov 1793	James Lasley		Ire/x	BRJM	376	---
18 Aug 1797	Elizabeth Latham[Chapman]	James	Va1768/x	HSAN	687	---
00 000 1809	Lucy Latham[Blackwell]	James & Mary(Briggs)	Va1768/Va1772	HSAN	687	---
00 000 0000	Maria Latham[Constant]			HSAN	687	---
00 000 1818	Mary Latham[Constant]			OPLO	86	1819
00 000 1864	R.B. Latham			HLOG	534	1866
00 000 0000	T.W. Latham			BHAN	167	---
00 000 0000	Nancy Lattimer[Wallace]		NC/x	PCHR	212	1853
00 000 0000	Jonathan Lawle~	Gibbon		AMEN	19	---
00 000 0000	J.E. Lawson			HSAN	803	1828
00 000 1794	William P. Lawson					

BIRTHDATE	NAME OF BIOGRAPHEE	PARENTS/BIRTHPLACE/BIRTHDATE	SOURCE/PAGE	DATE
00 000 0000	Christina Leach[Eoff]		PHCC 340	1849
00 000 0000	Matthew Ledbetter	Rev. Wiley	BRJM 402	---
00 000 1811	Charles B. Lee	Charles	PBRJ 703	---
00 000 0000	E.A[Lee]	Va/x	HCHA 183	---
00 000 1847	J.H. Lee		OCHA 91	1851
00 000 0000	Squire Lee		HCHA 183	---
00 000 0000	America Leforgee[Chenoweth]		PPDM 735	---
00 000 0000	George Leiber		HHEN 471	---
00 000 0000	Isaac Lemaster		BCHR 929	---
00 000 0000	P.W. Lemaster		HMEM 827	---
00 000 0000	George W. Lester		HADM 745	---
01 Dec 1845	Fountain Lester		HMOR 686	1870
00 000 0000	Anna M. Letton[Becraft]		HMOR 694	---
00 000 0000	Henry M. Lewis		HADM 745	---
10 Nov 1835	James B. Lewis		HPIK 551	1837
00 000 0000	Mary Lewis[McDaniel]		HMEM 808	---
00 000 0000	Mary E. Lewis[Osborn]		HSAN 800	---
00 000 0000	Louisa[Lewis]		HMAC 268	1835
00 000 0000	Mary[Lewis]		HMAC 277	1835
28 Dec 1827	Minerva W. Lewis[Riggs]	William D & Nancy(Pitts) Ky01/Ky06	PBML 717	---
00 000 0000	Polly Lewis[White]		PBCO 367	1840
00 000 0000	W.M. Lewis		PAUP B269	---
00 000 0000	Reuben Lightfoot		HGJR 731	---
00 000 0000	Montague G. Lightner	Pa/Pa	PBAD 503	---
00 000 0000	Usher F. Linder		BRCM 448	---
24 Jul 1801	James Lindsay		PBRJ 282	---
00 000 0000	John P. Lindsay		HLOG 399	---
00 000 1789	Vincent Lindsey		PHCC 118	---
00 000 0000	Mrs. M.E. [Lindsey]		HLOG 494	---
00 000 1812	William Lively		PHCC 349	---
00 000 0000	Christianna[Link]		HMAC 273	1872

00 000 0000	James Lisenby		HDEW	187	1828
00 000 0000	John Linville		PBSM	551	---
00 000 0000	John Little	Va/x	BRML	120	1865
00 000 0000	J.S. Little		AMEN	19	---
00 000 0000	Dr. William D. Li-t-e		HLOG	363	---
16 Feb 1831	Fermetta T. Lloyd[Maxey]		HSAN	694	1834
00 000 1805	J.R. Lloyd		PPWA	248	1830
00 000 1800	Ann[Loar]		HMOR	326	1830
00 000 0000	George Loar		HMOR	326	---
00 000 0000	J.W. Lochridge		HLOG	485	---
26 Oct 1821	John H. Lockhart		PPME	139	---
00 000 1836	Jane H. Loftis[Gilbert]		PBWA	445	---
00 000 0000	Elijah Logan		LOGA	494	---
00 000 0000	Elizabeth W. Logan		HSAN	442	1819
00 000 0000	J.M. Logan	NJ/NJ	HSAN	442	1840
00 000 1805	William C. Logan	Joseph & Sarah	GHHA	614	---
00 000 1820	William Logsdon	James	HCHR	229	---
00 000 0000	M.C. Long		HCHR	260	---
00 000 0000	J.B. Long		HADM	399	1835
00 000 0000	David Locke		HADM	401	1830
01 Jan 1782	Sarah Lott[Thomas]		HFUL	878	---
05 Jul 1779	Elizabeth[Lowry]		PPDM	491	---
02 Sep 1825	William Lowry		PPDM	491	---
00 000 0000	Francis M. Lowry	Eli & Elizabeth(Davidson) Ky/Ky	PPDM	324	---
00 000 0000	Baron T. Lowry		PHPI	300	---
00 000 0000	Jane Lofton[White]	Benjamin F.	HGJR	275	---
00 000 0000	William R. Logan		PBSM	481	1849
00 000 0000	Eliza C[Logsdon]		CSBR	389	---
00 000 0000	Sarah Long[Smith]		PBMO	B29	---
00 000 0000	Mary E. Loossey[Graham] Stephen & Sarah(Richardson)		PBDK	353	---
00 000 0000	Sarah C. Lorton[Campbell]		HGJR	1124	1833
00 000 0000	George Lowe		HWAS	86	1832
00 000 0000	Mary A[Lowe]		HWAS	86	1843
00 000 0000	Dr. H.B. Lucas		HWAS	86	1855
00 000 1838	Martha A. Lucas		OPLO	86	1857
29 Mar 1830	Benjamir Luckett		HSAN	811	---

BIRTHDATE	NAME OF BIOGRAPHEE	PARENTS/BIRTHPLACE/BIRTHDATE	SOURCE/PAGE	DATE
24 May 1811	Gregory Lukins		PPME	360	----
00 000 0000	William Lumsden		BCHA	156	----
00 000 1803	Nelson R. Lurton		HGJR	326	c1827
00 000 0000	Hiram Luttrell		HMOR	623	----
25 Aug 1819	Balseer W. Lutz	Daniel & Diana Va/Va	HFUL	445	----
00 000 0000	William H. Lynam		KNOX	691	----
00 000 0000	Joel Y. Lynden		HLOG	547	----
01 Dec 1833	Drucilla Lynn[Wright]	Jefferson & Elizabeth(Casey) Ky/Ky	PBGO	B308	----
00 000 0000	Elizabeth Lyon[Hickman]		HSAN	1053	----
00 000 0000	Samuel McAfee		LOGA	901	----
00 000 0000	J.D. McBrayer		HLOG	436	----
00 000 0000	J.P. McBrayer		HLOG	436	----
00 000 0000	J. McBride		HSAN	442	1827
00 000 0000	Andrew McBroom	Joseph & Phebe(Young) Va/Oh	GHHA	887	----
28 Apr 1815	William McBroom		PVED	216	----
11 May 1837	Amanda McCall[Bennett]		HWCL	8	----
00 000 1790	Elizabeth McCammon[Boon]		BRBM	69	1815
00 000 0000	Andrew E. McCartney	James Va/x	HFUL	922	----
00 000 0000	Daniel McCauley		CJRI	796	----
00 000 0000	Dr. J.D. McCauley		HWAS	84	1852
00 000 0000	J.W. McCauley		HGHR	262	1867
00 000 0000	Martha McClbben[Richardson]		HPEO	794	----
27 Feb 1816	Catherine McClin[Hall]	Rev.David W & Nancy	HWCL	364	----
00 000 1796	Margaret McClintock[Victor]		PBML	944	----
00 000 0000	James McClure		HMCD	811	1832
00 000 0000	James McClure		PBWO	408	----
09 Jul 1799	John McClure		PBML	876	----
00 000 0000	Milton McClure		HMAC	267	1835
00 000 0000	Samuel McClure		PHPI	518	----
00 000 0000	Sarah McClure[Duff]		LOGA	666	1828
00 000 0000	Sarah J. McClure[Venard]		HMCD	696	1830
00 000 0000	James C. McCollum Abraham		BRCM	88	----
00 000 0000	Mary I. McCollum[Smith]		HGHR	261	1865

	Name		Place	No.	Year
00 000 0000	Rev. Elam McCord		LOGA	497	---
00 000 1836	Christian L. McCormick Alfred G.		BRJM	311	1834
00 000 1830	James R. McCormick John & Jane W(Lochridge)	Pa/x	HMOR	624	1830
26 Oct 1811	James A.McCown James & Ann(Wood)	Ky1801/x	HEDG	695	---
00 000 0000	Caroline McCoy[Grimsley]	Ky/Ky	HSAN	670	---
00 000 0000	Elizabeth McCoy[Ratcliff]		PBAD	376	1844
00 000 0000	G.A. McCoy[Whiteside]		CSBR	391	---
00 000 1834	John McCoy		HADM	401	---
00 000 0000	John McCoy		HADM	746	---
00 000 0000	William McCoy	Daniel & Agnes	Va/Va	PBAD	504	---
31 May 1806	Martin D. McCray		PBWH	217	---
00 000 0000	Charley McCumber		HFUL	805	---
00 000 0000	Huldah[McCumber]		HFUL	805	---
00 000 0000	Reese McCurdy		HLOG	365	---
00 Mar 1808	Ezekiel McCurley	Joseph & Rebecca	HMOR	596	---
00 000 0000	William McDaniel		HMEM	808	---
00 000 0000	George McDonald		HLOG	365	---
00 000 0000	Henrietta McDonald[Ruggles]		GHHA	815	---
00 000 0000	James B. McDonald		PBHE	516	---
00 000 0000	Margaret E. McDonald[Pinkerton]		HGJR	1083	---
00 000 0000	Mary J. McDonald[Peck]		BCHR	959	---
00 000 0000	William P. McDonald		PPME	492	1849
00 000 0000	Rachel McDougal[Blair]		HMAD	584	1852
00 000 0000	Abigail McDowell[Vinson]		PVED	392	---
00 000 0000	Abigail McDowell[Vinson]		PPVE	524	---
00 000 0000	Jane W. McDowell[Allen]		PBKN	473	---
00 000 1832	Greenberry McBlfresh		HMOR	327	1834
00 000 0000	Joseph H.McElvain Robert	Pa/x	PBRJ	673	---
00 000 0000	James McFarlar		BRJM	423	---
00 000 0000	Margaret McElvain.Patton]		HSAN	775	---
00 000 0000	A.N. McGee		PAUP	B238	---
00 000 0000	J.M. McGee		HJAC	131	1858
00 000 0000	William McGlothlin		HSAN	766	---
00 000 0000	Mary McGrew[Scnger] James		HWCL	168	---
00 000 0000	Joseph McIntire		HPIK	827	1831
00 000 0000	Charles McIntcsh		TAZE	624	---

BIRTHDATE	NAME OF BIOGRAPHEE	PARENTS/BIRTHPLACE/BIRTHDATE	SOURCE/PAGE		DATE
00 000 1813	William McHenry		HENR	B400	1820
00 000 0000	Margaret McKashey[Young]		CJRI	344	----
00 000 0000	William MacKey		HLOG	364	----
00 000 0000	Samuel McKee		HMAD	562	1848
00 000 0000	Alexander McKinney		PHPI	487	----
00 000 1823	Elizabeth A. McKinnie[Jones]		HSAN	1025	----
00 000 0000	Jane McKittrick[Wallace]		PBCO	424	----
10 Feb 1815	James J. McKernan		PLAS	415	----
00 000 0000	Samantha McKernan[Peter]	Hugh & Amanda	PLAS	415	----
00 000 1827	J.H. McLain		OCHA	91	1852
00 000 0000	Mary J. McLurg[Bellville]		BMCL	939	----
00 000 0000	Eleanor McMillin[Morrow]		PEPE	553	----
00 000 0000	George McMurray		HADM	400	1829
00 000 0000	George McMurray		HADM	746	----
00 000 0000	Wilson S. McMurray		HADM	746	----
00 000 0000	J.U. McMurtry		CJRI	797	1851
00 000 0000	William McMurtry		PHKX	B462	----
00 000 0000	Samuel McNabb		HMEM	358	----
00 000 0000	Robert McNeely		HMEM	700	----
00 000 0000	Robert T. McNeely		PPME	166	----
00 000 0000	William McNeely		AMEN	23	1822
00 000 0000	Addison McPheeters		PBSM	643	----
00 000 0000	Andrew McPherson		HCHR	261	1870
00 000 0000	S.A. McQuown[Dora]		COLE	544	----
00 000 0000	Leonard McReynolds		BMCL	1186	----
00 00c 1802	Leonard McReynolds		BRML	361	1815
00 000 0000	Eleanor McRight[Overbee]		HWCL	28	----
00 000 0000	Jane[McRoskey]		HMAC	268	1857
00 000 1816	Jordan McSpawn		HPIK	692	1838
00 000 0000	James McVay		AWOO	8	1849
00 000 0000	E.S. Mabry		HFAY	96	1854
00 000 0000	Elizabeth Mace[Kincaid]		HGJR	898	1811

Date	Name	Parents/Spouse	Origin	Code	No.	Year
11 Apr 1828	William H. Mack	William		COLE	601	1833
08 Mar 1792	Alexander C. Mackey	Walter	Scot/x	PBMB	164	---
00 000 0000	John W. Maddox			PBDP	730	1812
00 000 0000	William M. Maddox			HMAC	267	1835
00 000 0000	Edward D. Maddux	George B & Judith(Neal)	Va/x	BRML	255	---
02 Jan 1816	Abraham Madison	LeRoy & Teziah(Lindsay)	Va/Va	HGJR	847	---
00 000 1826	George W. Mahill	John	Pa/x	PBWA	352	---
00 00c 1796	Ben Major			PBWO	283	1834
00 000 0000	Caldwell Majors			PVED	851	---
00 000 0000	Mary A. Majors[Hart]			HSAN	767	---
00 000 0000	Rachel Malone[Dunlap]			HMCD	982	1841
00 000 0000	Tabitha Manner[Short]			PPME	375	---
00 000 0000	Belle Manns[Coss]			HPIK	613	---
10 Feb 1805	Sarah Manser[Brown]			PHEF	B227	---
00 000 1819	James Mansfield			HMOR	327	1828
00 000 0000	Joseph Mansfield			KNOX	692	---
16 Dec 1795	Samuel Mansker	John & Margaret(Robinson)		PBRJ	603	---
00 000 0000	Esther O.[Markham]			KNOX	692	---
00 000 0000	Benjamin Marks			PBKN	193	1835
17 Sep 1863	Charles Marshall	Robert M & Elizabeth(Foreman)		BRJM	524	---
00 000 0000	D. Marshall			HMEM	568	---
00 000 0000	F. Marshall			HMEM	568	---
00 000 0000	S. Marshall			HMEM	568	---
00 000 0000	Andrew Martin			AMOU	6	1851
00 000 1789	Archer Martin			BRML	340	---
00 000 1850	B. Martin			HMAC	269	---
00 000 0000	F.M. Martin			HHEN	297	---
00 000 1802	George Martin	Joseph & Nancy(Thompson)	Ire/Ire	PBML	1062	---
00 000 0000	H. Martin			PHPI	386	1854
00 000 0000	Henry Martin			VTBU	368	1830
00 000 0000	James Martin			HMOR	667	---
00 000 0000	John Martin			PPME	308	---
00 000 0000	John G. Martin			HMAD	565	1831
00 000 0000	Lizzie Martin[Ashlock]			HGJR	871	---
00 000 0000	Lucinda_Martin[Martin]			HWAS	83	1857

BIRTHDATE	NAME OF BIOGRAPHEE	PARENTS/BIRTHPLACE/BIRTHDATE	SOURCE/PAGE	DATE
00 000 0000	Nancy Martin[Graves]		HCAS 203	----
04 Mar 1822	S.F. Martin	Nehemiah & Drusilla(Cottrell) Va/Va	HPIK 619	c1824
00 000 0000	Samuel Martin		HGJR 854	----
26 Dec 1811	Samuel Martin		PBCO 556	----
00 000 0000	Martha[Martin]		HMAC 269	1850
00 000 0000	Sarah Martin[Francis]		HADM 759	----
00 000 0000	Susan Martin[Logan]		PBSM 481	----
00 000 0000	Thomas Martin		HMEM 616	----
00 000 0000	W.E. Martin		ACAS 22	1846
00 000 1828	W.W. Martin		ACLA 72	1848
00 000 0000	William Martin	Hutson Va/x	HPIK 769	----
00 000 0000	Solomon Mason		PBML 215	1805
00 000 1830	Hardin Massie	Thomas & Polly(Suttle) Va/Va	GHHA 631	1847
00 000 0000	John G. Massie		HPIK 848	----
00 000 0000	James N. Masterson		HLOG 485	----
00 000 0000	John W. Masterson		HLOG 485	----
00 000 0000	Mildred Mastison[Foley]		BRCM 507	1835
00 000 0000	William Matkin		PVED 581	----
00 000 0000	John A. Matheny		HFAY 97	----
00 000 1849	Mary Matheny		PFAY 87	1880
00 000 1815	Richard Mathews		HMOR 326	1821
00 000 1799	Col. Samuel T. Mathews		HMOR 326	1821
00 000 1817	S.J. Mattingly		HMOR 326	1824
00 000 0000	Jason Mattox		PBSM 513	----
00 000 0000	Dr. William C. Maul		HLOG 474	----
00 000 1830	John C. Maxcy		HSAN 694	1834
00 000 0000	Peter Maxey	Ky/Ky	PHPI 440	----
00 000 0000	Jesse H. May	Anderson	BRCM 204	----
00 000 0000	Thomas G. May		HCHR 260	1862
00 0c 1810	Sarah Mayhall[Jackson] Timothy		PBCW 395	----
26 Jul 1830	F.W. Meacham	Andrew & Elizabeth(Jones) NC/Ky	PBWA 216	1838
00 000 0000	Elizabeth Meade[Logsdon]		HCHR 262	----
28 Mar 1798	Henry Meadows		PBWA 661	----
12 Mar 1822	M.C. Meadows		PPWA 345	1829

Date	Name	Notes		Code	No.	Year
30 Sep 1819	A. Means			PPWA	345	1846
06 Feb 1824	Mary Means[Henderson]			PBML	500	--
00 000 0000	Harvey Mederia			HCHR	266	--
00 000 0000	J.W. Merrill			AMOU	6	1831
00 000 0000	E. Meritt			AMOU	6	1865
00 000 0000	Joseph W. Messick			HSTC	316	--
19 Sep 1823	Julia Messick[Crow]			HSAN	795	--
00 000 0000	B[Metcalf]			HMAC	275	1855
00 000 0000	J.D. Metcalf			HMAC	275	1855
12 May 1834	James D. Metcalf	William & Huldah(Davis)	Va/Ky	HMAC	192	--
00 000 1838	Thomas Metcalfe	Melville & Amanda(McIntyre)		BRMA	398	--
00 000 0000	Eliza A[Miles]			HMAC	269	1835
00 000 0000	J.R. Miles			HMAC	269	1832
00 000 1790	Abraham Miller	Joseph		PPVE	1055	--
00 000 0000	Andrew J. Miller			PVED	403	--
00 000 1818	Daniel Miller			HCHR	32	1823
00 000 1801	E.T. Miller			HMOR	326	1817
00 000 0000	Evelyn Miller[Prather] Cornelia			PPVE	195	--
00 000 0000	F.P. Miller			ACAS	23	1843
00 000 0000	G.H. Miller			HSAN	441	1830
00 000 0000	George Miller			HMCD	985	1831
00 000 0000	Henry Miller			HCHR	211	--
00 000 0000	J.S. Miller			HCHA	176	1867
00 000 1789	Jacob Miller			HSAN	829	1824
20 Jan 1827	Jeremiah Miller			LOGA	853	--
00 Jan 1805	John Miller			PBWA	563	1851
00 000 0000	John Miller			HLOG	536	--
06 Oct 1820	Martin Miller			HCHA	33	1825
00 000 0000	Mary E[Miller]			HMAC	268	1857
00 000 0000	Polly Miller			HSAN	441	1830
00 000 0000	R.A. Miller			AMOU	6	1868
00 000 0000	R.A. Miller			AMOU	8	1868
00 000 0000	R.P. Miller			HMAC	268	1857
00 000 1852	Rainey Miller			OCHA	92	1857
00 000 0000	Sallie Miller[Sharp]			HSAN	1020	--

BIRTHDATE	NAME OF BIOGRAPHEE	PARENTS/BIRTHPLACE/BIRTHDATE		SOURCE/PAGE	DATE
00 000 0000	Samuel Miller			PEDK 540	----
12 Jan 1826	Samuel Miller			HMCL 1030	1835
00 00c 1816	Wyatt Miller			CJRI 311	----
00 000 1843	H. Millhouse			ACLA 72	1849
00 000 0000	Minerva Mills[McNeil]			PBMO B24	----
13 Aug 1792	Rachel Mills[Wilson]			PBRI 283	----
00 000 0000	William E. Milstead	Edward & Mary N(Hinchee)	Ky/Ky	CASS 931	----
25 Feb 1829	William E. Milstead	Edward & Mary N(Hinchee)	Va/Va	HCAS 350	----
10 Jul 1832	Williamson P. Minter			BRML 668	----
04 May 1809	Abigail Mitchell[Culton]			VTBU 316	----
00 000 0000	Elvira Mitchell[Carnahan]			HMCD 738	----
00 000 0000	Levi Mitchell			HMAC 268	1831
00 000 0000	Lucinda Mitchell[Hole]			HMEM 762	----
00 000 0000	Nancy Mitchell[Keenan]			PBML 395	----
00 000 0000	W.A. Mitchell			ACAS 19	1828
00 000 0000	William B. Mitchell			HLOG 416	----
00 000 0000	Sally Mitts[Hexmon]			HSAN 797	1830
00 000 0000	Tillman Mockbee			PBMC 557	----
00 000 0000	Elizabeth Modrell[Curtis]			PBCO 245	----
00 000 0000	Elder S.H. Moffett			BCLA 701	----
00 000 0000	Catherine Moler[Breckinridge]			HSAN 877	----
00 000 0000	James K. Monroe			ACAS 19	1848
00 000 0000	Flora Montgomery[Walker] Thomas & Polly			HMCD 1157	----
00 000 0000	H.W. Montgomery			AMEN 23	1829
25 Apr 1802	Lydia A. Montgomery[Watkins]			HCAS 353	----
00 000 0000	Mary Montgomery[Walden]			PBSM 271	----
00 000 0000	Thomas Montgomery			LOGA 588	----
00 000 0000	Thomas J. Montgomery			HMEM 733	----
00 000 0000	William Montgomery			HMAD 416	1809
28 Jan 1818	Elizabeth[Moon]			BGLS 200	----
00 Jan 1811	Alexander Moore			PPWA 304	1833

Date	Name	Parents/Spouse	Place	Code	No.	Year
00 000 0000	Elijah T. Moore			CJRI	545	---
00 000 0000	Emma E. Moore[Parker]			BEFF	835	---
00 000 1830	J.B. Moore			HADM	846	1836
00 000 0000	Nancy Moore[Fanning]			HMAC	275	1861
00 000 0000	Nancy Moore[Rose]			CSBR	385	1839
00 000 0000	Olympia Moore[Henderson]			HMAC	268	1833
00 000 0000	Col. Robert S. Moore			HMEM	591	---
14 Jan 1839	Sarah Morey			PPWA	345	1852
00 000 0000	George Morgan			HCHR	---	1865
00 00c 1789	Isaac Morgan			BRKI	1309	---
00 000 0000	John Morgan	Lambert	Va/x	HCHR	259	---
00 000 0000	Sarah Morgan[Wilson]			PBRJ	267	---
00 000 0000	W.W. Morgan			HLOG	494	---
00 000 0000	William M. Morgan			ACAS	22	1832
00 000 0000	Winnie Morgan[Speers]			HMEM	745	---
00 Apr 1804	James Morris	Joseph	Md/x	PBDP	708	---
00 000 0000	John Morris			HPIK	501	---
00 000 0000	Joshua Morris			ACAS	19	1835
00 000 0000	Louisa Morris[North]			PBDP	323	---
00 000 0000	Lucy Morris[Todd]			HPIK	509	---
00 000 0000	Minerva Morris[Docley]	Samuel & Martha	Va/Va	PBML	1086	---
00 000 0000	Elizabeth A. Morrow[Malone]			HCAS	212	---
09 Sep 1833	John E. Morton	Charles M & Mary L(Hawkins)	Va/Va	HPIK	501	1824
00 000 1804	Mary[Morton]			HMOR	326	---
00 000 1796	Armstead Mosely			GHHA	682	---
00 000 0000	Charles Moses			VTBU	198	---
00 000 0000	John W. Motley			HPIK	771	---
00 000 0000	Levi Moulton			BGLS	386	---
16 Jun 1843	Robert L. Mountjoy	Robert F & Susan T.		LOGA	709	---
29 Jun 1822	William Mountjoy			BLOG	412	1834
29 Jun 1822	William Mountjoy			BLOG	354	1834
00 000 0000	William Mountjoy			TAZE	491	---
00 000 0000	William Mountjoy			HLOG	494	---
00 000 0000	John L. Mount			PHCC	180	---
00 000 0000	F.G. Mourning	John & Hannah(Ball)	Ire/Va	GHHA	560	1839
00 000 0000	Allan Mcutray			HWCL	66	---
00 000 0000	Jacob N. Moyers			HGSH	809	---

BIRTHDATE	NAME OF BIOGRAPHEE	PARENTS/BIRTHPLACE/BIRTHDATE		SOURCE/PAGE	DATE
00 000 0000	John W. Muir			HLOG	416	----
00 000 0000	Margaret Mullen[Grayson]			PBML	522	----
09 Feb 1835	Martha A. Mullens[Raker]			HFUL	837	1855
00 000 0000	Harvey Mullkin			PHPI	385	----
00 000 0000	Elizabeth Mundy[Waddle]			PBML	472	1827
00 000 0000	D.K. Munson			AMOU	8	1854
00 000 0000	Edward Murden			HJAC	130	1833
00 000 0000	Josephine E[Murden]			HJAC	129	1847
00 000 0000	William H. Murden			HJAC	129	1829
00 000 0000	Daniel Murphy			AMOU	8	1854
00 000 0000	J.W. Murphy			HCHR	260	1867
13 Apr 1841	John W. Murphy	Miles & Sibbie(O'Hair)	Ky1818/x	PBCO	325	----
00 000 1815	Liberty Murphy			ACLA	72	1854
00 000 1818	Miles Murphy	William & Matilda(Biles)		PBCO	325	----
14 Dec 1830	Eli Murray	William & Margaret(Bird)	NC1785/1799	HMCD	635	1848
00 000 1824	Elizabeth Murray[Pearson]			HPIK	733	----
00 000 0000	J.C. Musick			HLOG	494	----
00 000 0000	Mary A. Musick[Judy]			LOGA	583	----
00 000 1854	Albert Naegelin	Emile & Annis(Threvenin)	Fr/Fr	GHHA	618	----
00 000 0000	Elizabeth Nall[Edgar]	Gabriel & Fanny(Tuttl)		BCSB	139	----
00 000 0000	Larkin Nall			HLOG	536	----
00 000 0000	R.P. Nall			HLOG	536	----
00 000 0000	R.T. Nash			PPVE	477	----
00 000 0000	Diadama Neal[Gill]			CJRI	351	----
00 000 0000	Elmira Neal[Keys]			PBML	288	----
00 000 0000	Thomas Neal			BRCM	319	c1808
00 00c 1800	Thomas Neal			PBML	558	----
00 000 1820	A.J. Neathercy			PFAY	87	1844
00 000 0000	Jesse Neece			CMCD	459	----
00 000 0000	Jesse Neece			HMCD	269	----
00 000 0000	Sarah Neel[Jones]			PPDM	825	----
00 000 0000	Catherine Neely[Reel]			PBCO	533	----
00 000 0000	William H. Nelms			HMEM	568	----

Date	Name	Parents/Notes	Code	No.	Year
00 000 0000	Nancy Nelson[Mansker]	Basil & Elizabeth(Chattan) Va/Va	PBRJ	603	---
00 000 0000	Malissa Nesbit[Burton]		BRMA	429	---
00 000 0000	David Nesler		HLOG	485	---
00 000 0000	Felix Nesler		HLOG	485	---
00 000 0000	A.K. Netherton		HMAC	277	1840
00 000 0000	Julia A[Netherton]		HMAC	277	1830
00 000 0000	Louise Newbarn		ACLA	73	1856
00 000 1843	Jane Newcomb[Lowry] William		PHPI	300	---
00 000 1807	Rebecca Newell[Neve]		PPVE	47	---
00 000 1805	Matilda Newman[Killman]		BCHR	851	---
30 Sep 1835	Louisa Newton[Kenredy]	Henry & Martha(Haggard)	PBML	601	1836
30 Sep 1835	Louiss Newton[Wilson]	Henry & Martha(Haggard)	PBML	601	1836
00 000 1821	John G. Newton	Uriah & Mary(Haley) NC/NC	HGSH	922	---
00 000 0000	J.J. Nicholson		AMOU	8	1858
00 000 0000	J.H. Nickles		HLOG	368	---
00 000 0000	Jennie Nivens[Sims]		PBSM	323	---
09 Apr 1857	Elvere Noble[Sutton]		HLOG	466	---
00 000 0000	Sallie A[Noble]		HLOG	495	---
00 000 0000	Joe Noe		PPPI	509	---
00 000 0000	Matilda Noel[Jones]		BRML	307	---
00 000 1795	Matilda Noel[Jones]		BRML	615	---
00 000 1795	Matilda Noel[Jones]		BMCL	1118	---
00 000 0000	Matilda Noel[Jones]		PBML	1190	---
00 000 1834	Silas Noland		ACLA	73	1856
00 000 0000	Emma Norfleet[Boggs]		MACL	295	1870
00 000 1816	Wesley Norman		PBMO	B26	---
00 000 0000	James Norris		PVED	561	---
00 000 0000	James H. Norris		HMEM	666	---
00 000 0000	James H. Norris		HWAS	85	1825
26 Feb 1829	John M. Norris		PPWA	345	1848
00 000 0000	Joseph Norris		HMEM	666	---
00 000 0000	Sarah P[Norris]		HWAS	85	1825
00 000 0000	A.D. Northcutt		HCHR	265	---
00 000 0000	Silas Nowlin		PBMC	521	---
00 000 0000	Margaret Oakwood[Fox]		PPVE	919	---
00 000 0000	John Oatman		CBKA	616	---

BIRTHDATE	NAME OF BIOGRAPHEE	PARENTS/BIRTHPLACE/BIRTHDATE	SOURCE/PAGE	DATE
00 000 0000	Balus Odell		HWCL 111	---
23 Aug 1841	Hugh L. Oder	George & Sarah(Logan)	PBMC 725	---
07 Jan 1843	Clara E. Odor[Ward]	George Ky1814/x	PBMC 500	1853
00 000 0000	W.G. Odor		AMOU 8	---
00 000 0000	Lemuel Offelle		HMEM 358	---
00 000 0000	James Ogden		KNOX 698	---
00 000 0000	William O'Harra		HADM 399	1846
00 000 0000	Charity Olive[Tabor]		HMAD 565	1828
14 Nov 1829	Catherine Omer[Stout]	Peter & Rebecca(Hawes)	HADM 750	1854
23 Mar 1820	Jacob Omer	Peter & Rebecca Ky/Ky	HADM 748	1851
00 000 0000	Teresa Onan[Hagan]		PHKX B804	1841
00 000 0000	Dr. Harvey O'Neal		HMEM 568	---
11 Oct 1811	Samuel O'Neal		HSAN 800	---
21 May 1804	Joel Onion	William Md/x	HFUL 957	1810
26 Jul 1801	William Orchard	Alexander & Sally(Owens)	PBCO 234	---
29 Jul 1814	Elizabeth Orendorff[Kimler]	William & Sallie(Nichols) Ga/x	PBML 1175	---
28 Dec 1812	James K. Orendorff		HMCL 930	1817
00 Dec 1814	Thomas H. Orendorff		TAZE 506	1827
00 000 1831	Thomas W. Orlon	Thomas & Mary(Ashby) Ky/Ky	GHHA 602	1854
00 000 0000	Catherine Orr[Vinson]		PBAD 300	---
00 000 0000	William Orrendoff		HLOG 368	---
00 000 0000	Martha J. Osborne[Epperson]		CWCD 353	---
00 000 0000	James Overton		HMEM 591	---
00 000 0000	Asal Owen		HMCD 567	---
20 May 1835	Dr. Benjamin F. Owen	Va/Va	PCHR 260	---
00 000 0000	Hellen E. Owen[Van Hoorbeke]		MACL 298	1870
00 000 0000	Asal Owen		CWCD 466	1841
02 Feb 1826	Robert Owen		PPWO 642	---
00 000 0000	Elizabeth Owens[Pate]		PVED 381	---
00 000 0000	Mary[Owsley]		HLOG 369	---
18 Dec 1806	George W. Pace		BRCM 43	---
00 000 0000	William I. Pace		HMCD 810	1830

	Name		State	Code	No.	Year
00 000 1796	William Padfield	William	Md/x	HSTC	351	----
00 000 0000	John Padgett	Jerry		BMCL	1226	1850
00 000 0000	Alfred Fadgitt			PVED	596	----
00 000 0000	Elizabeth Page_Hall			BMCL	1070	----
00 000 0000	James Pantier	Philip		HMEM	748	----
18 Jul 1752	Reina Paris[Campbell]			HLOG	460	----
00 000 0000	George A. Parish			HADM	746	----
00 000 1818	J.A. Park			HMOR	327	1831
00 000 0000	John N. Parker			HLOG	524	----
00 000 0000	Mandless Parker	Caleb	Ky/x	PBMC	729	1855
00 000 1848	Julia A[Parker]			OCHA	92	----
00 000 0000	Richard T. Parker			HLOG	524	----
00 000 0000	William C. Parker			HLOG	524	----
00 000 1832	Thomas Farrick			HADM	818	----
00 000 1822	R.D. Parrott			HMOR	327	1835
00 000 0000	John M. Parson			HLOG	454	----
00 000 0000	James Pasley			GPPD	A555	1835
00 000 0000	Thomas C. Patrick	Thomas C.	Ky/x	PVED	1010	----
00 000 0000	Bethsheba Patter[Johnson]			BMCL	1115	1826
00 000 1823	A.C. Patterson			HMOR	327	1830
00 000 1816	Franklin Patterson			HMOR	327	1830
00 000 1796	Maj. Gershom Patterson			HGJR	338	1797
00 000 1841	Dr. J.M. Patterson			OCHA	92	1892
00 000 0000	Jane Patterson[Scott]			HMEM	742	----
00 000 0000	John W. Patterson			HMEM	346	----
00 000 0000	Levi Patterson	James	Va/x	PBSM	220	1835
00 000 0000	S.A[Patterson]			HWAS	86	----
00 000 0000	T.J. Patterson			PFAY	87	----
00 000 0000	McCady Patterson[Sprouse]			HENR	B71	----
00 000 0000	William Patterson			HMEM	346	----
00 000 1800	William Patterson			HMOR	327	1829
00 000 1810	William J. Patterson.			HMORE	327	1830
00 000 1770	William Pattison			BLOG	579	----
00 000 0000	Cynthia Patton[Hoover]			HPIK	457	1829
00 000 0000	Mathew Patton			HSAN	775	1820

BIRTHDATE	NAME OF BIOGRAPHEE	PARENTS/BIRTHPLACE/BIRTHDATE		SOURCE/PAGE	DATE
27 Dec 1814	Dr. G.H. Paugh			BEFF	664	---
00 000 1832	H.A.J. Paul			OPLO	86	1850
00 Mar 1832	H.A.J. Paul	Edmund & Rachel(Gray)	Ky/Ky	BLOG	382	---
30 Mar 1832	H.A.J. Paul	Edmund & Rachel(Gray)	Ky/Ky	LOGA	854	---
00 000 0000	C.T. Pavey			PJEF	B27	---
00 000 0000	Frederic Payne			HCHR	262	1850
00 000 0000	William B. Payne			ACAS	22	1864
24 Aug 1824	William B. Payne	Fleming & Susan(Hightower)		ACAS	40	---
00 000 1852	Alexander Peak			PFAY	87	1852
00 000 0000	William W. Pearce			HMAD	565	1815
20 Jun 1815	William W. Pearce	James & Lucinda(Alison)		HMAD	554	1815
00 000 0000	Charity Pearcy[Lively]			PHCC	349	---
28 Apr 1848	Margaret Pedigo[Lair]			PPWA	291	---
00 000 0000	Presley Peek			HCHR	37	---
00 000 0000	B.B. Pegram			HLOG	369	---
00 000 1832	Fred Pell			OCHA	92	1856
04 Feb 1837	James M. Pelly			HMCD	1002	1848
00 000 1803	Joel Pennington			HMCD	793	---
00 0c 1799	James A. Penrod			PAUP	B180	---
00 000 0000	John D. Perline	John H & Margaret(Pennybaker)	NY/Ky	HFAY	59	---
00 000 0000	E.B. Perkins			HLOG	547	---
06 Jan 1819	Captain William Perkins			BRJM	124	---
00 000 0000	Hickson Perrill			VTBU	269	---
00 000 0000	George Perry			ACAS	23	1871
00 000 0000	Dr. Lewis M. Perry		1796/x	HLOG	454	---
00 000 1826	Zerilda Perry[Munsell]	John & Charity(Depew)		BMCL	1210	1848
00 000 0000	Amanda E[Peter]			HMAC	268	1848
00 000 0000	W.T. Peter			HMAC	268	1831
00 000 1823	Joseph Peters			OCHA	92	1830
00 000 1817	Sarah Peters			HMOR	327	1827
00 000 1818	John J. Pevehouse	John	Pa/x	BCSB	428	---

Date	Name	Parents/Spouse	Place	Code	No.	Year
00 000 0000	Amelia S. Peyton[Barker] Louis & Sarah(Roach)			GHHA	649	1830
00 000 0000	George W. Peyton Louis & Sarah(Roach)			GHHA	649	1830
00 000 0000	James I. Peyton Louis & Sarah(Roach)			GHHA	649	1830
00 000 0000	John Peyton Louis & Sarah(Roach)			GHHA	648	1830
00 000 0000	Joseph A. Phelps			HMEM	568	----
00 000 1824	Francis A. Phillips			HPIK	582	----
10 Jan 1828	James A. Phillips Joseph & Sarah(Jackson)		Md/Ky	HPIK	620	1830
00 000 0000	M.S. Phillips			AWOO	5	----
00 000 0000	Martha Phillips[Ross]			HFAY	57	----
00 000 0000	Nancy Phillips[Wirter]			BEFF	704	----
00 000 0000	Elizabeth Pickerill[Dunham]			HLAS	B312	----
00 000 0000	Jesse Pierce			HPIK	502	----
00 000 0000	Millie Pierce[Motley]			HPIK	771	1849
00 000 0000	Clement Pierceall			AMEN	22	1874
00 000 1820	N.A. Piersall			ACLA	73	----
00 000 0000	Willis C. Pierson			PPPI	158	----
00 000 1829	Winslow Pilcher			PFAY	87	1829
00 000 0000	Winslow Pilcher			HFAY	95	1829
00 Dec 1799	Andrew Pinkerton			HGJR	1062	----
00 000 1869	J.W. Pinkston			OCHA	92	1880
00 000 1860	J.W. Pinkston			CHAM	1004	----
00 000 0000	Edward H. Piper			HWCD	1111	----
00 000 1813	Israel Piper Thomas			HGJR	879	----
00 000 0000	Thomas Pirtle			PBML	748	----
00 000 0000	Hattie A[Pitman]			HMAC	276	1865
00 000 0000	William Pitts			PBML	1179	----
00 000 0000	J.I. Plain			HMAC	267	1831
00 000 0000	Eleanor Ploehous			HADM	400	1831
00 000 0000	John W. Plummer			ACAS	22	1850
00 000 0000	Eliza Poe[Sefton]			HWCL	B228	----
00 000 0000	Julia Pogue[McPheeters]			PBSM	643	----
00 000 1828	Amanda Poorman			ACLA	73	1836
00 000 0000	Nelson M. Pope			HMAC	277	1834
00 000 0000	John Poplett Thompson			PHKX	B759	----
14 Aug 1818	James Porter William & Sarah		Ky/Ky	HMOR	669	----
25 Mar 1826	Dr. William D. Porter Seth & Cynthia(Davis)		Ky/Ky	PPVE	856	----

BIRTHDATE	NAME OF BIOGRAPHEE	PARENTS/BIRTHPLACE/BIRTHDATE		SOURCE/PAGE	DATE
00 000 0000	Catherine Poston[James]			PPPI 439	---
00 000 1811	James M. Potter			PBMB 129	c1830
00 000 0000	John Poulter			PVED 1046	---
00 000 0000	James Powel	John	Ky/x	HGJR 995	1821
00 000 0000	Elizabeth Powell[Sanders]		NC/x	PCHR 404	---
00 000 0000	Roxline Powell[Logan]			LOGA 494	---
00 000 0000	William Powell			HLOG 486	---
00 000 0000	George Power			HSAN 441	1821
00 000 0000	E.D. Powers			AMEN 23	1829
00 000 0000	Elizabeth G. Powers[Tackett]	William & Nancy	Ky/Ky	BCHA 74	---
00 000 0000	Sarah Powers[Shepherd]			PBDP 500	---
00 000 0000	John Pranty			ACAS 19	1828
00 000 0000	Jeremiah Prather	Jonathan		PPVE 195	1847
00 000 0000	S.J. Pratt			AMEN 23	1850
00 000 1816	Cyrus A. Preston			PBMB 493	---
00 000 0000	Martha Prewett[Hoskins]			PBCO 324	---
00 000 0000	Corilla Price[Sterrett]			BGLS 608	---
00 000 0000	Louisa Price[Hunt]	John & Mary(Cotney)	Ky/Ky	CJRI 498	---
27 Jul 1790	Abraham Prickett	George & ---(Anderson)	Eng/x	HMAD 353	1808
00 000 0000	William S. Prince			HLOG 370	---
00 000 0000	Susan[Pritchett]			HMAC 273	1877
00 000 0000	John Pruitt			LOGA 842	---
00 000 0000	Mahala[Pruitt]			LOGA 842	---
00 000 0000	Maxy M[Prutsman]			BHIQ B167	---
00 000 0000	Martha Pugh[Whitfield]			PBSM 566	---
00 000 1817	William Pulliam			OCHA 92	1865
00 000 0000	John Purdum			PBML 623	---
00 000 0000	Adeline Purdy[Wilson]			HMCD 376	---
00 000 0000	Presley Purdy			HMCD 930	1834
00 000 0000	James Purkapile			AMEN 22	1824
00 000 0000	William Purkey			HLOG 495	---

Date	Name	Notes	Code	No.	Year
00 000 0000	George Purvis		AMOU	8	1830
00 000 0000	William Purvis		AMOU	8	1826
00 000 1814	Alfred Quick		BHAN	203	1834
00 000 0000	Martha Quiet[Blair]		HPIK	807	1831
23 Oct 1851	B.F. Quinn	S.M & Sallie(Boulware)	HMCL	1031	1852
27 Oct 1818	Borthana Quinn[Park]		HMCL	1030	1853
00 000 0000	H.W. Quinn		HMCL	1031	----
00 000 0000	S.M. Quinn		PBML	294	----
00 000 1835	A. Quisenberry		OPLO	86	1835
00 000 1828	Albert Quisenberry		OPLO	86	1835
00 000 0000	Albert Quisenberry		HLOG	495	1848
00 000 1823	Allen Quisenberry		OPLO	86	----
00 000 0000	Allen Quisenberry		HLOG	495	----
19 Oct 1823	Allen Quisenberry	Edward S & Polly(Thealkill) Va1786/x	BLOG	423	1843
00 000 0000	Arthur Quisenberry		HLOG	370	----
00 000 1835	Arthur Quisenberry	Edward Va/x	BLOG	437	1835
00 000 0000	H.C. Quisenberry		HLOG	537	----
00 000 0000	John Quisenberry		HLOG	495	----
00 000 0000	R.R. Quisenberry		HLOG	537	----
00 000 0000	T.H. Quisenberry		HLOG	537	----
18 Dec 1829	Thomas H. Quisenberry Edward S & Lucy		LOGA	712	----
00 000 0000	W. Quisenberry		HLOG	495	----
00 000 0000	Harriet Raffurty[Rhoads]		HMAC	273	1833
00 000 0000	Margaret Rainay[Baldridge]		MACL	294	----
00 000 0000	Louisa Rainey[Whan]		BRCM	325	----
00 000 0000	Margaret Rainey[Baldridge]		BRCM	210	----
00 000 0000	Elizabeth Ralston[Pearson]		HPIK	733	----
00 000 0000	Elizabeth Ralston[Dawdy]		PBKN	256	----
00 000 0000	J.N. Ralston		HADM	401	1833
00 000 0000	Hon. James H. Ralston		HPIK	386	----
00 000 0000	James H. Ralston		HMCD	331	----
00 000 0000	Judge James H. Ralston		GSER	147	----
00 000 0000	John C. Ramey		HMAC	268	1835
00 000 0000	Samuel Ramsey		GHHA	542	----
00 000 0000	Samuel Ramsey		GHHA	602	----

BIRTHDATE	NAME OF BIOGRAPHEE	PARENTS/BIRTHPLACE/BIRTHDATE	SOURCE/PAGE	DATE
00 000 0000	Sarah Randle		HCHR 262	1869
07 Nov 1797	Benjamin Randolph		HMCD 1137	1840
00 000 0000	Lucinda Randolph[Keath] James		PBAD 361	1833
00 000 0000	Augustus T. Rankin		HLOG 486	---
00 000 1822	D.J. Rankin		OCHA 92	1828
00 000 0000	I.N. Rankin		HLOG 417	---
00 000 0000	W.L. Rankin		AMEN 19	1838
00 000 0000	Fanny E[Ransdell]		HLOG 437	---
00 000 1814	A.B. Ratcliff	Joseph & Mary(Bryant) Va1781/Va1782	PBAD 376	---
00 000 1804	Isabella Ratcliff[Long] Joseph & Mary(Bryant) Va1781/Va1782		PBAD 376	---
00 000 1821	John H. Ratcliff	Joseph & Mary(Bryant)	PBAD 203	---
00 000 0000	James Ratekin		HLOG 371	---
00 000 1816	William Ratikin		HMOR 327	1829
29 Apr 1824	G.B. Ray		PPWA 351	1846
00 000 0000	Garland Ray		PPWA 298	c1835
00 000 0000	Harriet E. Ray[Brooks]		PBWA 205	---
00 000 1793	Mary Ray[Johnson]		PBCW 491	---
18 Feb 1819	Orville Ray	Hickerson & Sarah(Kelly) Va/Va	PBWA 565	---
00 000 0000	Samuel Ray		HSAN 441	1825
00 000 1824	Woodford Ray		PBWA 658	---
00 000 0000	Margaret Rayburn[Henline]		PBML 785	---
31 Oct 1798	Margaret Rayburn[Henline]		HMCL 1021	---
00 000 0000	Robert Rayburn		HLOG 475	---
14 Nov 1848	Mary C. Razor[Hurt] William Ky/x		BMCL 1106	---
00 000 0000	Frank Redden		HMCD 858	---
00 000 1837	A.M. Reddick		OCHA 92	1865
00 000 1808	J.N. Redding		HMOR 328	1822
20 Jan 1837	Mary Reddish[Yelton] Joseph		HEDG 691	---
14 Sep 1817	Zedock Reddish Va/Ky		HGJR 386	---
00 000 1830	L.L. Redman		ACLA 73	1841

			Name	Parents	Birthplace	Code	No.	Year
00	000	1820	Abraham Reed			HMOR	328	1822
00	000	0000	Ann J. Reed[Reynolds]			KNOX	701	---
00	000	1808	Burrus A. Reed			PBWA	442	---
00	000	0000	Elizabeth Reed[Wallace]			HADM	751	---
00	000	0000	Isaac Reed			PPME	340	---
00	000	0000	Joseph Reed			HPIK	502	1857
00	000	0000	Joseph Reed			AMOU	8	---
00	000	0000	Nathan Reed			PBPE	549	---
00	000	0000	Sarah Reed[Lambert]	John	Va/x	BGLS	710	---
00	000	1815	Stephen H. Reel			HMOR	327	1826
00	000	1819	T.M. Reed			OPLO	86	1843
00	000	0000	Timothy Reed			HLOG	475	---
30	Nov	1806	Sarah H. Reeds[Tinsley]			COLE	580	---
14	Feb	1793	Henry Reel	John & Catherine(Stooky)	NY/NY	PBCO	533	---
00	000	1801	Albert G. Rees	John	Oh/x	BGLS	337	---
23	Feb	1817	E.M. Rees		Va/x	HMOR	647	1839
00	000	0000	Elizabeth Reese[Barritt]			PHPI	411	---
00	000	0000	G. Reeve			HHEN	332	---
00	000	0000	L. Reeve			VTBU	203	1832
00	000	0000	Sampson Reeves	George		BRJM	243	---
00	000	1796	Jesse Renfro	James		HMAD	85	1810
00	000	0000	Redin Renfrow			HWCL	B55	---
00	000	0000	Benford Reno			HMAC	268	1841
00	000	0000	Martha[Reno]			HMAC	268	1842
00	000	0000	William Reno			HMAC	268	1842
00	000	0000	Elizabeth[Reynolds]			HLOG	495	---
09	Jan	1846	Euphrasia Reynolds[Kirk]			HMCL	1017	---
00	000	1834	James Rhea	William & Ann		GHHA	925	1850
00	000	0000	B.C[Rhoads]			HMAC	268	---
00	000	0000	C.C. Rhodes			HMAC	268	---
00	000	0000	William H. Rhoads			HWCL	273	1833
00	000	0000	Jane Rhodes[Cravens]			HWCL	108	---
00	000	0000	Elijah Rice	William	Oh/x	PVED	710	---
00	000	0000	Emily Rice[Walton]	Ezekiel & Fanny(Garnett)	Va/Va	GHHA	527	---
23	Sep	1840	Fantleroy Rice	Corban & Elizabeth	Ky/Ky	KNOX	702	---

BIRTHDATE	NAME OF BIOGRAPHEE	PARENTS/BIRTHPLACE/BIRTHDATE	SOURCE/PAGE	DATE
00 000 0000	George P. Rice	Va/x	PBPE 386	----
00 000 0000	Harriet Rice[Scott]		GHHA 605	1850
00 000 0000	Lovina Rice[Lyman]		KNOX 691	----
00 000 0000	Matilda Rice[McDow]		HGJR 435	----
01 Mar 1848	Tilford Rice		PPWA 298	1869
00 000 0000	William B. Rice		PBMB 186	----
00 00c 1798	Obadiah Rich		BRJM 321	----
00 000 0000	William Richards		HLOG 486	----
06 Nov 1811	Amos Richardson		HCHR 34	----
00 000 0000	C.P. Richardson		HMEM 568	----
21 Oct 1816	Henry Richardson		PPWA 292	1853
00 000 0000	Isaac Richardson		HCHR 264	1827
31 Mar 1804	Jane Richardson[Orchard]		PBCO 234	----
00 000 0000	Manda[Richardson]		VTBU 203	----
00 000 0000	Matilda[Richardson]		VTBU 203	----
00 000 0000	Rebecca Richey[Marshall]		PBPE 610	----
00 000 0000	S.H. Richey		PBRJ 254	----
00 000 1813	A.P. Rigg	George & Sarah	HMOR 328	1829
13 Dec 1813	A.P. Rigg		HMOR 648	1829
00 000 0000	Archibald P. Rigg		HGJR 990	----
00 000 0000	John L. Riley		HLOG 486	----
16 Mar 1827	Nimrod Riley	James & Delila(Gibson) Va/Va	PBCO 234	----
00 000 0000	Sarah Riley[Wade]		EFAY 821	----
00 000 0000	Samuel Ritchey		KNOX 702	----
00 000 0000	Mary[Ritchie]		HMAC 273	1855
24 Nov 1803	Elizabeth Ritter[Lykins]		PPME 360	----
00 000 0000	John Ritter		BMCL 923	----
00 000 0000	W.G. Ritter		HLOG 372	----
00 000 0000	Sarah Robbins		HSAN 442	----
00 000 0000	James Roberson		PHKX B874	1839
27 May 1814	Absalom Roberts	William & Elizabeth(Cox) SC/SC	PBJD 699	1834
29 Jan 1835	Addison B. Roberts	James & Sallie(Cox)	HMCD 587	----

Date	Name	Parents / Notes	Origin	Code	No.	Year
00 000 0000	Anna[Roberts]			HFUL	498	----
00 000 0000	Eliza Roberts[Jones]			BHAN	158	----
00 000 0000	Francina Roberts[Bryant]			PBCO	405	----
25 Dec 1823	H. Roberts		SC/x	HADM	930	1835
07 Aug 1802	Jane Roberts[Phillips] Jesse			PBMB	501	----
00 000 1808	John Roberts			HFUL	498	----
00 000 1808	Nathan E. Roberts Archibald			HWCL	100	1810
00 000 1839	H.G. Robertson			PFAY	87	1863
00 000 0000	Simon Robertson			CJRI	270	1830
01 Oct 1822	Zachariah Robertson Zachariah & Elizabeth(Jones)	Ky/Ky	PVED	719	----
01 Oct 1822	Zachariah Robertson Zachariah & Elizabeth(Jones)	Ky/Ky	PPVE	276	----
00 000 0000	Zacharaih Robertson			PPVE	840	----
07 Apr 1818	S. Robertson			HMEM	796	1836
00 000 0000	Julia Robine[Ritchey]			HGJR	475	1815
08 Feb 1836	Amelia T. Robinson[Fawlings] James J & Margaret(Gaines)			PBSM	667	1821
00 000 0000	D.P. Robinson			HSAN	442	1863
00 000 0000	E[Robinson]			HJAC	131	----
00 000 1820	Eliza Robinson[Cooper]			PEMO	B102	----
00 000 0000	George Robinson			HLOG	418	----
00 000 1793	Sen. John M. Robinson			EFAY	454	----
00 000 1805	Martin K. Robinson			BEFF	847	1834
22 Mar 1788	Rachel Robinson[Runyon]			PPVE	608	----
00 Oct 1798	John W. Rodgers			CJRI	315	----
00 000 0000	Joseph W. Rodgers			HMOR	328	1826
00 000 0000	Catherine J. Rodman[Morgan] James		Ire/x	PBCO	381	----
00 000 0000	Uriah C. Roe			BROG	62	----
00 000 0000	Fanny Roll[Mason]			PVED	817	----
00 000 0000	Melinda Rollins[Claypool]			PPME	416	----
00 000 0000	Mary Rose[McKever]			MACL	299	1831
00 000 0000	R.H. Rose			CSBR	385	1839
00 000 1804	Orpah Rosebrough[Ayres]			BLOG	510	----
00 000 1822	J.H. Ross			PFAY	87	1850
00 000 0000	Joshua W. Ross			HFAY	57	----
00 000 0000	Meredith B. Ross			CJRI	245	----
09 Dec 1801	Samuel Ross			COLE	631	----
00 000 1844	John M. Rothwell			OPLO	86	1865

BIRTHDATE	NAME OF BIOGRAPHEE	PARENTS/BIRTHPLACE/BIRTHDATE	SOURCE/PAGE	DATE
00 000 1822	Martha Routt[Newton]		PBML	552	----
22 May 1822	Martha E. Routt[Newton]		HMCL	1025	----
00 000 0000	Catherine Rowland[Bushy]		HCHR	264	----
00 000 0000	Emily Rucker[Sanders]		BCHR	972	----
00 000 1825	Nancy J. Rucker[Redman] John	Ky/x	HCAS	309	----
00 000 0000	Thomas Rucker		HSAN	442	1832
00 000 0000	Jacob Ruggles		GHHA	815	----
23 May 1788	Daniel Runyon Daniel & Rachel(Runyon)	1750/1752	PPVE	608	----
00 000 0000	Lucinda Rush[Herring]		GHHA	537	----
00 000 1807	Mary A. Rush[Hoes] Isaac	Pa/x	PBMO	B202	----
00 000 0000	Eliza S. Russell[Clarke] Samuel		PBWA	501	----
00 000 1818	William H. Russell John	NC/x	PBMO	B322	c1823
00 000 0000	James Rutledge Robert	SC/x	PBML	426	1820
00 Nov 1814	Jane Rutledge[Buckles]		HMCL	877	----
00 000 1810	Robert Rutledge		BRML	427	1826
00 000 0000	Adam H. Ryan		PHKX	B884	1848
00 000 1836	T.M. Sallee		ACIA	73	1873
00 000 0000	James Sample David	Scot/x	BRML	567	1857
01 Aug 1857	Samuel H. Sadler Joseph G.	Ky1832/x	HLOG	558	1858
00 000 1798	Andrew Samples		HMOR	329	1824
00 000 1798	Andrew Samples David & Mary(Townsend)		HMOR	579	1808
00 000 1824	Sarah A. Sampson[Tebbill]		PHPI	457	----
00 000 0000	Thomas Sams		PAUP	B238	----
00 000 0000	Alfred Samuels		HLOG	437	----
00 000 0000	John Samuels		HMAC	268	1839
00 000 0000	George W. Sanders		PPVE	883	----
00 000 0000	John Sanders John	NC/x	PCHR	404	----
00 000 1829	John Sandidge Daniel & Pamelia(Tate)	Va1804/Va03	BCSB	289	----
05 Jan 1849	Levi Sandusky		BRKI	1394	----
00 000 1838	Jeremiah Sarver Christopher & Caroline(Wright)Ky/Ky		PFAY	88	1839
00 000 0000	G.M. Saunders		HSAN	441	1828
00 000 0000	J.S. Saunders		HSAN	442	1824

Date	Name	Parents/Spouse	Birthplace	Code	No.	Year
00 000 0000	Polly Saunders[Kircaid]			PBHE	239	1836
00 000 0000	Jacob Sauter			HLOG	509	----
00 000 0000	Rebecca Sawyer[Lirder] John			COLE	551	1850
00 000 0000	Sarah S[Sawyer]			HMAC	269	----
00 000 0000	Sassander Sawyer			BCHA	599	----
00 000 1808	Thomas Scanland	William	Ky/x	BCSB	262	----
00 000 0000	John Scheets			HLOG	538	----
00 000 0000	Ephraim Schultz	David	Ger/x	BRCM	351	----
00 000 0000	William Scobee	Robert & Elizabeth(Crawford)	Va/Va	PBML	1086	----
00 000 0000	Rhoda[Scobey]			HPIK	583	----
00 000 0000	Charles C. Scott			HMEM	742	----
00 000 1840	E.R. Scott			OCHA	92	1871
02 Feb 1816	Moses Scott	William & Mary(Ryle)	Ky/Ky	GHHA	605	1850
00 000 0000	Nancy Scott[Williams]			BRJM	520	1836
00 000 1846	Pauline Scott[Provine] Martin		Ky/x	HFUL	926	1849
27 Oct 1846	Perry A. Scott	Moses & Harriet(Rice)	Ky/Ky	GHHA	606	1849
00 000 1812	Peter Scott			ACLA	73	1836
00 000 1827	R.H. Scott			ACLA	73	1864
04 Jan 1822	Walton K. Scott	Martin & Sarah	Ky/Ky	KNOX	704	----
00 000 0000	Z.P. Scott			HMOR	557	----
00 000 0000	Carter T. Scroggir	Humphrey		LOGA	808	1811
00 000 0000	Robert Scroggins			HGJR	854	1828
00 000 1823	I.P. Scrogin			BMCL	1285	----
00 000 0000	Lemuel B. Searcy	Charles	Ky/x	HMAC	226	----
00 000 0000	Mary Sears[Prater]			HFAY	80	----
00 000 0000	Apphia Seaton[Butler]			GHHA	551	----
16 Aug 1829	G.K. Seaton	C.D & Elizabeth(Payne)	Ky/Va	GHHA	543	----
00 000 0000	J.H. Seaton			VTBU	245	----
00 000 0000	James H. Seaton			VTBU	245	----
00 000 0000	Jane Seaton[Kelley]			GHHA	538	----
00 000 0000	Mary J. Secrest[Mershon]			HCAR	457	----
00 000 1826	B.J. See			ACLA	73	1851
00 000 0000	Jemima Selby[Bushy]			HCHR	264	----
00 000 0000	Orpha Self[Kelner]			HSAN	1017	----
00 000 0000	Hon. John Semple			PHEF	A140	----

BIRTHDATE	NAME OF BIOGRAPHEE	PARENTS/BIRTHPLACE/BIRTHDATE	SOURCE/PAGE COLE	DATE
16 May 1819	Thomas Senteney		648	----
00 000 1840	J.J. Sewell		ACIA 73	1855
00 000 0000	Elizabeth Seybold[Grigsby]		HMCD 882	----
00 000 0000	John G. Shastig		PBMC 507	----
00 000 0000	John G. Shastig		HPIK 700	----
00 00c 1798	George H. Shaw		BRBM 386	1828
18 Apr 1836	M.J[Shaw]		PPWA 262	1852
31 Dec 1832	Thomas S. Shaw	William & Alice(Nesbit)	TAZE 658	1865
00 000 1810	Isaac Sheets		HMOR 329	1829
00 000 1821	Daniel Shelton		PFAY 88	1829
05 Oct 1830	Mary Shelton[Means]		PPWA 345	----
06 Sep 1821	S.T. Shelton		PPWA 306	1837
20 May 1828	Lucinda Shepard[Downtain]		HMOR 734	----
00 000 0000	J.B. Shepherd		AMOU 6	1856
00 000 0000	James W. Shepherd		HEDG 655	1811
00 000 1827	Joseph Shepherd		HMOR 329	1830
07 Nov 1832	Preston Shepherd	---- & Anna(Brown)	PBMO B171	----
00 000 0000	Robert Shepherd		PBIP 500	----
00 000 0000	Nancy J. Sheplar[Martin]		HMOR 667	1830
00 000 1824	G.G. Sheppard		PFAY 88	1847
00 000 0000	William Sheppard		HMOR 650	----
00 000 1805	David Shields		HFUL 961	----
00 000 0000	John W. Shields		HLOG 447	----
00 000 0000	Benjamin Shipley		BRBM 633	----
00 000 0000	Columbus Shipp		AMEN 23	1856
11 Oct 1832	D.M. Shipp	Walker & Rebecca Ky/Ky	HFUL 719	1855
00 000 1828	Role Shipp		PPME 368	----
00 000 0000	Jacob Shire		HLOG 516	----
01 Jan 1841	Henry Shirley		HLOG 538	----
00 000 0000	James W. Shirley		HLOG 538	----
00 000 1841	S.H. Shirley		OPLO 87	1846

Date	Name	Parents / Notes	Code	No.	Year
00 000 0000	Joseph W. Short		HLOG	526	---
00 000 0000	Col. Purnell Short		HGJR	861	c1831
00 000 0000	William B. Short		PPME	375	1817
00 000 1816	Hannah Shrout[Hom]		PBCO	391	---
00 000 1827	William Shryock	John & Sarah	CJRI	581	---
00 000 0000	James W. Shumale		HLOG	447	---
02 Sep 1816	Jesse Siddenes		PHEF	B214	---
00 000 1808	Andrew W. Simmons		PPWA	250	1833
00 000 1826	Calvin D. Simmons		HMCH	588	1834
00 000 0000	David M. Simmors		HMOR	328	1828
00 000 1803	Enos Simmons		PBAD	142	---
00 000 0000	Hiram Simmons	Robert & Flora(Chenworth) Md1779/Va87	GHHA	623	---
28 Sep 1833	Martha Simmons[Groom]		GHHA	613	---
00 000 1810	Sarah Simmons[Yoakim]		HSAN	1014	---
10 Jul 1803	William J. Simmons		PLAS	460	1837
00 000 1814	W.W. Sims		HMOR	730	---
00 000 1819	William Sims		HGSH	823	1835
00 000 0000	Silas Simms		HMOR	329	1827
00 000 1831	Wesley Simms		HMOR	329	1827
00 000 0000	John J. Simons		HSTC	380	---
00 000 0000	Nancy Simons[Ray]		PBWA	658	---
00 000 0000	Virginia[Simons]		HSTC	380	---
00 000 1823	Frances H. Simpson		HMAC	273	---
00 000 1810	J.N. Simpson		HCHR	262	---
10 Jul 1803	Lydia Ann[Simpson]		CBKA	406	1821
00 000 0000	Milton Sims	Thomas & Lucinda(Hudson) Ky/Ky	CJRI	522	---
00 000 1830	W.W. Sims		HMOR	730	---
00 000 0000	William Sims		HGSH	823	1835
00 000 0000	Mary J. Singleton[Rigg]		CSBR	391	1867
00 000 1860	Catherine Skaggs[Chism]		PBMO	B214	---
21 Jul 1860	Martha J. Skeen[Humphreys]		PCHR	444	---
00 000 1795	Catherine Skelton[Jenkins]		PBCO	363	---
00 000 0000	James M. Skinner	William & Miriam(Noland) x/Clark	BMCL	1295	---
00 000 0000	Jesse Skinner	James M & Millie(Wilson)	BMCL	1295	---
00 000 0000	William Slack		BRJM	409	---
00 000 0000	William Slack		BRJM	244	---
00 000 0000	Barbara Slafor[Wilson]		PBML	1072	---

BIRTHDATE	NAME OF BIOGRAPHEE	PARENTS/BIRTHPLACE/BIRTHDATE	SOURCE/PAGE	DATE
00 000 1845	Mary Slater		OCHA 93	1854
00 000 0000	John J. Slater		HGSH 659	----
15 Nov 1822	Roseann Slater		PIAS 417	1822
00 000 0000	Richard Slaton		HADM 401	1823
11 Jan 1813	William Smalley		PPVE 642	----
00 000 0000	Asbury Smallwood		HDEW 340	----
00 000 0000	William Smedley		AMEN 23	1829
00 000 0000	William Smedley	Thomas	PPME 306	----
00 000 0000	Nathaniel Smiley		TAZE 411	----
00 000 0000	Aberland Smith		HPIK 480	----
00 000 0000	B.F. Smith		HLOG 376	----
00 000 0000	Cynthia A[Smith]		HCHA 261	1870
00 000 0000	David J. Smith		HLOG 475	----
00 000 0000	Elizabeth Smith[Kennedy]		HGJR 287	----
00 000 0000	Frances Smith[Nash]		PPVE 477	----
00 000 0000	George Smith		GSBR 393	1836
00 000 0000	Greenberry B. Smith		HSAN 717	1831
00 000 0000	Harvey Smith	Ky/x	HMOR 651	----
00 000 0000	J.C. Smith		HADM 400	1836
00 000 0000	James Smith		HADM 750	----
00 000 0000	James Smith		HWAS 86	1828
00 000 0000	James B. Smith	Warren/x	BGLS 727	----
00 000 1806	James P. Smith		HMOR 674	----
00 000 0000	John Smith		HLOG 475	----
00 000 0000	John M. Smith		BCHR 988	1825
00 000 0000	Laura Jane[Smith]		HWAS 86	----
00 000 0000	Lucy A.[Smith]		HPIK 480	----
00 000 0000	Martha[Smith]		GSBR 393	1834
00 000 0000	Mary Smith[Roberson]		PHKX B874	----
00 000 0000	Mary A. Smith[Scott]		PBCW 346	----
00 000 0000	Mary E. Smith[Whitecraft]		HCHR 267	----

Date	Name	Parents	Origin	Code	No.	Year
02 Sep 1833	Nathaniel F. Smith	John A & Cynthia S(Floyd)	Va/Va	TAZE	511	c1836
00 000 0000	Nicholas W. Smith			HPIK	411	----
00 000 1854	P.P. Smith			OPLO	87	1886
00 000 1830	Rebecca J. Smith			OPLO	87	1832
00 000 0000	Rhoda Smith[Wiley]			PBML	456	----
00 000 1829	Robert S. Smith	John & Elizabeth(Swift)	Va/x	TAZE	511	1834
00 000 0000	Roland Smith			HLOG	487	----
00 000 0000	S.B. Smith			ACAS	22	1870
00 000 0000	Samuel Smith			VTBU	206	----
00 000 0000	Samuel B. Smith			TAZE	484	----
00 000 0000	Sarah Smith[Hays]			PBML	884	----
00 000 1788	Summers G. Smith			PHEF	B233	----
00 000 0000	Dr. Thomas M. Smith			LOGA	334	----
00 000 0000	William Smith			HLOG	558	----
00 000 0000	William Smith			HGJR	881	----
11 Dec 1814	William Smith			HMOR	750	----
30 Oct 1835	William H. Smith	Willis & Phoeble(Taylor)	Ky/Ky	PBRJ	780	1831
00 000 0000	Abraham Smock	Henry	Ger/x	PBSM	555	1833
00 000 0000	A.M. Smyser			AMOU	6	----
00 000 1812	F.G. Snapp			PPWA	250	----
00 000 1812	David Snider			PHCC	158	----
00 000 1824	John Snodgrass			CJRI	318	----
00 000 1800	Samuel Snodgrass	Hugh		BRCM	600	1818
23 Jan 1850	Wiley A. Snow	Calvin N & Sallie(Bridgeman)	Al/x	BRJM	123	----
00 Feb 1811	Rebecca[Songer]			HWCL	169	----
00 000 0000	Thomas I. Sorter	John & Margaret(Sweazy)		HMGD	314	1849
00 000 0000	Susan Souther[Hudson]			PBSM	651	----
00 000 0000	Nancy W. Spalding[Cole]			CELW	350	1877
00 000 0000	Neppie Sparks[Flackburn]	Matthew & Prudence(Conway)		BCSB	369	1830
00 000 1825	M.A[Spates]			HMOR	328	1830
00 000 1823	Preston Spates			HMOR	328	1830
18 Apr 1822	G.C. Spears			PPME	205	----
00 000 0000	Isaac Spears			HMEM	745	1829
00 000 0000	W.G. Spears			PPME	253	----
00 000 0000	Winnie M. Spears[Reed]			PPME	340	----
00 000 0000	Olivia Spence[Lightner]			PBAD	503	----

BIRTHDATE	NAME OF BIOGRAPHEE	PARENTS/BIRTHPLACE/BIRTHDATE	SOURCE/PAGE	DATE
00 000 0000	John Spillman		PHCC 366	1811
00 000 0000	Jane Spivey[McDonald]		PBHE 516	----
00 000 0000	Nancy Spradling[Almond]		PBWA 255	----
28 Sep 1805	Caroline A. Springer[Brown] Charles		HMOR 658	1828
30 Jun 1828	Israel Spurgin		PPWA 251	1849
00 Apr 1814	Samuel Squires		PPWA 291	----
00 000 1829	Martha A. Stacy		HMOR 328	1829
00 000 1827	Thomas P. Stacy		HMOR 329	1827
00 000 0000	W.T. Stamper		AMOU 6	1843
23 Jun 1824	J.B. Standard	Gideon & Sina(Wyatt)	HMCD 798	1832
00 000 1820	E. Stanfield		ACLA 73	1832
00 000 0000	Stephen Stanley		PPPI 124	----
00 000 0000	Mary J. Stapp[Miller]		PBSM 584	1829
00 000 0000	Elizabeth[Stead]		HMAC 272	----
00 000 0000	Elizabeth H. Steel[Hazlett]		HCHR 263	----
00 000 0000	Samuel Steel		HHEN 306	----
00 000 0000	L.J. Steele		HPIK 508	----
00 000 0000	Lucinda Steele[Caldwell]		PBDP 285	----
00 000 1818	Dorcas B. Steely[Isbell]		HJOD 712	----
00 000 0000	Mary A. Steers[Gaunt]		PAUP B305	----
00 000 0000	Sarah E[Steidley]		HMAC 267	1835
10 May 1816	J.W. Stephenson	James & Margaret(Clinton)	HPIK 850	1819
00 000 0000	James Stephenson		HSTC 375	----
00 000 0000	James Stevens		HFUL 964	----
00 000 0000	Jasper Stevens		HMCD 609	----
00 000 1816	William Stevens		HMCD 606	----
00 000 1809	Benjamin F. Stevenson		HMOR 328	1829
00 000 1804	E.J[Stevenson]		HMOR 328	1828
00 000 1809	Elliott Stevenson		HMOR 328	1828
00 000 1813	Fleming Stevenson		HMOR 328	1828
00 000 0000	James Stevenson		HMOR 328	1829
00 000 0000	Sarah A. Stevenson[Bennett]		HSAN 695	----
00 000 1814	William Stevenson		HMOR 328	1829
00 000 1813	William Stevenson		HMOR 329	1829

00 000 1856	G.E. Stewart		OCHA	93	1857
17 Mar 1818	James Stewart	Peter & Tamar(Hancock) De/Md	HPIK	508	1825
00 000 0000	Lydia Stewart[Heady]		CJRI	562	----
00 Mar 1824	Nancy A. Stewart[Blackburn]		HHEN	416	1848
26 May 1803	Andrew Stice		HMOR	559	----
00 000 1810	Allen Stockton		HMOR	328	1830
00 000 1809	Eliza Stockton[Cavender]		HMAC	277	1841
00 000 0000	Thomas Stokes		PAUP	B85	----
00 000 0000	George Stone		HMEM	358	----
00 000 0000	J.L. Stone		HLOG	377	----
00 000 0000	John Stone		HMEM	358	----
26 Dec 1831	Nancy H. Stone[Gilbert] Stephen Ky/x	COLE	615	----
00 000 0000	William A. Stone		HMEM	346	----
00 000 0000	G.W. Stoner		PHPI	492	----
00 000 0000	Frances Stoner[Smith]		PPDM	882	----
00 000 0000	Mary Stoops[Hanna]		CJRI	567	----
00 000 0000	Samuel A. Stoops		PBML	808	----
00 000 0000	William Stotts		HMEM	346	----
27 Jan 1825	William Stout		HADM	750	1854
00 000 0000	Lurane Stow[Spear]		HFUL	708	----
00 000 0000	Mary L. Stowers	David L & Elvira(Sites) Ky/Ky	PBCO	384	----
00 000 0000	John R. Strange		LOGA	836	----
00 000 1819	B.F.W.Stribling		HMOR	329	1827
00 000 0000	Benjamin Stribling		CHAM	1034	----
00 000 0000	Frances Stribling[Mitchell]		HMEM	770	1828
00 000 0000	I.M. Stribling		ACAS	22	1827
13 Jan 1821	Isaac M. Stribling	Benjamin & Millie(Horn) Va c97/Va c97	CASS	964	1830
00 000 0000	John Stringfield		HLOG	487	----
00 000 0000	Parker Stringfield		HLOG	487	----
06 Apr 1807	William M. Stringer	---- & Elizabeth	HGJR	900	----
00 000 1810	Adora Strode[Jones]		PBWA	365	----
00 000 1819	Caroline Stubblefield[Campbell]		BCSB	221	----
00 000 0000	Andrew Stucker		KNOX	708	----

BIRTHDATE	NAME OF BIOGRAPHEE	PARENTS/BIRTHPLACE/BIRTHDATE	SOURCE/PAGE	DATE
00 000 1831	E.A. Stukts		ACLA 73	1854
00 000 1827	John T. Sturgeon		FFAY 88	1854
00 000 0000	Sarah J. Sturgeon[Bridges]		BCHR 852	----
00 000 0000	Alexander D. Stutsman Jacob & Mary(Berkey) Pa/Pa		BCSB 325	----
00 000 0000	Nancy Suduth[Downing]		HSAN 795	----
11 May 1824	Dr. James M. Suggett William & Elizabeth(Castleton)Va/Ky		HWCL B208	----
00 000 0000	Polly Summers[Bennett]		PBDP 292	----
00 000 0000	Robert Summers		HFUL 839	----
00 000 0000	Robert Summers		KNOX 708	----
22 Nov 1825	Elizabeth Sumner[Lamer]		PAUP B161	----
00 000 0000	Elizabeth Sumner[Hammett]		PBPE 531	----
00 000 0000	Alice Sutherland[Cash]		PSTC 342	----
14 Aug 1816	Peter J. Sutton Jonathan		PBDP 975	1826
00 000 0000	Francis Swan		HGJR 286	1814
18 Oct 1812	Monroe Swank Joseph		BROC 341	----
00 000 0000	Stenia Swearins[Watkins]		PPME 402	----
00 000 0000	Phoebe Sweet[Tankersley]		HPIK 466	1821
00 000 0000	William C. Swiney		HWCL 932	1836
00 000 0000	James Tade		BROM 461	----
00 000 0000	F. Taggart		HMAC 267	1833
00 000 0000	R.A. Talbot		HLOG 559	----
00 000 0000	Edward Tankersley		HPIK 466	1821
00 000 0000	Catherine Tennehill[Shoupe]		MACL 188	----
00 000 1826	William Tapscott		ACLA 73	1840
00 000 0000	A.A. Taylor		HGHR 267	----
00 000 0000	C.Q. Taylor		HLOG 487	----
00 000 0000	Elizabeth Taylor[McAdams]		HADM 805	----
00 000 1818	Isaac Taylor		HSAN 441	----
00 000 0000	J.C. Taylor		HLOG 487	----
00 000 0000	J.W. Taylor		HSAN 442	1833
00 000 1795	Jane E. Taylor[Elliott] John G.	Va/x	HSAN 660	----
00 000 0000	Joseph B. Taylor		AMOU 8	1857
00 000 1833	M.S. Taylor		HADM 401	----
00 000 0000	Mary Taylor[Gordon]		HSAN 766	1825

Date	Name	Spouse/Parents	Birth	Code	No.	Year
00 000 0000	P.A. Taylor			BRCM	293	----
00 000 0000	R.A. Taylor			HLOG	559	----
00 000 0000	Simon H. Taylor			HPIK	509	----
00 000 0000	Thomas Taylor			PPVE	116	----
00 000 1814	William Taylor			HMOR	329	1821
00 000 0000	William Taylor			CJRI	811	----
00 000 0000	William Taylor	John J.	Md/x	GSBR	303	1829
00 000 0000	Dr. William L. Taylor			PPME	222	----
00 000 0000	Z.T. Taylor			HLOG	300	1872
00 000 0000	Z.T. Taylor			HLOG	487	----
00 000 1852	Z.T. Taylor			OPLO	87	1871
00 000 1831	James Terhune			PPME	483	----
00 000 0000	James Terhune			PPME	408	1853
00 000 0000	James B. Terhune			CJRI	524	----
00 000 0000	John S. Terhune			CJRI	523	----
00 000 0000	Mary Thatcher[Garwood]			PBKN	584	----
00 000 0000	Isaac Thomas			BHAN	234	----
00 000 0000	Nathan Thomas			HFUL	878	----
00 000 1807	Robert Thomas	James & Sarah(Childers)	Ky/Ky	GHHA	925	1829
00 000 1802	William Thomas			HMOR	329	1826
17 May 1806	Benjamin W. Thompson		Va/Va	HFAY	60	1817
00 000 1847	C.M. Thompson			OCHA	93	1866
01 Jan 1823	Harrison Thompson			HEDG	--	1849
00 000 0000	J. Bradley Thompson			AGAS	22	----
00 000 1814	J. Bradley Thompson			HMOR	329	1827
00 000 0000	James Thompson			PVED	745	1827
00 000 0000	James Thompson			PVED	899	----
00 000 0000	L.H[Thompson]			HMAC	274	----
00 000 1799	Mary Thompson[Bagby]	James & Nancy		PAUP	B311	1868
00 000 1811	R. Davis Thompson			HMOR	329	----
00 000 0000	Sally Thompson[Smart]	Henry & Mary(Ray)	Ky/Ky	HMAD	453	1829
00 000 0000	W.F. Thompson			HMAC	274	----
00 000 0000	William M. Thompson, Esq.			HGHR	35	1868
00 000 0000	Eliza P. Threlkeld[Jones]	Elder Thomas		PBCO	352	1832
00 000 0000	William Threlkeld			HGSH	831	1857
00 000 1835	Amanda J. Thuman[Helton]	Marshall		PBSM	391	----

BIRTHDATE	NAME OF BIOGRAPHEE	PARENTS/BIRTHPLACE/BIRTHDATE	SOURCE/PAGE	DATE
19 Jul 1854	Newton Tibbs	Aaron & Mary A(Wilcher)	PHCC 127	1860
00 000 1854	Newton Tibbs		ACLA 73	1860
00 000 0000	Alice C. Tilley[Deputy]		CELW 354	1876
00 000 0000	Martha L. Tilton		HFAY 97	1845
00 000 0000	Elizabeth Timmons[Duvall]		HGSH 537	----
00 000 1821	John L. Tincher		EFAY 523	----
00 000 0000	Lorinda Tingle[Parkinson]		MACL 295	1861
00 000 0000	Lucy J. Tingle[Evans]		BRCM 54	1850
00 000 1811	Jane Todd[House]		PBWC 303	1835
00 000 0000	Phebe Todd[Wegle]		BCSB 579	c1835
00 000 0000	William Todd		HPIK 509	----
00 000 0000	Isaac Tomlinson		BLOG 624	1841
00 000 0000	Isaac Tomlinson		BLOG 298	1840
00 000 0000	Isaac Tompkins		VTBU 218	----
20 Dec 1815	Thomas W. Thompson		PPWA 251	1853
00 000 0000	Eliza J. Trabue[Boggess]	Va/x	HMAC 274	1835
00 000 0000	Joseph H. Trabue	Haskin	BRMA 129	----
00 000 0000	W.C. Trabue		PHPI 397	----
00 000 0000	Jesse Tracy		PBHE 221	----
00 000 0000	Penelope Traughber[Hodge]		PPDM 635	----
00 000 0000	Joel C. Traylor		PBMB 130	c1844
00 000 0000	Nancy Trent[Saddoris]		BROC 403	----
21 Jun 1845	Cora L. Triplett	Lee & Martha(Anderson) Va/Ky	PPVE 609	----
00 000 1806	Rev. W.D.R. Trotter		HMOR 329	1830
00 000 1828	Martha A. Truman		OCHA 93	1838
00 000 0000	Margaret Trumbo[Wigginton]		BLOG 539	----
00 000 0000	Polly E. Tucker[Traylor]		HSAN 778	----
00 00c 1800	Rebecca Tucker[Ruddell]		PBCO 423	----
02 Jun 1824	John P. Tull		GHHA 634	1846
00 000 1816	George Tureman		HMOR 329	1827
00 000 0000	George Tureman		ACAS 22	1827
00 000 0000	George W. Turley		HLOG 487	----
00 000 1812	Osben Turley	Charles & Sarah(Cheatham) Montgom/x	LOGA 814	1829

	Name	Parents/Spouse		Code	No.	Year
00 000 1826	Elijah Turner	John & Martha(Williams)	NC/x	HGSH	950	----
00 000 0000	Rev. John L. Turner			HMEM	665	1840
00 000 0000	Nathan Turner			HFUL	815	1831
00 000 0000	Starling Turner			AMEN	19	1831
00 000 1814	Henry Turney			FFAY	88	1816
22 Aug 1833	Nancy J. Tyler[Horsley]	John W & Elvira(Oxley)Fayette/x		PPDM	790	----
00 000 0000	Julia A. Underwood[Nicholson]			PBMC	489	----
00 000 0000	N. Underwood			VTBU	272	----
00 000 0000	Elizabeth Utterback[Quick]			PBDP	506	----
00 000 0000	Hattie Van Bibber[Burchett]			HLOG	553	----
00 000 0000	Thomas Vandeveer			HGJR	882	1831
00 000 0000	Martha Vandyke[Harmon]			PBCO	470	----
00 000 0000	L.J. Van Hook			PHPI	458	1864
00 000 1796	Mathias Van Kirk			PBWA	310	----
00 000 0000	---- Van Winkle			HMOR	329	1829
00 000 0000	Ransom Van Wirkle			HMOR	584	----
08 May 1798	Edmund C. Vance	Tobias & Nancy(Jack)		HMOR	562	----
00 000 0000	Jane Vance[Holmes]			HMOR	690	----
00 000 0000	J.H. Varble			AWOO	8	1860
00 000 0000	S.G. Varble			AWOO	8	1860
00 000 0000	William K. Varble			AWOO	8	1860
00 000 0000	A.H. Varney			HLOG	378	----
00 000 0000	J.E. Vaughan			HLOG	510	----
00 000 0000	Erastus Vaughn			BRMA	39	1871
00 000 1858	M.M. Vaughn			OPLO	87	1874
23 Sep 1791	J. Van Sandt			PHEF	B249	----
00 000 0000	Thomas Vaughn			CJRI	337	1856
04 Apr 1838	Henry C. Vawter	J.D & Sarah(Foster)		TAZE	661	1847
00 000 0000	M.A. Veeden[Eirk]			HLOG	435	----
00 000 1841	Wesley Veirs			OCHA	93	1883
00 000 0000	John Venard			HMCD	696	1830
00 000 0000	William Venard			HMCD	696	1830
00 000 0000	Henson Vinson			PPVE	524	----
00 000 0000	Henson Vinson			PVED	392	----
00 000 0000	Isaac D. Vinson			PBAD	300	----
00 000 0000	Sarah Vinyard[Pinkerton]			HGJR	1006	----
00 000 0000	Thornton Violett			HMOR	628	----
00 000 0000	William Voorhies	William		PHPI	495	----

BIRTHDATE	NAME OF BIOGRAPHEE	PARENTS/BIRTHPLACE/BIRTHDATE	SOURCE/PAGE	DATE
00 000 0000	Louisa[Waddington]		HJAC 130	1830
00 000 0000	James H. Waddle		PBML 472	1827
00 000 1829	John Wade		HPIK 510	---
04 Jun 1823	Z. Wade	Josiah & Frances Va/Ky	HPIK 710	1830
00 000 0000	Arabella Waggenner[Allensworth]		TAZE 710	---
00 000 0000	John D. Waggoner		HGJR 290	---
00 000 0000	Gincey Wagner		HMAC 277	1834
00 000 1813	Mary B. Wakefield[Nichols] Charles	Ky/x	PBCW 579	---
00 000 1816	Alexander Walker		HMOR 330	1827
00 000 0000	Catherine Walker[Stone]		PPME 178	---
00 000 0000	Cyrus Walker		CSER 149	---
00 000 0000	David Walker		HMEM 346	---
14 Jul 1833	Elizabeth Walker[Harrison] Hugh & Nancy(Givens) Ky/Ky	HFUL 831	1835
00 000 1822	Jesse B. Walker		PHPI 562	---
00 000 1822	John Walker		PFAY 88	1831
00 000 0000	John M. Walker		AMEM 23	1853
00 000 0000	Joseph M. Walker		HMEM 346	---
00 000 0000	Nathan D. Walker		PAUP B151	---
00 000 0000	Pinkney H. Walker		HPIK 389	---
00 000 0000	Sarah Walker[Steele]		HPIK 508	---
00 000 0000	William Walker		HMEM 346	---
00 000 0000	Nancy J. Walkup[Pile]		COLE 553	1855
00 000 0000	H.H. Waller		VTBU 260	---
18 Jun 1809	Allen Wallace Josiah & Mary(Mason)	HADM 771	---
00 000 1828	Cylon I. Wallace Allen & Ann	PBAD 446	---
00 000 0000	David Wallace		PBCO 424	---
00 000 0000	Delia J. Wallace[Simmerman]		PHEF B253	---
00 000 0000	Elizabeth Wallace[Chambers]		HWCL 10	---
00 000 0000	Elizabeth Wallace[Baldridge] Michael	Ky/x	PBWC 222	---
00 000 0000	James A. Wallace		HADM 400	1835
00 000 0000	James H. Wallace		CJRI 570	---
00 000 0000	James H. Wallace		BHAN 167	---
11 Feb 1827	John Wallace		PPWA 235	1832

00 000 0000	Mary A. Wallace		HADM	400	1835
00 000 0000	V.P. Wallace		HJAC	131	1844
00 000 0000	W.A. Wallace		HADM	400	1835
00 000 0000	William M. Wallace		HADM	751	----
00 000 0000	Cyrus Waller		HSAN	93	----
00 000 0000	Elizabeth Waller[McMurray]		HADM	746	----
00 000 0000	H.H. Waller		VTBU	260	----
00 000 0000	Dr. James Walshe		HLOG	379	----
00 000 1859	R.M. Walters		OPLO	87	1878
00 000 1834	John Walton	Frederick & Emily(Rice) Mason/Ky	GHHA	527	----
09 Nov 1818	Simeon B. Walton	William & Barbara Va/Va	GHHA	606	1840
00 000 0000	Wesley Walton	Frederick & Emily(Rice) Mason1809/Ky	GHHA	527	----
05 Aug 1814	William G. Wa-trip		HGJR	944	1819
00 000 0000	Eliza Ward[Hungate]	William & Elizabeth(Thaxton)	GHHA	904	1833
00 000 1826	May J. Ward		ACLA	73	1854
00 000 0000	Nancy[Ward]		HJAC	129	1835
00 000 0000	Ann M. Ware[McNeely]		HMEM	700	----
00 000 0000	Maria Ward[McNeely]		PPME	166	----
00 000 0000	David Warmer		BMCL	1337	1869
00 000 1841	Dr. A.R. Warren	Judge & Elizabeth(Bardridhe) Canada/Ky	TAZE	709	----
00 000 0000	Isabella Warren[George]		HCHR	265	----
00 000 0000	Martha Warren[Lindsey]		PHCC	118	----
00 000 0000	Daniel Waters		HLOG	379	----
00 000 0000	L.H. Waters		GSBR	150	----
00 000 1821	Z. Waters		HMOR	330	1825
00 000 0000	J.H. Wathon		AWOO	8	1835
23 Jul 1797	Elijah Watkins		HGAS	353	----
00 000 0000	James Watkins		PPME	402	----
00 000 0000	James W. Watkins		HFUL	816	----
00 000 0000	Ann Watson[Adkill]		PPVE	983	----
00 000 0000	D.J. Watson		HCHR	266	----
15 Mar 1825	Hiram Watson	John & Mary(Johnson) Va/Ky	HGJR	1098	----
00 000 0000	James T. Watson		HCHR	266	----
00 000 0000	John H. Watson	John W & Frances(Place) Va1777/x	PBCW	289	----
00 000 0000	Madeline Watson[Alvey]		HSAN	957	----
00 000 0000	William G. Watson		HCHR	266	----
00 000 0000	Elsie Watts[Mills]	Gabriel Ky/x	PHEF	B252	----
00 000 1853	James Watts		OCHA	93	1871

BIRTHDATE	NAME OF BIOGRAPHEE	PARENTS/BIRTHPLACE/BIRTHDATE	SOURCE/PAGE		DATE
00 000 0000	Laura A[Weaner]		HFAY	97	1825
00 000 0000	John Weatherford		HMOR	564	---
00 000 0000	Sarah Weaver[Raney]		PVED	581	---
00 000 0000	G.W. Webb		HLOG	379	---
00 000 0000	Nancy D. Webb[Fisher]		PBSM	331	---
00 000 1830	George G. Webber		OCHA	93	1833
00 000 0000	Jeptha Wegle		BCSB	579	o1835
00 000 0000	Mason Welch		PHPI	562	---
00 000 0000	James Welch		HFUL	709	---
00 000 0000	Judge W.R. Welch		HMAC	267	1861
07 Mar 1802	Absalom Wells	Md/x	HEDG	676	1822
00 000 0000	Ruth Wells[Elliott]		HPIK	680	---
00 Sep 1809	Samuel Wells	Philip	HGJR	996	1834
00 000 1770	William Wells		EFAY	582	---
00 000 0000	Col. A.S. West		HMEM	568	---
00 000 0000	George West		PBML	883	---
00 000 1831	H.C. West		OCHA	93	1851
00 000 0000	Benjamin Wheeler		HPIK	467	1834
00 000 0000	C. Wheeler		HMAC	268	---
00 000 0000	Catherine Wheeler[Willson]		BRMA	87	---
00 000 0000	Charles Wheeler		PPPI	157	---
00 000 0000	Dr. E.D. Wheeler		HJAC	128	1864
00 000 0000	Garland Wheeler		PEMC	464	1834
00 000 0000	Mary Wheeler[Hancock]		PHPI	448	---
00 000 0000	Wesley Whip		HMEM	358	---
24 Dec 1831	Ann E. White[Gayle]		HLOG	555	1866
00 000 1825	Elisha G. White		PFAY	88	---
00 000 0000	J. White	Ky/x	AMCH	63	1836
00 000 0000	James White	Stephen	PBMB	348	1817
00 000 0000	N.B. White		HSAN	441	1831
00 000 0000	W.H. White		AMEN	23	1826
00 000 0000	W.H. White		HLOG	539	---
00 000 0000	J.A. Whitecraft		HCHR	267	---
00 000 0000	Elzira Whitlock[Mitchell]		HGJR	978	---

Date	Name	Parents	Location	Code	No.	Year
20 Apr 1809	Elizabeth Whitman[Songer]			HWCL	228	---
27 Mar 1824	W.H. Whitman			PPWA	306	1830
00 000 1799	John Whorton			HMOR	330	1830
00 000 0000	Benjamin V. Wible			PBCO	315	---
00 000 0000	Cyrus Widick	George		PHPI	525	1826
00 000 0000	Marjorie Wiggins[McBride]			HRMA	252	---
00 000 1827	John Wigginton			QPLO	87	1855
12 Jan 1835	John W. Wigginton	Sidney & Elizabeth	Trimble/Trimble	HSAN	872	---
00 000 0000	M.G. Wight			HCHR	261	1867
00 000 0000	Mary A. Wilborton[McCarty]	Judge		PPWO	553	---
00 000 0000	John S. Wilburn			HMEM	568	---
00 000 0000	Patrick H. Wilche_	Josiah	Ky/x	BROC	81	1845
15 Feb 1825	Ellis Wilcox[Rhea]			HSAN	970	---
00 000 0000	John M. Wilcox			HMCH	264	---
00 Jan 1814	Ann Wilhite[Yager]			HMAD	491	---
00 000 0000	Reuben Wilkenson			PCHR	246	---
25 Aug 1833	George Wilkinson	James & Metis(Post)	Ky/Ky	HGJR	969	---
00 000 1825	H.C. Wilkinsor			BRGM	434	---
00 Oct 1820	Judge Ira O. Wilkinson			BRKI	1503	1845
00 000 0000	Nancy Wilkinscn[Barbre]			HSAN	888	---
00 000 0000	Reuben Wilkinson			HCHR	204	---
00 000 0000	Arah Williams[Eckarts]			HSTC	218	---
00 000 0000	Elias Williams			HMOR	601	---
00 000 0000	Elizabeth Williams[Harrold]			PEDP	495	---
20 Sep 1829	Henry C. Williams	Levi & Mary(Reed)	Madison94/Madison96	BHAN	484	---
00 000 0000	Isaac J. Williams			TAZE	561	---
00 000 1804	Joel G. Williams	Thomas	Ky/x	PBAD	280	---
00 000 0000	John Williams			HSAN	442	1824
03 Apr 1812	Joseph Williams			PPME	251	1823
00 000 0000	Mary Williams[Price]			HWCL	69	---
00 000 0000	Dr. Richard F. Price			BCLA	847	---
00 000 1822	Samuel Williams			HMOR	330	1827
00 000 0000	Sarah A. Williams			HMOR	601	---
27 Apr 1841	Thomas Williams			PHCC	355	1851
00 000 0000	Juliett Williamson[Cox]			PBHE	384	---
00 000 0000	Thomas Williamson			PHKX	B993	---
00 000 1792	William Williamson			HMOR	330	1834

BIRTHDATE	NAME OF BIOGRAPHEE	PARENTS/BIRTHPLACE/BIRTHDATE	SOURCE/PAGE	DATE
00 000 0000	B.F. Willis		HWAS 86	1858
00 000 0000	Hannah Willis[Reed] Wright & Judith(Wireman) Md/Va		HWCL 134	----
00 000 0000	Hannah Willis[Flinn]		BCSB 388	----
00 000 0000	W.E. Willis		AWOO 8	1834
00 000 0000	Anna Willoby[Montgomery]		PBWO 394	----
00 000 1823	Eliza J. Wills[Bell]		HSAN 1062	----
00 000 1819	John M. Willson	Isaac & Rebecca Ky/Ky	BRMA 87	c1833
00 000 1834	Aaron Wilson	Aaron & Queenie(DeBall) Va/Union	HGSH 586	----
00 000 0000	Catherine Wilson[Junken]		PBCO 300	----
00 000 0000	Darwin Wilson		HLOG 380	----
00 000 1802	Elizabeth Wilson[Van Kirk]		PBWA 310	----
00 000 0000	Emily Wilson[Gibson]		CJRI 578	----
00 000 0000	Henderson J. Wilson		HLOG 380	----
00 000 0000	James Wilson		HLOG 380	----
00 000 1821	John Wilson		HMOR 330	1823
00 000 1815	John M. Wilson		HMOR 330	1824
00 000 0000	John M. Wilson		HMAC 268	1834
00 000 0000	Louisa[Wilson]		HMAC 273	1876
00 000 0000	Nancy Wilson[Lackey]		PHCC 309	----
00 000 0000	Naomi Wilson[Wheeler]		HMAC 268	----
00 000 0000	Robert T. Wilson		HLOG 477	----
00 000 0000	Thornton Wilson		BGLS 708	1825
00 000 0000	W.H. Wilson		HCHR 267	----
00 000 0000	William Wilson		HPPB 371	1854
00 000 0000	William Wilson		PBRI 283	----
08 Mar 1791	A.C. Winchester		HMAC 270	1866
10 Jan 1839	Hon. Henry C.Withers William		HGJR 678	----
00 000 0000	R.H. Withrow		HSAN 441	1825
00 000 0000	William Withrow		HSAN 442	1824
19 Sep 1822	Allen B. Wood		HGJR 837	----
00 000 0000	F. Wood		HLOG 380	----
17 Feb 1825	John C. Wood	Aman & Sarah(Baker)	HGJR 836	----
00 00c 1828	Mary S. Wood[Brown]		BRMA 333	----

Date	Name	Parents / Notes	Birthplace	Code	No.	Year
00 000 0000	S.S. Wood			AMOU	8	1833
00 000 0000	Samuel Wood			HMAD	439	---
00 000 0000	Sarah Wood[Varner]			HPIK	416	---
00 000 0000	T.C. Wood			AMOU	8	1834
00 000 1808	Thomas Wood			HMAD	490	1828
00 000 0000	William Wood	Jesse	Va/x	PBKN	409	---
00 000 0000	William Woodburn			GHHA	768	1834
00 000 0000	Alphonso Woods			HLOG	380	---
00 000 0000	Catherine Woods[McCaleb]			HLAS	B337	1832
00 000 0000	Hiram Woods			PBCO	462	---
00 000 0000	J.P. Woods			HMAC	267	1858
00 000 1818	Martha Woods[Shoemaker]			PBCO	366	---
02 Jul 1816	Samuel C. Woods	Michael & Martha	Ky/Ky	HMOR	629	---
22 Sep 1851	Jemison Woodson			PBCO	227	---
28 Jan 1833	Septimus S. Woodward	Henry & Mary(Ball)		PBWA	582	1830
00 000 0000	Fielding Woola-idee			HMAD	456	1830
00 000 0000	Fielding Woola-idee			HMAD	582	---
00 000 0000	Mary A. Workma[Plain]			HCHR	266	---
00 000 1816	America A. Wortham[Lawson]			CJRI	331	1840
00 000 1822	John Wray	Isaac & Mary(Carlton)	Ire/Ire	PBWA	586	---
06 Jun 1822	Josephus Wray	Isaac & Mary(Carlton)	Va/Va	PBWA	553	1827
00 000 1834	Jemima[Wright]			PFAY	88	1835
20 Apr 1780	Joseph Wright			PBWO	B308	1814
00 000 1813	Joseph Wright			PBWO	B300	---
30 Nov 1800	Elder Morgan Wright	William		BEFF	889	1852
00 000 1832	Richard Wright			OCHA	93	1888
00 000 0000	William Wright			HPIK	461	---
00 000 0000	William Wright			HMAC	267	1835
00 000 1808	William Wright			HMAC	267	1829
01 Sep 1846	Zipporah Wright[Stringfield]	William T & Amanda(Hooton)	Ky/Ky	PBWL	1067	1849
00 000 0000	John Wrigley			HMCD	704	---
00 000 1817	Colman Wyatt			GHHA	769	---
00 000 1809	E.M. Wyatt			HMOR	330	1828
00 000 1824	James L. Wyatt			HMOR	330	1829
00 000 0000	Rebecca[Wyatt]			HMOR	655	1822
00 000 0000	Thomas Wyatt			HMOR	630	---
00 000 0000	W.T. Wylie			HLOG	488	---
13 Feb 1820	Joseph E. Wyne	B.F & Mary A(Doyle)	NJ/Ire	HMCD	320	1834

BIRTHDATE	NAME OF BIOGRAPHEE	PARENTS/BIRTHPLACE/BIRTHDATE	SOURCE/PAGE	DATE
00 000 1787	Mary A. Yator[Layton]	Henry & Nancy Ger/Ire	PBCO 278	c1839
03 Aug 1836	N.B. Yelton		HEDG 691	1828
00 000 0000	William Yoacum		HSAN 442	----
00 000 0000	Solomon Yocum		HFUL 710	----
28 Jul 1817	Catherine Yokum[Hart]		PBCO 394	----
00 000 1821	Eleanor York[Carns]		PHKX B96	----
00 00c 1803	J.W. York	Jesse & Betty(Wright) Ky/Ky	GHHA 563	----
00 000 1790	Elijah Young		BRJM 425	----
26 Mar 1807	Elizabeth Young[Wells]	Jacob	BKAN 657	----
00 000 0000	Emily Young[Whitehead]		PHCC 54	----
00 000 0000	Ezekiel B. Young		HGHR 260	----
00 Aug 1789	J.E. Young		AMEN 19	1836
00 000 0000	John Young		HWCL 125	----
00 000 0000	Marces I. Young		HGHR 34	1829
00 000 0000	Nancy[Young]		HGHR 260	1829
00 000 0000	R.A. Young		AMEN 19	----
00 000 0000	Richard M. Young		HMQD 330	1836
00 000 0000	Robert S. Young		PJEF B138	----
00 000 0000	Sarah Young[Purcell]		HGHR 262	1854
00 000 0000	Col. Thomas S. Young		HGHR 34	1854
00 000 0000	Louisa Yount		BWCL 970	1829
00 000 1822	J. Yowell		ACLA 73	1824
00 000 0000	John Yowell	James	HWAC --	----

-252-

Boulton(cont.)
Jesse A. 123
Boulware, Hardin 118
May J. 118
Nancy 172
Ruth(McWilliams) 118
S.A[Quinn] 172
Taylor 118
Bourland, Miles 172
P.G. 172
Rachel(Slaten) 172
William 172
William W. 172
Bourn, Elijah 172
Bowden, Sarah[Solomon]
116, 135
Bowen, B.F. 39
Jeremiah 172
John 172
M.A. 173
N.A. 39
Nancy J[Van Sandt] 173
Paulina[Johnson] 141
Bowers, Jane E. 173
Bowlds, Jane[Fulkerson]
135
John 135
John N. 135
Bowles, Amelia[Garden]
159
David 173
Lemuel 68
Matilda J(Kenney) 42
Mourning[Nichols]173
Bowling, George W. 55
Turner J. 55
Bowyer, William 26
Box, Mary[Williams] 110
Boyd, A.C. 173
Andrew 82
Arthur 94
Drury B. 33
Elizabeth[Fruit] 57
Elizabeth(Hurd) 33
Elizabeth(Pierce)57
Elizabeth(Wiley)149
G. 57
George 57
Hardy 57
J. 123
James 149
Jemima(Kitson) 149
Lucy A[Major] 57
L.C(Bailey) 123
Mary[Johnson] 173
Mary[Torian] 57
Mary E[Bridges] 173
Rebecca(Maze) 95
S.G. 110
Samuel G. 110
Samuel L. 82
Stephen 149
Susan 57
Thomas H. 33
W.J. 123
W.P. 173
William 149
Boyer, Frederick 140
J.H. 173
John K. 140
Naomi(Kester) 140

Boyle, John 97
Nancy[Ashcock] 173
Sarah(Green) 97
Boyles, Hugh H. 159
James C. 114
John 114
Bozarth, Alfred B. 57
Cynthia(Taylor) 57
John 57
Milton 57
Braber, Matthew 173
Bracken, Abigail[Hornback]
33, 34
Eliza[Montgomery] 173
Elizabeth[Kays] 173
Elizabeth(Mappen)33
George W. 33
James H. 33
N.W. 33
Robert 33
Theophilus 33
Brackett, Sarah E[Stanley] 173
Braddus, Sarah[Samuell] 60
Braden, Christian[Blair] 173
Bradford, Adaline M(Semple)65
Bradley, Elijah 33
Elizabeth(Crowder) 91
Hiram 39
Luellen[Johnson] 76
Martha(Hornback) 33
Mary[Greenawalt] 109
Mary(Markwell) 39
N.C[Reynolds] 131
Nancy J[Booth] 39
O.P. 33
Rebecca(Smith) 131
Ruth M(Patrick) 136
Thomas 91
Tobias S. 131
William 131, 191
Bradshaw, Cornelius G. 149
J.F. 173
Nancy[Huston] 173
Brady, James 158
Susannah[Henson] 158
Brake, Ann[Briggs] 173
Bramel, Elias 123
Elisha 123
Rebecca(Morse) 123
Bramson, Emeline(Baily)
159, 168
Hezekiah 159
J.M. 159
Jane(Cooledge) 181
Bramwell, Catherine(McDonald)
82
William C. 128
Brandenburg, David 61
James 91
Samuel 61, 173
Brannan, Alzena B[Costley]
173
Dudley 173
Mary 173
Thomas 173
Branom, J.W. 114
Bransford, Nancy G[Parrott]32
Brantley, Leah[Crisp] 64
Brasfield, James E. 118
T.H. 118, 173
Thomas H. 118

Brassfield, W.R. 173
Bratton, Archer 173
Brawley, Elizabeth
(Carr) 165
Brawner, Nancy[Thomp-
son] 118
Bray, Catherine
(Ranard) 144
Nathan 144
William 144
Breckenridge, James E.
39
Nancy(Ellis) 39
Oliver H.P. 39
Breckinridge, Catherine
(Moler) 216
Preston(Collins)123
Bredwell, Elizabeth(Col-
lins) 123
Susan(Collins) 123
Breeden, William 173
Breeze, Margaret
[Farmer] 189
Brengman, Margaret N.
[Head] 103
Brent, George 86
Brents, Emeline[Ray] 65
Samuel 173
Brentz, William C. 173
Bretz, Mary L[Westen-
berger] 173
Brewer, Ambrose 122
Delia(Hough) 156
Delilah(Hough)156
M.J. 122
Mary[Barton] 169
Rebecca(Gowen) 122
W.T. 173
William 156
William H. 156
Brewster, Elizabeth[Cook]
28
Bridges, Eliza(Ellis) 39
Elizabeth[Brownell] 94
Elizabeth A[Stewart]164
George 94
Hannah[Baker] 164
John 39
Joseph I. 173
Mary E(Boyd) 173
Bridgett, Mary(Shaffer)
68
Thomas 68
William M. 68
Briggs, Ann[Brake] 173
Charles L. 159
Charlotte 159
Elizabeth[Mitchell] 158
Jane[Corbin] 83
Martha(Hartis) 51
Mary[Latham] 160, 207
Sarah J(Sturgeon) 238
Susan(Clements) 112
Bright, Elizabeth(Morrison)
112
Henry 112
John H. 46
Maria(Gentry) 112
Martha A[Caldwell] 57
Mary[Lillard] 47
Reuben G. 112

Craig(cont.)
  Robert 131, 182
  S.A[Hersman] 94
  Whitney 67
  William 182
Craill, James J. 182
  William 182
Crain, Amanda(McMillan)114
  Amsted 114
  Eliza[Stevens] 182
  Jane E(Porter) 51
  Sarah 114
  Sirilia M[Ewing] 114
  Wesley T. 114
  William 114
Crampton, Lulu[Craig] 182
Crane, B.S. 102
  Emma A[Verry] 182
  Fanny G[Jackson] 96
  Hannah(Johnson) 102
  Lafayette 182
  Mary A[Huff] 114, 182
  William 102, 182
Crask, Annie L[Attebury]84
Cravens, Elijah 183
  Jane(Rhodes) 227
  Y.B. 183
Crawford, Alexander B. 131
  Alice(Thompson) 145
  Alzira(Dougherty) 137
  Charlotte(Riggs) 131
  David 137
  Eliza J[Vandever] 66
  Elizabeth(Howard) 159
  Elizabeth(Huddleston) 137
  Elizabeth[Roby] 136
  Elizabeth[Scobee] 231
  Harrison 145
  James B. 145
  Jane[Horney] 49
  John 137, 159
  John W. 159
  Mary A[Cockern] 183
  Priscilla 66
  R.O. 131
  Sarah L[Bilderback] 110
  Screpta(Daugherty) 40
  Thomas 40, 137
Creal, Edward G. 65
  Elijah 65
  Temperance S(Wilburn) 65
Cree, Sally[Cash] 133
Creel, Charles 26
  Malinda[Hamilton] 26
  Silas 26
Crewdson, Mildred A[Bernard]
  114
Crews, Alexander 31
  Elizabeth R. 183
  Jesse 183
  Matthew 31, 183
  Nancy(Blair) 31
  Nancy(Carter) 177
  William 183
Crigler, Love E(Ballard) 106
Crim, Jesse 149
  John 149
  Lucinda(Churchill) 98
Crisler, Adam 37
  Alm 37
  Mary(Shafer) 38
  Silas 37
Crisp, Andrew J. 64

John 64
  Leah(Brantley) 64
Crockett, Eliza(Ware) 40, 146
  W. Keen 40
  William 40
  William D. 69, 146
  William K. 146
Cromwell, Rachel 183
Crook, Ardia[Janes] 203
  Ardra[Janes] 203
Crooke, George W. 183
  Sylvenie 183
Cross, Alvin 183
  Martha(Forbes) 190
  Solomon 183
Crossly, Elizabeth[Brown] 175
Crosswhite, Polly[Coons] 69
Crosthwait, Samuel T. 156
  W.Y. 156
  William Y. 156
Crouch, Sarah[Wood] 64
Crow, Annie[Dunniway] 81
  Frances[Armitage] 86
  John 46
  Mary(Little) 47
  Mary A[Kermicle] 50
  Susan[Peak] 81
  W.D. 183
Crowder, Caroline[Foster] 183
  Elizabeth[Bradley] 91
Crownover, Rachel[Fisk] 100
Crum, Mial M. 78
Crumbaugh, Daniel 183
  Henry 97
  James H.L. 97
  Martha(Robinson) 183
  Mary E. 183
  Montgomery 40
  Sarah(Baldock) 97
  Solomon 40
Crume, James W. 122
Crump, Elizabeth[McGinnis] 137
  William C. 137
Crutchfield, Martha A[Lawson] 183
Culbertson, James 74
  John B. 112
  Sarah(Weaver) 74
  W.G. 74
  William G. 74
Culley, Huldah J(Moore) 117
  Jasper 117
  M.M. 117
Cullom, Permelia[Brown] 183
  Shelby M. 163
Culp, Samuel B. 137
  Thomas 137
Culton, Abigail(Mitchell) 216
Cummings, D.W. 94
  Henry B. 123
  J. 183
  John 146
  Samuel 146
Cummins, Elizabeth(Price) 95
  James 194
  John 94
  Lydia 194
  Moses 183
  Rebecca A(Scott) 183
  Robert 194
  Robert S. 183
Cunningham, Elizabeth(Yates) 85
  Elizabeth C(Yocum) 85

Emeline(Cooper) 122
  J.R. 85
  James 154, 183
  James T. 85, 91
  John 85, 154
  Joseph 94
  Margaret[Rainey] 183
  Mary(Humes) 94
  Matthew J. 183
  Nancy 122
  Nancy(Taylor) 91
  Robert 122
  Robert L. 122
  Samuel 122
  William 183
  Wright 91
Cure, David 183
Curl, Elizabeth[Curry] 183
Currens, E.T. 47
Curry, Alexander 146
  Amanda(Price) 147
  Amanda M(Price) 147
  Benjamin A. 102
  Christopher S. 102
  Elizabeth(Curl) 183
  Elizabeth(Nutter) 146
  Elizabeth(Robinson) 83
  George 87
  H.P. 87, 183
  J. Daniels 83
  James M. 128
  Malinda(Murphy) 183
  Martha G(Clements) 179
  Mary[Smith] 183
  Mary(Wilcox) 87
  Nicholas 83
  Priscilla[Omer] 104
  Richard S. 183
  Robert N. 146
  Thomas 102, 183
  William M. 141
Curtis, Elizabeth(Modrell)
  216
  Ellen[Kirk] 125
Cushing, Susan E.P. 183
Custer, Bridget[Wilson] 81
Cutright, Nathaniel 69

Dabbs, Samuel 183
Dailey, Mary[Standerfer]183
Dale, John 183
  Nancy(Hall) 195
Dallam, Francis A. 183
  Frank A. 183
Dalton, Elizabeth[Epperson]
  118
Dalzell, B.F. 183
Damron, Charles 183
  Wilson 183
Dance, Frances A[Haselwood]
  83
Dancy, F. 184
Daniel, Sarah G(Jackson)61
  T.J. 61
  Willis 61
Daniels, J.A. 184
  Lockie B[Flint] 112
Danner, Adelea M[Swiney]
  79
Darnall, Aaron 184

-261-

Drennon, Henrietta(Wimberley)
  157
Driskell, J.M. 128
  Judith(Mayo) 79
Drury, John J. 46
  Robert 46
  Robert M. 187
Ducker, Charles 54
Duckwell, F.W. 52
  May F(Sanders)53
Duff, Andrew M. 187
  Belle F(Johnson) 203
  Sarah(McClure) 210
Dukes, Elizabeth[Groves]
  134
  Sarah M. 113
Duley, Hiram 75
  Sophia(Northcott) 75
  W.W. 75
Dunbar, A. 75
  A.P. 75
  Cora(Holloway) 116
  George 187
  Malinda(Logsdon) 119
  Martin 118
  Millie(Collins) 180
  Washington 187
Duncan, Amelia[Wightman]
  149
  Catherine[Street] 151
  Clara C[Willim] 55
  Clark 114
  Darius 187
  Editha(McKay) 136
  Eliza W. 187
  Elizabeth[Sterne] 143
  Euclid M. 159
  Henry 187
  James 187
  James T. 187
  John H. 122
  Joseph 40
  Martha[Poland] 81
  Martha G(Clements) 179
  Mary(Booth) 39, 172
  Mary C[Gardner] 157
  Millie[Phelps] 120
  N.A. 187
  Ruhamah(Frizzell) 122
  S.S. 187
  Samuel 122
  Sarah E[Barnett] 69
  William 187
Dunham, Elizabeth[Jasper]
  144
  Elizabeth(Pickerill) 223
Duning, John M. 187
Dunlap, Andrew 187
  C.M. 69
  Charles M. 69
  E.P. 187
  Edmund P. 75
  Esther[Carpenter] 102
  George N. 69
  Latin W. 69
  Martha[Ruddell] 128
  Matilda F(Belt) 74
  Onie(Green) 69
  Rebecca M(Bell) 69
  Stephen 75
  William 69

Dunn, Alexander W. 75
  Andrew 47
  Benjamin I. 118
  Elijah 94
  Elijah T. 187
  George T. 128
  John 55
  Junetta(Marrs) 129
  Margaret[Peters] 187
  Martha[Feagan] 47
  N.L. 187
  Nancy[Gristy] 87
  Nathaniel A. 118
  S.K. 94
  S.W. 94
  Sarah(Foster) 94
  Sarah A(Elliott) 47
  Sophia W(Irvin) 118
  Thomas 103, 187
  Thomas J. 47
  Z.M. 187
  Zephaniah 187
Dunniway, Anna 62
  Annie(Crow) 81
  David 62, 81
  Elizabeth 62
  John W. 81
Dunseth, A.A. 75
  Mary(Burnside) 176
Dupuy, A.G. 89
Durben, Joseph P. 187
Durbin, Joseph 118
Durham, Sarah[Oglesby] 59
Durk, William A. 66
Durning, James 52
  Jane(Maxwell) 52
  John 52
Duvall, Benjamin F. 187
  Elizabeth(Timmons) 240
  James W. 143
  Martha(Butler) 155
  Melinda W(Colvin) 143
  Moses 155
  Prometheus M. 143
  Sarah E(Watson) 143
  William 187
Dycus, Andrew 155
  George 155
  Margaret 155
Dye, Alice[Mayhugh] 187
  Fanny(Biggars) 123
  Ross P. 124
Dyer, Martha A. 187
  Nancy[Salisbury] 187
Dyhouse, Almirna[Grafton] 124
Dyke, Mary A. 187
Dykes, Mary[Tomlinson] 73
Dyson, Mary F(Irwin) 203

Eads, Chamock 187
  Coleman 163
  J.A. 187
  Jacob H. 163
  John 69
  Margaret[Hoffman] 118
  Nancy(Tuttle) 163
Eakins, Joseph S. 75, 188
Ealer, Lucy[Powell] 38
Earl, Jane[Robeson] 188

Early, Sarah(Faris) 109
  T.L. 164
Earp, Julia[Sandusky]44
Easley, Ambrose 188
  Elizabeth(Haggard) 188
  James 188
  May F. 188
  W.W. 188
East, Drusilla(Hudson)41
Eastham, Annie O. 188
  George A. 188
  W.E. 112, 188
Easton, Daniel 188
Easum, Catherine(Tyler)
  103
  Charles A. 103
  William 103
Eaton, Adam 31
  Delia[Peddicord] 125
  George S. 188
  Martha[Ervin] 69
  Martha Jane[Sisson]188
  W.S. 103
Ebberman, Annie[Honn]138
Eberhardt, Catherine 188
Eberman, Mary[McCoy] 138
Eberwein, Carrie[Hoffman] 89
Eccles, Henry 128
  Jane L(Anderson)86
  Joseph T. 128
  Polly(Gaunt) 128
Eden, Catherine(Can) 34
  Catherine(Cann) 34
  John P. 34
  John R. 34
Eddine, Mildred[Huffman]
  165
Eddings, Catherine[Lyons]
  79
Eddy, Burilla 66
  James 66
  John W. 66
  T.O. 99
Eden, J.E. 188
  John 188
Edgar, Elizabeth(Nall)
  218
  G.W. 188
  George 79
  James 96
  Lowry J. 96
  Martha A(Brown) 96
  Sarah(Trowbridge) 96
Edie, Mattie[Lafferty]
  188
Edlin, Eliza[Gill] 149
Edmondson, Elizabeth
  [Montague] 129
  Mary[Nelson] 83
  Sarah A[Haggard] 62
Edrington, D.E. 188
Edwards, Abigail[DeSpain]
  87
  Ambrose 188
  C.S. 188
  Elizabeth[Griffith] 165
  James L. 188
  Lucy E[King] 112
  Margaret[Todd] 89
  Martha[Hardy] 31

-265-

Frasier, Anna(Sammons) 78
  Hiram 78
  Weeks 78
Frayser, P.C. 191
  Virginius 191
Frazer, George 95
  Lafayette H. 95
  Lemuel G. 95
  Nancy J[Ritter] 66
Frazier, J.W. 153
  Jane[Dowdy] 191
  Nancy[Dawdy] 191
  Thomas 191
Frederick, Edna[Stivers]105
Freeland, Rachel[Ruggles]43
Freeman, Martha[Marby] 53
  Stephen F. 144
  William S. 144
Friend, Ephraim 191
  Rachel 191
  W. 91
  William 191
Frith, Jemima[Oliver] 112
Frizell, Elizabeth[Chester]
53
Frizzwll, Ruhama[Duncan] 122
Frost, James P. 28
  Margaret[Walker] 28
  Nancy[George] 191
  Sarah(Holloway) 28
  William B. 28
Fruit, Elizabeth(Boyd)57
  Elizabeth A(Vawter) 101
  James 191
  Judith F(Willson) 116
Fry, Bernhardt 70
  Elizabeth[Harris] 70
  Elizabeth[Hershan] 95
  G.W. 95
  Jacob 70
  Joseph 40
  Letitia D(Devore) 185
  Milton 191
  Thomas 191
Frymire, Eves[Bruner] 49
  John H. 49
  Polly(Bruner) 49
Fugate, John W. 83
Fulkerson, J.F. 191
  Rachel[Wilson] 140
Fulks, Sarah A. 159
Fullenwider, J.H. 191
  J.N. 191
  William S. 191
Fullinwider, Harriet(Neil)
149
  Henry 149
  John N. 149
Fulton, Amy(Hagden) 195
  Isaac 75, 191
  Nancy 191
  Sarah(Moore) 62
Funkhouser, Elizabeth(Newman) 159
  John 159
  Preston L. 159
Fuqua, G.F. 191
  William W. 75
Furgason, Martha[Goff] 96

Furguson, Elizabeth[Thompson]44
Furs, Henrietta[Glass] 115

Gaines, Coleman 191
  H.P. 191
  Henry 191
  Margaret[Robinson] 229
Galbreath, Jane(Reed) 153
  Phebe(Foreman) 138
  William H. 138
Galewood, Myra[Haines] 31
Galliher, B.N. 75
  Margaret(Laird) 111
Galloway, Anna[Harbert] 191
  David 191
  Joseph 191
  Mary[Guyot] 66
  Mary E[Miller] 70
  Mary(Johnson) 191
Gannaway, Elizabeth(Williams)85
  John 85
  John J. 85
  Mary[Williams] 86
Gannis, Leah[McClure] 191
Gano, John P. 146
Gant, Jane(Holt) 136
  Thomas 136
  William 136
Gardner, Amelia(Bowles) 159
  Asa B. 159
  Catherine 31
  Catherine(Lair) 67
  Electa R(Richmond) 107
  James 67
  Jemima R(Wallace) 161
  John 157
  Louis W. 107
  Samuel D. 159
  Thomas 67
  Thomas G. 191
  William M. 191
  Winfield S. 107
Garland, Lovina[Hopper] 109
Garner, J.S. 146
  James H. 62
  Minnie E(Roberts) 164
  Paris 146
  Sarah L(Pierce) 146
Garland, Lovina[Hopper] 109
Garnett, Fanny[Rice] 227
  Ann E(Graves) 37
  Joel G. 37
  William 37
Garrard, W.M. 41
Garrett, Annie[Thomas] 136
  B.J. 191
  Catherine(Yates) 26
  Loven 26
  Mary(Guthrie) 194
  Polly(Reid) 132
  Robert 26
  W.D. 191
  William 131
Garrison, Aaron 191
  Clarissa[Wall] 191
  Elijah 191
  Lucy(McColun) 191
  Rosa[Flatt] 190

  Sally(Allen) 167
Garvey, Maria(Elliston) 142
  Samuel 142
  William F. 142
Garwood, J.R. 191
  Mary(Thatcher) 239
  Sarah[Spain] 191
Gasaway, Peter 192
Gash, Ann(Wood) 192
  John 191
  John J. 129, 191
  John S. 129
  Thomas(Jackson) 129
Gaskins, Wilson G. 192
Gates, Elvira[Foster]192
  Flora 70
  Frank W. 134
  Henry 134
  John 192
  Joseph T. 192
  Lucinda 192
Gatewood, Myra[Raines]32
  William J. 159
Gatlen, Lucinda[Roberts]100
Gattan, Joseph 192
Gatton, B.H. 192
  H.P. 192
  Z.W. 192
  Zachariah W. 192
Gaunt, Ambrose G. 100
  Joseph W. 100
  Maria(Mott) 100
  Mary A(Steers) 236
  Polly[Eccles] 128
  Thomas 100
Gayle, Ann E(White) 139,
244
Gearhart, Allen R. 136
  Ellen 136
  Thomas 136
Gebhart, Allen 192
  Eliza(Feather)154
  Mary(Feather) 154
  Nellie(Robbins) 192
  Thomas 192
Gee, I.G. 153
  Isaac G. 153
  Malinda(Billingsby) 153
  Melinda(Billingsly) 153
Geest, Martha 58
Gentry, Maria[Bright] 112
George, Ann(Sharp) 34
  Catherine(Whaley)36
  Edwin 70
  Elizabeth(Anderson)167
  Elizabeth[Rigg] 29, 30
  H.R. 131
  Henry 34
  Isabella(Warren) 243
  Lefty[Tyler] 73, 74
  Magdalen[Jones] 92
  Mary E[Shake] 192
  Nancy(Frost) 191
  R.W. 192
  Thomas J. 34
German, James 192
Gex, Lucille[Pullen] 81
Gibney, Mary J[Pierce]
107

Gibson, Anna[Hewitt] 58
  Andronica[Hewitt] 58
  Chrissie[Jones] 155
  Crissy(Jones) 155
  David 81
  Delila[Riley] 228
  Eliza[McGinnis] 38
  Elizabeth 87
  Emily(Wilson) 246
  Frances[Hodgen] 92
  G.W. 124
  George W. 124
  John 87, 124
  John H. 81
  Mary(Marrow) 81
  Z.J. 84
  Zachariah J. 87
Gilbert, James 192
  Jane H(Loftis)209
  Nancy H(Stone)237
  P.M. 192
  Simon 192
Gilbertson, Laura(Long)59
Gill, Amelia[Williams]113,
  133
  Bade 149
  Captain 131
  Diadema(Neal) 218
  Eliza(Edlin) 149
  Elizabeth(Trabue) 166
  James 131
  Zachariah 149
  Zachariah E. 149
Gilland, Polly[Barnes] 169
Gillaspie, James H. 99
  Juliette(Halloway) 131
  S.G. 192
  Simon 131
  William H. 131
Gillespie, Margaret(Field)47
  Rebecca[Gould] 70
Gillham, Elizabeth(Walker)53
  John 54, 192
  Robert 54
Gilliham, Eli D. 54
  Elizabeth(Walker) 54
  Robert 54
Gilliland, John W. 192
  Margaret[Moore] 153
  Robert 192
  William P. 192
Gillman, Sarah[Fetters] 110
Gillmore, James L. 133
  Jeremiah 133
  Mary(Lansaw) 133
Gillum, Polly[Cowden] 192
Gilmer, D.H. 192
  Sallie T[Capps] 61
Gilmore, Alexander 91
  Andrew H. 159
  David S. 91
  Ephraim M. 155
  James L. 192
  Jeremiah 133
  Lucinda[Jacobs] 192
  Martha F[Wright]159
  Mary(Landsaw) 133
  Millie(Mudd) 91
  P.R. 159

Thomas D. 159
  William 133
Gimlin, Elizabeth[Burleson] 192
Ginter, William O. 34
Gittings, Kinsey 161
  Mary(Clemmons) 161
  William H. 158, 161
  William K. 158
Given, Rebecca[Holman] 51
Givens, George R. 41
  James 119, 192
  Julia 192
  Julia(Carter) 177
  Lydia 192
  Martha[Logan] 112
  Martha(Miller) 119
  Nancy[Walker] 242
  T.H. 192
  Thales H. 119, 192
Gladson, John A. 55
  Richard 55
  Sarah(Scruggs) 55
Glasgow, Adam 107
  Douglas 107
  Mary A(Stevenson) 107
Glasman, Mary(Beam) 103
  P.C. 103
  Peter 103
Glass, Harrison 75
  Henrietta(Furrs) 115
  James L. 117
  Kittie(Nolan) 117
  T.V. 117
Glassco, Enoch 91
  Madison 91
  Rachel 91
Glasscock, Asa 75
  J.P. 193
  John P. 75
  Mary(Penquite) 75
Gleason, John 107
  Mary 107
  Mary[Small] 107
Glenn, G.W. 193
  Isaac D. 193
  Jacob 193
  James 70
Glenny, Kate B. 193
Glore, James H. 141
  Milburn 141
  Sarah(Clark) 141
Glover, Matilda[Adam] 193
Goar, Clement 91
  Elizabeth[Hart] 91
Gobble, Elizabeth J(Sweeney) 56
Goddard, Abbott 193
Goff, Amy(Trent) 87
  E.M. 87, 193
  Elizabeth[Pulliam] 153
  Iredell 193
  James 96
  John R. 193
  Martha(Furgason) 96
  William 87, 193
Golden, James F. 119
  Julia A[Stagner]119
Goldman, Jacob 62
Goldsby, Elizabeth(Hingley) 87
  J.B. 87
  James 87

William M. 87
Gonterman, Caleb 193
  Jacob 193
Gooch, James M. 144
  Mary(Eoff) 144
  Stephen C. 144
Goodan, David C. 41
  Eleanor[Jones] 34
Goode, Jinse(Walker)58
  William B. 58
  William H. 58
Goodin, Elizabeth[Van
  Meter] 93
Gooding, Cornelius 75
  Mary(Jones) 41
  Robert 75
Goodloe, Susan[Johnson]119
Goodman, Elizabeth[Adams]
  158
  Nancy 193
  Sarah(Maxey) 193
  Thomas 193
  William 193
Goodnight, Margaret[Moore]
  112
Goodrick, R.A. 193
Goodson, Nancy 193
  Sarah(Maxey) 193
  William 193
Goodwin, Evalina(Johnson)
  204
  J.C. 193
Goram, Nancy[Clark] 114
Gorden, Elizabeth[Adams]
  131
  Lydia E(Ribelin) 131
  Rachel(Baker) 131
  Rachel R. 131
  Randall 131
Gordly, Mary[Lee] 70
Gordon, Elizabeth[Adams]
  131
  James 124
  Mary[Fowler] 161, 193
  Mary(Taylor) 238
  Patrick H. 115
  William 193
Gore, Amanda(Graff) 153
  Cinderella(Keller)205
  James 100
  John 153, 156, 193
  Michael 193
  Regina(Tevler) 100
  Robert 153
  Sophia 156
  Sophia(Barten) 156
  W.F. 193
  Walton 193
  William F. 156
Gorin, Jerome R. 58
  John D. 58
  Mattie(Thomas) 58
  Sanford P. 193
  Virginia C. 193
Gorum, Nancy[Clark] 114
Gosins, Mary[Clardy]193
Gosnell, George K. 95
  Sarah(Campbell) 94
Gosney, Mary E[Tobias]193

Grooms, Elizabeth[Prit-
  chett] 132
Ground, Mary[Huffman]159
Grover, Anna[Putnam] 111
  Henry P. 124
  Joseph 124
  Mahala[Harper] 124
  Sarah(Putnam) 124
Groves, Catherine[Gates]
  134
  Elizabeth(Dukes) 134
  Elizabeth[Thompson] 34
  John R. 34
  Louisa 34
  Sampson 134
  Solomon 134
Grow, Wilson D. 150
Grubb, David 194
  Jacob 159
  Sallie(Rice) 159
  Virgil 159
Gruelle, Martha A[Threlkeld]
  95
Grundon, Gertie(Bayne) 170
Gudgel, Abraham 62
Guess, Lizzie(McCosland)120
  Mary E(Chrisnand) 69
  W.F. 119
Guest, John B. 112
  Tabitha[Lane] 130
Guinn, Elizabeth(Henson)199
  Simeon 194
Guliher, George 58
  Isaac 58
  Sarah(Gibson) 58
Gulley, Emily[Clevinger]
  194
Gum, J.B. 87
  Jemima 194
  Jesse 194
  Mary(Dills) 186
  Thomas D. 194
  William 194
Gun, George C. 26
Gunnell, J.T. 58
  James L. 58
Guthrie, Eleanor[Johnson]
  103
  J.J. 194
  John 194
  John P. 194
  Mary[Garrett] 194
  Mary[Welsh] 105
  Sarah(Johnston) 194
  William L. 194
Guy, Benjamin 194
  Benjamin F. 194
  George 194
  Rebecca(Flors)194
Guyot, Mary(Galloway) 66
Guyton, Cornelia E[Walden]
  141
Gwyn, Cinderella(McCaslin)52

Hackett, George F. 147
  Levi 147, 195

Malinda[Ford] 69
Merill F. 70
Peter 195
Hackley, Ann M[Jeffries] 85
  Elizabeth 85
  James L. 85
  John 85
  John R. 85
  Kittie B[Diehl] 85
  Susan(Thomas) 85
  Susanna 85
Haden, Virginia F. 195
Hadley, John 195
  William 195
Haff, Sophia[Carver] 128
Hagaman, Albert 34
  Charlotte 34
  John 195
Hagan, A.T. 195
  Elizabeth(Cook) 136
  George H. 136, 195
  Leonard 136
Hagden, Amy[Fulton] 195
Hagerty, J.T. 95
  John T. 95
Haggard, Charity(Baldwin) 58
  D.D. 58
  David 62
  David J. 62
  Dawson 58
  J.R 62, 195
  Martha[Newton] 195
  Sally[Lander] 59, 62
  Sarah A(Edmonson) 62
Haghey, J.W. 195
Hail, William S. 153
Haines, Christopher 31
  Fletcher 31, 195
  Mary A(Thompson) 60
  Myra(Galewood) 31
Hainline, George 131
  George W. 131
  Green 195
  Henry 195
  Jacob 131
  John 131
  John D. 131
  Susan[Batterton] 118
  Thomas(Cockerek) 131
  William C. 131
Hale, James V. 195
  Isaac 90
  Louisa[Kincaid] 34
  Mary[Jarvis] 119
  Nancy[Butler] 154
  Susan 195
Haley, Joseph A. 195
  Nancy A. 195
Hall, Alonzo 70
  Angeline(Hammond) 131
  Benjamin J. 122
  Benjamin L. 150
  Buelah[Pugh] 59
  Candis(Miller) 32
  Cynthia A(Willis) 163
  David T. 195
  E.C. 195
  Elizabeth(Jackson) 122

Evaline(Pickrell) 150
George 195
J.D. 195
James H. 70
John 158
John W. 131
Julia(Harber) 31
Leonard 131
M.W. 195
Mary 49
Mary(Sellers) 195
Micajah 195
Michael W. 31
Nancy 82
Nancy[Dale] 195
Nancy(Sherley) 32
O.H. 150
Phineas C. 195
Robert S. 31
Sallie A(Pritchett)70
Sarah[Pyle] 59
Sarah[Smith] 116
Sidney 82
Sylvester 49
William 49, 122
Halloway, Juliette[Gil-
  laspie] 131
Halsted, Mary E[Case]70
Ham, George A. 195
  Hezekiah 195
  James 195
  Martin 195
  Mary A.195
Hambaugh, Henry 136
  Rebecca(Morris) 136
  Stephen D. 136
Hamblen, Benjamin D. 91
Hambrick, J.W. 196
Hamilton, A.J. 196
  Allen 195
  Andrew J. 195
  E.H. 195
  Elijah 195
  Elizabeth A[Morgan] 138
  Harrison 26
  J.M. 195
  John C. 95, 195
  Levi 26
  Lloyd F. 195
  Malinda(Creel) 26
  Richard M. 195
  S. 26
  Saline 195
Hammer, Addison W. 196
  Elizabeth(Webb) 62
  Frederick 62, 196
  George 144
  Lucien W. 62
  Mary J. 196
  William L. 62, 196
Hammett, Anna(Oliphant)
  159
  Elizabeth(Sumner)140
  John 159, 196
  William 159
Hammond, Angeline[Hall]
  131
  Mary M[Walker] 28

-270-

Hammonds, Sarah[Clark]196
Hampton, Amanda[Haynes]196
  John J. 196
  John L. 196
  Martha M[Waters] 91
  Rosanna[Jack] 81
Hancock, Elizabeth[Anderson]
  196
  Elizabeth B[Kinsall] 196
  Levi E. 29
  Marie[Wilhoit] 142
  Mary(Wheeler) 133
Haney, John R. 70
  Lydia[Keeling]92
  Margaret 70
  Nancy[Groom] 62
  William 70
Hankins, Cheston 196
  Gilbert 150
  Gilbert B. 150
  Martin A. 196
  Rebecca(Caress) 150
Hanks, James 133
  John 196, 197
  Milly[Pruitt] 98
  William 131, 133, 196,
  197
Hanley, Joseph 103
  Mary(Ripple) 103
  Samuel 103
Hanna, Jane[Council] 196
  P.K. 196
  Philip K. 196
Hannah, Dovey E[Grey] 58
  Jane[Grey] 58
Hannahs, Anna[Kelley] 110
Hanning, Daniel 70
  Maria[Levitt] 70
Hansford, Ann[Palmer] 150
Hanson, Catherine[Craig] 70
  James 124
  Samuel 124
Harbaugh, Elizabeth[David-
  son] 196
  Polly[Patterson] 134
Harber, Julia[Hall] 31
Harbest, Joseph B. 196
Harbison, Baxter D. 150
  David 150
  Martha D(Venable) 150
  Moses 196
Harbor, Sarah[Graham] 75
Harbour, Elizabeth(Lind-
  ley) 59
  Samuel 82
Harbur, Levi 82
Hardesty, Sarah F[Ballard]41
Hardey, John 158
  Mary A(Riley) 158
  William M. 158
Hardin, Ellen(Colelasure)86
  George W. 34
  Lewis W. 158
  Mary[Butler] 26
  Patsy(Fleming) 138
  Sally D[Perrin] 50
  Victor M. 162
  William 34, 135

Harding, Abel 26
  Andrew 31
  Green 26
  Isabella(Beard) 31
  Julia(Bettisworth) 26
  Martin 31
  Paschal 31
  Peyton 31, 196
  Sarah 31
  William 31
Hardisty, J.V.M. 196
  Jerome 196
Hardwick, Eliza[O'Hair] 134
Hardy, I.E. 31
  Isham 31
  J.E. 31
  Martha(Edwards) 31
Hargise, William 196
Hargrave, George B. 51
Hari, J.B. 124
  John 124
  Mary 124
Harlan, Catherine 58
  Catherine[Wheeler] 60
  Columbus 58
  E. 58
  E.W. 196
  Elijah 58
  Elizabeth 196
  Frances(Ranch) 58
  George B. 130
  George T. 130
  J.N. 58
  James 58
  John 58
  L.L. 196
  Lebin L. 130
  Lucinda C. 196
  Mary A(Kelly) 130
  Nancy(Greenup)130
  Sallie M. 196
  Wesley 130, 196
Harland, Clarissa C[Huffman] 130
  Elizabeth[Greenup] 130
Harlen, Jacob 31
  Sarah(Combs) 31
  Wesley 31
Harlow, Elizabeth[Kemble] 117
Harmon, Elizabeth 47
  Henry 31
  John 197
  Nancy[Ellis] 47
  Samuel 47
Harness, Christina(Smith) 41
  Isaac 41, 197
  Jacob 41
Harney, James 197
  Nancy[Hopkins] 41
Harp, Jacob 197
  Millard 197
  Polly[Feather] 154
Harper, C.W. 197
  Cyrus A. 70
  Harriet(Sterling) 70
  James 110
  John S. 70
  Mahala(Grover) 124
  Stephen 197
Harrel, Edward F. 197

Harrington, Lively[Catton]
  67
  Matilda(Hinch) 58
Harris, Alexander C. 159
  Amanda J[Murray] 129,
  197
  C. 136
  Charles 87
  Chatham H.D. 197
  Cyilene[Hinhaw] 197
  D.M. 197
  Edward 136
  Elizabeth(Fry) 70
  Elizabeth(Shrewsbury)50
  H.D. 197
  H.L. 106
  Harriet(Paseley) 197
  Harvey L. 106
  John 115, 197
  Lizzie[Scott] 101
  Lucy W(Buck) 79
  Margaret[Lowder] 93
  Martha[Cleek] 37
  Mary(Northfleete) 159
  Mary E[Deal] 159
  Mary(Ahern) 79
  Nancy 197
  Nancy(Hismith) 197
  Patsey[Allen] 144
  R. 197
  R.E. 197
  Rachel(Mills) 32
  Sarah 87
  Sarah(Wells) 136
  W.P. 197
  William 197
  William P. 87
Harrison, Ann E[Terhune] 78
  Barton L. 110
  Eleanor[Young] 29
  Elizabeth[Stipp] 95, 197
  Elvira[Wight] 197
  Francis M. 110
  James 110, 197
  Julia A[Jewell] 197
  Melinda[Courtney] 57
  Sarah 197
  Sarah C(Lee) 110
  V.M. 73
  William C. 197
Harrold, Susan E. 54
Harry, Martin M. 110
Hart, Benjamin 144
  Catherine C(Yocum) 91
  David 129, 197
  Elizabeth[Goar] 91
  Elizabeth[Lester]197
  George M. 79
  Jacob 91
  James 197
  James L. 85
  John 144, 197, 198
  John M. 153
  Joseph 197
  Martha[Deckard] 91
  Mary[Roger] 197
  Matilda(Goar) 91
  Miles H. 91
  Milligan 197

Hart(cont.)
Nancy(Blankinship) 144
Oliver 85
Solomon 129
Thomas 191, 198
Thomas W. 79, 198
Zoranda 85
Hartis, Martha[Briggs] 51
Hartley, Eli 26
James 197
Nathan 26
Thomas 197
Hartsock, Mary[Threlkeld]
197
Harvey, Frances 58
Joel 58
Mildred 58
Hascall, Hannah M[Brown]
197
Haselwood, Frances A(Dance)
83
James 83
Thomas A. 83
William K. 83
Haskell, Emma 197
Hassett, Frances(Church)97
James 97
James J. 97
Hasson, J.M. 110
Margaret(Riley) 110
Theophilus N. 110
Hatche, J.H. 197
Hatfield, Mary(Lemaster)99
Sarah[Howard] 197
Hathaway, Dorotha[Owens]111
Hauss, Herman C. 197
Havenhill, George 85
Havenhill, Oliver 85
Haw, Susan[Downing] 124
Hawes, Herman C. 197
James M. 197
Hawkins, Crosby 197
Elizabeth(Ballar) 75
Elizabeth(Ballard)75
Gregory 75
Gregory R. 75
O.D. 75
Oliver D. 75
William 197
William B. 37
Haws, George W. 78
Hay, Angeline B[Hull] 62
Celia 58
Charles 70
Jane B[Vance] 60
Jemima(Coulter) 70
John 58, 70
Milton 70
Peter G. 58
Rachel F[Hall] 155
Haycraft, Hannah(Parker)91
James J. 91
John 91
Martha[Reno] 87
Nancy[Vertress] 93
Hayden, Elisha 198
Jennie(Reeves) 198
Joan[Kessick] 75
Nancy[Tracy] 198

Nancy[Yeager] 162
Robert W. 198
Ulysses G. 198
Hayes, Charity[Perry] 107
Elizabeth(Henderson) 100
George W. 198
Jefferson 160
Maria J(Head) 162
Haynes, Anne(Hensley) 31
Baxter 31
S.H. 198
William 31
Hays, Henry 198
William H. 162
Hazelwood, Martha[Cheaney] 97
Head, Benjamin 103, 198
Harrison 162
John H. 162
M.H. 103
Margaret N(Brengman) 103
Maria J[Hayes] 162
Martin H. 103
William T. 162
Headington, Laban 198
Temperance[Williams] 198
Headleston, Mary N. 41
Headley, W.B. 198
Heady, Benjamin 198
Rebecca L[Lycan] 136
Stillwell 136
Susan(Stowbreaker)136
Heafer, Edgar M. 146
Elizabeth C(Clark) 146
Napoleon B. 146
Hearn, Campbell S. 165
James 198
Jane(Alexander) 165
John C. 198
Nancy(Dix) 198
Heath, David 113, 198
Samuel 113
Heaton, James W. 84, 99
John 99
John C.B. 99
Lorinda J(Lindsay) 84
Nancy 198
Sarah(Malin) 99
Heavenhill, Ann[Prunty] 136
George 91, 136
Hiram 91
Martial 136
Sally 91
Hedden, Simon 70
Hedger, Margaret[Moore] 147
Hedges, Anna(Brown) 66
Catherine T. 41
Catherine T[Moreland] 42
Dorcas[Banta] 41
James 41
Mary E[Colvin] 41
Peter 41
Susan(Miller) 41
Heinline, Mary[Bulson] 198
Helms, Agnes 70
Caroline[Rees] 125
Heltsley, John 198
Henderson, A.M. 37
D. Pat 198
Elizabeth[Hayes] 100
Elizabeth(Hendrickson)110

Elizabeth[Smith] 139
Elizabeth[West] 139
Elizabeth P. 198
Hannah[Clark] 57
Henderson 198
James H. 82
Jerome B. 110
John 198
John P. 82, 198
John W. 198
Patsie D[Anderson] 83,
198
Sarah P[Rea] 110
William H. 82
William P. 110
Katie O[Abrogast] 110
Hendrick, Catherine E(West)
45
Elijah 75
Jonathan 198
Martha(West) 45
Sarah[Jackson] 160
Hendricks, Cynthia(Wilson)
95
Ellen[Luckett] 198
Europe 198
John 95
John T. 95
Lorley 198
Lovicy G[Roberts] 198
Samuel 198
Thomas 198
W.S. 198
Hendrickson, Elizabeth[Hen-
derson] 110
Hendrix, Catherine(Thomp-
son) 34
Jacob 34
John 34
Hendron, James 199
Hendry, Catherine(Ruddell)
43
Henline, China[Burt] 199
David 37
George 119, 199
James J. 37
John 37
Mary 37
Mary(Darnell) 37
Susan[Batterson] 118
William B. 37
Henly, Emily[Morris] 199
Henninger, A.E. 124
M.I. 124
Henry, A.B. 41
A.M. 99
Andrew G. 41
Betsey(Mills) 41
E.R. 70
Elijah 199
Elizabeth(Alexander) 41
Elizabeth[Nicholson] 82
Greenup 41
Jesse 129
John 41, 199
John T. 71
Joseph W. 99, 100
Lucy(Shumacke)100
Margaret H[Hester] 155
Richard 70

Hensley, Amis(Anderson)
  Anne[Haynes] 31
  Archibald P. 124
  Byers 199
  Elijah 199
  Emilla[Black] 100
  Evan S. 131, 199
  J.A. 131
  J.W. 131
  John A. 199
  Julia A(Hudson) 97
Henson, Catherine[Craig]
  199
  Elizabeth[Guinn] 199
Herbert, America A[Florer]
  199
Herell, Elizabeth[Camron]
  199
Herndon, Benjamin 58
  James W. 58
  Nancy 58
  Richard 199
  Richard F. 199
Herrin, Andrew 101
  Celia[Leech] 163
  David 101
Herron, Elizabeth[Rankin]53
  James 199
Herrott, J.W. 199
Hershan, Elizabeth(Fry) 95
  George 95
  Henry 95
Hersman, America[Means] 95
  Elizabeth(Fry) 41
  George 95
  Henry 41
  Jacob 41
  Rebecca A(Knox) 99
  S.A(Craig) 94
  Sarah E[Baxter] 70
Hess, L.W. 199
Hessey, William 103
Hester, Elizabeth(Matthews)
  58
  John 58
  Mary M[Shearer] 58
Hett, George 103
  Joseph 103
  Sarah 103
Hewitt, Andronica(Gibson)58
  Ann(Gibson) 58
  Aurelius M. 58
  William T. 58
Hewlett, Alfred M. 103
Heyatt, Alice[Farmer] 57
Hiat, Rachel[Lomax] 160
Hibler, Elizabeth F[Lewis]
  138
Hickman, Eliza A(Wither-
  spoon) 64
  Elizabeth(Witherspoon)64
  George T. 199
  Joseph E. 64
  Lewis 70
  Rodney 70
  Sarah[Lawhorn] 56
  Thomas B. 71
  Thomas G. 71
  William 64
  William B. 64

Hicks, Argus 106
  Martha[Johnson] 31
  Sallie(Myers) 106
  W.H. 106
Hieronymous, Alvira(Darnell)119
  Enoch 119
  James 199
  William 119, 199
Hiett, William 119
Higgins, Hiram 199
  James 199
  John 71
  John L. 71
  Nancy 37
  Nancy[Yates] 65
  W.H. 37
  William 31, 37
Highfill, Sophrona[Jayne] 143
Hightower, Susan[Payne] 106
Hilbert, Marvin 199
Hildreth, A.K. 41
  Alvin K. 41
  Elender[Rogers] 43
  John 199
  Junius B. 41
  Sarah(Ritter) 41
  William H. 41
Hill, Charles 92, 199
  David 113
  Emily H. 99
  Henry 199
  Isaac 119, 199
  J.H. 199
  James 71
  Jesse 71
  John T. 199
  John W. 119
  Louisiana(Pemberton) 109
  Maria(Porter) 119
  Mary[Perry] 103
  Mary(Maxwell) 150
  Mary A. 71
  Mary A[Leigh] 199
  Mary C(Cope) 71
  Phebe L[Beatty] 71
  R.E. 199
  Rodney P. 99
  Samuel 199
  William M. 150
  William 199
  William E. 113, 199
  William F. 150
  William L. 119
Hilligoss, J.W. 75
  John W. 76
  Mary(Darnall) 76
  Thomas 75, 76
Hills, John 26
Hinch, George 199
  Matilda[Harrington] 58
  William 199
Hinds, Charity 200
  Joseph 200
Hingley, Elizabeth[Goldsby] 87
Hinkle, Jesse 150
  Jessie(Oglesby) 150
Hinton, Lewis 200
Hise, Frances B[Leach] 200
  George 200
  Nancy 200

Hitch, Alexander 103
Hite, J.T. 200
  John S. 200
Hitt, Daniel F. 41
  Jesse 200
  Julie[Holmes] 200
  Margaret(Smith) 41
  Martin 41
  Rebecca K(Brown)102
  Samuel M. 41
Hix, George 200
  Gerrit 200
  Martha 200
  William 200
Hobbs, Henrietta[Brown]127
  Henrietta(Brown) 135
  Henson 200
  Hinson S. 200
  Mary L(Young) 200
  Solomon 200
Hockaday, Eugene 89
Hockensmith, Andrew J. 200
  Mary(Parks) 200
  Vienna[Foster] 200
Hodgen, Frances(Gibson) 92
  Robert 92
Hoffman, Carrie(Eberwein)
  89
  Charles P. 89
  John E. 89
  Margaret(Eads) 118
  Mary J[Juett] 71
  Michael 71
  Syba 71
Hogan, Catherine[Ballard]
  200
  Elizabeth[Quimby] 130
  Katie[Ballard] 106
  Mary E[Anderson]200
  William 106
Hogans, Rachel[Bybee] 61
Hohimer, Elias 87
Hoke, Barbara 200
  George 200
  John 200
  John A. 200
  Leonard 200
  P.E. 200
Holden, A.G. 200
  Catherine[Williams] 121
  Lydia A. 150
  Parmilia[Rogers] 104
  Salena(Yates) 30
Holland, A.E. 115
  Agnes E(Wimpey) 116
  Ann(Shemwell) 200
  Henry 200
  James 200
  Julia A. 200
  N.M. 200
  Jeremiah 200
Holliday, A.D. 56
  Charles 200
  Charles L. 200
  June R(Kiner) 103
  Margaret(Taylor) 139
  Nancy[Robertson] 200
Hollingsworth, Charles L.
  103
  Joseph 103
  Margaret(Beeler) 103

Hollis, Allen R. 106
  Berly 106
  Elizabeth(Woods) 106
Holloway, Charles 200
  George 41
  George W. 200
  Harriet(Tade) 200
  Lucy E(Smithson) 63
  Martha[Rankin] 41
  Nancy H[Robertson] 200
  Robert 41, 200
  Sarah[Frost] 28
Holman, B.F. 200
  D.H. 51
  Joseph 51
  Rebecca(Given) 51
Holmes, John M. 87
  Mary 200
  Mary(Miller) 122
  Nathan 122
  Thomas 122, 200
  William 200
Holstlaw, D.S. 200
  Daniel 31
  Daniel J. 31
  Daniel S. 200
  Mary(Smith) 31
  Richard 31
Holt, Jane[Gant] 136
Homes, Rebecca[Wrigley]200
Honn, Absalom 138
  Andrew A. 138
  Anna 138
  Annie(Ebberman) 138
  Annie(Erverman) 138
  Daniel 138
  Daniel W. 138
  David 138
  Hannah(Shrout) 44
  Martha J[Hulse] 138
  Matilda(Woods) 121
  Miranda(Moler) 138
  Nancy E(Hook) 138
  Peter K. 138
  S.D. 138
  Samuel D. 201
Hood, Betsey[Maxwell] 159
Hook, Mathias 138
  Matilda(Huddleston) 138
  Nancy E[Honn] 138
Hooper, Dudley 109
  Jacob 109
  Lida 201
  Lovina(Garland) 109
  William 162
Hooton, Lydia A[Miller]119
  Mary J. 62
  Nicholas 62, 119
Hopkins, Ann[Rice] 89
  Elizabeth[Worth] 28
  Garrett V. 41
  John 201
  Lemuel 41
  Nancy(Harney) 41
  Samuel 41
  Samuel A. 41
Hopper, Annie[Martin] 42
Horine, Harrison 106
  John 106
  Margaret(Bash) 106
  Sarah[Houser] 106
Horn, W.H. 201
Hornback, Abigail(Bracken)
  33, 34
  John 34, 41
  Margaret[Canterbury] 74

Martha[Bradley] 33
  Sarah E[Killion] 34
  Solomon 201
Hornbeck, Margaret[Alkire] 38
Horney, Jane(Crawford) 49
Hornsby, Joseph 150
  Robert J. 150
Horrell, James L. 201
Horton, Ann[Lobb] 87
Hoskins, Lowry 201
Hostetler, John 201
Houchin, Alexander 100
  Edwin R. 100
  Elizabeth G. 201
  Jackson 67
  Lucinda[Taylor]67
Houck, Lucinda A. 58
Hough, Delia[Brewer] 156
  Delilah[Brewer] 156
Hougham, Bettie A(Dozier) 67
Houghton, Catherine D[Purkipile]
  124
  Charles P. 124
  Elizabeth(Vandeventer) 124
  William C. 124
House, Ann(Whitecraft) 34
  Fielding 34
  Margaret[Kincaid] 34
  Mary E. 115
Houser, Elizabeth[Hoover] 106
  Harrison 106
  Peter 106, 201
  Sarah(Horine) 106
Housh, David 41, 201
Houston, Caleb 201
  Delilah(Weldon)47
  Joseph 47
  Levi 47
Houts, C.J. 201
Hover, Alonso J. 201
Howard, Benjamin 47
  Ellen 201
  Elizabeth[Crawford] 159
  Hannah[Cotton] 136
  Ignatius 119, 201
  Joseph 47
  Lavina(Sageser) 107
  Letty[Webb] 121
  M.M. 201
  R.S. 119
  Robert S. 119
  Rachel[Buckner] 47
Howe, B.F. 138
  Catherine 138
  J.S. 76
  Joseph 201
  Reuben 138
Howell, A.D. 201
Howk, B.D. 71
  Mary(Mitchell) 99
Howser. John 201
Hoxey, Christopher 201
Hoxsey, Jiney G(Lyon) 52
  Mary(Martin) 120
Hoye, Elizabeth 156
  Henry 156
  John T. 156

Hubbard, Elizabeth(Parks)
  119
  John 119
  Polly[Francis] 70
  Thomas 119
Huckelby, Elizabeth
  [Walker] 49
Huddleston, Elizabeth J
  [Crawford] 137, 138
  John 92
  Matilda[Hook] 137
  Melvina[Clark] 114
  Samuel 92
Huddlestun, Barnett G.
  201
  James W. 201
  Susan(Winter) 201
Hudgen, Robert 201
Hudson, Drusilla[East] 41
  Fannie(Brochman) 119
  George W. 124
  James E. 201
  Jesse 106
  John 119
  Julia A[Hensley] 97
  Lydia[Coyle] 118, 119
  Nathan 124
  Isaac 201
  Sarah A(Fisher) 124
Huey, John 37
  Martha(Jones) 59
  Matilda(Rice) 37
  Phebe E[Jones]58
Huff, Aquilla 129
  Ben J. 201
  Elizabeth 201
  George N. 201
  Mary A(Crane) 114
Huffaker, Israel 163
Huffman, Alexander 165
  Clarissa C(Harland) 130
  Daniel P. 95
  Elizabeth(Switzer) 95
  George D. 201
  I.E. 201
  Isaiah E. 165
  John W. 201
  Mary(Ground) 159
  Mildred(Eddine) 165
  Milford E. 130
  William A. 130
Hufford, Eliza A[Fouts]
  201
  George 201
Hughes, Albert 103
  Daniel T. 76
  James 76
  John A. 201
  Phebe[Parker] 147
  Richard T. 201
  Robert 201
  Sarah[McClain] 142
  Sarah A(Taylor) 151
  W.C. 201
  W.W. 41
  William 41
Hughey, John R. 64
  W.A. 64
Hulbertson, E.F[Hilliar]201
Hulett, Anna[Swihart] 201

-274-

Hull, Angeline B(Hay) 62
  Julia V(Martin) 54
  Martha J[Devol] 202
  Samuel 202
Hulse, Otho 202
  Thomas 202
Hume, E.W.S. 38
  Margaret 202
  W.A. 202
Humes, Mary[Cunningham] 94
Humlong, Elizabeth[Gregg]47
Humphrey, Alfred 53
  B.N. 202
  F.G. 202
  Frances(Nay) 141
  John 202
  John M. 141
  Margaret 136
  Mary 202
  Samuel 136
  Samuel A. 136
  Thomas B. 53
  Western R. 141
  William D. 202
Hundley, J.B. 156
  James J. 129
  Uriah(Dorsey) 156
  William B. 156
Hungate, Abonijah 162, 202
  Charles C. 162
  Harrison 162
  John 162
  Mary(Coffman) 162
Hunley, A. 87
Hunsaker, Elijah 58
Hunt, Eliza C(Wilson) 71
  Elizabeth(Wright) 160
  Hannah(Davis) 202
  John 160
  John R. 202
  Joseph 202
  Mary[Rigg] 115
  Mary(Tierney) 105
  Sarah[Prater] 160
  Silas W. 71
  Thomas B. 71
Hunter, A.C. 202
  Benjamin A. 202
  Caroline(Willis)163
  David P. 115
  Elizabeth[Donner] 202
  G.D. 202
  James A. 202
  James B. 202
  Lucy[Self] 52
  Mary B. 202
  Sophia[Tudor] 106
  William 202
Hupp, Nancy[Spencer] 93,
  202
Husband, Elizabeth 202
  Elizabeth J[Yowell] 58
  Evalina 202
  Hamm 202
  Martha 202
  Polly 202
  Sarah 202
  Jane 202
Huston, James 58

Hutchason, Lucy A[Wilson] 87
  T.S. 87
Hutcheson, John W. 115
  Mary A(Wallace) 105
Hutchins, Elizabeth[Vawter] 66
  George W. 65
  Jane(Pace) 65
Hutchinson, E.T. 58
  Nancy[Porter] 51
Hutchison, Ann[Wilson] 203
  James B. 156
Hutton, John 131
Hynes, Barbara(Chenault) 136
  Thomas W. 136
  William R. 136

Idson, Mildred[Johnson] 49
Iles, Ann(Foster) 34
  Elijah 203
  Elizabeth[McDannold] 34, 35
  Thomas 34
Ingels, Bartlett H. 71
  Mary B.F[Chambers] 203
Ingles, Mary E[Pritchett] 41
  Nathan H. 41
  Permelia(Jacoby) 41
  William 41
Inman, H. 203
  Henry 203
Ingle, Elizabeth 76
Ingraham, Elizabeth[Silvers]162
Ingram, Hancil 203
  James 134
  Nancy A(Reno) 134
  W.T. 134, 203
  William T. 134
Irvin, Elizabeth J[Barnett] 41
  John 41
  Mary[Miles] 115
  Sarah(Wilson) 41
Irving, Gracie[Woodburn] 203
Irwin, Charles N. 71
  Elizabeth J. 41
  John M.C. 71
  Martha(Newman) 71, 129
  Mary F[Dyson] 203
Isaacs, Abraham 203
Isbell, Elliott T. 160
Isgrig, Nancy A[Clark] 40
Isgrigg, Hannah[Pattison] 203

Jack, Nancy[Vance] 241
  Rosanna(Hampton) 81
  Samuel 81
Jackson, Adaline(Pearl) 110
  Amanda 203
  Andrew 109
  Andrew J. 96
  C.C. 160
  Elizabeth[Allen] 101, 149
  Elizabeth[Graham] 122
  Elizabeth[Kelley] 203
  Elizabeth[Little] 142
  Fanny G(Crane) 96
  F.J. 203

Fanny G(Crane) 96
Frederick A. 95
H.T. 110
Henry L. 110
James 203
James S. 79
Jane(Shearer) 203
Jeannetta[Tyler] 203
John 92, 109
John E. 124
Mary(Gray) 194
Milton 203
N.H. 160
Oliver R. 92
Permelia[Rodgers] 203
Polly(Carter) 177
Sarah(Hendrick) 160
Sarah(Mayhall) 79, 214
Sarah(Price) 92
Sarah[Phillips] 223
Sarah G[Daniel] 61
Thomas[Gash] 129
Vincent 203
William 79, 95
William H. 96
Jacob, Elizabeth[Wright] 50
Jacobs, H.S. 203
  John 203
  Lucinda(Gilmore) 192
  Mary[Calvin] 203
  Nancy(Gwinn) 203
  Samuel 103
Jacquess, Elizabeth(John-
  son) 95
  Isaac 95
  Isaac N. 95
James, Adam 95
  Alexander C. 138
  Catherine(Poston) 72, 224
  Elizabeth A[Lee] 144
  Mary[Lane] 146
  Mary(Richards) 95
  Mary A(Robinson) 138
  William W. 138
Jamison, Catherine[Mills]42
Janes, Ardia(Crook) 203
  Ardra(Crook) 203
  Jesse 203
  John 203
  Mary[Lane] 146
  Walter 203
Jansen, Gerhard 95
Jared, Alsey K[Watt] 203
Jarrett, Caroline(Watt)161
  Catherine(Dowell)127
  Martha A(Grant) 97
  Samuel 127
  Wilson 127
Jarvis, Ephraim 119
  James 119
  John 119
  Mary(Hale) 119
  Polly(Ray) 121
  William 119
Jasper, Elizabeth(Dunham)
  144
  Louisa J[Lester] 203
  O.D. 144
  Thomas 144

Linder(cont.)
  Melissa[McCartan] 92
  Rebecca(Sawyer) 231
  Usher F. 208
Lindley, Elizabeth[Harbour]
  59
  Simon 59
Lindsay, Abraham[Madison]
  213
  James 208
  John P. 208
  Lorinda J[Heaton] 84
  Martha A. 81
  Michael 81
  V.T. 81
Lindsey, Elizabeth L[Neville]
  59
  James 59
  James A. 59
  Jean(Scott) 59
  John 59
  Mrs. M.E. 208
  Martha(Warren) 243
  Mary[Williams] 95
  Robert 147
  Stewart 147
  Vincent 208
Link, Christianna 208
Linn, Mahala(McDavid) 42
  Philip 42
Linton, William D. 104
Linville, John 209
Lisenby, Benjamin G. 130
  Charles S. 130
  Elizabeth J. 130
  James 209
  Margaret(Simpson) 120
Liston, George 122
  Joseph 122
  Martha(Bland) 122
Liter, Catherine 71
  Eliza[Taylor] 44
  Joseph 42
  Mary[West] 45
Litherland, Sarah J(Tite)129
Little, Eliza M(Morgan) 77
  Elizabeth(Jackson) 142
  Henry 142
  J.S. 209
  John 209
  John M. 104, 142
  Mary[Crow] 47
  Mary(Newcomb) 76
  Samuel 76
  Samuel M. 76
  Samuel N. 76
  William D. 209
Littlepage, Nancy E. 101
Littleton, Eleanor[Rowe] 55
Lively, Charity(Pearcy) 222
  D. 104
Livingston, Margaret[Winter]
  127
Lloyd, Fernetta T[Maxey]209
  J.R. 208
Loar, Ann 209
  George 209
Lobb, Ann(Horton) 87
  Chapman 87
  Richard W. 87

Lochridge, J.W. 209
Lock, George 42
  John W. 42
Locke, David 150, 209
Lockhart, John H. 209
  Robert E. 76
  Temperance[Roberts] 162
Lockridge, Eleanor K[Wilson] 138
Loftis, Jane H[Gilbert] 209
Lofton, Jane[White] 209
Logan, Allen 112
  Anna[Anderson] 152
  Benjamin F. 209
  Elijah 209
  Elizabeth[Allsman] 105
  Elizabeth(Layer) 82
  Elizabeth W. 209
  Hugh 82
  J.M. 209
  John 153
  Joseph 209
  Martha(Givens) 112
  Martha J[Layton] 82
  Nancy 88
  Rebecca J(Jennings) 27
  Roxline(Powell) 224
  Samuel 153
  Samuel F. 112
  Sarah[Oder]220
  Susan(Martin) 214
  Tifflin P. 157
  William C. 209
  William R. 209
Logsdon, Aaron 119
  Eliza C. 209
  Elizabeth(Beheimer) 119
  George 119
  James 209
  John W. 96
  Joseph 119, 120
  Lucy(Parker) 120
  Malinda[Dunbar] 119
  Maria(Remus) 96
  Mary E(Johnsey) 96
  Mary E(Johnson) 96
  Perry 120
  Robert 96
Logston, Patience[Flatt] 31
Loman, Isaac 120
  James 120
  Lucy(Parker) 120
Lomax, E.H. 160
  Rachel(Hart) 160
Long, Eliza Y[Ball] 116
  Griffin 116
  Isabella(Ratcliff) 226
  J.B. 209
  James 136
  John C. 59
  Laura[Gilbertson] 59
  M.C. 209
  Peter 162
  Rebecca S(McCormick) 59
  Sarah[Smith] 209
  Thomas 136
  Winston L. 59
Longmate, Octavia(Mount) 150
Longshore, Julia A. 95
Loossey, Mary E[Graham] 209
  Sarah(Richardson) 209

Stephen 209
Lorton, Samuel C[Camp-
  bell] 209
Lott, James 63
  Sarah[Thomas] 209
Lovelace, Mahala[Doyle]
  187
Lowder, George W. 95
  Margaret(Harris) 93
  William 93
Louderbach, Margaret[Rigg]
  122
Low, Elizabeth[Beckham]
  159
Lowe, George 209
  Mary A. 209
Lowrey, Jane[Overstreet]
  106
Lowry, Baron T. 209
  Eli 209
  Elizabeth 209
  Elizabeth(Davidson) 209
  Elizabeth A. 66
  Jane(Newcomb) 219
  William 209
Loyd, Julia A[Rucker] 108
Lucas, Cynthia A(Whitman)
  97
  Elijah 147
  H.B. 209
  Marsham 96
  Martha A. 209
  Sarah[Hendrick] 140
  Sarah A(Keith) 92
  Susan(Jones) 45
Luckett, Benjamin 209
  Ellen(Hendricks) 198
Luckins, Jesse 76
  John T. 76
Luken, George M. 104
  Mary B(Bills) 104
  Samuel S. 104
Lukins, Ann[Kincaid] 35
  Ann(Rector) 76
  G. 76
  Gregory 76, 210
  Jesse 35
  Peter 76
Luman, Eliza[Lanteman]111
Lumsden, Lucy(Keelen) 205
  William 210
Lurton, J.H. 147
  M.E(Striding) 44
  Nelson R. 210
Luttrell, Hiram 210
Lutz, Balseer W. 210
  Daniel 210
  Diana 210
Lycan, J.G. 133
  J.V. 133
  Lydia(Ogden) 134
  Rebecca L(Heady) 136
Lykins, Elizabeth(Ritter)228
Lyles, Albert R. 29
  Moses M. 29
  Sarah J(Walker) 29
Lynam, William H. 210
Lynch, Nancy[Anderson]
  86
Lynden, Joel Y. 210

-280-

Lynman, Lovina(Rice) 228
Lynn, Drucilla[Wright]210
  Elizabeth(Casey) 210
  Jefferson 210
Lyon, Elizabeth[Hickman]210
  Elizabeth[Roe] 116
  Elizabeth[Wood] 93
  Elizabeth A[Roe] 116
  Harrison D. 150
  Henson 150
  Jiney G[Hoxsey] 52
  John 27
  Nancy(McCoun) 150
Lyons, Catherine(Eddings) 79
  John U. 79
  Samuel 111
  William 79
  William D. 79

McAfee, Samuel 210
McAllister, Catherine(Kennedy) 129
McArtee, W.H.H. 125
McAtte, Keziah[Jones] 125
McBrayer, J.D. 210
  J.P. 210
McBride, Charles 129
  Eliza J[Bloomfield] 129
  J. 210
McBroom, Andrew 210
  Joseph 210
  Phebe(Young) 210
  William 210
McBurnie, James V. 104
  W.S. 104
McCaffrey, Margaret[Milligen] 108
McCall, Amanda[Bennett] 210
McCammon, Elizabeth[Boon]210
McCann, Eliza(Young) 63
  Mary[Young] 133
  Neal 71
  Plaza 71
  Polly A[Chowning] 115
  Sarah[Young] 133
McCartney, Andrew 210
  James 210
McCarton, Melissa(Linder) 92
McCarty, Milburn 122
McCaslin, Cinderella[Gwyn]52
  Gray 52
  Hugh 52
  James 52
  Jane 52
  John O. 52
  Martha 52
  Mary 52
  Rachel 52
  Sallie(Robinson) 52
  Thomas 52
  William R. 52
McCauley, Daniel 104, 210
  J.D. 210
  J.W. 210
  Mary A(Jeffrey) 104
  N.L 104

McCausland, Elizabeth[Craft] 35
McCibben, Martha[Richardson]210
McClain, B.T. 95
  Elizabeth[Coley] 123
  George 95
  John 27
  Sarah 95
  Sarah(Hughes) 142
McClair, May A(Shelburn) 151
  William H. 150
McClendon, John 97
  Sarah(Pratt) 97
  Young E. 97
McClernand, Fatima 49
  John 49
  John A. 49
McClin, Catherine[Hall] 210
  David W. 210
  Nancy 210
McClintick, W.L. 132
McClintock, Margaret[Victor]210
  William 138
McClure, Eliza D[Kinkade] 65
  Elizabeth(Taylor) 60
  Frances(Dickerson) 106
  Greenup 150
  James 210
  James A. 106
  John 27, 210
  Lorrin[Thompson] 150
  Mary(Marcumpsey) 150
  Milton 210
  Nancy(Wheeler) 104
  Samuel 104, 210
  Samuel L. 65
  Sarah 210
  Sarah J. 210
  Thomas 27
  William 104
McCollom, Henry B. 65
  Nancy(Davidson) 65
McCollum, Abraham 210
  James 112
  James C. 210
  Mary I[Smith] 210
McCombs, Elizabeth[McCutchen]115
McConahy, Matilda J(Olverson)05
  Perry 71
McConnell, Martha E[Henry] 42
McCord, Charles A. 59
  Elam 211
  Mary(Lane) 130
McCormick, Alfred G. 211
  Andrew 136
  Ann(Short) 88
  Christian L. 211
  Flora[Wilcox] 55
  James 211
  James A. 211
  Nancy[McGee] 59
  Sarah[Amis] 136
McCosland, Lizzie[Guess] 120
McCoun, Nancy[Lyon] 150
McCown, James 136
  Jonathan 136
McCoy, Agnes 82, 211
  Caroline(Grimsley) 211
  Daniel 82, 211
  Elizabeth[Ratcliff] 211
  G.A. 211

  James 138
  John 82, 138, 211
  Mary(Eberman) 138
  Mary E(Murphy)117
  William 211
McCray, Martin D. 211
McCrory, James 95
  William E. 95
McCrosky, Susan[Walker] 27
McCrory, James 42, 95
  Sarah(Vance) 42
  William E. 95
McCrosky, Susan[Walker] 27
McCubbin, Eleanor 88
  Joseph 88
  William G. 88
McCuddy, Isaac 165
McCullough, Peter 76
  Polly M[Perry] 76
McCumber, Charley 211
McCune, James 138
  Margaret[Shawhan] 44
  Sarah J[Nichols] 138
McCurdy, Reese 211
McCurley, Ezekiel 211
  Joseph 211
  Rebeca 211
McCutchen, Elizabeth(Combs) 115
  Finis 115
  Hugh 115
McDade, William 51
McDaniel, William 211
McDannald, Elizabeth(Means) 111
McDannold, Elizabeth(Iles) 34, 35
  Elizabeth(Means) 111
  John 35, 132
  Reuben 132
  Thomas A. 35
  Thomas I. 35, 132
  Thomas L. 35
McDavid, Mahala[Linn] 42
McDonald, Catherine[Bramwell] 82
  Fannie[Artis] 61
  George 211
  Henrietta[Ruggles] 211
  Hugh 92
  James B. 211
  John 92
  Margaret E[Pinkerton] 211
  Martha J. 164
  Mary(Larue) 92
  Mary J[Peck] 211
  Nancy[Datin] 37
  W.P. 35
  William P. 211
McDougal, Rachel[Blair]211
McDowell, Abigail[Vinson] 211
  Archibald 155
  Euphemma[Sandusky] 44
  James 27
  James A. 27
  Jane[Sandusky] 42, 44
  Jane W[Allen] 27
  Lucinda(Rippeto) 27
  Margaret[Drennan] 52

Mayhugh, Fielding 125
  Jane(Dixon) 125
  John 125
Mays, Martha[Carter] 91
Maze, Rebecca[Boyd] 95
Meacham, Andrew 214
  Elizabeth(Jones) 214
  F.W. 214
Mead, Andrew J. 99
  Mary(Scott) 99
  Richard H. 99
  William 99
Meade, Elizabeth[Logsdon]214
  Mary J(Briscoe) 46
Meadows, Elijah J. 160
  Henry 214
  Jane(Cobb) 160
  Lemuel C. 160
  M.C. 214
  Mary[Kilgore] 49
Means, A. 215
  America(Hersman) 95
  Elizabeth[McDannald] 111
  Elizabeth[McDannold] 111
  George W. 111
  Harriet(Debell) 75
  J.R. 111
  James H. 59
  John 111
  Mary[Henderson] 215
  Owen A. 111
  Phebe[Dickson] 110
  Robert 111
  Sarah(Rumsey) 111
Mederia, Harvey 215
Meek, Bazel 71, 145
  Ellen(Roberts) 71, 145
  H.H. 145
  Henry B. 145
  Joseph 71
Menough, Hiram B. 79
Meredith, Martha A(Delanay)
  112
Meriwether, E.B. 155
  F. 115
Merrell, Andrew 125
  Elizabeth(Stout) 125
  Jacob 125
Merrifield, Julia[Reed] 92
Merrill, J.W. 215
Merriman, Jacob H. 82
Merritt, E. 215
  John W. 49
  Lucretia(Pyle) 49
  N.P. 49
Mers, Andrew W. 77
  Samuel 77
  Tenna(Plank) 77
Mershon, Hannah[England]34
  T.O. 77
Messick, Abraham 59
  Joseph 215
  Joseph W. 59
  Julia[Crow] 215
Metcalf, B. 215
  Eliza(Peter) 104
  Elizabeth(Jones) 101
  Huldah(Davis) 215
  Huldah A(Davis) 101

J.D. 215
J.L 101
James A. 53
James D. 215
James L. 101
Jane A(Graham) 53
R.J. 101
Richard J. 101
Robert E. 53
Thomas F. 53
Thomas M. 101
William 101, 215
Metcalfe, Amanda(McIntyre) 215
  John A. 150
Melville 215
  Thomas 215
Meteer, Mary J[Morse] 35
Michaels, M.F(Bell) 94
Midcap, Elizabeth[Cox] 49
Midgett, Mary E(Kendall) 92
Mileham, Ann(Dougherty) 83
  Ebenezer 83
  Samuel 83
Miles, Alexander 115
  Eliza A. 215
  Ellen I[Marshall] 80
  J.R. 115, 215
  James I. 80
  John 92
  Maria R[Price] 166
  Mary(Irvin) 115
  Traleton C. 80
Millen, Frederick 120
  Sarah[Ware] 120
Miller, Abarilla(Barnes) 125
  Abraham 215
  Andrew J.215
  Benjamin P. 88
  Candis[Hall] 32
  Cornelia 215
  Dabner 150
  Daniel 215
  E.T. 215
  Edmund P. 88
  Elizabeth 150
  Elizabeth[Keller] 104
  Elizabeth[Williams]50
  Elizabeth[Wiseheart] 93
  Erastus 89
  Evelyn[Prather] 215
  F.P. 215
  Frederick A. 54
  G.H. 215
  George 115, 215
  George H. 115
  H.L. 125
  Henry 215
  Henry M. 106
  Isabella(Moore) 59
  J.L.F. 157
  J.S. 215
  Jacob 215
  Jacob H. 42
  James 59, 71, 132
  James M. 153
  Jane 153
  Jane(Levesque) 42
  Jeremiah 150, 215
  John 32, 42, 215

John A. 42
John H. 150
John R. 42
John W. 157
Joseph 215
L.A. 89
Lydia A(Hooton) 119
Martha[Givens] 119
Martha(Winlock) 88
Martin 215
Mary(Owent) 115
Mary E(Galloway) 70
Mortimer M. 54
Nancy[Phillips] 72
Permilia(Tapscott) 32
Polly 215
R.A. 215
R.P. 215
Rainey 215
Rebecca[Jones] 150
Reuben 150
Robert 125
Robert P. 89
Sallie[Sharp] 215
Samuel 216
Sarah(O'Hara) 71
Sarah A. 54
Sarah A(Anderson) 48
Solomon 27
Susan[Hedges] 41
Uriah K. 42
William 71, 88, 106
William T.M. 59
Wyatt 216
Millhouse, H. 216
Milligan, Sarah[McKenzie]71
Milligen, Margaret(McCoffrey)
  108
Mills, Artemisia(Carl) 40
  Betsey[Henry] 41
  Catherine(Jameson) 42
  James 83
  John H. 42, 83
  Minerva[McNeil] 216
  Nathan 42
  Patsey[Scrogin] 44
  Rachel[Harris] 32
  Rachel[Wilson] 216
  W.A.A. 83
Milner, John 85
Milstead, Edward 216
  Nancy N(Hinchee)216
  William E. 216
Miner, Betsey(White) 71
  Charles 71
  John 106
  Rufus 71
  William 106
Minnis, Hester A(Outhouse)59
  James 59
Minter, Williamson P. 216
Mitchel, Ebenezer B. 158
  Elizabeth(Briggs) 158
  Peyton 158
Mitchell, Abigail[Culton]
  216
  Andrew K. 35
  Anna B[Pilcher] 115
  Bedford 160

Mountjoy, Frances M(Stout)30
   George 30
   W.D. 30
   William 217
Mourning, Ann(Jones) 27
   F.C. 217
   Hannah(Ball) 217
   John 217
   Lewis 27
   William H. 27
Moutray, Allan 217
Moyers, Jacob N. 217
Mozley, Agnes(Golloway) 84
   Archibald 84
   John N. 84
Mudd, Arabella S(Cass) 88
   Henry L. 88
   Millie[Gilmore] 91
   W.A. 88
Muelheim, Grace F(Lander) 59
Muelheims, Mrs. G.L. 59
Muir, John W. 218
Mulberry, J.B. 147
   James 147
   Judy Ann(Laforce) 147
Mullen, Margaret[Grayson]218
Mullens, Martha A[Raker] 218
Mullican, Rachel 32
Mulligan, James 56
   Joseph H. 158
Mulkin, Harvey 218
Mundy, Elizabeth[Waddle] 218
Munsell, Zerelda(Perry) 107
Munson, D.K. 218
   Sally[Turney] 139
Murden, Edward 218
   Josephine E. 218
   William H. 218
Murdoch, Mary[Brown] 48
Mure, George A. 72
Murphey, Davis 127
   Lucinda(Conn) 127
   William M. 127
Murphy, Daniel 218
   J.W. 218
   James H. 117
   John 112
   John W. 218
   L. 112
   Malinda[Curry] 102
   Mary E[McCoy] 117
   Matilda(Biles) 218
   Michael A. 165
   Miles 133, 165, 218
   Rachel J(Butler) 117
   Sarah J(Powers) 134
   Sibbie(O'Hair) 165
   Thomas 112
   William 133, 218
Murray, Amanda J(Harris)129
   Eli 218
   Elizabeth[Pearson] 218
   John B. 88
   Margaret(Bird) 218
   Milly(Kennedy) 156
   Milton A. 38
   William 88, 218
Musgrove, William F. 104

Musick, Hannah 165
   J.C. 218
   Jesse 165
   John 165
   Mary A[Judy] 218
Myers, Abraham 66
   J.C. 82
   J.L. 80
   Jacob 66
   Jacob W. 59
   Jordan 82
   Joseph C. 82
   Mrs. M.R. 80
   N. Amelia(Banton) 82
   Sallie(Hicks) 106
   Sarah[Anderson] 37

Naegelin, Albert 218
   Annis(Threvenin) 218
   Emile 218
Nall, Charles H. 165
   Elizabeth[Edgar] 218
   Fanny(Tuttl) 218
   Gabriel 218
   Julia(Griffin) 140
   Juliet(Griggin)140
   Larkin 140, 218
   R.P. 218
   Richard P. 140
Nash, R.T. 218
National, Isaac 32
   Vickrey 32
Nave, Elizabeth 66
   Sarah D. 160
Nay, Frances[Humphrey] 141
   Nancy(Bennett) 141
   Sanford 141
   William 141
Naylor, Benjamin 27
   Benjamin F. 27
   Benjamin T. 27
   Resin 27
Neal, Abijah D. 43
   Ann(Yeamin) 43
   Diadama[Gill] 218
   Elmira[Keys] 218
   George W. 43
   Jacob 43
   James M. 43
   John T. 43
   Margaret[Williams] 136
   Martha[Ruddell] 43
   Matilda 43
   Sarah[Cheaney] 74
   Tavener 43
   Thomas 218
Neathercy, A.J. 218
Neece, Jesse 218
Neel, E.G. 51
   Lucy(Wand) 51
   Sarah[Jones] 218
   Wade 51
Neely, Catherine[Reel] 218
   Jane[McElvain] 153
   Jane[McElvin] 153
   Mary(McCoart) 72
   Mary[Spears] 88

   Robert F. 72
   W.J. 72
Neil, Harriet[Fullinwider]
   149
Nelms, William H. 218
Nelson, Annie(Smith) 132
   Basil 219
   Elizabeth(Chattan) 219
   Enoch K. 83
   Mary(Edmonson) 83
   Nancy[Mansker] 219
   Susan[Dooley] 132
   Susan J[Dooley] 132
   William 132
   William K. 83
Nesbit, Malissa[Burton] 219
Nesbitt, Enelia[Fraizer] 95
Nesler, David 219
   Felix 219
Netherton, A.K. 219
   Abram 104
   Abram K. 104
   Amy(Ashbaugh) 104
   Julia A. 219
   Rebecca[Kellar] 141
Nevil, William 32
Neville, Elizabeth L(Lind-
   sey) 59
Nevitt, Mary(Edlin) 50
   William 50
   William G. 50
Newbarn, Louise 219
Newberry, Mary J[Martin] 32
Newcomb, Jane[Lowry] 219
   Margaret[Wilson] 78
   Mary[Little] 76
   William 219
Newell, Ann(Solomon) 153
   Elizabeth C[Solomon]153
   James 153
   Rebecca[LeNeve] 95
   Rebecca[Neve] 219
   Susan C[Taylor] 153
   T[Fletcher] 32
   William 95
Newman, Charity 104
   Elizabeth[Funkhouser]159
   John 104
   Matilda[Killman] 219
   Welch 104
Newport, Joseph 38
   Maria(Scholes)38
   Noble C. 38
Newton, Henry 219
   John G. 219
   Louisa[Kennedy] 219
   Louisa[Wilson] 219
   Lucinda(Fletcher) 115
   Martha(Haggard) 219
   Mary(Haley) 219
   Uriah 219
   W.H. 156
   William H. 98
Nicholas, Elizabeth[Speed]47
   H. Clay 43
Nichols, Catherine[Ruddell]
   43
   Dulcibela(Berry) 125
   Elizabeth(Perkins)72

Potts, Richard F. 80
  William B. 80
Poulter, John 104, 224
Powel, James 224
  John 224
Powell, A.M. 98
  Elizabeth[Sanders] 224
  Elizabeth[Stevens] 38
  Elizabeth(Williams) 80
  Hezekiah 38
  Hiram 108
  Lucy(Ealer) 38
  Margaret[Darnell] 72
  Martha(Barron) 90
  Oner R. 108
  Rebecca[Yocum] 133
  Roxline[Logan] 224
  Thomas M. 139
  Virginia R[Martin] 108
  William 224
  William A. 38
Power, E.D. 72
  Eleanor(Defman) 72
  Elizabeth(Stogedill) 72
  George 72, 224
  James 72
  John 77
  John C. 77
  Martha S(Thompson) 36
  Mary[Darnell] 72
  Sarah[Donaldson] 33
  William 72
Powers, E.D. 224
  Elizabeth G[Tackett] 224
  Nancy 224
  Sarah[Shepherd] 224
  William 224
Poynter, Elizabeth(Davis) 32
  James T. 32
Prall, Mary[Reid] 72
Prance, Susan[Bruner] 49
Pranty, John 224
Prater, Mary S. 160
  Sarah(Hunt) 160
Prather, Jeremiah 224
  Jonathan 35, 224
  Sarah(Ritter) 35
  Uriah 35
Pratt, S.J. 224
  Sarah[McClendon] 97
Pray, Margaret(Canaday)100
Preston, Lucy[Stone] 27
Prewett, Martha[Hoskins]224
Pribble, Melinda[Huddleston] 142
Price, Amanda[Curry] 147
  Corilla[Sterrett] 224
  Edith[Cummins] 95
  George W. 160
  J.F. 166
  Jacob F. 166
  James B. 160
  James R. 147
  John 163, 224
  Maria R(Miles) 166
  Mary(Cotney) 224
  Mary(Johnson) 163
  Mary(Wall) 160
  Peter B. 160

  Richard 163
  Robert 72
  Sarah[Jackson] 92
  Sophia[Brockman] 147
  William D. 98
Prickett, Abraham 72, 224
  George 224
Prince, William S. 224
Pritchett, Elizabeth(Grooms)132
  Gilbert 132
  Lewis 132
  Lydia(Wilson) 43
  Mary E(Ingles) 41
  Susan 224
  Thomas A. 43
  William 43
Proctor, Lafayette 77
  Sarah(McKee) 77
  William 77
Pruitt, Jane(Moredock) 49
  John 224
  Mahala 224
  Willis 98
Prunty, Ann(Heavenhill) 136
  Robert M. 136
  William T. 136
Prutsman, Maxy M. 224
Pugh, Beulah(Hall) 59
  Charity[Perry] 107
  John 59
  Jonathan H. 35
  Martha[Whitfield] 224
  Thomas 59
Pullam, Margaret[Blackwell] 158
Pullem, Lucille(Gex) 81
Pulliam, Elizabeth(Goff) 153
  James 151
  Samuel 151
  Susan(Greer) 151
Pullian, Lucy[Brooks] 96
Purcell, Elizabeth[Lander] 59
Purdum, John 224
Purdy, Adeline[Wilson] 224
  Presley 224
Purkapile, Catherine D(Houghton) 124
  James 224
Purkey, William 224
Purvis, George 225
  William 225
Putnam, Ann(Grover) 111
  Daniel K. 111
  John 125
  Joseph G. 111
  Sarah[Grover] 124
Pyle, Abner 59
  David 129
  Lucretia[Merrit] 49
  Rachel 129
  Ralph 129
  Sarah(Hall) 59

Quick, Alfred 225
Quiet, Martha[Blair]225
Quimby, Elizabeth(Hogan) 130
  George E. 130
  James B. 130

Quinn, B.F. 225
  Berthana[Park] 120
  Borthana[Park] 225
  Elizabeth(Moberly) 120
  H.W. 225
  Hiram 120
  Hiram W. 120
  Nancy(Kennedy) 92
  Rachel[McMaster] 92
  S.M. 225
  Thomas 92
Quisenberry, A. 225
  Albert 60, 225
  Allen 60, 225
  Arthur 60, 225
  Edward 225
  Edward S. 60, 225
  H.C. 225
  John 225
  Lucy(Cator) 60
  Lucy(Catour) 60
  Nancy(Thoroughkill) 60
  Polly(Threalkill) 225
  R.R. 225
  T.H. 225
  Thomas H. 225
  W. 225
  William(Burt) 37

Radford, Benjamin 60
  Frances T(Lawrence) 60
  R.N. 60
Rafferty, D.K. 88
  Elizabeth(Kean) 88
  James 88
  John 88
  M.C. 108
  Mary S(Benedict) 106
Raffurty, Harriet[Rhoads] 225
  James 132
  Nancy(Booth) 132
Ragland, John 64
Railsback, Nancy E[Kennedy] 62
Rain, Nancy[Neal] 43
Rainay, Margaret[Baldridge] 225
  Maria 85
Raines, Christopher 32
  Fletcher 32
  Myra(Gatewood) 32
Rainey, Louisa[Wham] 225
  Margaret[Baldridge]225
Raker, Daniel M. 63
  Nelson 63
  Susan E(Chaney) 63
Ralston, Elizabeth[Dawson] 225
  Elizabeth[Pearson] 225
  J.N. 225
  James H. 43, 225
  Koseph N. 43
Ramey, Jane[Patterson] 27
  Samuel 225
Ranch, Frances[Harlan] 58

Rice, Ann(Hopkins) 89
Benjamin 88
Catherine[Dickerson] 106
Corbin 227
Edwin 227
Elijah 227
Eliza[McMurtry] 92
Elizabeth 227
Elizabeth(Bayley) 154
Elizabeth[Welch] 107
Emily[Walton] 38, 125,
227
Ezekiel 227
Fanny(Garnett) 227
Fantleroy 227
George P. 228
Hannah(Underwood) 151
Harriet[Scott] 228
James 89
Jasper 88, 154
Lovina[Lynman] 228
Matilda[McDow] 228
Mary(Jones) 65
Polly A[Kearn] 81
Sallie[Grubb] 159
Sallie[Stevens]104
Sarah P[Kyle] 88
Seaton, S. 151
Strother G. 151
Thomas H. 89
Tilford 228
William B. 228
Rich, Obadiah 228
Richards, Martha A(Adair)166
Mary[James] 95
Richardson, Amos 60, 228
C.P. 228
Henry 228
Isaac 228
John W. 121
Louisa 60
Lucy[Stansifer] 38
Manda 228
Matilda 228
Nancy[Lender] 92
Reason 121
Jane[Orchard] 228
William A. 72
Richey, Andrew J. 151
Elizabeth(Biggs) 151
Rebecca[Marshall]228
Robert 151
S.H. 228
Richmond, Electa R[Gardner]
107
Roswell 108
Ricketts, Caroline[Lamb]125
Ricks, John B. 157
William S. 60
Ridens, Sarah M[Over] 63
Rigdon, Dicie(Hurst) 111
Eli T. 111
Matilda J[Grayson] 111
Rigg, A.P. 228
Archibald P. 228
Elizabeth(George) 29, 30
Emily J(Watts) 121
George 228
James M. 122
James N. 30, 151

James M. 122
James N. 30, 151
Margaret(Louderbach) 122
Margaret(Utterback) 30
Peter 30, 129
Richard 29, 30
Sarah 228
William T. 29
Riggs, Charlotte[Crawford] 131
Eleanor C[Routt] 77
George W. 77
Millicent[Couchman] 40
Minerva W(Lewis) 76
Nancy 89
Nancy(Pitts) 77, 111
Robert J. 89
Russell 89
Samuel 89
William M. 77
Riley, Ann[McKinney] 112
Delila(Gibson) 228
Elizabeth[Adams] 137
H.H. 92
James 228
John L. 228
Margaret[Hasson] 110
Martha(Payne) 43
Mary A[Hardey] 158
Sarah[Wade] 228
T.H. 139
Rimbey, Mary A(Vertrees) 93
Ringo, Catherine B[Lewis] 76
Jane[Swope] 151
Ringold, Jane[Swope] 151
Rippetoe, Lucinda[McDowell] 27
Ripple, Mary[Hanley] 103
Risk, Amanda[Allen] 147
Ann(Dougherty) 147
John 147
Ritchey, Catherine(Bronson) 147
James 72
Nancy B. 147
Samuel 228
Ritchie, Mary 228
Ritter, Elizabeth[Lykins] 228
George L. 151
James 72
Nancy J(Frazer) 66
John 228
Nancy J(Frazer) 66
Rebecca(Woodgate) 72
Sally H[Hildreth] 41
Sarah[Prather] 35
W.G. 228
William T. 72
Ritty, A[Roberts] 92
Robards, Eleanor O[Myers] 72
Robb, Lydia(Waller) 162
Matthew 162
Thomas 162
Robbins, D.F. 54
Sarah 228
Roberson, James 228
Robert, Celeste F[Candy] 69
Roberts, A(Ritty) 92
Absalom 228
Addison B. 228
Anna 229
Azariah 43
Bainbridge H. 50

D.D. 38
Eliza[Jones] 229
Elizabeth(Cox) 228
Ellen[Meek] 71, 145
Francina[Bryant]229
H. 229
Isaac 43
James 228
James E. 50
Jane[Phillip] 229
Jesse 229
John 229
L.W. 72
Lucinda(Gatlen) 100
Mary[Barnes] 118
Mary(Gilmore) 88
Mary J[Barclay] 118
Minnie E[Garner]164
Nancy(Bowles) 39
Nathan 229
Penelope 164
R.S.D. 99
Richard B. 72
Richard S.D. 99
Sallie(Cox) 228
Sarah(Simmons) 99
Squire 164
Temperence(Lockhart)
162
Robertson, C.M. 115
Elizabeth(Jones)229
H.G. 229
Harriet(Key) 155
Isom 160
J.P. 155
Jesse B. 155
Lucy[Sample] 88
Martin 115
O.P. 160
Robert 43
S. 229
Sarah(Morton) 115
Simon 229
Z. 43
Zachariah 95, 229
Robinet, Julia[Ritchey]229
Robinson, Amelia T[Raw-
lings] 229
D.P. 229
E. 229
Eliza[Cooper] 229
Elizabeth[Barry] 30
Elizabeth[Curry] 83
George 229
Hannah E. 151
James 60
John M. 229
Martin K. 229
Mary A[James] 138
Polly[Thurman] 66
Pressley 53
Rachel[Runyon] 229
Ruth[Runyon] 126
Sallie[McCaslin]52
Sarah 60
Sarah H[Parks] 73
Robison, Jane[Watson] 30
Margaret[Whiting] 74
Roby, Frances A(Barnes)
102

Roby(cont.)
James R. 67
Lawrence 151
Rochester, Sidney 109
Rogers, Catherine W(Richey)
81
John W. 229
Joseph W. 229
William O. 43
Rodman, Catherine J[Morgan]
229
Roe, Elizabeth(Lyon) 116
Elizabeth A(Lyon) 116
Uriah C. 229
Roety, Elizabeth[Peugh] 82
Rogers, Ann W[Lander] 59
Anna[Deering] 74
Chilton 136
Elender(Hildreth) 43
Elias 104
Elizabeth[Clapp] 136
Elizabeth(Shelton) 136
Greenberry 136
J.A. 43
James T. 162
Jane[Deventer] 43
John 43
John G. 32
Miles 92, 104
Parmella(Holden) 104
Samuel R. 140
Sarah(Morgan) 140
Thomas M. 140
W.O. 43
Rohrer, Artemisia(Asbaugh)
115
Jacob 115
James H. 115
Roland, Mary A[Scott] 126
Roll, Fanny[Mason] 229
Rollins, Melinda[Claypool]
229
Romine, Elizabeth[Junior]
153
Roney, James 141
Mary(Aiken)141
Sarah[Tyler]141
Roper, Frances F[Davenport]
157
Henry C. 157
Nancy(Lewis) 157
Rose, Dreaury 85
Drury 85
Eliza(Champ) 82
George W. 82
James 73
Mary[McKever] 229
O.H. 101
Phoebe(Coulter) 73
R.H. 229
Samuel 73
William B. 82
Rosebery, Charles 151
Meekee[Cook] 151
Roseberry, James A. 104
Rosebrough, Orphah[Ayres]
229
Ross, Betsy(Baskin) 73
Elizabeth[Chenoweth] 86

J.H. 229
James W. 73
John 126
Joshua W. 229
Margaret(Clark) 79
Meredith B. 229
Nancy[Pinnell] 141
Nancy A(McMullen) 150
Samuel 229
Samuel B. 73
Rothwell, John M. 82, 229
Matilda 82
Thomas 82
Rotramel, David 115
Henry 115
Keziah(Simpson) 115
Margaret[Coad] 115
Routt, Byram 77
Eleanor C(Riggs) 77
James 77
John 77
Martha[Newton] 230
Martha E[Newton]230
Rowe, Edward 55
Eleanor[Coake] 55
Eleanor(Littleton) 55
Elexor 55
Rowland, Catherine[Bushy] 230
John 65
Wade 65
Winfred 65
Rucker, Alice J[Suggett] 151
Carter 27
E. 108
Emily[Sanders] 230
Ezekiel 84
George W. 154
Isaiah 27
John 230
Julia(Bennett) 154
Julia(Reese) 84
Julia A(Loyd) 108
Morning 84
Nancy 27
Nancy J[Redman] 230
Thomas 230
William M. 108
Ruddell, Armen(Phelan) 43
Catherine[Hendry] 43
Catherine[Nichols]43
George 43
George H. 43
J.D. 43
John M. 43
Martha(Dunlap) 128
Martha(Neal) 43
Stephen 43
Susan(David) 43
William 43
Zalmon 43
Rudy, J.O. 104
P.O. 104
W.H. 104
Ruggles, Jacob 48, 230
Rachel(Freeland) 43
Thomas 43
Rumsey, Sarah[Means] 111
Runyon, Daniel 126, 230
Rachel 230

Ruth(Robinson) 126
Sally[Worthington]127
T.H. 126
Rush, Abraham 151
Ezekiel 32
Isaac 230
Leonard 32
Lucinda[Herring] 230
Mary(Mattox) 151
Mary(Willis) 163
Mary A[Hoes] 230
Posey 151
Russell, Eliza S[Clarke]
230
Hiram 88
John 230
John L. 88
Margaret[Phelps] 88
Merritt A. 88
Nancy[Moore] 97
Samuel 230
William H. 230
Rutledge, J.M. 98
James 230
Jane[Buckles] 230
Robert 230
Ryan, Dulcina 35
Mildred[Vivion] 63
Moses 35
Nannie[Chowning]35
Ryerson, Charity[Johnson] 129
Ryon, Mildred[Vivion] 63

Saddoris, Nancy(Trent)240
Sadler, Joseph G. 230
Samuel H. 230
Sagester, Henry 107
Joseph 107
Lavina[Howard] 107
Nancy(Woodard) 107
Said, Martha[Record] 143
Susannah[Record] 143
Salisbury, Nancy(Dyer)186
Salle, T.M. 230
Salmon, Emma[Bacon] 108
Jacob 108
Saltonstall, Samuel R. 147
Sammons, Anna[Frasier] 78
Samoniel, Edward 104
Samuel 104
William 104
Sample, David 230
James 230
Samples, Andrew 230
David 230
Mary(Townsend) 230
Sampson, Hannah[Wiley]83
Sarah A[Tebbill] 230
Sams, Sarah 30
Thomas 230
Thomas M. 30
Samuell, Lydia(Blunt) 31
Samuels, Alfred 230
John 230
Sander, Nancy(Gregson)194

-293-